BATTERING STATES

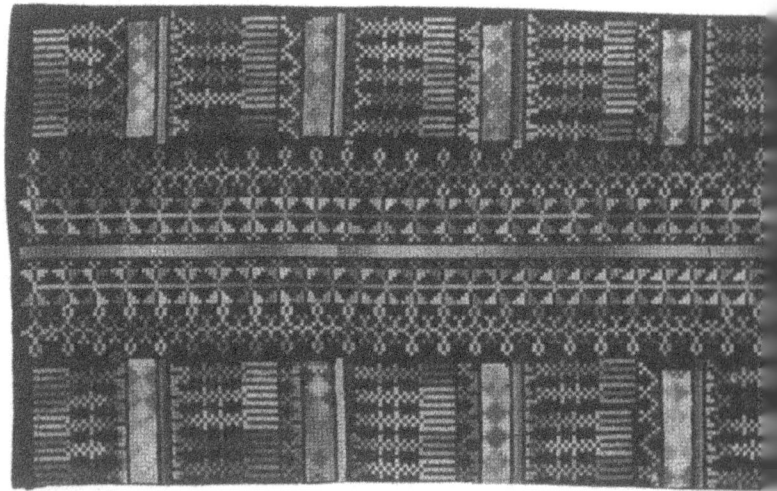

Battering States

The Politics of
Domestic Violence
in Israel

Madelaine Adelman

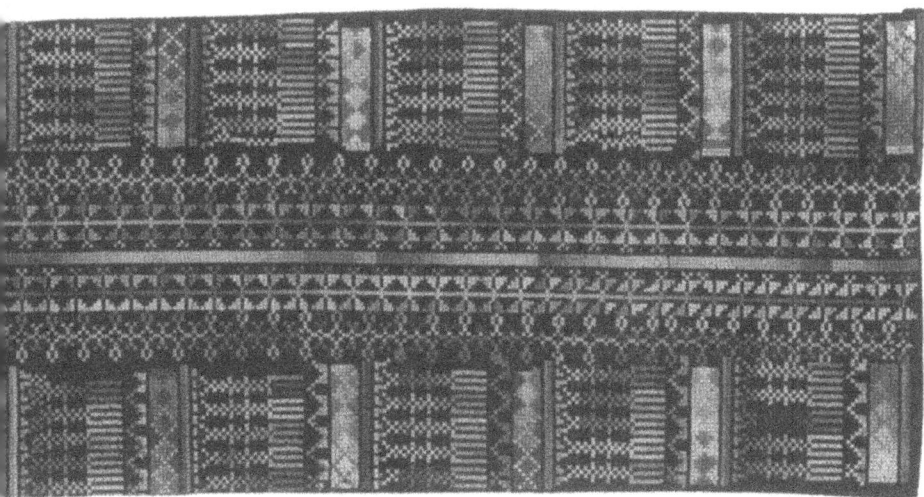

Vanderbilt University Press
Nashville

Frontispiece: Traditional Bedouin embroidery

Library of Congress Cataloging-in-Publication Data on file
LC control number   2016007510
LC classification number   HV6626.23.I75 A34 2016
Dewey class number   362.82/92095694—dc23
LC record available at *lccn.loc.gov/2016007510*

ISBN 978-0-8265-2131-6 (paperback)
ISBN 978-0-8265-2130-9 (hardcover)
ISBN 978-0-8265-2132-3 (ebook)

For my sisters.

Contents

Acknowledgments

THE RITUAL OF PREFATORY REMARKS CONVEYS meaningful messages, both about the behind-the-scenes production of the book as well as its author (Ben-Ari 1987). Being aware of these conventions has made me particularly self-conscious about my presentation of self and others within this component of the book. Nevertheless, I will draw on the textual tradition and attempt, but surely fail, to suitably acknowledge the many people who have generously shared their intellectual, personal, and material resources with me over the years.

I earned my undergraduate and graduate degrees at Duke University, the most beautiful and challenging campus imaginable. I am indebted to Anne Allison, miriam cooke, Virginia Dominguez, Karla Fischer, Richard Fox, Ernie Friedl, Roger Kaplan, Bruce Lawrence, Jean O'Barr, Mack O'Barr, Ellen Plummer, Orin Starn, and others from the Department of Anthropology and the Program in Women's Studies.

At Arizona State University, where cross-disciplinary conversations are more than encouraged, my thinking and writing are much improved because of former and current colleagues and students in the School of Justice Studies (now Justice and Social Inquiry); Jewish Studies Program; Religious Studies; Center for the Study of Religion and Conflict; Institute for Humanities Research; School of Social Work; School of Politics and Global Studies; Film & Media Studies; School of Human Evolution and Social Change; School of Film, Dance, and Theatre; and School of Social Transformation, including Elizabeth Segal, Nancy Jurik, Gray Cavender, Marjorie Zatz, Julia Himberg, Nancy Winn, Miriam Elman, Mary Bernstein, Jennifer Culbert, Michael Musheno, Souad Ali, Carolyn Forbes, Laurie Perko, Joel Gereboff, Linell Cady, Carolyn Warner, Miki Kittilson, Yasmin Saikia, Hava Tirosh-Samuelson, Ilene Singer, Rachel Leket-Mor, and Dawn Beeson; and I appreciate the career and scholarly guidance over the years from Anne Schneider, Marie Provine, Marjorie Zatz, Mary Margaret Fonow, and Beth Swadener.

The Association for Political and Legal Anthropology (APLA) at the American Anthropological Association, and the multidisciplinary Law and Society Association have been intellectual and professional homes, where I have been formed by the kinship and collegiality offered by so many, including Sally Merry, Lisa Neumann, Donna Coker, Phoebe Morgan, Jennifer Curtis, Sarah

Hautzinger, Andrea Ballestero, Kate Sullivan, Susan Coutin, Carol Greenhouse, Susan Hirsch, Mindie Lazarus-Black, Rebecca Torstrick, John Conley, Jennifer Weis, Hillary Haldane, Erik Harms, and Catherine Besteman. The collaborative scholarship of Becky Dobash and Russell Dobash inspired this research. Scholarly circles at Martha Fineman's innovative Feminist Legal Theory Workshop at Emory University and the Schusterman Center for Israel Studies at Brandeis University also offered resources for and feedback on my work.

I thank the founding editor of *Violence Against Women*, Claire Renzetti, for shepherding publications that helped form my thinking for Chapters 3 and 4. I also thank Elizabeth Segal, founding editor of the *Journal of Poverty*, for inviting me to explicitly incorporate political economy into my work, which launched ideas for Chapter 5. The manuscript reflects the reviewers' incisive reading and comments, and I recommend that others work with the generous staff at Vanderbilt University Press, and with Ideas on Fire founder Cathy Hannabach, who developed the index.

The book is set within and possible because of the broadly defined feminist movement against gender violence in Israel, where a number of justice provocateurs (Aiken 2001; Cavender and Jurik 2012) and NGOs welcomed me, including Isha l'Isha Haifa Feminist Center, Kayan-Feminist Organization, Haifa Rape Crisis Center, Women for Women Haifa Shelter for Battered Women, and Haifa Crisis Shelter for Women. I am grateful for Marilyn Safir's friendship, insight, hospitality, and guidance, and I have benefitted greatly from engagement with activists and researchers working in the region, including Nathalie Brochstein, Amalia Sa'ar, Edna Erez, Nadera Shalhoub-Kevorkian, Hannah Safran, Michal Mor, Rula Deeb, Zvi Eisikovits, Muhammad Haj-Yahia, and many others. I also could not anticipate how much my work with the Gay, Lesbian & Straight Education Network (GLSEN) and education scholars and advocates would influence my thinking about social movements.

I would be lost without my extended family, who sustained me along the way, including Lauren Kotkin, Cory Greenberg, Marilyn Jarvis, Cheryl Reiss, Nora Haenn, Deanna Cavelli, Jen Robinson, Rebecca Stanier-Shulman, Ellen Ben-Naim, Deborah Waxman, and Christina Ager. Fellow ethnographic travelers Liz Faier, Sharon Lang, Patricia Woods, and honorary anthropologist and comrade Shoshana (Cohen) Ben-Yoar were invaluable during and after my fieldwork. Several additional "logical" family members nurtured me along with the research and writing process: Bahney Dedolph cheered me on and offered learned feedback; Nancy Jurik and Marjorie Zatz contributed impossible-to-reciprocate emotional and intellectual labor; Liz Segal's friendship and hospitality were rivaled only by her intellectual gifts and institutional savviness; Nora Haenn reanimated and expertly shaped my writing; Brian Shire and Matt Heil helped me navigate the integration of activism and academics; Lauren Kotkin is the sole person who lent her sharp eye to every iteration of the manuscript; and Julia Himberg shared the pain (and pleasure) of writing, celebrating each step in the process. Amy Ettinger's love and encouragement accompanied me, and this book, from aspiration to reality.

They don't call it a "body of writing" for nothing: I benefitted greatly from my ASU-subsidized membership to the Lincoln Downtown YMCA; my health insurance, which granted me access to physical therapists at the Mayo Clinic, including the amazing Sandy Flatten; and the friendly staff at the Wildflower Café at 44th Street and Indian School Road in Phoenix.

My parents and ninety-seven-year-old grandmothers have been patient champions of this project. I dedicate this book to my sisters, Michelle Buckman and Melanie Kinard, whose love (of family) has sustained me throughout.

Note on the Cover Illustration

THE FIRST THING A PROSPECTIVE READER SEES is the front cover of a book. Like most authors, I wanted the cover to be attractive and to reflect the core subject matter: the relationship between domestic violence and the cultural politics of the state. I welcome readers to make their own interpretation, of course, but here is my take on the design.

Overall, the three horizontal stripes are meant to evoke the imagery of a flag, a symbol that signals the establishment of a state, along with its official currency, stamps, anthem, and so on. A state flag represents the polity and marks its territorial sovereignty. The symbols or colors that make up the flag itself connote belonging to or exclusion from the state. As the state's most well-known symbol, a flag stands in for the state, and thus it is metaphorically fought for, or materially desecrated to communicate rejection of the state's ideology, boundaries, or policies. In Israel, the Ministerial Committee on Symbols and Ceremonies determines the contours of annual state rituals, where the flag plays a visible role. Similar to other states, legislation in Israel regulates who can use the flag and for what purposes. On the cover of this book, the blue stripe corresponds to the blue in the Israeli flag; and the green references the Palestinian flag.

The "stripe" in the middle is a photo I took of a piece of embroidery that I purchased during a visit to the Association for the Improvement of Women's Status, an NGO and social enterprise located in Lakia, a small town in the Negev. Lakia is located only a dozen miles from Be'er Sheva, the "capital" of the Negev, but it has more in common with the other six towns founded by the state in order to settle and "civilize" the Bedouin people. The NGO was founded by and for Bedouin women to help address the persistent poverty, isolation, and lack of infrastructure in the region, which includes unrecognized Bedouin villages as well. More information about the project and its organizational partners is available on their website, along with the option to purchase items from their online catalog (*desert-embroidery.org*).

There is much to say about the selection of the fabric shown on the cover. It is a newly commodified piece of material culture, its stitching, colors, and design derived from Bedouin women's clothing. As such, it could too easily contribute to the touristic search for "cultural authenticity" or be read as emblematic of a seminomadic tribe putatively frozen in time. A critic might argue that its place-ment on the cover pulls attention away from the prevalence of domestic vio-lence among non-Bedouin communities in Israel, and in doing so, may reinforce stereotypes about Arabs or Muslims and violence against women. However, my intention is to convey that Bedouin women who are battered by their husbands are one of the most vulnerable communities in Israel and that their everyday encounters with the state, and their resulting differential citizenship, embody the argument outlined in the book. Namely, how statecraft—how a state defines itself and its status among other states, how it organizes its governance and legal systems, how it defends its borders, and how it forges its economy—shapes domestic violence. Finally, by including this beautiful swath of cloth, and the network of victims and survivors, family members, activists, scholars, artists, law-yers, educators, and policy advocates embedded within it, I also want to amplify the critical role played by women who mobilize collectively for social change.

1 | The Politics of Domestic Violence

AFTER WE GRADUATED, a friend from college invited me to join her at an orientation session for Rape Crisis of Durham, North Carolina,[1] a nonprofit organization that provides 24/7 support to victims and survivors of sexual violence and prevention education to the community.[2] Without giving it much thought—I was a feminist and pretty good in a crisis—I joined the organization. Over the next four years, I responded to women's calls to the hotline, which came mostly in the evening and late night hours. I once met with a young woman at a hospital emergency room. I met with another woman down at the courthouse so she could take a look at a courtroom in anticipation of a hearing. Mostly, I spoke to women on the phone, sometimes for a few minutes and sometimes for more than two hours.[3] As a counterbalance to direct service with victims and survivors, I also participated in policy advocacy: I was one of many voices demanding that the state's marital rape exemption (one of the last two in the country) be overturned, for example, and I helped my university, inspired by the Anita Hill hearings, to update its sexual harassment policy. Eventually, I turned this advocacy work on violence against women into my research focus, but only after a serendipitous encounter in a Jerusalem bathroom.

During the summer of 1990, I conducted preliminary fieldwork in Jerusalem. It entailed studying Hebrew in the mornings with new Israeli immigrants, mostly from the former Soviet Union, a few Palestinian Arabs wishing to improve their language skills and market potential, and a handful of Christians from Denmark living in Jerusalem who hoped to obtain permanent resident status. Once a week in the evening, I studied colloquial Palestinian Arabic with a teacher from Beit Safafa at the Jerusalem-stone YMCA building, along with a small group of primarily left-wing, middle-aged Israeli Jews. In the afternoons, I interviewed people or took advantage of the Hebrew University's library to learn more about the education system in Israel (then the focus of my research).

By July of that summer, it was hot in Jerusalem. Middle East hot. Wearing a T-shirt, khakis, and sandals, I walked from my apartment building on Reuven Street in Bak'a, leaving the mild breeze that swirled through its fourth-floor windows, and made my way to the (Jewish) center of town overlooking the walled Old City. The sloping streets were crowded with groups of young people wearing

1

jeans and colorful tank tops; the girls, often linked arm-in-arm, sporting danger-ously high-heeled chunky black sandals and talking loudly, click-clacked toward their destinations. Sharing the sidewalk were older *haredi* Jewish women pushing baby carriages loaded down with small children and plastic bags bulging with food. They wore full-length dresses with long sleeves, heads covered with a dark scarf or a wig. Older children, also dressed with dark stockings or pants and long sleeves, walked alongside the carriages, following their mothers' shopping routes. I reached King George Street and watched for bus number no. 9 or no. 4a, either of which would take me to the main campus of the Hebrew University of Jerusalem.

I planned to escape from the oppressive heat in the university's air-conditioned library. After passing through a perfunctory security-guard search of my backpack at the entrance to the university, and another to enter the library,[4] I went directly to the women's restroom to ring myself out from the unaircon-ditioned bus ride. There I came upon what ultimately changed the focus of my research: strategically placed on the mirror above the sinks with the half-broken faucets, and at eye-level on the inside of the stall doors pockmarked by etched graffiti, were stickers with the message "You are not alone." These stickers from the Jerusalem Rape Crisis Center hotline sparked for me links between my then home in North Carolina and my prospective research in Israel.[5] Over the next two years, I mulled the intellectual and logistical possibility of shifting my research to the relationship between gender violence and the state. When I returned to Israel in 1992 for another summer of language study and fieldwork, this brief encounter had transformed my research agenda into what has become a lifelong study of the politics of domestic violence. This book represents the culmination of my research.

Battering States is an interdisciplinary, ethnographic study of the politics of domestic violence—an analysis of when and how intimate partner violence intersects with cultural politics of the state.[6] The book examines this intersec-tion in Israel, where a number of factors bring the connections between the state and domestic violence into stark relief: the presence of a contentious mul-tinational and multiethnic population; competing and overlapping sets of reli-gious and civil family law; state securitism and political violence that permeate people's everyday lives; and a growing gap between the wealthy and the poor. The exact combination of these factors is unique to Israel, but they are typical of states with a diverse population in a time of globalization. In this way the example of Israel offers insights wherever the political and personal impinge on one another.

The book addresses how the business of nation- and state-building—what political scientists refer to as "statecraft"—informs the enactment, experience, and explanation of violence within intimate relationships. Specifically, I analyze how the family is configured through cultural difference by the state, how political violence shapes domestic violence, and how the political-economic context engenders domestic violence.

Battering States counts among the first long-term ethnographic analyses of domestic violence inside or outside of the United States (Adelman 2010).[7] It serves as an example of social research that conjointly considers the everyday lives of Jewish and Palestinian Israelis. As an "engaged anthropologist" (Low and Merry 2010), I conducted ethnographic research in Israel over the course of two decades, 1992–2012. This time horizon is meaningful because it tracks with the grassroots development and subsequent state adoption of domestic violence as a social problem in Israel. It also coincides with the state's transformation from the presumption of relatively robust social welfare supports to a market-based global economy. And it parallels the growing critique of its personal-status law system and the cyclical rise and fall of political violence and the peace process in the region. The book captures these significant shifts through a cultural analysis of the relationship between the state and domestic violence.

ETHNOGRAPHIC PERSPECTIVES ON DOMESTIC VIOLENCE

Ethnographic research is a continual process that comprises a number of methods of data collection and production (Dewalt, Dewalt, and Wayland 1998). Cultural immersion is accomplished through participation in and observation of everyday life, ranging from personal conversations to media coverage of extraordinary events. Although its foundational practices remain, the logistical nature of ethnographic research has been transformed by technology over the past two decades.

The first time I visited Israel, it was 1988, and I was a junior in a study-abroad program for undergraduates at the Hebrew University in Jerusalem. I walked from the noisy dorms down Churchill Boulevard, passing a British military cemetery along the way, to the much quieter Hyatt Hotel, where I used tokens in their payphones to initiate a collect call to my family; during the same semester, a friend from high school sent me a (decidedly retro but the only near-instant form of communication) telegram to congratulate me: "Duke in Final Four." I used prepaid cards to call the United States when using public phones, exchanged airmail letters with friends, and relied on my apartment phone (no voice mail) to coordinate my research schedule in Jerusalem during the summers of 1990 and 1992. When I spent the summer of 1991 in an Arabic-language immersion program at Middlebury College, no technology other than flashcards was allowed at all. In Haifa conducting fieldwork between July 1993 and June 1994, I was able to secure an e-mail address because I was enrolled in a language immersion program at the University of Haifa. This was a less-than-instant form of communication because I could use it only on a set of computers on campus, and few people I knew had e-mail addresses at the time.

When I returned to Haifa between November 1994 and March 1995, I signed a contract with NetVision in order to access a dial-up Internet connection at home. This enabled me to exchange updates with a few friends and mentors. To manage research logistics during the summer of 1999 in Haifa, I purchased a local cellphone with prepaid minutes. When I returned to Israel for fieldwork during winter break in 2005, I added wireless Internet connections to my repertoire. By 2011 I was using FaceTime to stay in touch with friends and family, and e-mail, texts, and a rented international phone with a local number to make research plans. In between research trips, the Internet made it possible to follow up on research leads and continue to collect data.

Ethnographic research on domestic violence, which has the potential for much personal resonance, conducted within a contested state such as Israel requires cultural vigilance, social empathy, and emotional reflexivity during every step of the process, from developing a research question to disseminating research findings (Lee and Renzetti 1990). Before I developed substantive components of the study, I formulated several of its key parameters. I was committed to posing locally relevant research questions (see Chapter 2); I was keen to avoid further jeopardizing participant safety during the research process, and to avoid maternalistic approaches to their safety and well-being; and I envisioned integrating various forms of advocacy and activism into my fieldwork. Underlying these parameters was my goal to generate an inclusive research sample reflecting the complexity of the state's population in order to collect and produce diverse stories about domestic violence.

Research Design

Ultimately, I concentrated my work in the Israeli port city of Haifa and the rural region of the Western Galilee, although I also conducted research in Tel Aviv, Jerusalem, and Be'er Sheva, visiting NGOs, interviewing frontline workers, and attending workshops and conferences. These spaces reflect the variety and intersection of social identities in Israel, including ethnic (e.g., "western" Ashkenazi to "eastern" Mizrahi Jews), national (e.g., Palestinian to Israeli), religious (e.g., secular Muslim to fundamentalist Jewish), migration (1948 Palestinians to new Israelis), and regional class (rural poverty to urban elites). Because social distinctions structure everyday life and battered women's experiences of and responses to domestic violence, the Haifa region enabled me to observe life along a geographical continuum and to seek out a diverse group of battered women to interview.

I volunteered within a number of NGOs for extended periods of time in order to learn about the local advocacy landscape, to establish trust with key community leaders, and to pursue my own commitments to social change. At the local shelter, for example, I volunteered with the residents' children; at the regional hotline for battered women, I underwent training and answered the phone along with a team of experienced advocates, and participated in a new grassroots court-watch program, in addition to observing in a legal advocacy clinic and women's center. It was through daily and weekly contact with these individuals and organizations that I was able to locate, reach, and gain the confidence of experts such as lawyers, religious leaders, and private psychologists—some of whom arranged meetings for me and their clients. Few of the women I interviewed had requested police assistance; none had pending criminal cases; and many of them were exposed to the legal system only via their advocate or divorce lawyer. The resulting study is thus a unique, culturally contextualized perspective on the politics of domestic violence in Israel.

The book is based on interview-generated narratives, a collection of cultural texts, and local engagement in domestic violence advocacy and everyday life. First, the core of the analysis is based on narratives gathered from forty-nine women from various social locations in Haifa and the Galilee region about their experiences of domestic violence; the majority of these women had never entered a shelter or contacted the police. Between 1993 and 1995, I interviewed twenty women who were currently or had been previously assisted via hotline, the women's center, or other NGO staff members for needs related to domestic violence and/or divorce. Of these women, three were Muslim, three were Catholic, two were Ethiopian, two were recent Russian Jewish immigrants, seven were Mizrahi Jews, and three were Ashkenazi Jews. Five other women (one upper-class Ashkenazi Jewish mother, three working-poor Mizrahi Jewish women with children, and one working-poor Russian immigrant who identified as Christian) were referred to me by a social worker as women who had recently left the local shelter for battered women. I also interviewed three hotline volunteers, two women's activists, and a neighborhood friend, all of whom had struggled with divorce-related domestic violence. Local friends identified and arranged for me to speak with four additional women, including a Druze woman, two Ashkenazi Jews from kibbutz, and a Mizrahi woman.

In the summer of 1999, I interviewed an additional fourteen women. I spoke with one working class Ashkenazi mother referred to me by the new local emergency shelter for battered women and a young Muslim mother of three referred to me by the original local shelter. I interviewed four additional Jewish women from Haifa and towns in northern Israel who responded to my ad in a women's center newsletter. An Islamic court judge arranged for me to speak with five Muslim women from the Haifa area; a team of social workers organized a meeting with me and two Muslim women from villages near Nazareth; and a local friend invited me to speak with another Muslim woman from a town in the Galilee region. Women discussed how multiple identities and social locations (e.g., being religious and a mother, being a new immigrant and unemployed, being both a member of the national minority as well as a feminist) informed their pathways to safety and justice.

I also conducted interviews with about twenty "front-line workers" (Wies and Haldane 2011), such as lawyers, social workers, scholar-advocates, and activists in Haifa, Tel Aviv, and Jerusalem, who reflected on the state of their respective fields and their work on domestic violence. I also spoke with paid staff and volunteers of domestic violence service organizations as well as psychologists, community religious leaders, lawyers, family court and religious court staff and judges, and members of the Israeli parliament. To grasp the history of Israel's complicated family law system from the Ottoman Empire to contemporary times, I read primary sources such as parliamentary debates, proposed and accepted legislation, and High Court of Justice rulings as well as secondary legal history sources. I also consulted sociolegal scholars, university law school librarians, and a high school history teacher. Regional nongovernmental organizations in Haifa as well as statewide NGOs served as critical resources for my research.

A second set of data is a collection of cultural texts tied to domestic violence. This set of data includes official policies and regulations, legislative debates and associated legislation, court rulings, state and international reports, and NGO-generated reports and related ephemera such as press releases, posters, pamphlets, stickers, and signs. These texts represent a range of perspectives on domestic violence as a social problem and how they have changed over time. Other texts include local university and nongovernmental organization-based research on domestic violence in Israel, which has helped shape statewide public policy. I systematically reviewed several Israeli newspapers from 1993 to 1999 and then kept on top of relevant media coverage using online searchers and alerts of key public events such as the peace process, elections, political violence, as well as domestic violence–related topics considered newsworthy, such as domestic violence homicides, which have informed popular understandings of domestic violence.[8] I also collected materials such as intake files, newsletters, and annual reports from these and other organizations.

The third set of data is based on participation in and observation of everyday life, annual and sporadic public events and NGO activities. This set of data includes holiday celebrations; political demonstrations; turning points in policy-making; organizational planning and programming activities and volunteer trainings; and unstructured conversations on the street and among neighbors, friends, colleagues, and advocates. I also observed or participated in one-off events such as the conference to close out the International Year of the Agunah, held in Jerusalem in 1994. The Women's League sponsored a meeting of the International Study Group on the Future Intervention with Battered Women and Their Families, which convened in Haifa in March 1995. I participated in the daylong workshop for practitioners and activists (see Edleson and Eisikovits 1996). Taken together, these data form the foundation of an innovative approach to domestic violence where people's sense of their everyday experiences are placed at the center of the analysis, complemented by layers of local knowledge originating within both the mainstream and the marginalized, ranging from official texts to informal observations.

Safety and Well-Being

Identifying prospective research participants proved challenging because of the silence, stigma, and safety issues associated with domestic violence. Beyond women residing in the shelter where I volunteered, whose staff made the ethical decision to bar me from interviewing, there is no "club" or natural gathering place for battered women. They do not form or belong to a community of their own. Nor did I live in a setting or have the time for a chance encounter with domestic violence, which might erupt within a particular household (e.g., Lancaster 1992). Pragmatic spaces for studying domestic violence include health care such as public clinics, emergency rooms, and social service agencies (e.g., Stark 1979). Frontline workers such as doctors, nurses, and social workers serve clients every day who disclose or cloak their experience with domestic violence. Because I was interested in being somewhat useful during my research, and had no expertise with regard to health concerns, these locales did not make a good match.

My background in sociolegal studies meant that the police or courts presented an obvious field site. However, the majority of research on domestic violence takes place within populations culled from these institutions. Moreover, I rarely heard hotline volunteers talk about the police, and even the few times they did, it was to criticize their response and/or their collusion with relatives who were batterers. I had the opportunity to escort only one woman to the police station during a particular volunteering period of approximately ten months. Being interested in women's experiences of domestic violence beyond policing, I visited the regional Na'amat's Center for the Prevention of Family Violence, and WIZO's walk-in legal clinic for women. However, neither was prepared to absorb a volunteer or was able to refer me to clients. In the end, women I interviewed had sought help in the organizations in which I volunteered or visited, were networked with circles of colleagues or friends (or friends of friends of friends) I made in town, or responded to ads I placed in the feminist center newsletter.

My interviewee recruitment mechanisms were not always effective, primarily because of the damaging and threatening nature of domestic violence. I maintained a list of reasons why women rejected my interview requests: lives with husband and cannot get phone calls at home from strangers; cannot invite someone over to be interviewed; cannot leave the house to be interviewed; is embarrassed to talk about the violence; does not want to remember the awful time in their lives; is too involved in the daily struggle of making it to take time to talk to me; has no energy to start from the beginning of the story; has recently reconciled with her husband and is unwilling to jeopardize the relationship by talking about it with an outsider. When I tried to contact a woman enrolled in a Haifa Feminist Center support group for women getting divorced, the facilitator told she had stopped participating because her husband would not let her out of the house; the few times she had come to the group, it was obvious to the coordinator that she had been beaten up.

Talking with victims and survivors of gender violence raises logistical and ethical issues to consider. Battered women as well as formerly battered women can be vulnerable to ongoing abuse and violence or to the effects of domestic violence, and research can exacerbate this vulnerability. Yet presuming that battered women or survivors of domestic violence are too tender or breakable to participate in research is condescending and inaccurate. What concerned me most was ensuring that participation in my research would not extend or intensify any danger or social sanction an interviewee might encounter in the future. Women who have survived intimate partner violence can best discern their own risk, and so I followed their guidance as to when and where to host an interview. It was least risky when meeting in Haifa's congested neighborhoods, more risky when meeting in a less central neighborhood or in a village, town, or kibbutz outside of the city, where my presence was easily noted and questioned. The women I worked with varied in their presentations of self: lonely, generous, savvy, creative, tenacious, loving, enraged, humorous, and resilient. None was either meek or tentative about wanting to know about me. It was rare not to be asked upfront about my marital status, religion, ethnicity, motivation, and how I intended to use their stories. I responded to their straightforward queries, and sought to locate and legitimize myself by talking about being either a student or professor conducting research and doing advocacy work in the United States and in Israel.

The women I interviewed did not need protection from me, but research codes of ethics are built to protect study participants, so the people conducting the research are generally on their own in terms of their personal well-being. Insights into how identities such as gender, sexuality, or race/ethnicity inform ethnographic research were especially helpful given the contested nature of belonging in Israel (Alcalde 2007; Lewin and Leap 1996; Ortbals and Rinker 2009). In a similar vein, the reflections of scholars on the dangers associated with fieldwork in conflict zones (Nordstrom and Robben 1995; Huggins and Glebbeek 2009) were instructive as was the wisdom of those who have faced the emotional hazards of conducting research on domestic violence (Stanko 1997; Pickering 2001; Coles et al. 2014). The affective life of research can be both productive and constraining. Consider, for example, the value of the "hidden ethnography" of emotional exchanges between researcher and participants in the shadows (Blackman 2007; McLean and Leibing 2007), which are particularly vivid when studying either people whose politics we find repugnant (e.g., Blee 1998; Presser 2005) or people with whom we more easily empathize. On the other hand, in a recent study, seven out of every ten trained surveyors employed to gather data for the first national survey of domestic violence in Israel dropped out of the project because of "difficulty in coping with the highly emotionally charged content of the questionnaire" (Eisikovits, Winstok, and Fishman 2004, 735).

Beyond generalized concerns with personal safety, it was my training and experience as a rape crisis volunteer in Durham and the four months I spent becoming a volunteer at the antiviolence hotline for battered women in Haifa—which included how to cope with and distinguish between the emotional pain of women who call, and my own, and how to be aware of potential exposure to becoming collateral damage (Dobash and Dobash 2015)—that provided me not only with pragmatic advice but also with the camaraderie of women committed to doing similar work.

Stories for Social Change

Storytelling is surging in popularity, at least according to my Stitcher podcast app, which accompanied me during walk-breaks while writing this book. Here in Phoenix, open-mic and curated, live storytelling events have popped up all over town. Regional and thematic film festivals continue to attract large audiences, despite the technological capability that allows us to demand that stories be sent to our personal screens, wherever we are. Instead of closing its doors because of Amazon's drone delivery system, the independent bookstore in town recently opened another branch location. Meanwhile, popular role-play video games enable gamers to become part of a story-in-the-making, while virtual reality–based treatment for PTSD helps patients relive traumatic stories with a witness to guide them safely through them. In a similar, but less structured way, my older sister provides her therapy clients with a safe space to tell and craft revised versions of their stories. My younger sister and her best friend take their personal experiences, recast them into bawdy stories set to music, and then perform them in front of crowds who laugh until they cry, self-identifying with the duo's creative send-ups of real-life scenarios. People enjoy hearing other people's stories. And most enjoy telling their stories to other people, which is one of the reasons why I became an anthropologist.

Anthropology and its signature mode of ethnographic research have given me the chance not only to seek out other people's stories, but also to reflect on what makes a "good story," along with the cultural rules and rhetorical strategies that determine who can tell which kind of story about what to whom, and for what purpose—that is, what has been called "the politics of storytelling" (Shuman 1986, 2005). Candidates standing for election, for example, tell prospective voters stories of overcoming adversity. Advocates mobilize constituents via problem-based tragic stories that end with proposed solutions. Fundraisers catalyze donors with stories of organizational success. Children express moral stories of righteousness and blame. Survivors of political violence recount their experiences of innocence and suffering during a truth and reconciliation hearing. These context-specific and genre-based stories effectively circulate in various venues because of their association with credibility, authenticity, the "local" and the "real." Well-told stories make concepts or unknown issues come alive and pique curiosity; resulting insights may stick better because stories trigger emotional responses in ways that PowerPoint bullet points simply do not. The emotional engagement that stories offer is behind their emancipatory potential as well. Other people's stories may offer a listener a new perspective on an established idea or offer a new idea and, along the way, stir reflexivity and empathy in a listener or reader.

Despite our inability to explain "the pervasiveness of storytelling" or "the existence of particular forms of storytelling in particular places or periods," storytelling is commonly claimed as one of the universal characteristics that makes us uniquely human, as a means to "transform the inexplicable into the meaningful" (Shuman 2005, 10). The turn to the study of narratives and to storytelling as an epistemologically legitimate source of evidence within social research indicates either their enduring centrality or our enduring belief thereof. The question remains as to the liberatory potential or effectiveness of sharing one's story in the name of social change, and the inherent risks and limitations in doing so (Polletta 2006).

What is common to the study of domestic violence, regardless of disciplinary approach or geographical location, is the challenge to translate the lived experience of suffering and violence into a legible language because injurious pain is subjective and can be inexplicable. Anyone who has tried to describe it to a loved one or a doctor grasps how difficult it can be for the one who listens to really "get" it. Elaine Scarry (1985, 4) calls this the chasm between the certainty of "having pain" and the doubt felt when "hearing about pain." Complicating translational matters is that domestic violence is a stigmatized and privatized form of violence, whose definitional boundaries are a moving and hazy target. Its manifestations have only recently been deemed socially unacceptable or criminalized, or even named, and they cause both seen and unseen wounds for which victims are often held accountable.

In the domestic violence world, the very idea of "telling your story" has become a genre for the purposes of self-healing and social change, akin to the coming-out story for LGBT people or unauthorized immigrant youth, echoing ACT UP's AIDS activist slogan that "Silence = Death." Telling stories about stigmatized topics or by people who have been tainted socially by their identity or victimization is a subversive strategy, a means to "break the silence" on a taboo subject. Fittingly, the names of several books on domestic violence signal the desire to breach a tacit norm by talking about that which has been deemed unsuitable to tell, such as *Scream Quietly or the Neighbors Will Hear*, *Silence Is Deadly*, *Speaking the Unspeakable*, *The Shame Born in Silence*, and *Breaking Down the Wall of Silence*.

I have observed stories about domestic violence being used in a number of ways to produce empathy in an audience: a (formerly) battered woman tells her life story to help train hotline volunteers, submits an application for an order of protection detailing what happened to her, gives testimony at a legislative hearing, or serves as a witness in the criminal case against her intimate partner. I also have harnessed the power of domestic violence stories in my classroom, where students read first-person accounts of victimization or "getting free," watch a documentary about women incarcerated for killing the men who beat them, analyze newspaper stories about domestic violence homicides, or discuss the themes in fictional stories or popular songs they bring to class. In an effort to integrate student exposure with (simulated) experience, I facilitate the "In Her Shoes" activity developed by the Washington State Coalition Against Domestic Violence, which asks participants to take on a role, based on actual women's stories, to make constrained choices as they navigate safety in their home and community (Adelman et al. 2016).

The alleviation of victim blaming and the ultimate goal of social transformation may be pursued, in part, by the telling of one's story of domestic violence, in this case, to a researcher. Personal stories about domestic violence may be particularly subversive, or perhaps jarring to listeners, given the shame and silence that have been required of its victims. The disjunctive nature of women telling personal stories of violence may simultaneously tap into the authenticity associated with such disclosure, while making women vulnerable to critique for telling stories that either do not conform to culturally valued narrative tropes or do not reinforce dominant models of victimhood (Maynes, Pierce, and Laslett 2008).

Women battered by their intimate partners have multiple salient identities, competing needs and interests, and differential access to resources, all of which exist alongside the domestic pain (Sa'ar 2007). Thus constant caution is required to avoid representing women as a uniformly vulnerable class of people who are always already victims or to avoid repeating storylines that unintentionally "generate expectations of battered women's fortitude that are unrealistic" (Polletta 2009, 1491). Monolithic narratives with either an overabundance or absence of agency also may limit the public's ability to accept the range of experiences women have when faced with an intimate partner who batters them. Research can "emphasize the diverse experiences women have of sexual violence, rather than thinking that we must conceptualize what we find in common as grounds for legitimacy" (Heberle 1996, 72).

In this book I share stories from different points of view,[9] such as victims and survivors of domestic violence, frontline workers, advocates and activists, and representatives of the state; and stories told by people from distinct as well as overlapping social locations based on national identity, religion, religiosity, ethnicity, citizenship, or geography. Along the way, I include a range of narrative styles or modes: ethnographic, confessional, chronological, empirical, mediated, bureaucratic, legal and transformational, as well as stories about the ordinary and the exceptional. I also relate stories that typically are missing or marginalized when discussing domestic violence.

Embedded within the ritual of storytelling is the presumed social distance between narrator and listener. The story is the mechanism intended to bridge that distance. As a stand-alone mechanism, such storytelling may contribute to the development of interpersonal empathy: a physiological and emotional response combined with a sense of the other person's world, all the while noting the experience is theirs, and not yours (Segal 2011). However, depending upon the social distance, the context, and the relations of identity and power between narrator and listener, personal stories may also reinforce stereotypes, elicit disgust or pity, make some feel overwhelmed, hopeless or guilty, or encourage people to feel entitled, prepared and able to "rescue" vulnerable "others." Because of this and other unintended consequences, appropriating someone's story, whether they share it directly or indirectly, can be exploitative, or even worsen the problem.

Pedagogically it is recommended to address the conditions that create opportunities and inequalities behind the violence, also known as "contextual understanding of systemic barriers," and help people imagine what it is like to be part of another group, referred to as "macro perspective taking," so they can identify (and perhaps take) potential ameliorative steps toward social change, what my colleague Elizabeth Segal terms "social empathy" (Segal 2011, 2013). Yet given the depths of entrenched structural inequalities, the multiple stories of suffering and social problems we hear every day, and our increasingly short attention spans and memories, I question an overreliance on storytelling in the name of social change.

I was struck by the assumptions, costs, and limitations inherent in storytelling as a mechanism of social change in a blog entry recently posted on "Africa Is a Country." The entry profiled Mutasim Ali, an asylum seeker from Darfur, Sudan, who has lived in Israel since 2009, much of that time in a detention center. Ali is an accomplished social justice advocate, fighting for the right of asylum seekers to stay in the country with official authorization. Talya Swissa, the blogger-interviewer, explains his advocacy work:

Mutasim told his asylum story many times. He shared it at universities and political forums, as well as in community centers in South Tel Aviv while working with the African Refugee Development Center (ARDC). Yet according to him, the success of such individual narratives is limited and temporary in Israel. "I can't even count the times I told the story of how I became an asylum seeker, sometimes in large and prestigious forums. It doesn't help and it's degrading." Mutasim held several meetings with the residents of South Tel Aviv, yet whenever he felt there was a breakthrough and that a dialogue had begun, some politician would come along and incite the population against Africans. He therefore no longer believes in the power of his personal asylum narrative in influencing public opinion, at least not without ending the ambiguous and unclear policies towards the asylum population. When asked about his strategy to promote the rights of asylum seekers, Mutasim said that it is a question Israelis should ask themselves. "We the asylum seekers do not have much left to do. The next protest should come from the Israeli public. It is not only about the African population. You [Israelis] should ask yourself what kind of society you want to live in."

Mutasim Ali points to the exhaustion of strategically crafting and telling and retelling one's story as a means to persuade people seemingly far removed from the justice problem at hand, or who perceive themselves as distant from or having no part in creating his experience of injustice.

Simply sharing a multiplicity of battered women's stories is not sufficient to effect social change, in part because these stories are not consumed within a neutral context untouched by social hierarchies and skeptical publics. Cultural stereotypes and ethnocentric comparisons, which are, for example, embedded in every storytelling context, too easily displace violence from one community to another, enabling a chain of deniability whereby the marked, socially weaker link's violence is labeled as collectively normative, while violence attributed to the unmarked, socially stronger link is labeled as an individual aberration. Upon hearing that I was studying domestic violence, neighbors and taxi drivers in Israel would recommend that I conduct research with a socially marginalized community to which they did not belong: "the Mizrahim," "the haredim," "the Russians," or "the Arabs." Each marked group was serially described as a combination of either primitive, violent, or criminal.

In contrast to the presumption of rampant domestic violence among Russian immigrants, who were commonly classified as conniving alcoholics, for example, appositional cultural myths regarding the putative innocence and purity of unmarked "model minority" groups circulated as well. I still astonish Jewish people who disconcertingly utter the refrain that they thought that "Jewish men don't batter their wives" (B. Swirski 1991a). Judeophilic Christians in the US similarly express disbelief and then disappointment when I explain that, yes, domestic violence occurs among both secular and religious Jewish Israelis.

Others seek to distance their own community from violence because of its location along a parallel chain of vulnerability. The entrenched association of Arabs and violence led an accomplished senior scholar of the Middle East to urge me to pursue a different topic or to not include Palestinian Arabs within the research purview: "Do we need yet another study of Arab men being violent?" she asked me. Indeed, Rhoda Kanaaneh and Isis Nusair (2010, 13) argue that "gender violence among Palestinians in particular functions as a kind of 'colonial scandal' (Dirks 1997, 209); it is fetishized by the Israeli media and used as proof of Palestinian backwardness—justifying the supposedly liberal state's control and civilizing mission." Evidence of this tension was revealed to me when a religious leader ended a research interview with me by expressing the hope that I would "say only positive things" about his people.

Emerging from similar concerns about exposure, although I conducted research in a city known for its small but vibrant lesbian community,[10] domestic violence was not and has not yet become part of its primary activist agenda. Nor was sexism or gender violence an early priority among Palestinian women who faced discrimination as members of a national minority (Espanioly 1991, 150). Embattled communities, whether based on religion, nationality, or sexual orientation, may prioritize external hostility over intracommunal forms of violence. Unfortunately, when communities treat domestic violence like dirty laundry that must be hidden in order for them to be perceived of as civilized or respectable, it devalues and compromises women's lives.

Yet violence is never completely hidden. Family, friends, neighbors, shopkeepers, and coworkers all know about domestic violence by witnessing it, hearing about it, or perpetrating it, as do frontline workers such as doctors, nurses, social workers, law enforcement officers, and religious and community leaders. Elizabeth Stanko (2006, 549) argues, "There is record after record of violence in so many places. . . . Why do we insist on speaking about the hidden when we can be documenting and challenging what we do see in a more comprehensive and systematic way?" In order to better understand why domestic violence was such a salient issue, this study seeks to reveal how domestic violence became culturally knowable and to trace the visible but opaque relationship between the state and domestic violence.

THEORIZING THE STATE

Scholars across the social sciences and the humanities differ in how we conceptualize "the state," to the point that defining what is meant by this phrase can be an exhausting and somewhat elusive intellectual journey. The state is just one form of social control, organized governance, or political system, based on kinship, territory, commerce, or sovereignty, which humans have invented over time in support of collective life (Vincent 1990). For my purposes here, what is notable is that the very notion of "the state" has a history. The modern state as we know it—in essence, a type of political entity that qualifies for membership in the United Nations and serves as a conduit for economic exploitation and accumulation—is a relatively recent human innovation.

What currently counts as a state bears some resemblance to but is not a reproduction of the kind of polities formed, say, during Egyptian rule in the third millennium BCE, after the collapse of the Western Roman Empire, within the Iroquois Confederacy, throughout the Ottoman Empire, or in the early era of postcolonialism and nationalist self-determination (Opello and Rosow 2004; Lewellen 2003). Nor are contemporaneous states generic or unitary. Indeed, "[T]he difficulty in studying the state resides in the fact that the state—as unified political subject or structure—does not exist; it is a collective illusion, the reification of an idea that masks real power relations under the guise of public interest" (Aretxaga 2003, 400). The state is made up of a heterogeneous set of actors with varying interests and authority and is experienced differently depending on one's social location and the context and place of one's encounter with "the state." States nested today within global capitalism can neither be described nor are they experienced homogenously.

Yet common among states is the notion of "statecraft": future-oriented efforts required to perpetuate a state rather than have it devolve into a historical fact of the past (Devetak 1995, 21 in Ping 2005, 16). Statecraft creates a sense of belonging (or dispossession) as well as possibilities for well-being, or harm (Aronoff and Kubik 2013; Sharma and Gupta 2006; Migdal 2013). The construction of domesticity and the governance of domestic violence are just two aspects of the cultural work of statecraft.

DOMESTIC VIOLENCE STUDIES

Intellectual starting points for the contemporary study of violence in the family can be traced to writing in the medical and psychiatric fields on "the battered child syndrome'" (Kempe et al. 1962) and "the wifebeater's wife" (Snell, Rosenwald, and Robey 1964). Both studies examined victims to better understand these newly visible forms of violence. This tendency continued for decades. The systematic study of marital violence or wife beating entered the academy through two research tracks illustrated by the distinction in titles of these two foundational texts: *Violence in the Family* (Steinmetz and Straus 1974) and *Violence Against Wives* (Dobash and Dobash 1979).[11] The family violence track, which originated in the medical study of parental abuse of children, now includes interpersonal violence across the lifespan, from child abuse to sibling abuse to spouse abuse to elder abuse (Kurz 1998; Barnett, Miller-Perrin, and Perrin 2011). Family violence researchers generally align with positivist social science epistemological and methodological claims related to objectivity and rely on survey data (Straus, Gelles, and Steinmetz 1980). This is due in part to the need to demonstrate that reliable and valid research on the topic using nonclinical samples was possible. Early on, family violence researchers pointed to "battered husbands" and violent women as a key problem in the United States. Family violence research continues to question the validity of gender asymmetry.

In contrast, the violence-against-women track originally placed woman battering within a feminist gender-based analysis including sexual harassment and rape (Dobash and Dobash 1979, 1992; Martin 1976; Schechter 1982; Stanko 1985). It now has an even broader conceptualization of gender violence (Merry 2008). Gender violence scholars tend to embrace a more reflexive and interpretive orientation to the relationship between researchers and research subjects and have used both quantitative and qualitative data. A critical area of domestic violence research attends to its intersections with gender, race and ethnicity, immigration, poverty, ability, and sexual orientation (Sokoloff and Dupont 2005).

Over the years, discipline after discipline has "discovered" domestic violence, and it has become a legitimate object of academic study. However, a debate remains between feminist and nonfeminist research over the political nature of the production of knowledge about domestic violence (Adelman and Coker 2016; Renzetti 1997). Feminist legal scholars in the United States taught the first few courses on domestic violence in law schools in 1988, yet accredited schools of social work still are not required to deliver a stand-alone course on domestic violence (Adelman and Coker 2016). Today some scholars retain a connection while others maintain a firewall between their research and advocacy work (Weis and Haldane 2015) or eschew engagement with social movements or applied work altogether. The domestic violence studies literature has grown so unwieldy that many researchers fail to benefit from cross-disciplinary insights. Yet major trends in the literature transcend disciplinary boundaries and coalesce around methodological, research design, and justice concerns.

A dominant trend within domestic violence studies is a body of unwittingly decontextualized research that tends to extract violence from the everyday life in which it is produced: that is, large-scale surveys to study crime and victimization (Straus, Gelles, and Steinmetz 1980; Brush 1990). The strength of the survey approach is the production of easily shared state or multistate snapshots, such as reports published by the Centers for Disease Control (Black et al. 2011), Israel's Ministry of Public Security (Regev and Shiri 2012), Statistics Canada (2013), the United Nations Statistics Division (2015), and the World Health Organization (García-Moreno et al. 2005), which often carry with them the imprimatur of "official statistics" (Ellsberg et al. 2001, 4; Ellsberg and Heise 2005). This approach also results in comparable data sets by using tools such as the Conflict Tactics Scale. Surveys document the frequency, extent, and pervasiveness of domestic violence and produce persuasive quantitative data for policy and evaluative purposes, but they also result in relatively two-dimensional or flattened insight into the experience and effects of domestic violence. Moreover, they highlight the limitations of applying culturally specific terms in a one-size-fits-all way.

Similarly, psychological studies, based on self-report surveys, interviews, or experiments, seek to classify violent personalities and compile predictive characterological models of pathological batterers and victims (e.g., Dutton 1995; Bancroft and Silverman 2011). Psychological studies of domestic violence, often based on gender symmetry, offer etiological explanations, including genetic, neurological, interpersonal, situational, emotional, developmental, and trauma-based dimensions, which may offer new avenues for research, but mainly reject feminist perspectives when they do so (Dutton and Corvo 2006; also see Duluth's response by Gondolf 2007 and Dobash and Dobash 1992).

A second trend in domestic violence studies is a wealth of research that relies on the experiences of "captured" populations, that is, women and men who have interacted with the legal system or social services in response to domestic violence. This site-specific focus is due to the centrality of criminal and legal processes in the regulation of domestic violence and the relative ease of access researchers have to people, for example, in policing, perhaps the most common point of entry into the domestic violence regulatory system (e.g., Miller 2005; Sherman and Cohn 1990). Courts, too, have been a viable space for learning about domestic violence and recruiting family members for research (e.g., Durfee 2011; Fischer and Rose 1995; Merry 2001; Ptacek 1999). Despite restrictions placed on institutions like prisons, domestic violence researchers have generated critical knowledge about the disproportionately small number of convicted and incarcerated domestic violence offenders, and the prevention and intervention initiatives aimed at them (e.g., Dobash and Dobash 1999, 2011; Gondolf 2012; Presser 2005).

Unfortunately, this approach limits our understanding of domestic violence to the relatively small minority of people who can be found in these regulatory and therapeutic spaces. Whether intentional or not, the overwhelming majority of this research has focused on women victims rather than men who batter (Dobash and Dobash 1999). These studies likely examine the endpoint of the most vulnerable, under-resourced women and men, leaving unexamined the full range of people's experiences. Additionally, the criminalization model of research has carved out a deviant rather than normative stance toward battering: it is what criminals do, rather than respectable citizens. Regardless of intention, this research oversamples poor families and people of color, populations disproportionately criminalized by a combination of biased justice systems and under-resourced communities (Websdale 2001). Commonly excluded from research are those who either reject state-based interventions or are denied access to them, such as undocumented immigrants, middle-class or elite white women, and LGBT people. *Battering States* avoids these constraints by studying a diverse population, many of whom have had minimal contact with either legal or social service systems.

A third trend in the study of domestic violence is whether the state is a suitable partner for solving the problem of intimate partner violence. Scholars and advocates critique an overreliance on state-based solutions because they create unintended consequences: the disproportionate imprisonment of poor men and women of color (INCITE 2006); unrealistic expectations for women to end their intimate relationships in order to be free from violence (Merry 2001); disempowering policies that transfer decision-making from the batterer to the state (Bumiller 2008; Goodmark 2010); and the depoliticization of the battered women's movement more generally (Lehrner and Allen 2009; Schneider 2000).

Others argue that the criminalization of domestic violence has legitimized women's claims for state-based protection, but has done little to ameliorate the conditions that entrap women in intimate partnerships (Coker 2001; Potter 2008; Richie 1995, 2012). Scholars have uncovered a pattern of states that pass but fail to implement anti-domestic violence laws-on-the-books (Hajjar 2004; Lazarus-Black 2007). The global anti-gender violence movement is implicated, too, in the debate over animating state responsibility for domestic violence as violations of women's human rights (Merry 2006; Montoya 2013; Weldon 2002). The healthy debate continues as to whether or how domestic violence is best addressed vis-à-vis the state. However, rather than determining its suitable role, *Battering States* considers how the cultural politics of the state itself shape domestic violence.

RETHINKING THE "DOMESTIC" IN DOMESTIC VIOLENCE

The approach taken by this study demands a redefinition of the term domestic violence and a reorientation of the concept from an individual perspective toward a macro-level analysis. The redefinition indexes theoretical and pragmatic issues based on the phrase's multiple meanings, and it serves as a key to the relationship between the family and the state. First, the term "domestic" in domestic violence is a synonym for the anthropological concept of kinship-based social relations. One common contemporary pattern is the household formed through marriage, reproduction, and labor, where socioeconomic power is arranged hierarchically by gender and generation. Non-anthropologists refer colloquially to this bundle of social relations as a family, hence the overlap in meaning among the phrases "domestic violence," "family violence," "relationship violence," and "intimate partner violence." The "domestic" in domestic violence refers narrowly to kin-to-kin violence between family members, as opposed to violence among non-kin beyond the residential household.

Thus differentiated from public forms of violence, domestic violence is set aside as a privatized phenomenon, often "invisible and ignored," if not sanctioned affirmatively (Fineman and Mykitiuk 1994, xiii). This is because a gendered ideological distinction between public and private demarcates where the apolitical, natural "family" ends and the political, man-made "state" begins (Ross and Rapp 1981). Feminist anthropologists analyzed the distinction between "private" and "public" to explain what they perceived as the universal devaluation of women's status and female oppression (Reiter 1975; Rosaldo and Lamphere 1974).

The family then becomes a metaphor for or a microcosm of the state in that the distribution of power in the family mirrors normative social relations within a state. According to the ideological distinction between public and private, states are charged with maintaining public order, rendering the home—and any violence within it—as beyond their jurisdiction (Gordon 1988). State inaction or noninterference based on this sociolegal doctrine of privacy, whether explicit or implied, becomes a choice about the nature of family values, and whose safety matters within a state's borders.[12] In keeping with this logic, states around the world have had to be cajoled to even recognize domestic violence as a social problem and then forced to consider it a matter within their regulatory purview.

Second, despite the traditionally hands-off nature of the state when it comes to domestic violence, the state has been and continues to be involved in the domestic sphere of life in any number of ways. The family and its associated ideology of familism—idealized and yet malleable notions of the family—are critical to processes of state-building and reformation (Haney and Pollard 2013; Barrett and McIntosh 1982). The state helps determine how the normative family is structured, how its membership is determined, and the configuration of its social responsibilities. The state "makes" and regulates families because of its control over rules about who counts as kin—who can marry whom, which relations belong in a family, what kind of reproduction is legal, which families can be reunited across political borders, and who is supposed to care for whom; thus it determines who qualifies for membership in and who is eligible for the benefits associated with the state's political family (Stevens 1999, 6). States do so, for example, by refashioning the moral order of domestic life and gender relations within the realm of the family, as part of the development of new colonial settlements, or in the building of postcolonial states (Lazarus-Black 1994; Merry

1996). States also commonly manage sexual relations, reproduction, and marriage in an effort to guard against sullying the purported purity of racialized hierarchical boundaries among the governed population (Pascoe 2009). Justifications for states waging war, too, are made in the name of protecting women, the family, or the "homefront" (Russo 2006).

The state values certain family forms over others, such as heterosexual and nuclear families; and it gives advantages to some families over others; in Israel, for example, it gives advantages to Jewish families over Palestinian families and to citizen families over migrant worker families. The state also treats various family members differently (e.g., men versus women, or children versus adults) through marriage, health and welfare, immigration, employment, and military policies. In short, in a set of patterned ways, the family engenders states at the same time that the state engenders families.

Third, the term "domestic" also signals the internality of a state, often thought of as a national collective or homeland, as contrasted with international relations. Because of this, political candidates at the national level need to demonstrate their expertise in domestic as well as foreign affairs. In essence, production of the domestic—home and homeland—is about creating boundaries of difference and commonality: insiders belong and thus are deserving of the state's resources from within and protective power against outsiders. The resulting doubled space of domesticity, both the home and the homeland, are mutually constitutive and come about and are maintained through various violent processes and everyday cultural practices. Nationalist discourse, for example, formed in response to a real or perceived threat from an external source (colonialism, Western imperialism, genocide, global capitalism, etc.) can invest women, a signifier of the family, with what Chatterjee (1989, 622) refers to as "the dubious honor" of representing cultural tradition or embodying the nation. Cultural tradition and national identity are often transmitted symbolically through motherhood (Peterson and Runyan 2010). Mothers physically and socially reproduce the nation either in support of or in opposition to the state (Berkovitch 1999; Kahn 2000; Kanaaneh 2002); men protect and defend the feminized home front as warriors (Enloe 2007).

An image of the traditional family also can be used politically to assert a state's culturally authentic domestic landscape. It was not until 2015 that the US Supreme Court rejected the notion of same-sex couples forming families as un-American (Canaday 2009; Lugg and Adelman 2015), and postcolonial states in the global south and within the former Soviet Union have mobilized "the traditional family" against the putative foreign enemy of "homosexuality." Family life that conforms shores up state power; flawed families can be blamed for political failure or labeled as traitorous (Parson 2013; Haney and Pollard 2013). Bringing the family back into the state helps reveal the politics of domestic violence: how violence in the home is produced alongside the culture of the state.[13]

With regard to domestic violence, the state remains a central locus of both concern and advocacy. Yet conventional theories of the state across the philosophical spectrum ignore domestic violence because of their focus on either national (domestic) politics or the international life of the state rather than on how the discursive construction of the "domestic" informs life at home. Consequently, rather than focus on individual characteristics to explain domestic violence, or individual interventions to address domestic violence, this new level of analysis entails the point where gendered intimate partner violence intersects with imposed or embraced cultural constructions of the state, that is, the politics of domestic violence.

THE MEANINGS OF "VIOLENCE" IN DOMESTIC VIOLENCE

Domestic violence studies reflect a strong undercurrent of ahistorical presumptions about and decontextualized perspectives on its object of study. Scholars across the disciplines who conduct research on domestic violence and use related concepts such as abuse, battering, controlling behaviors, domination, injury, interpersonal aggression, sexual violence, suffering, trauma, victims and victimization do so often under an implied assumption that the meanings of these complex concepts are self-evident or shared across time and place, rather than considering the social conditions that produce the very category of "domestic violence" or continual contestations over or gaps in its meaning (Dell and Korotana 2000; Stanko 2006). Even what it means to be a victim of domestic violence is a contingent cultural transaction. What domestic violence means among frontline workers varies, and it differs again when described by survivors, witnesses, or perpetrators of domestic violence.

The very meaning of violence cannot be extracted from the context in which it occurs (Merry 2008). The category of domestic violence is emergent, contested, and multiple, accessible through a combined bottom-up and top-down analysis of the problem within the "larger social matrix in which it is embedded" (Farmer 1996, 261). Anthropologist and sociolegal scholar David Engel (2001, 3) takes yet another step back in the analytic process: "When we say that an individual has suffered an injury, we implicitly refer to a self that is constituted in a particular way and is therefore vulnerable to particular kinds of harm. . . . Because such concepts are socially constructed, they vary significantly across different social settings." In Israel, similar to other sites engaged with the global anti-gender violence movement, that context is a transnational field where normative definitions of domestic violence used for personal or advocacy purposes circulate as the bureaucratized result of long-term social movement organizing (Merry 2006; Hemment 2004). Although the variation in meaning can make it difficult to conduct comparative research, Elizabeth Stanko (2006, 552) argues that it is "this fluidity that provides the space for disrupting violence, altering its impact on people's lives and on the way in which we give meaning to it in society at large."

What I have named as "the politics of domestic violence" is thus in partial response to the call for anthropologists to "resocialize" the study of structural violence by reintegrating biology (the body and its suffering) along with history and political economy (the "materiality of the social") into our analyses of suffering and violence (Farmer 2004, 307–08). *Battering States*, then, is an attempt to connect what Farmer terms the "ethnographically visible"—here, the public recognition of domestic violence as a social problem in Israel, the everyday lives of battered women across the country, or the number of women killed by their husbands or ex-husbands each year according to law enforcement—to "the social machinery of oppression," in this case study, the dynamic decision making related to becoming and being a state. *Battering States* analyzes the embodiment of domestic violence along with the material and ideological conditions that make it possible. Within this culturally contextualized view, domestic violence is studied as a social phenomenon rather than as an individual problem, as a process rather than as an event (Lawrence and Karim 2007, 11), and as being integral to a state's historical development and future direction rather than distanced as a cultural problem associated only with its marginalized citizenry.

THE GOVERNANCE OF DOMESTIC VIOLENCE

States are implicated in the governance of domestic violence—giving domestic violence its meaning, structuring its manifestation, and shaping its management—in uneven and often messy ways, both direct and indirect, by setting the family aside as a space beyond its purview; by rejecting domestic violence as a problem worthy of investment or refusing to intervene when asked; by reforming idealized domestic relations when overseeing marriage and divorce law or distributing economic resources; by defining the parameters of acceptable forms of domestic violence when criminalizing domestic violence and punishing offenders; by coproducing new subjectivities of the battered woman and the violent man through the adjudication and social-service processing (Merry 1996); by funding domestic violence resources either "in-house" or via community-based partnerships (Singh 2012); by participating in events organized against domestic violence; by endorsing international instruments related to domestic violence; and by importing or exporting best practices related to domestic violence. This continuum of public engagement with domestic violence uniquely depends on place and time. To be sure, the governance of domestic violence has never resulted in the eradication of the problem; public responses to it have ranged between silence and affirmation, and between limited and infrequent intervention.

Anthropological accounts of the governance of domestic violence vary accordingly. Ethnological evidence documents that most societies establish and police the line, either formally or informally, between acceptable and unacceptable forms of men's violence against their wives, although what constitutes "acceptable" is a category contingent on contextual interpretation (Adelman 2010). The widely used experimental/feminist ethnography, *Nisa* (Shostak 1981), for example, which recorded repeated acts of what may have been considered acceptable forms of punishment or violence, did so unreflexively; this not only naturalized the behavior but also dismissed it as a legitimate, analytical problem available for study. Colonial imposition of new ideas about marriage and masculinity, along with new standards surrounding sexuality and sobriety, shaped nineteenth century Hawaiian courts' ideas and practices regarding unacceptable levels of husbands' use of violence against their wives (Merry 2000). Examining research on domestic violence from a historic or comparative perspective supplies ample evidence that states have been drawn into the regulation of family life in a variety of ways, some more narrow than others.

Contemporary ethnographic research also finds ambivalent governance of domestic violence even after legislative steps have been taken to ameliorate it (Lazarus-Black and Merry 2003). States can create "an illusion that it is representing the common interest by passing legislation to protect persons who experience domestic abuse while in reality it provides them with very little protection" (Lazarus-Black 2007, 91; Hajjar 2004). States, too, make battered women's suffering and resistance largely invisible through pervasive state violence, coupled with a weak sense of citizenship (Alcalde 2010a and 2010b; Lancaster 1992; Menjivar 2011; Shalhoub-Kevorkian 2009).

State violence also can be an integral part of the project of state-sanctioned family life (Parson 2013). The polity's policing of its physical as well as cultural borders engenders domestic violence (Abraham 2000; Adelman 2003; Adelman, Erez, and Shalhoub-Kevorkian 2003), so too does the existence and execution of public policies that distinguish deserving from undeserving families (Adelman 2004a; True 2012). I extend this work by rendering relevant hidden data sources and untold stories about the governance of domestic violence.

Battering States begins with the premise that the state has had, and continues to have, a contentious and dynamic relationship with domestic violence (Adelman and Morgan 2006; Morgan, Adelman, and Soli 2008). The second-wave feminist slogan "the personal is political" drew attention to domestic life—and men's violence against women in the family—as worthy of cultural analysis, political organizing, and public investment. This brought and still brings a critical perspective to the study of domestic violence because it shifts the explanatory framework for domestic violence from isolated victims of individual men's deviancy to socially structured patterns of behaviors.

I build on this analysis by arguing its obverse, that the "political is personal"— that is, statecraft configures "the domestic" and makes possible the living conditions within it, including domestic violence. As previously noted, the ideological distinction between the domestic and the "not domestic" has created difficulties for activists and policy makers attempting to bring attention to domestic violence (Duggan 2003; Fineman 1991, 1995); in contrast to the public sphere, the home is assumed to be a harmonious shelter and beyond the reach of state intervention. Ironically, this promise of privacy has been broken most often when it comes to families within marginalized communities, whether poor, people of color, or members of religious or national minorities (Richie 1995, 2015; Erez, Ibarra, and Gur 2015).

In this book I conduct an audit across several common areas of statecraft to reveal how domestic violence can be, unexpectedly, the product of and informed by political concerns that are typically not included in discussions about intimate partner violence; nor is intimate partner violence commonly found in scholarly conversations about the state. These concerns include how a state defines itself and its status among other states, how it organizes its governance and legal systems, how it establishes sovereignty and defends its borders, and how it forges its economy. In Israel, for example, where a legally pluralistic system helps to determine not only one's religious and national identities, but also the state's rationale for existence, marriage and divorce are under the sole jurisdiction of state-funded religious courts. Meanwhile, either the state's religious or family courts can adjudicate issues such as child custody and support, property division, and spousal support. This arrangement provides husbands, but not wives, legal prerogatives to control the status of their marital relationships, and all too often, the ability to hold women hostage in marriage, with few if any exit strategies (Adelman 2000; Weiss and Gross-Horowitz 2012). In this way a combination of family law's cultural underpinning of the state and the state's configurations of family law constructs a clear and legal pathway to domestic violence.

Instead of evaluating the effectiveness of the state as a locus of activism for the anti-domestic violence movement, or as an injurious form of protection to battered women, the book asks how the very process of building and maintaining a state shapes domestic violence. It does so within a relatively new state in the Middle East, which has been mobilized against domestic violence to help transform a personalized injury into a public concern. In this way the study complements but does not reproduce the emerging critique of the current orientation of the anti-domestic violence movement and its location within the penal or surveillance state.

ISRAEL AS A CASE STUDY

The modern state of Israel is a uniquely productive and challenging place to study the connections between statecraft and domestic violence because of its violence-scarred geopolitical location and domestic diversity, its engagement with twentieth century postwar nationalism and twenty-first century global capitalism, and its contribution to the new global anti-gender violence movement within a context of contested legal and religious pluralism. As a result, it is impossible to tell a unified narrative about or even describe the state's demography, history, or geography without conditional phrases, multiple viewpoints, or explanatory digressions. For example, the state's official commemoration of its founding on Independence Day is contrasted with the Palestinian counter-commemoration on the same day, what they mark as a catastrophe: Al-Nakba Day (Adwan, Bar-On, and Naveh 2012; Masalha 2005). Therefore attempts to offer streamlined commentary for the purpose of introducing the Israeli case study will be frustratingly incomplete because of its contested complexity. The overwhelming majority of qualitative research on Israeli society focuses on either Jewish or Palestinian citizens, perhaps because of convenience, language, lack of access, or lack of interest. Research on Palestinians in Israel often charts either their advancement because of state policies or the discrimination against them by the state. That said, research that offers nuanced analyses or integrated perspectives on Israeli society have guided this study.

Geographically, at about 8,000 square miles (excluding the West Bank and Gaza Strip), Israel, which sits on the eastern shore of the Mediterranean Sea, is similar in size to Slovenia, El Salvador, or the state of New Jersey. According to armistice lines established in 1949, sometimes referred to as pre-1967 borders or the Green Line, Israel abuts Lebanon to the north and Syria to the northeast; resource and land disputes persist across both borders. However, Israel's southwest border with Egypt and its eastern border with Jordan have been settled through peace treaties. Still, the state of Israel contains, administers, or occupies noncontiguous Palestinian territories comprising the 140-square-mile Gaza Strip located at the southern edge of Israel's coastline and the West Bank (of the Jordan River) located inland, between Israel and Jordan. The status of Jerusalem and its borders remain contested, too. Within the Green Line, Israeli population density is high, but varies by region: Tel Aviv/Yafo is twice as dense as Haifa, and the Tel Aviv district is one hundred times more populated than the southern district of the Negev desert, anchored by the small city of Be'er Sheva.

Similar to other new states, Israel is a country constituted by layers and waves of wanted as well as unwanted indigenous and immigrant communities, with an entrenched yet critiqued melting pot model of assimilation. As a result, Israel's heterogeneous population can be sorted according to national identity, religion (and religiosity), ethnicity and country of origin, generation, and geography (Dominguez 1989).

Israel's Central Bureau of Statistics (2015) issues an annual report that includes a catalog of identities considered salient to the bureaucratic state. The state's primary classification is "national," meaning Jewish or Arab. According to its most recent calculations, out of a total of 8.345 million people, 6.251 million or 74.9 percent were identified as Jews, 1.730 million or 20.7 percent were identified as Arabs, and 364,000 or 4.4 percent were categorized as "Other." CBS population reports account for Jewish Israeli citizens living in Judea and Samaria (referred to as the West Bank or "the occupied territories" by those critical of the state's political relationship to this area of land), but not this region's Palestinian residents. The state's Jewish population also is sorted by an immigrant's continent or country of origin; those born in Israel are sorted by the continent or country of origin of their father. The CBS distinguishes among Jews from "Europe/America," Africa, and Asia. The desire to categorize people by "continent of origin" stems both from the immigrant-based growth logic of the Israeli state and from ethnic and political divisions among Mizrahi, Sephardi, and Ashkenazi Jews (Dominguez 1989). The term "Mizrahi," that is, "eastern," describes a person's location-based identity, and refers to Jews living in or from the Middle East and North Africa. Similarly, the term "Sephardi," that is, "of Spain" or Spanish, points to the geographic diaspora of Jews who were expelled from Spain and Portugal at the end of the fifteenth century, and who then migrated to the Middle East, Latin America, and elsewhere. The term "Ashkenazi" describes Jews who live in or whose families hale from Central and Western Europe; Ashkenazi immigrants from English-speaking countries such as Canada and South Africa are known colloquially in Israel as "Anglo-Saxons." Overall, the categories of national and religious identities overlap officially for Jewish Israelis, while their ethnic identities vary. In contrast, the state's "Arab" national category can be disaggregated into several religion-based communities, including Muslim (and Bedouin), Christian, and Druze citizens of Israel; although not captured in CBS reports, many Muslim and Christian Arabs, and some Druze, identify as part of the Palestinian nation alongside their religion affiliation. Still, what Palestinian Arab and Jewish citizens share in common is a range of religiosity from secular to fundamentalist.

Over time, the CBS has changed who gets counted and how they get counted in population reports. Since 1995, for example, officially falling into the "other" category are non-Arab Christians (Christians not from an Arab country or Christians whose fathers were not born in an Arab country), members of other religions, and those without an official religion identity (CBS 2015, 30–37). For the most part, those in the "other" category are immigrants from the former Soviet Union (FSU) who qualified for citizenship based on a family member's classification as Jewish by the Ministry of the Interior. Many of these Jewish citizens from the FSU classified as Jewish by the Interior Ministry, however, are not recognized as such by the state's rabbinical court system, meaning they are unable to marry within the state. Since 2008, authorized foreign workers living in Israel for more than a year are no longer counted in the general population, although their number is calculated within the state's labor statistics.

The unsettled nature of its population and boundaries, its ongoing wars and conflicts, and its high profile international relations, including the large aid package it receives annually from the US, and the frequent criticism it receives from the United Nations, means that Israel is often discussed in the news. Because of this, Israel is most often linked with political rather than domestic violence. The silence regarding domestic violence is due in part to persistent myths of gender equality in Israel, where women (at least Jewish women), it is said, live on egalitarian socialist kibbutzim and serve in the army. In fact, the percentage of Jewish Israelis who have lived on a kibbutz or other utopian agricultural settlement has always been very low, and most have shifted toward or even embraced the capitalist economy. The "equality bluff," has been a barrier, among others, to pursuing and securing gender equality for women in Israel within and beyond military service (Swirki and Safir 1991).

Other cultural myths inform people's assumptions about domestic violence in Israel, too, casting cultural culpability for domestic violence on so-called "primitive" and racialized communities (Razack 1998) such as Palestinian, Russian, or Mizrahi Israelis; some assume that religion (i.e., being religious or simply being Jewish) or living in a face-to-face community would mitigate the prevalence of domestic violence in Israel; still others reason that religious fundamentalism would make one vulnerable to domestic violence. Few imagine secular middle-class Ashkenazi Jewish Israelis as having a problem with domestic violence. Israel's diverse population and the stereotypes and inequalities distributed unevenly across it present a compelling cultural space for considering the production of domestic violence along with the construction of the state.

Because of the disputed nature of Israel's heterogeneity, and enduring inequities associated with it, the cultural politics of the state remain contentious, ranging from the colors of the flag to the languages spoken in court, to the level of state budget allocations to local councils. These inequalities, mapped onto social differences, have made it difficult to effectively name, organize against, and intervene into domestic violence in Israel. Not surprisingly, scholarship has begun to reveal tensions associated with a universal approach to domestic violence within a multicultural society, particularly when there are historical patterns of state-based differential treatment of its residents and citizens (Adelman, Erez, and Shalhoub-Kevorkian 2003; Erez, Ibarra, and Gur 2015; Parson 2013; Shalhoub-Kevokian 2009). *Battering States* builds on this research by analyzing the relationship between domestic violence and a range of distinction-based inequalities, both in terms of vulnerability and various pathways to justice.

Becoming a State

Established in 1948, Israel is a relatively young state, making it possible to trace continuities and changes over time while still maintaining a focus on the state's contemporary configuration. The state's origins stem from multiple and competing forms of Jewish nationalism and religious belief, which manifested during the mid-to-late nineteenth century mainly in Europe: not all Jewish national movements—or Jews—aspired to establish a state in Palestine, or elsewhere. However, Zionist approaches to Jewish nationalism that did so encountered an Ottoman Empire embedded within a global economy comprising a diverse and quickly changing population, which soon was fought over by European powers. Inextricable links among family, religion, and the state persisted during subsequent transformations in regional governance.

The Ottoman Empire was built over the course of centuries of successive military, religious, and economically inspired conquests of territory across Europe, North Africa, and the Middle East; and at its peak, thirty-six million people lived under its rule (Davison 1963, 61) in territory beyond the Danube to the north and the Persian Gulf to the east. To ease governance of such an unwieldy territory, over time the empire was divided into a hierarchy of geographically nested administrative units (Cooke 1968; see also Heyd 1960 and Maoz 1975a). Except for a brief Egyptian occupation (1831 to 1840), the Ottomans reigned over the Palestine region, primarily referred to as Southern Syria, until the British invaded Jerusalem in 1917.

During its heyday, Islam was the empire's dominant religion. However, the Ottoman millet system permitted those of *dhimmi* status—i.e., members of recognized religious communities, such as Jews, Christians, and Armenians—to be subject to their respective communal laws and courts. Such communities, which were referred to as *ra'aya* or "protected flock," were "allowed to govern [themselves] as long as members . . . paid taxes to the state" (Starr 1994, 239). Foreign nationals, or non-*ra'aya* residents, from recognized Christian European powers in Palestine were subject to their respective courts at home under the capitulatory system. Capitulatory refers to the *capitula*, or chapters of the "contract" awarded by the Ottoman Empire granting trading rights to foreign powers, such as France (in 1535), Britain (in 1580), and Russia (in 1774) who, by the nineteenth century, had established foreign consulates in Palestine to serve their constituents

(Blumberg 1985, 16; Starr 1994; Inalcik 1994; and Kafadar 1995). This pluralistic arrangement meant that communal authority varied within and beyond the Ottoman Empire, as did one's sense of belonging to the empire.

By the nineteenth century, the Ottoman Empire began to crumble because of expensive wartime territorial losses and growing nationalism and communalism that had the empire's diverse population agitating for self-rule, or at least a more equitable share of the empire. In the shadow of rising European powers, rulers initiated reforms to economically resuscitate and modernize the ailing Ottoman Empire. A particularly intense period of reorganization ("*tanzimat*") took place between 1839 and 1867, which focused on Ottoman political unification via centralization and standardization. By 1876 the empire had begun to incorporate key elements associated with the modern bureaucratic state. By the turn of the century, Muslims made up only 60 percent of the population, the power of the *ulema* or Islamic religious authorities had been downgraded, and the millet system was weakened. A transformation of the relationship between the government and the governed had begun from differentiated subjects of empire to equal citizens within a shared state.

The upstart Young Turk revolutionaries (1908–1918), buoyed by an emerging women's movement, understood the "modern family" and republican motherhood as central to advancing state development. By August 1914, the capitulatory system was eliminated, and universal and secular personal status law was called for (Eisenman 1986, 62). Within a few years, two controversial *irades* were put in place by an imperial *karar* (a decision of the Council of Ministers) on November 7, 1917: the Ottoman Law of Family Rights, or OLFR, and the Ottoman Law of Procedure for Sharia Courts, or OLPSC (63). The reforms aimed to soften, simplify, and standardize strict Hanafi interpretations of Islamic family law in order to enable destitute war widows to remarry, and elite women to choose or terminate love-based marriages (Altinbas 2014, Tucker 1998).

These transformations occurred against the backdrop of the Balkan Wars and World War I, when secular family law reform was understood as a common pathway to modernization (Abramov 1976, chap. 3; Eisenman 1978). The controversial reforms reorganized Ottoman identity from one based on sectarian affiliation to one that would apply equally to all its citizens—with Muslims assuming the privileged, unmarked category of the empire, non-Muslim residents retaining the marked identity of protected minorities, and foreign nationals maintaining their fundamental, but welcomed, otherness.

The Ottoman Empire was dismantled when the British were awarded a mandate over Palestine by the League of Nations as part of the peace treaties that ended World War I. Thirty years of British rule (1917–1947) brought subtle but meaningful changes to the region carved out of three adjacent Ottoman-era *sanjaks* (administrative districts)—Jerusalem, Nablus, and Acre—what became known as Mandatory Palestine. The British military administration (1917–1922), and later their postwar civil administrative authority (1922–1947),[14] served in a caretaker role for their temporary colony, jockeying between Arab and Jewish interests, with each interest group ultimately pursuing political control over (or in) Palestine. The British were determined to downgrade the nationalist character and stress the religious character they observed among the existing Arab community and the growing Jewish population.

The British rejected the proto-Turkish model of universal secular nationalism by selectively reinstituting and more narrowly applying to Muslims the family law reforms developed at the end of the Ottoman Empire. This reflected the colonial administration's strategy of governance through division. The British policy on personal status laws may have sought to weaken Palestinian national unity by encouraging separate religious identifications in Mandatory Palestine, but Muslim and Christian Arabs navigated the intersection of communal and national identities, among others, as members of a nascent Palestinian nation (Haiduc-Dale 2013). Eventually, a Palestinian national identity emerged with the capacity to exist alongside or to envelop more than one contextually salient identity, be it religion, region, or family (Khalidi 2009). At the same time, control over personal status law became part and parcel of Palestinian leadership efforts to secure political autonomy.

The British encouraged religious identification among Jews in Mandatory Palestine as well, which exacerbated tensions among the heterogeneous Jewish population. The British created a central authority, the Rabbinical Council, headed by two Chief Rabbis, which oversaw the rabbinical courts where Jewishness was determined by Orthodox personal status law (Abramov 1976, 95).[15] The Rabbinical Council's authority was restricted to those persons whose names were listed in the official register of *Knesset Yisrael*, the organized Jewish community in Palestine (Zucker 1973, 108). However, Mandatory policy enabled Jewish persons to "opt-out" of the collective (Badi 1959; M. Cohen 1987, 76). Jewish foreigners and noncitizens, numbering in the thousands, were exempt as well, and echoing the capitulatory system, could arrange civil marriages with consular officers (Abramov 1976, 179). These options spotlighted fissures among the Jewish population: Ashkenazi-Mizrahi/Sephardi, veterans-newcomers, religious-secular.

By the mid-1940s, however, when the establishment of a Jewish state, pending approval by the United Nations, was most promising, nationalists mobilized the unifying power of personal status law as a means to secure political autonomy. With the United Nations Special Commission on Palestine (UNSCOP) scheduled to conduct an inquiry as to the political aspirations of the Jewish community, the anti-Zionist ultra-Orthodox Agudat Yisrael, which did not support the establishment of a Jewish state, threatened to meet separately with UNSCOP (i.e., not as part of the Jewish Agency delegation). The decidedly socialist and non-religious Jewish leader David Ben Gurion urged the dissenting party to enable the Jewish Agency to represent the "the entire nation" (Friedman 1995, 62).

Agudat Yisrael agreed to "support the cause of a Jewish state if their religious demands were guaranteed in the state constitution" (63). Although Ben Gurion could not make such a priori promise, in June 1947 the Jewish Agency Executive sent a letter to the offices of World Agudat Israel that sealed at least the appearance of Jewish political unity. Ben Gurion offered what came to be seen as the "status quo": religious control over marital affairs, the Sabbath, kashrut, along with autonomy in education and freedom of religious conscience. In exchange, Agudat Yisrael agreed not to appear separately before UNSCOP, nor to articulate their ideological rejection of the nascent Israeli state. Soon thereafter, UNSCOP recommended partition of western Palestine into two sovereign political-territorial areas, one Jewish, the other Arab. This plan was adopted in UN Resolution 181 in November 1947, and on May 14, 1948, Ben Gurion declared the establishment of the State of Israel. Since then the state's political existence and its boundaries have remained contested by those opposed to its establishment, including Palestinians and much of the Arab and Muslim world; over time, the expansion and contraction of Israel's geographic boundaries, most pronounced subsequent to the 1967 War, have fomented dissension among Israeli Jews as to the proper dimensions of the state as well.[16]

Israel's identity was forged during a postwar period of growing anticolonial and nationalist sentiment and has yet to be settled: what it means to be an Israeli is a continual construction based on competing origin stories and visions for society, not limited to but certainly informed by the ongoing Palestinian-Israeli conflict (Kimmerling 2001). Indeed, political violence associated with the conflict is the focal point of most scholarship on Israel. This focus tends to elide the domestic realm by primarily identifying elections and wars as meaningful historical turning points rather than looking to transformations in the everyday life of individuals, families, and communities in Israel (e.g., Gilbert 2008; Grinberg 2010; Khalidi 2009; Pappe 2006; Sacher 2007; and Shapira 2012). Building on my research on the everyday life of Jerusalem (Adelman and Elman 2014), *Battering States* attends to political violence, and does so in terms of the securitization of domestic violence and of a hierarchy of victimizations found within the cultural politics of the state of Israel.

Stories about political violence in the region are replaced intermittingly by headlines celebrating Israel as the "startup nation," and its impressive array of scientific discoveries and innovations. However, like residents of other social welfare-based states, Israelis have observed a major shift in their economic life from guaranteed financial supports and public investment to one organized around market-based individual responsibility (Grinberg 2014; Nitzan and Bichler 2002). This has created new consumption patterns (Carmeli and Appelbaum 2004) as well as unprecedented levels not only of income inequality, as compared with other Organization for Economic Co-operation and Development (OECD) countries, but also high rates of family poverty that is stratified by nationality, ethnicity, gender, age, religion, and region—nearly one in five Israeli families live below the poverty line; this number jumps to over half among ultra-orthodox Jewish and Palestinian families in Israel (Khattab and Miaari 2013; Swirski, Konor-Attias, and Ophir 2014). Although state subsidies still exist in order to mitigate hunger, homelessness, ill health, and low wages, the safety net has waned while the number of residents requiring it has risen. Today Israelis face the dual punch of privatization and global capitalism on the one hand and an overall weakening of the public sector and its infrastructure on the other hand (Lavie 2014). By analyzing domestic violence from a political economy perspective (Adelman 2004a), *Battering States* engages in the broader conversation about the relationship between poverty and domestic violence, and what role states do, can, and could play in protecting its citizens' integrity and well-being.

Israel is a complex multicultural society with entrenched divisions found along national, ethnic, and religious lines. In an attempt to accommodate some of these divisions, as well as manage political power, it is a legally pluralistic state, particularly when it comes to the regulation of marriage and divorce. The government has ratified human rights instruments such as the UN Convention on the Elimination of All Forms of Discrimination against Women (CEDAW) (Freeman, Chinkin, and Beate 2012) but has exempted religious adjudication of personal status law from domestic and international oversight. It is a state with unsettled political boundaries and ongoing political violence; this diverts a significant percentage of the country's resources, which marginalizes internal concerns, such as domestic violence. The associated vulnerability to discrimination and violence is compounded by the widespread impoverishment of Israel's families.

These conditions have not gone unnoticed. The state has been challenged over time by grassroots demands for protection from domestic violence, expansion of women's, national, and ethnic minority rights, and realization of social justice for all families. Taken together, this context makes Israel a useful site for an ethnographic study of the politics of domestic violence and for the development of a new framework for studying the complex relationship among culture, the state, and domestic violence. This framework then can be leveraged comparatively in other contexts that may experience one or more of the preceding factors such as securitism, contentious citizenship, legal pluralism, and economic inequality. It also can contribute to transnational analyses of the now globalized flow of domestic violence—related ideas, systems, monies, and processes of social change. In this way *Battering States* bridges macro and micro studies of the cultural life of violence to examine the more quotidian embodiment of the state.

OVERVIEW OF THE BOOK

The book's central focus—a multidimensional and interdisciplinary conceptualization of the relationship between domestic violence and the cultural politics of the state—calls for the generation of contextualized local knowledge to produce a new "politics of domestic violence." In this way *Battering States* shares Sally Merry's (2008) combined anthropological and social problems approach to the study of gender violence. Namely, that the notions of "gender" and "violence" are culturally constructed, notwithstanding the embodied experience of both concepts; that public concern over gender violence typically emerges as a result of an organized social movement; and that the study of gender violence cannot be separated from the context in which it occurs. In her introductory text, Merry draws on ethnographic scenarios from across the globe (including my work on the militarization of domestic violence) in order to illustrate the complexity of gender violence, its relationship to other forms of institutionalized violence, and the social movements organized against it. *Battering States* advances this area of inquiry in a number of unique ways with an analysis of when and how gendered intimate partner violence intersects with cultural constructions of the state in ways that may be surprising to readers already familiar with more conventional studies of the Israeli polity or to those more familiar with mainstream approaches to domestic violence.

Domestic violence was not always considered by Israelis to constitute a social problem that warranted state attention. Every social problem that appears self-evident today is the result of an unanticipated history of transformation that requires a good victim, good timing, and good connections. A comparative example taken from Israeli history is instructive. Soon after the 1948 War, disabled Israeli soldiers fought and quickly secured recognition as wounded veterans. One of the first laws passed by the Knesset, and its first social security law, the 1949 Invalids' Law (Benefits and Rehabilitation), provided veterans with "relatively generous non-means-tested benefits" and "a variety of medical and occupational rehabilitation services, business and home loans, and access to personal social services and counseling" (Gal and Bar 2000, 581). Those benefits have grown more generous over time.

Yet, in the 1960s, when representatives of a state agency, the National Insurance Institute, lobbied for legislation that would protect people with disabilities, many of whom had similar injuries and needs, they were turned down (Gal and Bar 2000, 590). The difference? Veterans were perceived as heroes who had sacrificed their bodies for the good of the nation-state, and thereby deserving of its limited resources. Veterans made their "ask" when the memory of the war was still fresh in the minds of decision makers. They organized collectively to do so and were represented in one voice via a union-like NGO that was partly funded by the Ministry of Defense. Veterans had the support of citizens across the country, the majority of whom knew a soldier who had either been killed (about 1 percent of the population) or injured in the war. In contrast, people with disabilities were perceived of as a low-status group of disparate individuals. They lacked a compelling story that would resonate with decision makers who had limited exposure to or awareness of their needs, and people with disabilities had neither organizational capacity nor social capital with which to effectively advocate their request. National security trumped social security.

Those committed to transforming domestic violence from a personal injury to a social problem similarly needed to muster a deserving victim, deliver a memorable message about the person, develop and leverage social and cultural capital, and time their "ask" at politically opportune moments. In Chapter 2, drawing on social movement, social problems, and sociolegal theories of disputing and social change, I analyze this process, highlighting the major turning points and tipping point in what became the antiviolence against women movement. Central to the transformation are tensions between the family and the nation-state, which always have been part and parcel of the story of domestic violence in Israel. The chapter begins with a reflection on domestic violence under "pre-social problem" conditions and ends with the conundrum of success: after nearly four decades of constructing domestic violence as a social problem, its adoption and institutionalization brings with it perhaps anticipatable but not necessarily desirable outcomes. Today, for example, it is "possible to oppose 'domestic violence' and at the same time oppose all other efforts to restructure relations of dominance" (Ferraro 1996, 78).

Before there were systematic efforts to construct domestic violence as a social problem, individuals and couples brought their marital troubles to family members, community leaders, and communal courts where personal status law helped to guide people's expectations for spousal relations and determined ways to begin and end intimate relationships. Because family law consistently plays a central role in governments' "effort to create a community and define its borders" (Triger 2012, 369), in Chapter 3, I turn to a deeper analysis of personal status law and its relationship to domestic violence. *Battering States* tells an intrastate comparative story of familial ideology and forced reconciliation found within mandatory legal processes. The Israeli case echoes Mindie Lazarus-Black's (2007) findings about how battered women are embedded within webs of familial relationships, with recourse only to inaccessible, intimidating, and ineffective courts. However, in this chapter, I analyze women's experiences of personal status law (family law), rather than court-processing of civil or criminal domestic violence cases. Additionally, it is a study of communal-based legal pluralism and competing jurisdictions undergirding a contentious relationship between secular and religious visions of a state in the Middle East. Similar to lawyer and activist Susan Weiss and journalist Netty Gross-Horowitz's (2012; and see Woods 2008) beautifully written and expert study of divorce denial in rabbinical courts, I also analyze the Kafkaesque route Jewish women endure while seeking dissolution of their marriages in Israel. However, this book also integrates the experiences of Palestinian citizens of Israel who pursue divorce within Muslim, Druze, and Christian ecclesiastical courts.

I observe the relationship between domestic violence and the state by analyzing battered women's experiences of the constraints and opportunities found in personal status law, with a particular focus on divorce. In her study of Muslim family law, Ziba Mir-Hosseini (1993, 54) argues, "Divorce is often a key to a deeper understanding of marriage. Legally, it is at the point of divorce that approved marital behavior is rewarded and spouses who violate the norms are punished. Socially, divorce represents the point at which the inducements to leave prevail over the social and cultural forces that have so far kept the couple together." Indeed, Chapter 3 begins with my account of serving as an advocate accompanying a woman seeking a divorce from her husband in a Jewish rabbinical court and later on contrasts this experience with my observation of a divorce hearing in an Islamic *qadi* court.

In Chapter 3 I analyze why divorce—the very solution to domestic violence offered by many friends, family members, social workers, law enforcement officers, and judges—can be so difficult and dangerous for battered women. By asking what it looks and feels like to "just leave" a relationship, whether leaving constitutes a just process, or produces just outcomes for battered women, the chapter argues that, although divorce may be a key to ending a relationship, it also may extend or escalate domestic violence. The analysis focuses on how the amalgamated Israeli family law system paves a legal pathway for men's controlling and violent behaviors in ways both similar and different for Jewish, Muslim, Christian, and Druze women in Israel, many of whom are trapped in marriage by their husbands, and some of whom, perhaps unexpectedly, use marriage as a technique of resistance against domestic violence. This state of marital affairs contributes to Israel's enduring ideology of familism, even in the face of significant socioeconomic and cultural changes (Fogiel-Bijaoui and Rutlinger-Reiner 2013).

Family law is but one of several expressions of the relationship between domestic violence and the state examined in *Battering States*. Building on my earlier thinking on the militarization of domestic violence (Adelman 2003), in Chapter 4 I address the relationship between the security state and domestic violence. My analysis benefits from Nadera Shalhoub-Kevorkian's (2009) study of the militarization of violence against women among still-stateless Palestinians in the post-1967 occupied territories, where she demonstrates how women's bodies are managed in conflict zones—to be protected, and to be invaded—by nationalist as well as by occupying forces. *Battering States* addresses a related dynamic from a different perspective: that of Jewish and Palestinian Israelis within pre-1967 Israel. Multiple expressions of the politics of domestic violence are configured uniquely by the state within its borders.

National security may or may not contribute to personal security, so *Battering States* examines the interplay between state formation and domestic violence. Chapter 4 views the conventional responsibilities of the modern state, to secure its boundaries and the well-being of its citizens within them, from the perspective of domestic violence. The chapter starts with the "Gun Free Kitchen Tables" policy-reform campaign against pervasive "armed domestic violence" as a result of the post–Second Intifada proliferation of Israeli security guards' weapons at home (Mazali 2016b). I then juxtapose it with another cultural moment two decades prior: the euphoric period (for some) in the mid-1990s, when the "peace dividend," triggered by Prime Minister Yitzhak Rabin and Chairman Yassir Arafat's public handshake, promised to enhance domestic environmental, economic, and gender justice. The chapter analyzes what role national security arrangements, including security guards, law enforcement officers, and military soldiers, may play in the perpetration and public understanding of domestic violence. The chapter ends with an analysis of how an everyday logic of national security creates culturalized hierarchies of vulnerability and victimization in states experiencing high levels of political violence. This approach allows *Battering States* to offer a nuanced analysis of differential (or "disjunctive") citizenship, drawn not only by gendered boundaries but also by distinctions of religion, nationality, geography, and social class in a highly contested state.

Battering States aligns with emerging political analyses of domestic violence that link individual experiences to macro-level policies and structural inequalities within states in flux or transition, politically and economically (e.g., Parson 2013). This applies equally to the security state as it does to political economy. Development and globalization scholars have argued, for example, that women's increased access to wages in the global economy may alter the configuration of gender relations at home, seemingly for the better, as women "gain greater personal autonomy and independence while men lose ground" (Sassen 1998, 91). Yet universal claims such as these require both a local perspective and a domestic violence–based analysis. Initiatives such as the UN program on Gender and Poverty Reduction make it critical that domestic violence researchers and advocates around the globe engage empirically with the notion of political economy. An anthropological political economy is inherently historical, focusing on how "experience and meaning are shaped by inequality and domination," which are themselves produced at the "conjunctions of local and global histories" (Roseberry 1990, 49). In other words, Roseberry, and others like him, advocate for richer appreciation at the local level of the complex and interlocking ideologies and institutions necessary to produce and sustain ever-changing processes of global capitalism.

I pose a seemingly irrelevant question to open Chapter 5: What does the price of cottage cheese have to do with domestic violence? I first examine recent collective calls for social justice in Israel, sparked symbolically by the rising cost of domestic life, including staples such as dairy products. This nascent social justice movement emerged in response to the withdrawal of the state's original presumption of relatively robust social welfare supports for poor families, which has been replaced over time by a winner-takes-all market-based global economy. After clarifying what I mean by "political economy" and the difference between "economics and domestic violence," and what I have termed the "political economy of domestic violence," I review from four different angles how the state's decisions about its economy produces domestic violence. The first looks at the production of differential citizenship alongside domestic violence, particularly among Palestinian women in Israel. The second examines the state's "ambivalent familism" in the face of neoliberalism that renders Mizrahi women, among others, vulnerable to domestic violence and impoverishment. The third reveals how the new global economy in which Israel competes leads to new categories of domestic violence victims, including noncitizen foreign workers and spouses, trafficked women, and refugees. The fourth and final viewpoint returns to the relationship between domestic violence and the price of cottage cheese by considering explicit tensions between national security and social justice. I close the chapter by analyzing how shelters for battered women reflect a political economy of domestic violence.

The political economy of domestic violence is the final of several key areas of statecraft examined in *Battering States*. The book points to transnational connections between violence against women and structural inequalities produced through factors such as neoliberal economic globalization (Adelman 2004), but rejects treating women as a constant variable within studies of gender violence and political economy (True 2012). Ethnographically, we know that women are not similarly situated; my book argues that any intervention into violence against women will require locally meaningful approaches that incorporate the domestic needs of residents as well as the external-facing position of the state. In addition, although multiple forms of gender violence are linked, I demonstrate that the pathways to justice may vary, depending on the form of the violence, as well as the social locations of those directly and indirectly affected. Women are active agents in this study, albeit constrained by relative material immobility, cultural ideologies about family life, and unhelpful institutional resources (see Alcalde

2010a and 2010b). Women often must give meaning to and manage multiple forms of violence in their everyday lives: political violence, structural violence, and domestic violence.

The sixth and final chapter concludes the book with a reflection on key themes and contributions of the analysis to rethink the multiple relationships between domestic violence and the cultural politics of the state in Israel. Because the long-term ethnographic research behind *Battering States* was inspired by activism's contribution to the construction of domestic violence as a social problem, I trace what has been and what might be possible moving forward. I specifically look at three areas of "doing states" that create mutually constitutive and multilayered relationships between family formation and state formation. These linked processes are traced through an analysis of burgeoning cultural identities, persistent political violence, and the shifting political economy.

I argue that locally contextualized, ethnographic research on the politics of domestic violence can counter pervasive short-term, individualized, and often victim-blaming representations of, and solutions for, this severe and entrenched social problem. The chapter demonstrates three key insights. One, it explains how such an approach complements the still necessary large-scale research found across the social sciences. Second, it argues for the incorporation of the experiences of those found within and beyond regulatory and therapeutic sites. And third, it contributes uniquely to the debate on whether the state is a suitable partner for solving the problem of domestic violence.

Battering States argues for this multiscalar approach in order to create the possibility for complex historical and cultural comparative research on domestic violence. The chapter ends with a reflection on central themes and implications of the book for the production of knowledge about the politics of domestic violence over the next twenty-five years. *Battering States* suggests that pathways to safety and justice should be informed by the very structural inequalities and ideological considerations that produce and are produced by the state. This unique vantage point allows the book to examine how the cultural politics of the state shape women's experiences of domestic violence and efforts to transform public responses to domestic violence. In short, *Battering States* argues that cultural difference and context matter and that what is considered to be political is indeed personal.

2 | Moving from Personal Trouble to Social Problem

DURING THE SUMMER OF 1992, I lived in the converted porch of a two-bedroom apartment in the center of West Jerusalem. I researched the basics of Israeli criminal and family law and visited with members of rape crisis centers and shelters for battered women in Jerusalem, Tel Aviv, and Haifa. The trip to Haifa took place two days before I was to return home. I traveled three hours by bus to meet with members of the Haifa Feminist Center: Isha L'Isha, Woman to Woman. Nervous about the meeting and not familiar with the winding switchbacks of Haifa's streets, I got off the bus one stop too early and found myself climbing up Arlozorov Street. Soon enough my white pants and blue Gap T-shirt were no longer crisp. Again, humidity had me wilted beyond repair.

At the time, Isha (as members of the center often refer to it) operated out of a fourth-floor residential apartment with access to the roof and a stunning view of the Mediterranean. Reflecting its inclusive philosophy and limited budget, the center was located in the working-class and mixed Jewish–Palestinian Hadar neighborhood of Haifa, set in between Carmel, the mostly elite and Jewish part of the city, and the mostly poor and Palestinian residential and business district of Ir HaTachtit, the lower city. Upon entering the center, I first noticed a bulletin board with activity and event announcements and a small set of books, stickers, and buttons for sale. I was given a quick tour: in this corner here is the Rape Crisis office, there is the Hotline for Battered Women, the library and archives, and the all-important kitchen where volunteers and staff often wind up eating breakfast, lunch, and sometimes dinner. Later, I learned that the women help keep the refrigerator continually stocked with snacks like small tubs of 5 percent cottage cheese, hard yellow cheese, and pita bread, purchased from the *makolet* across the street.

After the tour of the center, I sat and spoke with Hannah Safran, one of its leaders, in the salon. The salon was the center's meeting room in which I would later be trained as a volunteer for the hotline, participate in weekend workshops, help monitor the temperamental computer, and help create posters for local demonstrations and marches. It was a rectangular-shaped room. Along three of its walls were low, dark couches made comfortable with the addition of over-stuffed, non-matching pillows. The air in the salon did not circulate well, and our conversation was frequently drowned out by the noise of diesel buses and trucks rising from the heavily traveled street four stories below. As I listened to Hannah describe the activities of Isha in her beautifully clear Hebrew, I became convinced that Haifa fit my parameters for a research site:

> I highly recommend that you select Haifa . . . here we have all of these activities under one roof [i.e., rape crisis, battered women's hotline, and women's center]. We also have connections to the municipality, the Ministry of Social Affairs, the Women's Studies Program at Haifa University, and we run a MediaWatch program. We also have in Haifa the first shelter and are trying to start a pilot CourtWatch program. We work at the grassroots level.

Assured that there would be opportunities for me to volunteer and partici-pate in their local advocacy efforts, by late afternoon, I was back on the bus to Jerusalem, satisfied that I had identified a more than suitable research site. My interests in the politics of domestic violence were reflected in the priorities of local, regional, and national NGOs, as well as in contemporaneous judicial decisions and legislative debates. As I explain momentarily, the timing of my research ensured that I would be immersed in a rapidly developing public con-versation about domestic violence.

My study of domestic violence emerged in parallel with several, sometimes competing, efforts to rework the cultural politics of the state in Israel. These efforts, motivated by feminist, Palestinian, LGBT, nationalist, peace and anti-occupation, religious, and social justice movements, have been organized around the production of new social problems ranging from national minority rights to poverty. Domestic violence was just one of many unsettled social problems competing for public attention in Israel (Best 2008). It was not a new social condition, for sure. Conditions or behavior such as domestic violence become social problems when previously unremarkable or seemingly inevitable injuries become reframed as unjustified and unjust (Bumiller 1987; Felstiner, Abel, and Sarat 1980–1981; Dobash and Dobash 1992; Kang 2015; Renzetti and Bergen 2005a). This reframing involves a patterned and accumulative set of transforma-tive events and processes, often stemming from social movement activity (Jenness 1995; Jurik, Blumenthal, Smith, and Portillos 2000; McAdam and Sewell 2001; Snow et al. 1986; Tarrow 1989). It is this transformation of domestic violence from personal trouble to social problem—how domestic violence became cul-turally knowable and what that knowledge consists of—that concerns me here (Tierney 1982; Weldon 2002). This chapter maps critical turning points in how "domestic violence" emerged as a salient cultural category within the contentious politics of nation- and state-building in Israel.

SOCIAL MOVEMENTS AND SOCIAL PROBLEMS

Social movements commonly strive for the public's acceptance of new social problems. This is an existential fight for the acknowledgment of heretofore-ignored social ills (Rose 1977). To gain visibility and legitimacy, advocates, known as claimsmakers or moral entrepreneurs, must persuade a range of stakeholders—victims, allies, influencers, and decision makers—that the social problem exists, that a person or entity is to blame for it, and that the people it primarily affects are worthy of public support (Madriz 1997; Schneider and Ingram 2005). "[T]he problem itself is not fully constituted until its victims are made apparent" (Holstein and Miller 1990, 117, in Adelman and Morgan, 2006, 33). Once a clear victim has been identified, claimsmakers must articulate that urgent efforts are needed to address the problem and that the recommended solution to the problem is viable, if not visionary (Best 2008; Kitsuse and Spector, 1973). In essence, social movements give ontological life to social problems by naming and imbuing them with meaning (Dell and Korotana 2000, 287; and see Hall 1997, 24). They do this most effectively by telling illustrative stories about them in culturally compelling ways (Ewick and Silbey 1998; Shuman 1986).

Such "narration is a form of social interaction that constructs and deconstructs reality. Narratives tell us the nature of the universe and how to make sense of our experiences. While some describe reality, others prescribe it, telling us not so much the nature of things but how things ought to be" (Morgan, Adelman, and Soli 2008, 427). Narratives—comprising images, statistics, and stories, drawing from both anecdotal and systematic study—make a personal experience such as domestic violence knowable, allowing people to think about their taken-for-granted attitudes or behaviors from an alternative perspective (Schon and Martin 1994). The resulting exposure to and potential learning, discussion, understanding, and action about other people's experiences may transform a nuisance previously unknown or hidden from others into a collective concern that requires public attention (Hilgartner and Bosk 1988).

Thus the production of knowledge about social problems is not limited to academic research, although it is surely part of the process; it is a multilayered and dynamic process of creating new ideas, awareness, and concern about issues like domestic violence through which people interpret experience, develop empathy for others, gain skills, and use their power to change society (Segal 2016; and see Segal et al., forthcoming). If successful, a new social problem takes shape as a cultural object whose experiential, emotional, and explanatory contours have been sculpted in tandem (and sometimes at cross purposes) by a range of participants and audiences: social movement members, nonprofit organizations, academic researchers, business leaders, government ministries, media coverage, policy makers, social service agencies, voters, and victims and family members. Of course, real-life examples do not fully conform to theoretical models, or when they do, not necessarily in the "right order."

The Israeli transformation of domestic violence into a social problem happens in stages; it is a piecemeal, discontinuous, and improvised process, notwithstanding the sophisticated ideas and plans that are generated. In the remainder of the chapter, I trace a thematic chronology of proactive and reactive turning points in the cultural production of domestic violence as a socially tangible object of public knowledge. I begin by taking a step back historically to notice how, during the Mandate period of British rule, when Jewish and Palestinian Arab residents strategize over their respective or shared political futures, both Palestinian Arab and Jewish women's organizations engage in nation-building through charity and social welfare work as well as through political party work. At the time, domestic violence, per se, is not a part of their agenda. Domestic violence is framed as a kind of marital trouble that an individual might discuss with family members or community leaders on an ad hoc basis, or bring to a communal court to harness the authority and sanctioning power of a religious judge. (These tactics are still employed by women today.) Eventually, the care of family life within communal courts becomes a catalyst for and a challenge to new ideas about marriage and domestic violence.

The next brief stage in the process, occurring nearly fifteen years into the life of the new state of Israel, moves domestic violence forward from an undifferentiated family matter to a particular criminal matter, but only momentarily, before being dismissed. A public conversation about domestic violence restarts in Haifa with the advent of the second wave of feminism in Israel: an emerging interest group that names violence against women as one of its key issues. During this third stage, public discourse is shaped, again, by national tensions, with domestic violence named as an "Arab problem," a cultural myth challenged only by the grassroots establishment of the first battered women's shelter in 1977.

Nascent social problems require "good numbers," preferably big ones, and compelling stories of "good victims" (ideally, sympathetic characters with dramatic yet solvable experiences) to help persuade decision makers and prospective allies that the problem is a legitimate one, deserving of their attention, so the fourth stage of the process is an analysis of the production of knowledge about domestic violence, from advocates to academics. I then turn to the fifth stage in the process when social-movement advocates begin to secure government acceptance if not full implementation of two foundational goals: financial support for shelters and social services, and policy plans for improved policing of domestic violence. The government at first frames domestic violence within the larger question of women's status in Israel, which at the time was an international question, advanced by grassroots feminists from below and the United Nations from above. This sixth stage in the process, a pivot to the global arena, starting with the UN Decade for Women and its series of unprecedented global conferences, ultimately offers diverse stakeholders in Israel new language, mechanisms, and networks for pursuing domestic violence as a violation of women's rights as human rights. Relations between Israel and the UN color the initial reception of this new framework.

The 1990s is a tipping point in the process when domestic violence matures as a social problem. A convergence of historical conditions ensues in this galvanizing seventh stage, which produces a range of political opportunities for domestic violence to effectively compete in the social-problem marketplace. Yet it is more accurate to say multiple or hybrid social-problem marketplaces. This is not only when concrete one-size-fits-all solutions are put into place, such as the first piece of domestic violence legislation, but also when a second generation of differentiated resources, and collaborations based on nation, ethnicity, and religion becomes possible.

The eighth and final stage in the analysis to date arrives with the new century, when domestic violence becomes institutionalized as a legitimate social problem. At this point, ownership of the problem is multiplying, and NGOs navigate a precarious relationship with the state: bureaucratic integration of new social problems can easily lead to their co-optation. At the same time, new victims of domestic violence begin making claims; responses to them originate at both grassroots and state levels. Through each stage, tensions and opportunities based on the relationship between the family and the nation-state always have been and continue to be central to the story of domestic violence in Israel.

A FAMILY MATTER

Who governs family life and how it is governed is central to contemporary Israeli debates over women's equality, national autonomy, and state-building, and it shapes the development of domestic violence as a social problem. In Israel, similar to other states, when men or women contravene normative behavior, intimate family life is subject to kin- and community-based critique and intervention (Agmon 2006). The phenomenon, if not the cultural category, of domestic violence existed before there was a word for it, before police were urged to treat it as a crime, and before international conferences were held to exchange best practices among NGOs. For centuries, women in the region turned to family members and religious community leaders qua mediators to help them navigate married life, and many still do. An Ethiopian Israeli woman, for example, explained to me how she would escape to her sister's house when her husband got too violent, but she lost that survival strategy after immigrating to Israel because her extended family was dislocated in the process. Rather than being a distinct category of concern, domestic violence was a family matter. Domestic violence may have lacked a unique name, but marital troubles were not invisible (Stanko 2006).

Married women turn to communal religious-based courts as well to address their husbands' use of unacceptable levels of violence or dereliction of martial duties (Hirsch 1998). A communal court is a logical forum for handling such matters because it is where personal status law—the regulation of marriage and divorce, and issues related to them—is adjudicated. This is significant for a number of reasons. First and foremost, these courts have been endowed by a succession of political rulers with enormous cultural power to confer religious identity and form social boundaries by determining what makes a family and how families are made. Personal status law determines who can marry whom, how spousal relationships should be enacted, and how they might be terminated. As such, personal status law produces belonging among or exclusion from one's kin, religious community, ethnic group, nation, and fellow citizens. Additionally, although communal courts are today funded by the state of Israel, their staff and participants often perceive them as a space set aside from or beyond the purview of the state; for some, it is how they enact their identity; for others it is a bulwark against the encroachment into family life of either the modern or exclusionary state.

The governance of the family within communal courts dates to the rise of the Ottoman Empire, when protected communities, such as Jews and Christians, enjoyed autonomy under Muslim rule; the status of communal courts was tweaked by the "Palestinian triangle of British, Arabs, and Jews" during the Mandatory period, when new administrative oversight was introduced (Shapira 2012, 74; Brownson 2008), and since the establishment of the Israeli state, the legal arrangement known as the "status quo" has been contested yet reaffirmed repeatedly by the parliament. The status quo agreement promised that rabbinical courts would have exclusive jurisdiction over marriage and divorce, similar to but not exactly the arrangement during the preceding (British Mandate) administration. With the establishment of the state, distinct Muslim, Christian, (and later) Druze courts also officially controlled their respective personal status law systems among Palestinian citizens.[1]

What may have started out as a series of political concessions has over time turned into a convenient strategy of sectarian cultural politics that has cemented alignment across family, religion, and the state by encouraging "horizontal homogenization" among Jewish Israelis and "vertical segmentation" among non-Jewish Israelis (Sezgin 2010, 639). In other words, personal status law suppresses religious differences among Jews, but emphasizes them among Palestinians within the new state. Upon its codification in law, the status quo also became a sacrosanct symbol leveraged by religious parties when courting or being courted to form a ruling government. Thus it is never an opportune time for systemic reform of personal status law in Israel. Nearly forty years after the status quo agreement was made, Minister of Justice Moshe Nissim reacted to "a proposal to reformulate regulation of personal status [in 1986] as follows: 'I cannot understand the heated controversy. I believe there are problems more important and difficult calling for solution. Israel has more serious challenges to cope with. Believe me, this issue, is not numbered among them'" (*Divrei Haknesset*, Mar. 19, 1986, 2276, in Yishai 1996, 188). To this day, marriage and divorce are exempted from every legal maneuver regarding gender equality, religious pluralism, or civil marriage.[2]

Palestinian middle- and upper-class women's benevolent associations that provided social welfare services to impoverished peasant families pre-dated the Mandate. During the British Mandate, an era of political and economic change, an internal, lively public debate among Palestinian women and men about the changing status of marriage (e.g., its high cost, should it be delayed or avoided altogether, arranged versus love matches) ensued in the Arab press (Fleischmann 2003, 84–85). At the same time, under the Mandate, women's movement organizations such as the Palestine Women's Union, later called the Palestinian Arab Women's Union, and the Arab Women's Committee (or Association) blurred the line between charitable works and political engagement in order to strengthen the Palestinian people (Peteet 1991, 46, 52, 54).[3] This included nationalist support during strikes and other rebellious efforts (Swedenburg 1995). The "new Palestinian woman" did not pursue women's rights, per se (Fleischmann 2003, 140). Yet women's actions within the embattled nation challenged the normative gender order and provided women with the skills, networks, and awareness required for future social critique of women's domestic lives (Peteet 1991, 65).

This continued after the 1948 War, when Palestinians who remained living in Israel did so under military rule (and cut off from refugees and those already living beyond the armistice line), and focused on issues such as land expropriation, poverty, and children and women's education. Women were members of nationalist political parties, organizations, and university student groups. They formed organizations such as the Women's Renaissance Movement in Nazareth, Haifa, and Acre (which later joined progressive Jews to become the Movement of Democratic Women), and autonomous groups like the Acre Arab Women's Association (Abdu 2009; Daniele 2014; Daoud 2009; Kanaaneh and Nusair 2010; Payes 2005). At the same time, Palestinian women's contribution to the nationalist struggle continued to find expression in the maintenance of cultural memory and identity through marriage and motherhood (Kanaaneh 2002).

Similar to Palestinian women's provision of neglected social services, during the "state-in-the-making" period of immigration and infrastructure-building prior to and under the British Mandate (Shapira 2012), Jewish women helped develop relief efforts for the sick, poor, children, mothers, and elderly members of the religious Old Yishuv and Zionist New Yishuv (Loewenberg 1989). Socialist Zionist Jewish women of the New Yishuv, who had originally considered "the woman question" resolvable through the establishment of a new state, began organizing to address gaps between the egalitarian ideology that inspired their migration and the realities they faced on arrival (Bernstein 1987); to do so they initially focused on self-transformation in order to become skilled agriculturalists but soon realized that change would require organizations of their own. Ultimately, this "separatist" approach was taken over by centralist leaders, and women's struggle for equality at work was transformed into a social service and welfare organization for working women (Izraeli 1981). At about the same time, the urban-based Union of Hebrew Women for Equal Rights in Eretz Yisrael, formerly The Women's List, pursued voting and election rights for women, provided legal aid services to "married women and their children in cases of family conflict," and fought the British Mandatory's (and later the new state's) allocation of exclusive jurisdiction over personal status law to the religious courts, even though this struggle "involved a certain amount of conflict between women's issues and national interests" (Azaryahu [1948] 1980, 42, 44; Levin 1999).

Upon establishment of the state, and in response to a large immigration of Jews from Arab countries, a clear hierarchy was instituted by Ashkenazi Israelis, such as the director of the Jewish Agency's Absorption Department, who commented about the need to uplift the "uncivilized" family lives of these new Mizrahi immigrants "by ending the rule of the strong-bodied, by restraining the feral control of the male" (Rozin 2011, 143).[4] Still, a distinct notion of domestic violence was not a priority around which Jewish women were mobilized in any systematic way.

Women organized to improve the living conditions of their respective communities during the British Mandate and within the new state, which included issues such as land ownership, labor rights, suffrage, and personal status law (including property rights) that affected them as women within a nationalist framework. These early organizing efforts by Jewish and Palestinian women built a foundation for later political organizing, when women also struggled with the inextricable relationship between nation- and state-building and women's lives.[5] Eventually, among other goals, reform of communal courts—both state- and religion-based—returned to the top of agendas of women's and feminist organizations.

Which courts "own" family matters, and thus one's relationship to the state, has had long-term effects on the ability to critique the cultural institution of marriage and advocate for comprehensive acceptance of domestic violence as a social problem. Within a communal court or during family reconciliation rituals (Lang 2005), domestic violence may be raised as a concern within a particular case involving a specific marital couple, but there is no institutional mechanism for it to be taken up as a public issue relevant beyond that family. Family matters, including violence, are handled behind closed doors, and men judges or mediators within them possess near-full discretion to solve the problem at hand, with the overarching goal of keeping the family together.[6]

Communal courts are run exclusively by men and segregated by religion, which means that natural social problem constituents—for example, women concerned with domestic violence—are already divided by their unique histories and disparate relationships to the state. Women who share the same religion may differ in terms of religiosity, political ideology, or social class, and thus may lack a common set of expectations about marriage or domestic violence. Because personal status law and family life are integral to perceptions of respectability and processes of nation- and state-building, drawing attention to domestic violence and other "dirty laundry," or expressing a desire to alter the regulation of family life, has pitted women against their simultaneous political interests as members of religious, ethnic, and national communities. This is particularly true as domestic violence became associated more explicitly with the Israeli state through demands for increased policing and public funding of shelters for battered women.

GOING PUBLIC

Reconstituting domestic violence from its status as an undifferentiated family matter into a particular matter suitable for public concern was not a simple process. Plenty of people may have been exposed to domestic violence, but public knowledge about domestic violence was limited during the first quarter century of the new state. No law set aside domestic violence as a unique crime. In turn, official statistics were not collected by law enforcement that could otherwise have documented the extent of the problem.[7] No organizations existed that were dedicated to serving victims or perpetrators of domestic violence. Nevertheless, frontline workers encountered individual women who sought relief from their intimate partner's violence. Each professional offered claimants discretionary resources at hand: a "talking to" by the police, counseling, and daycare subsidies from social workers, a doctor's medical attention, lawyerly advice, or religious encouragement to reconcile. These same professionals often blamed women as the cause of the problem that remained unnamed (B. Swirski 1991b, 322). It was difficult to raise public awareness or have the state pay attention in any systematic way, even after Member of Knesset Ada Maimon Fishman tried in 1953 and then a decade later when MK Beba Idelson sought information about how the police handled domestic violence.

In 1962 during Israel's Fifth Knesset, its tenth government was presided over by Prime Minister David Ben Gurion, the Mapai (Labor) leader who had held that position almost continuously since the establishment of the state in 1948.[8] It was, however, the last government he would head. Under Ben Gurion's leadership in this government, the Knesset revalued the lira to stabilize the national economy, oversaw the execution of the Nazi leader Adolf Eichmann, and prohibited the keeping and raising of pigs. Parliament members debated and then dismissed proposals to annul the State of Emergency Regulations that governed Arab citizens, and women members of Knesset submitted proposals for "equal pay for equal wages," and to reform spousal property laws (Braudo 2012). But on January 15, 1962, when long-time women's advocate and veteran Member of Knesset Beba Idelson (1885–1975) raised a parliamentary question about police response to women being beaten by their husbands, she was dismissed with a perfunctory response. That morning in the Knesset, Idelson addressed Minister of Police Bechor Shalom Sheetrit:

> Based on information that has come to me, and newspaper articles, the phenomenon of husbands beating their wives exists in the state. Complaints have been heard about these incidents that the police do not demonstrate compassion for [these] injured women. Therefore I respectfully ask his honor the Secretary, 1. What knowledge do the police have regarding this phenomenon? 2. In what form do the police provide protection to a battered woman? 3. Does the Secretary think that there are special measures that can uproot this plague?" (*Divrei Haknesset* 1962, 33: 1123)

Sheetrit responded to each of Idelson's questions in quick succession:

> 1. The police register incidents of battering of women by their husbands, but there are not many. 2. The assault of a woman is a criminal offense, and the police take care of it like any other criminal offense. Furthermore, on this subject special attention is paid when the battered woman, to a certain extent, is a prisoner captured by a violent husband. It's true that for the good of the family, she sometimes requests that we not open a criminal file, and require the couple to hire a lawyer, and there are times when law enforcement officers place themselves in the role of arbitrator to mediate between the spouses. However, when circumstances such as those are not new [for the couple], the police open a criminal file against the violent husband and ensure that the case will be handled as quickly as possible. 3. No, with regard to the last question, I don't see any need for that.

And with that, the session was terminated. The entire exchange takes up just four inches of column space in the Knesset minutes.

The dismissive response by the minister is not surprising given the history and orientation of policing at the time. The new state adopted the centralized and militaristic British colonial model of policing set in place during the Mandate, which focused on rule of law and administrative security over personal security, eschewing as well what became known as community policing; subsequent reforms to bring more attention to everyday crime control and prevention in Israel were thwarted by increased responsibility to guard national security and manage "challenges to state authority," as well as by the military leadership pipeline into law enforcement (Shadmi 1998, 231). Reinforcing police indifference to domestic violence on the job was the generalized sense within the government that, as a state, Israel faced higher-order troubles, along with utopianism that labeled social problems as incompatible with the new Zionist society, and ethnocentrism that labeled Palestinian and Mizrahi families as inferior; these converging ideologies relegated crime and "reduced a whole range of social and welfare issues to the margin of public and political domains" (Ajzenstadt 1998, 3).[9]

Despite its brevity, the query demonstrates the existence of this type of incident, and that men's violence against women in the home is a phenomenon known by the police and reported on by the media. The categories of "battered woman" and "violent man" are already meaningful, at least to law enforcement, and police have routinized, if not official, procedures for dealing with domestic violence. Most critically, MK Idelson indicates that women have communicated to her that they are satisfied with neither the violence against them nor how the police respond to it. This point in time marks an achievement: the transformation of a personal experience into a grievance (Felstiner, Abel, and Sarat 1980–1981). An injury has been named (battered women), and the source of the problem has been blamed (violent men). In addition, a Member of Knesset has made a claim that women need the state to provide a different solution (better policing), and she has framed the issue as an urgent one for the public to solve (it's a "plague").

If domestic violence were to be recognized as a social problem, it would require a larger and more organized group of "dissatisfied people" with "awareness that they share a situation which is in some important respects unjust" (Izraeli 1981, 96). Claimsmakers would need to persuade a public invested mainly in physical survival, economic viability, political representation, and a new state busy building its capacity to govern a diversely divided citizenry. When the next iteration of a feminist movement emerged in Israel in the 1970s, a small cadre of women repeated MK Idelson's message to try again to place domestic violence on the public agenda. This time, a combination of national and international conditions was ripe for the advancement of a new social problem: men's violence against women in the home.

REIGNITING THE CONVERSATION

A significant turning point in the fight to put domestic violence on the public agenda developed in the 1970s when new interest groups aired their grievances during a transitional period in Israeli politics. Military rule over its Palestinian citizens had been lifted by the state in 1966, releasing a national minority from social and economic immobility; within a year, territories occupied by Israel in the 1967 War enabled contact between Palestinians split by the 1948 War, raising anew questions about the fair distribution of state resources. At the same time, Israel's decisive "win" of the war ushered in the Gush Emunim Jewish settlement movement. Its messianic nationalism would affect the balance of power in the Knesset in terms of the formation of government coalitions and the legislative, policy, and budgetary decisions they would make for years to come. A spate of terrorist attacks—Munich, Entebbe, Nahariya, Maalot—compounded by significant military casualties during the 1973 War, escalated internal and external criticism of state affairs.

Identity-based politics coalesced during this period of instability. The Mizrahi Black Panther protest movement emerged in 1971. Following the 1973 War, Jewish women began to question why the state did not look to them as a productive resource during wartime. Palestinian nationalism was catalyzed: Yassir Arafat gained recognition as the sole representative of the Palestinian people in 1974, soon followed by the Soviet-backed UN resolution that "Zionism equals racism" in 1975. The first Land Day protest took place in 1976 against the expropriation of Palestinian land within the Green Line. In 1978 Peace Now was formed and mobilized tens of thousands of Israelis to urge the state to finalize the treaty with Egypt. These changes in state-citizen relations surrounded the "upheaval" in 1977 from Rabin's Labor government, felled technically by a breach of the status quo agreement, to the reign of Likud party founder Menachem Begin. Begin was a religion-affirming (if not terribly religious), territorially hawkish, and economically liberal Jewish candidate who was given a clear mandate by his working-class Mizrahi and religious Zionist supporters. So-called women's issues like domestic violence were not at the top of his priorities for the state.

Amidst these national dynamics that had various groups competing for public attention, a second wave feminist renaissance in Israel grew in Haifa (as well as in Jerusalem and Tel Aviv), the founding home for organizing against violence against women. In hindsight, they proved to be savvy and successful organizers, especially when it came to the victimization of women. Eventually, at a time when no distinct domestic violence services existed, a small group of feminists reignited the conversation by building a social movement infrastructure that adopted domestic violence as its key social problem: consciousness-raising education groups, knowledge and cultural production, organizational development, community outreach, policy advocacy, media relations, research, and electoral politics. They delivered a feminist critique of domestic violence to audiences at both the grassroots and the state levels, and received a mix of responses.

Marcia Freedman, a leader from the Haifa feminist contingent and a Member of Knesset representing the new Citizens Rights Party,[10] took their case against domestic violence to her colleagues at the Knesset. In her memoir Freedman describes the responses she received when asking for assistance from local organizations and government ministries in preparation for her proposed presentation on domestic violence to the Knesset:

> "Arabs beat their wives, not Jews," I was told by Haifa's Chief of Police. "They say that even if they don't know what she's done wrong, she'll know," he finished, smiling at me from across his desk, inviting me to share the joke. "No," I was told, "the police keep no statistics on complaints of domestic violence." "Do you ever investigate such complaints?" I asked. "Only when there's blood or broken bones," he said. "Then it's a matter for the police. Otherwise, we consider it to be a private family affair. We can't get involved in every argument between a husband and a wife." (Freedman 1990, 102)

Freedman received feedback as well from the Women's International Zionist Organization (WIZO), which operates a network of legal advice bureaus where volunteers consult with women on family law issues. WIZO fielded inquiries from women throughout the country: 80–85 percent of the queries in the Southern area (Jerusalem, Be'er Sheva, Eilat) were from women being beaten by their husbands, in the Tel Aviv-Yafo area it was 40 percent of the calls, and in the Northern District (Haifa, Galilee, and Golan) it was 50–55 percent; WIZO reported that, up to that point in 1976, they had assisted 1,500 women with regard to divorces, and over half (n=826) complained that they were regularly beaten by their husbands (*Divrei Haknesset* 1976, 77: 3538). Freedman eventually presented these data, after months of waiting for approval to do so.

Under Prime Minister Yitzhak Rabin, Freedman's request to place the topic of wife beating on the Knesset agenda was put off until July 14, 1976, when, during the 319th meeting of the Eighth Knesset, she was given permission to proceed. Her colleagues' initial disparaging responses are recorded in the minutes from the session. MK Freedman took her turn to speak, "Honorable speaker, honorable Knesset," but before she could finish the obligatory greeting, she was interrupted by MK Mordechai Ben-Porat (Alignment), who asked, "What about the second motion, about men battered by their wives?" MK Meir Pa'il (Moked) came back immediately with a one-liner, apparently intending to insult men who are victimized, "If a wife beats her husband, you are supposed to arrest the husband." Freedman retorted, "I am stunned that you find this topic so funny, and that proves exactly what I have to tell you today." MK Ehud Olmert (Likud) asked, "Why aren't all women present in the chamber?" Freedman drolly responded, "The sensitivity you are showing is very interesting" (*Divrei Haknesset* 1976, 77: 3537–38).[11]

She went on to report on the lack of official data about domestic violence in the country: "There are also no statistics collected by the Ministry of Welfare or the President's Bureau of Social Affairs office in spite of the fact that social workers have multitudes of cases of violent assaults. . . . In spite of the conspiracy of silence, it is possible to estimate that in Israel the number of battered women is measured in the thousands and not in hundreds" (*Divrei Haknesset* 1976, 77: 3538). MKs continued to critique Freedman. Akiva Nof (Likud) asked, "Why the discrimination in how you raised the topic? Why not talk about wives who beat their husbands?" Esther Herlitz (Alignment) questioned her commitment to equality because she was not talking in a gender inclusive way about intimate partners (*bnei zug*). Minister of Health Victor Shem Tov and the Minister of Police shared a joke at the expense of their colleague MK Groper (Likud): "If you haven't seen his wife, how do you know he isn't being beaten?" According to Freedman, MKs smirked and laughed throughout most of her presentation (Freedman 1990, 103).

Ultimately, Freedman concluded her comments by making several requests of her colleagues. These requests soon formed the aspirational goals around which the fight for public recognition of domestic violence coalesced: to align criminal sentencing for men convicted of beating their wives with those meted out to anyone convicted of a similar violent assault, to build a shelter for women so that they could be safe from their husband's retaliatory violence after reporting to the police, and to pressure the rabbinical courts to change their practices, "because it isn't *shalom bayit*, it is terror" (*Divrei Haknesset* 1976, 77: 3539). Freedman explained:

> We need to break the silence—by institutional authorities in power who come up against this problem and by battered women themselves. Toward that end, I request a discussion in front of the entire Knesset. I also request from the Minster of Police, that he will ensure that there will be sufficient protection and respectful interaction with women who are victims of family violence . . . and I call on battered women to identify themselves and raise their voices so that we will know who they are, how many there are and what their needs are.

She then added, "If I am allowed to make an additional modest request—I will ask my colleagues to stop telling jokes that are in bad taste about battered women" (*Divrei Haknesset* 1976, 77: 3539).

The Minister of Police Shlomo Hillel (Alignment)[12] was then given an opportunity to respond to Freedman's comments. At first, Hillel lamented that when matters have no other clear "home," they are sent to the police to be dealt with. Domestic violence, he said, is one of those unclaimed matters. Hillel then explained that men's violence against women was not a unique issue; if it *was* a problem it should be grouped with all the other violence in society. Hillel assured Freedman that the police properly handle each complainant, after which social workers with the appropriate expertise took care of them (*Divrei Haknesset* 1976, 77: 3540). Hillel urged the Knesset to drop consideration of the issue and not to send it to a committee, "I don't see what we can contribute here or in a committee" until specific proposals are brought to the debate (*Divrei Haknesset* 1976, 77: 3540).

At first glance, Hillel's dismissive response echoes the one MK Idelson received nearly fifteen years prior. However, the discussion in the Knesset did not end there. Surprisingly, MK Meir Pa'il argued that the issue deserved serious consideration from a committee, which could then forward concrete proposals to the Knesset. Although this may have been a strategy to further delay discussion of the issue, Pa'il emphasized that Freedman represented the new feminist movement in Israel, with which most if not all MKs were unfamiliar. Pa'il further argued that the issue should be sent to a subcommittee; otherwise, a parliament of men would be deciding to remove this subject from the agenda, which could be construed as perpetuating a patriarchal system. Whether this was said in jest or to pander, Hillel responded by clinging to his position that the parliament end consideration of the issue. His move to quash the motion was summarily rejected: MK Arieh Eliav (Independent Socialists) pushed back against Hillel, "I have seen hundreds of motions much less important sent to committee. What gives? What's with this stinginess?" (*Divrei Haknesset* 1976, 77: 3541).

In the end, Freedman withdrew her motion to have a full parliamentary discussion; the proposal to send the issue to a subcommittee was passed. Perhaps more importantly, the entire exchange was broadcast on the evening news, and in a country with only one television channel, Freedman's audience numbered in the millions (B. Swirski 1991b, 321). Ultimately, the subcommittee found few if any records of women's complaints to the police about their husbands, and they asked the police to conduct their own audit. Police found on average that only 15 percent of women's complaints resulted in a criminal file being opened, 60 percent of which were then closed because of lack of evidence or public interest (Avni 1990, 175–76). With this revelation from official sources, government framing of domestic violence as a family matter began to break down.

When new government elections were called for in May 1977, feminists—with the incumbent Marcia Freedman near the top of the candidate list—formed a Women's Party in order to run on a women's rights platform, ranging from workplace discrimination to violence against women. Although the Women's Party failed to reach the electoral threshold, its campaign produced a new potential constituent group, women, and raised the profile of new grievances such as domestic violence to be debated among other political parties and advocated for by the public (Levin 1999, 56). Anthropologist and feminist activist Esther Herzog, herself a leader of two women's parties in 1992 and 1999, argues that the 1977 Women's Party had long-term direct and indirect effects:

> [F]eminist messages . . . were transmitted to the public through the election broadcasts. Among the indirect achievements of the 1977 women's party was the nomination, for the first time, of an Advisor to the Prime Minister on Women's Status and the influence on the final report of the Prime Minister's Committee on Women's Status. That report became a crystalized version of the women's party platform. To this day it is used as a point of reference in relation to progress made in women's rights. (E. Herzog 2005, 446)

Indeed, domestic violence appeared matter-of-factly in the Prime Minister's Committee Report, and as Herzog notes, founders of the Women's Party went on to establish the first shelter for battered women in Israel.

The following November, after being unseated in the 1977 spring elections, Freedman and four feminist friends decided to open the first shelter for battered women, *Nashim l'maan Nashim* or "Women for Women." They rented and renovated a five-room apartment in the working-class Hadar neighborhood in Haifa and invited the press to visit the space. Within a month after the newspaper *Yediot Ahronot* and the magazine *L'Isha* published stories about the shelter in January 1978, including its phone number, women and their children quickly filled the shelter (Steiner 1990, 60). Two years later, Freedman and her friends had to secure a new home. No one would rent to the shelter, and they did not have the funds to purchase a place. The collective running the shelter rejected the Ministry of Welfare's offer of funds in exchange for depoliticizing the shelter (suggesting that they aim to keep the family together, hire professional staff, etc.), so they squatted in a decrepit, seemingly abandoned building in Wadi Nisnas, an Arab neighborhood in Haifa (Freedman 1990, 201; Steiner 1990, 60).[13] This televised spectacle helped mobilize various government ministries, which resulted in partial state funding. Remaining monies were secured through grants and donations from Israel and from abroad (Steiner 1990, 60). Receipt of limited state funding did not prevent the shelter from maintaining its feminist orientation of women's empowerment rather than client services. Soon after the Haifa shelter was established, grassroots feminists opened two others, in Herzliya (April 1978) and Jerusalem (Feb. 1981).

Shelters filled to capacity with women and their children revealed the extent of the problem and presented a short-term solution being tested in the United States and the United Kingdom at the same time. Media coverage provided readers with stories of the most vulnerable battered women who found their way to shelters, the majority of whom were Mizrahi women. One incident in particular solidified feminist claims about the need to protect women from violent men. On July 18, 1979, the day before his much delayed criminal trial, Carmela Nakash's husband killed her at the gate of the Herzliya shelter (which was subsequently named in Nakash's honor).[14] The public responded to her murder with "a major increase in donations to shelters" ("Shelters for Israeli Women," *Herizons* Jan./Feb. 1986; and see Freedman 1990, 202–23). Murdered women—mostly poor Mizrahi or Palestinian women, and later on, Ethiopian and Russian women—became the iconic "poster children" of domestic violence.

Growing visibility of local domestic violence initiatives led to an accrual of interest in the issue beyond grassroots feminist groups, including researchers and mainstream women's organizations (Tierney 1982). Na'amat and WIZO, the two largest women's organizations with children and family initiatives around the country, quickly got on board. They had indirectly provided services to battered women for years, through the provision of day care or legal advice, and now adopted domestic violence as a distinct problem that deserved dedicated resources. After the first shelters opened, WIZO partnered with the Ministry of Welfare and the Ashdod municipality to open a fourth shelter. On the occasion of the shelter's twenty-fifth anniversary, founder Michael Modai recalled " . . . how hard it was to convince people that it was necessary: they did not believe that Jewish men beat their wives. [I] went from town to town asking each mayor to provide a location for the shelter. All had some excuse until Ashdod mayor Tzvi Zilker finally agreed to give WIZO a kindergarten building" (Rockberger 2008–2009, 11). Both WIZO and Na'amat subsequently started Centers for the Prevention and Treatment of Family Violence. These mainstream, powerful women's organizations helped to legitimate domestic violence as a social problem (Abulafia, n.d). Domestic violence services also served as a data source to help researchers document it as an *Israeli* problem.

DOCUMENTING THE PROBLEM

An interest group or social movement seeking to transform a grievance of intimate partner violence into a social problem commonly needs culturally valued evidence; today this means poignant stories of victimization and recovery, combined with statistical explanation of the number and type of people affected by the problem. Such evidence helps to rationalize public intrusion into family life, disclosure of private information, and government regulation of formerly noncriminalized activities. Before any systematic research agenda existed, Israeli claimsmakers documented and disseminated grassroots-based statistics and stories in forums such as street protests, reports, newsletters, parliamentary hearings, and requests for donations. Along the way, these stories and statistics became social facts and political objects as they were taken up and recirculated (Condon 2013, 42).

Talk about the problem focuses on the victim as the main unit of analysis. Violent men commonly disappear in accounts of domestic violence; instead, it is the problem of "battered women" or "violence in the family." Profiles of courageous women who left their homes to stay in a shelter—who with the assistance of dedicated staff, rebirthed as independent women—are prominent on shelter brochures, in fundraising "asks," and at commemorative events. The women selected reflect the demographics of shelter residents: economically marginalized mothers, women with little formal education, Mizrahi women, "new immigrants" from Ethiopia or Russia, and, more recently, religious Jewish women. Few organizations highlight stories about Palestinian women, other than in materials distributed by a "mixed" or Palestinian-identified NGO. Women killed by their (former) intimate partners also are highlighted in public protests.

Although the number has increased over time, advocates, NGOs, and government representatives have tended to circulate a common number of women and children affected by domestic violence. In 1978 the Knesset Committee for the Status of Women estimated that between 30,000 and 60,000 battered women lived in Israel (Avni 1990, 171). A decade later in 1988 the Knesset Labor and Social Welfare committee pegged the figure at 100,000 or 5 percent of Israeli women (Edleson, Peled, and Eisikovitz 1991). By the mid-to-late 1990s, the figure had doubled. Media, women's organizations, and the state began to use two figures: about 10 percent of married women are battered, or "200,000 women" (Zacharia 1995; State of Israel 1997, 55; Israel Women's Network 1999), numbers that are still used when newspapers publish their annual stories in November to mark the International Day for the Elimination of Violence against Women.

The first systematic national survey determined a prevalence rate of about 10–13 percent of women who are physically assaulted by their intimate partner (Eisikovits, Winstock, and Fishman 2004), which they extrapolated to a total number of 141,740 battered women (E. Weiss 2002). This narrower framing of the problem was adopted in some quarters of the government: the Prime Minister's Office's Authority for the Advancement of the Status of Women and the Ministry of Immigrant Absorption point out in their brochure on family violence that "there are more than 145,000 battered women in Israel" (Prime Minister's Office 2011, 3). Still, until today, the phrase "200,000 women and 600,000 children" persists across claimsmaking genres, such as academic publications, newspaper articles, lobbying, media commentary, NGO websites, and fundraising pitches. An exception to this rule occurred on March 8, 2016, International Women's Day, when the NO2Violence Foundation indicated that 25 percent, or one in four women, suffer from violence in the home in Israel. Critics of the gendered construction of domestic violence in Israel, such as "fathers' rights" activists, oppose the use of what they term as repetitively cited "magic numbers" and "manufactured statistics."[15]

Advocacy-based and commissioned research also has been used to help domestic violence gain traction in the policy arena. NGOs present reports to the Knesset (e.g., Aharoni 2006) and international arenas like shadow reports to the CEDAW Committee. Members of Knesset and committees like the Knesset Committee on the Advancement of Women request that the Knesset Research and Information Center investigate topics such as hotlines for battered women (Vertsberger 2001a), treatment for men who batter (Vertsberger 2001b), or the implementation of laws that contribute to the prevention of violence against women (Teschner 2013). The Committee requisitions an annual report on the rates of violence against women, which it typically releases in honor of the UN International Day for the Elimination of Violence against Women (IDEVAW), November 25 (Bugensky 2013). The state submits research-based periodic reports to the committee to document compliance with the Convention on the Elimination of All Forms of Discrimination against Women.

Activist analyses, academic studies, and government reports on domestic violence emerged at the same time that the state's response to domestic violence was questioned and that shelters and support services for battered women were being established. Barbara Swirski, one of the founders and coordinators of the Haifa shelter, and later of the social justice and public policy research institute Adva Center, published some of the first work on wife beating in Israel, arguing that the establishment of the Haifa shelter enabled the public to "discover" the social phenomenon of men's battering of wives (B. Swirski 1981, 38). Swirski's Breirot Publishing House produced a series of groundbreaking studies and guides related to domestic violence (B. Swirski 1984, 1987; Epstein and Marder 1986; Steiner 1990).

Ronit Lev-Ari (1979) completed a master's thesis at Tel Aviv University based on interviews with women at the battered women's shelter in Haifa and with those who had requested help for domestic violence at WIZO's legal offices. She then went on to become the national director of Na'amat's division on domestic violence, and the Prime Minister's Advisor on the Status of Women. Michal Mor completed a social work master's thesis at the University of Haifa on "The Turning Point in Battered Women's Lives," in 1995 while working as the coordinator of the hotline for battered women in Haifa.[16] Early, and even much later, research focused primarily on Jewish-serving agencies, or it excluded Palestinian women, so that not until Palestinian women activists developed services and conducted their own research did the data better reflect the shared and unique experiences of Palestinian battered women (e.g., Working Group on the Status of Palestinian Women Citizens of Israel [WGSPWCI] 1997, 2005, 2010).

Scholars and NGOs continued to document the prevalence of domestic violence, determine who experiences what kinds of domestic violence, and identify its presumptive risk factors.[17] Because more than a few scholars engage in applied work, their research has directly shaped the meaning of domestic violence and forged its solutions while also documenting the institutional reach of new interventions. Circulation of these data helps to recruit and retain the attention of a broadly defined public, including politicians, civic leaders, and funders. Not only has university-based scholarship supplied students with new curricular content and research on these topics, but its imprimatur, along with the authenticity associated with locally generated data, also has helped to legitimate and advance the notion of domestic violence as a *domestic* issue. Research thus serves an integral role in the construction of domestic violence as a social problem.

POLICY REFORM VERSUS IMPLEMENTATION

After the establishment of the first few shelters, various government entities and women's organizations began to adopt domestic violence as a social problem within their purview of responsibility. This enhanced the legitimacy of the claims about the problem and the number and type of stakeholders newly committed to working on domestic violence, along with anticipatable outcomes: uneven policy implementation, particularly around policing, and insufficient public funding coupled with government oversight of NGO-delivered direct services (Edelson, Peled, and Eisikovits 1991; Halperin-Kaddari 2004). Between 1982 and 1984, the Ministry of Labor and Welfare formed a department to coordinate government subsidies of shelters and social services, first for victims and then for perpetrators of domestic violence (B. Swirski 1991b, 325). WIZO, in coordination with the municipality, Ministry of Labor and Welfare, and the National Insurance Institute, opened the Ashdod shelter in 1984. Building onto their legal services for women, Na'amat dedicated resources to treat and prevent domestic violence in Tel Aviv in 1983 and in Haifa and Jerusalem in 1989. A new nonpartisan education and lobby group, Israel Women's Network, established in 1984, identified violence against women as one of its core advocacy issues. By 1985 representatives from a growing number of voluntary organizations formed a Council for Battered Women to ensure a coordinated approach to policy reform, media campaigns, and public inquiries (Steiner 1990, 59).

Belying its heightened public profile, implementation of policy recommendations lagged. In 1988, a decade after the Namir Report was issued by Prime Minister Rabin's ad hoc Commission on the Status of Women in 1978,[18] the Israel Women's Network (IWN) found minimal progress had been made (Benson and Harverd 1988, 99–101). Namir's report of 241 recommendations included three regarding battered women:

Recommendation #186
In order to uproot the evil of family violence, special emphasis should be given in the schools to understanding that both spouses share family roles and that both spouses are equal and have equal rights to live a life free of threats and violence.

Recommendation #187
A   A law against family violence should be enacted.
B   Under this proposed legislation . . . paralegal social workers shall be appointed. They should take complaints, investigate them and present a memorandum to the court.
C   In cases where divorce proceedings have been initiated, the memorandum of the paralegal social worker shall be accepted as expert opinion by the Rabbinical Courts.

Recommendation #188
A   Shelters shall be established to take in battered women in order to provide them with immediate protection against the danger of physical injury by the husband.
B   Efforts must be made to gain the recognition of the Rabbinical Courts that these shelters are places of "refuge" and not "escape."
C   Shelters for battered women will fall under the supervision of paralegal social workers, to be appointed under the Family Violence Act.

Neither of the first two recommendations had been implemented at the time of the review. The first was too abstract to translate into action. More importantly, it also was directed at schools, a bureaucratic, politicized system of education divided by nationality, religion, and religiosity, each hostile to the introduction of new social problems for distinct reasons. The second recommendation, which suggested a distinct law against domestic violence, would take several more years to come to fruition. Reference to the rabbinical courts alludes to judges not taking seriously women's claims of domestic violence, an issue that remains today. The third recommendation was deemed as partially implemented by IWN, referring to the four existing shelters, but nothing to indicate how many there should be. The phrase "not 'escape'" refers to the notion of "*moredet*," a rebellious wife, in Jewish law. No comparable recommendation was made regarding religious courts that would provide support to Muslim, Druze, or Christian women in Israel, a pattern that runs through much of the early efforts to gain recognition for domestic violence as a social problem.

A decade after MK Freedman's Knesset Subcommittee's poor assessment of policing, Deputy Attorney General Yehudit Karp was asked to author what became a touchstone report for the visibility of domestic violence (Muhlbauer 2006). The Karp Report issued in 1989 reflects testimony from stakeholders such as shelter staff, women's organization leaders, social workers, law enforcement officers, and staff from the Ministry of Labor and Social Affairs. The committee was unable to obtain police data. Rooting her suggestions in Jewish perspectives on domestic violence, Karp urged the state to develop both criminal justice and therapeutic responses.[19] New guidelines were issued to the police to take domestic violence seriously and to collaborate with social welfare professionals.

Resistance among frontline workers is predictable when bringing new social problems and policies to large bureaucracies, such as law enforcement. Since Karp's well-known report was submitted, various government entities and designees have conducted additional inquiries, published reports, and issued directives to police officers to properly handle domestic violence. Despite several assessments that indicate lack of training, lack of adherence to guidelines, and lack of coordination between police and social services, such as one compiled by the State Comptroller in 1992, law enforcement has been slow to internalize domestic violence as more than a family matter (Halperin-Kaddari 2004, 199; Eisikovits and Griffel 1998). Commander Shalva Cohen, director of the Department of Education, Therapy and Rehabilitation in the Israel Prison Service, conceded in a 1995 report that "Israeli Society [sic] did not feel it could legitimately probe into the family fabric in defense of the victims of that violence. Only recently has it become accepted that women and children are not the husband's and father's to do with them as he likes."

Because policing had been identified as a key solution to domestic violence, the number of police complaints can be an indicator of public awareness and treatment of domestic violence as something more than a family matter. This information is available only since 1995,[20] when police began tracking domestic violence in their database. That year the police opened 19,228 files. The number of opened files rose to a high point of 22,540 in 1999 and returned to 19,615 files in 2003. For the last several years, the number has hovered between 20,342 (in 2011) and 22,289 (in 2014). In essence, the absolute number of files opened has stayed within a 15 percent differential, but the actual rate has decreased relative to a nearly one-third growth in population from 5.4 million in 1995 to 8.29 million in 2015. Today the Ministry of Public Security recognizes that only 34 percent of violent crimes (including sexual offenses) are reported to any state authority (Regev and Amram 2014, 9). Notably, annual police reports do not analyze domestic violence data against population size, which gives an appearance of minimal change.

Yet a second indicator drawn from police data—the number of arrests as measured against complaints for domestic violence—increased over time. In 1995 the arrest rate was 8.8 percent. The rate shot up in 1998 to 18.3 percent and climbed to 22.9 percent in 2002, reaching an all-time high of 31 percent in 2014. This reflects policy reforms to professionalize and regularize handling of domestic violence complaints through arrest policies, trained investigators, and risk assessment (IWN 2004, 188).

However, only 4 percent of domestic violence cases ever make it to court, and when they do, judges rely on personal rather than police risk assessments, and sentence offenders to lower punishments as compared to other offenses (Shoham 2013b, 3; Bogosh and Don-Yechiya 1999; Herbst and Gez 2012). This persistent "funnel effect" means that, even if inputs widen (i.e., arrests), outputs (i.e., prosecutions, convictions, and punishments) get narrower as the cases get processed. Policy reforms intended to make prosecutors "get tough" on domestic violence—e.g., making it more difficult to drop prosecution, charging crimes as felonies rather than misdemeanors, doubling penalties—can be undone by judicial processing (Buzawa, Buzawa, and Stark 2012, 249). Policy reform helped police to treat domestic violence as more than a family matter when it came to arrest, although the social problem work remains unfinished regarding steps before (reporting rates) and after (who gets charged and the disposition of their case).

If a goal of the social problem process is to see reporting rates increase, narrow policy reform may not be sufficient. Twenty years ago Erella Shadmi, a former high-ranking law enforcement officer and a criminologist, assessed the situation: "Police officers are aware that they're being asked to be tougher, but some of them still haven't read the rules. Sometimes they blame the wife for the assault, or say things like 'Why don't you go home and be a little nicer to him'" (Zacharia 1995). At the time, inadequate training on new policies exacerbated police attitudes. Ruth Rossing, a fundraiser for the Jerusalem shelter for battered women commented, "I'm sometimes horrified to hear cops, after spending three hours with us, stand up and say, 'The last time I hit my wife was because. . . . ' without batting an eyelash" (ibid.). Police stereotypes about women, Palestinians, and new immigrants likely color their treatment of domestic violence calls as well.

Nearly twenty years after the fundraiser's comment, and echoing Minister of Police Hillel's even earlier wish in 1976 to pass off domestic violence to social workers, frontline workers who manage domestic violence in Israel today using the dual therapeutic and penal approaches recommended in the Karp report—police and social workers—express frustration with their inability to solve the problem, and blame their professional counterparts: "While the police are expected [by social workers] to be a symbol of control and power, they become an advocate of care and social intervention [by quickly referring families to the social welfare system]; at the same time, the social agencies that are expected to care and intervene become advocates for the use of power and control [by law enforcement]" (Buchbinder and Eisikovits 2008a, 5). Domestic violence may have been officially designated as a social problem subject to state surveillance, but the dual approach has its respective representatives expressing an inadequate response from the other.

Despite a post-1973 War political context crowded with competing proposals for new social problems, and a state facing its perhaps worst economic crisis within a short period of time, a sometimes-coordinated set of social problem claimsmakers—grassroots activists, organizational leaders, frontline staff, elected officials, government ministers, victims, and their families—placed domestic violence on the public agenda, evidenced by its inclusion within the foundational Namir Report issued in 1978 by the ad hoc Commission on the Status of Women Knesset Committee. However, poor policy implementation plagued domestic violence policy reform from the beginning (Halperin-Kaddari 2004, 199), so the IWN follow-up report in 1988 was intended as a tool to help keep the state accountable. The state made minimal monetary investment but began to reform and develop policies related to shelters for battered women (Ministry of Welfare) and policing of violent men (Ministry of Public Security), framing domestic violence as a problem needing a combined therapeutic and penal response. NGOs—some explicitly feminist in orientation and others stemming more from the perspective of the helping professions of social work and counseling—continued to deliver direct services to women and their families by relying on both paid and volunteer staff, underwritten by a mix of government allocations and international and domestic donors. However, short-term safety in shelters combined with a dual mental health and criminal justice approach maintained social problem activities at a reactive stance, cleaning up the mess, rather than in a proactive mode to change the conditions that made the mess. While grassroots and state feminists continued to push for more substantive buy-in by the state and the general public, they were simultaneously gaining new ways to frame domestic violence as a social problem from within the international realm.

INTERNATIONAL PIVOT

Simultaneous to renewed Israeli activity associated with domestic violence, women around the world were brought together to study and ameliorate the status of women, broadly defined. The UN offered new language, audiences, mechanisms, and networks to help Israeli feminists navigate the fight for women's equality and highlighted the low profile given to "women's issues" by their state. Violence against women eventually became one of the emerging transnational network's most salient issues. The UN's global push for women's equality provided Palestinian and Jewish women with a global forum to make demands of the state, which revealed existing tensions between state-building and domestic violence. Yet, the UN's antagonistic relationship with Israel within the context of post-1967 Palestinian occupied territories diminished the value of that forum in its early stage, at least from the state's perspective.

Israel sent official representatives to the UN Women's Conferences spanning the UN Decade for Women held in Mexico City in 1975, in Copenhagen in 1980, and in Nairobi in 1985.[21] The Women's Conferences were not immune to the politics of the day: Cold War fissures, postcolonial divides, and clashes between economic development and legal rights. Although violence against women was not discussed formally in Mexico City, the effect of Israel's occupation on Palestinian women was on the table. The conference's final report included Resolution 32, dedicated to Palestinian and Arab women, which noted "the futility of speaking about equality of human beings at a time when millions of human beings are suffering under the yoke of colonialism" and called for the "the elimination of colonialism, neo-colonialism, fascism, zionism [sic], apartheid and foreign occupation, alien domination, and racial discrimination in all its forms" (UN 1976, 110). In November of the same year, the UN General Assembly approved Resolution 3379, which equated Zionism and racism. Several years later, the 1980 Copenhagen report's fifth resolution, which briefly called on states to "adopt measures to protect the victim of family violence and to implement programmes whose aims are to prevent such abuse" (UN 1980, 68), similarly reaffirmed that "political settlement in the Middle East was a precondition of an improvement in the situation of Palestinian women" (UN 1980, 151). The 1985 Nairobi final report touched on the topic of "abused women," commenting that "states should undertake to increase public awareness of violence against women as a societal problem" (UN 1986, 70), and returned as well, under the section on "Peace," to note: "The Palestinian woman as part of her nation suffers from discrimination in employment, health care and education" (UN 1986, 62).[22]

The UN's critical perspective on Zionism, in general, and Israel's occupation of Palestinian territories, in particular, permeated the UN's interactions with the state. However, the UN Decade for Women and its signature outcome, the Convention on the Elimination of All Forms of Discrimination against Women (CEDAW), adopted in December 1979 (UN 1979),[23] gave efforts to improve the status of women a "patina of respectability" (B. Swirski 1991b, 297). As a result, Prime Minister Rabin appointed a committee to assess the status of women in Israel, and under his successor's government, Israel was an early signatory to the Women's Convention in July 1980. The state then delayed its ratification until October 1991, as it did with four other major UN instruments, just two weeks after the United States and the Soviet Union called for and thus guaranteed repeal of Resolution 3379.[24]

The CEDAW blueprint comprising fifteen substantive articles outlines areas of life for participating states to audit for and ameliorate the existence of discrimination against women. Upon ratification of CEDAW, the State of Israel expressed reservations on Articles 7 and 16: only men may serve as religious court judges, and because of "the extent that the laws on personal status which are binding on the various religious communities in Israel do not conform with the provisions of that article." In doing so, the state declared it could not or would not remedy these forms of gender discrimination. After ratification, a state's initial periodic report becomes a baseline against which states then measure themselves every four years for increased compliance. NGOs may submit "shadow" reports to supplement official state reports. The CEDAW committee assesses these reports and returns "issues and questions" to the state to be discussed at their periodic meetings. The reporting and feedback components are tools to incorporate multiple voices to help move states closer toward the elimination of discrimination. CEDAW's enforcement mechanism is twofold: peer pressure derived from the symbolic power of conforming to the blueprint, and thus being counted among enlightened states that value women's equality, as defined by the supranational body (Montoya 2013); and encouragement from below by NGOs capitalizing on the "boomerang effect" of transnational networks (Keck and Sikkink 1998).

CEDAW opened debates over the meaning of women's equality and introduced new ideas about state accountability for human rights violations. Whereas human rights violations were previously construed as those acts perpetrated by the governing on the governed (i.e., relations between the state and individuals), CEDAW demanded that states regulate what happens among individuals within the state as well. This means, for example, that states are instructed to regulate relations within a family or community. By the 1990s states were held to a standard of "due diligence" in preventing, investigating, or punishing acts of violence against women.[25] The UN Special Rapporteur on Violence against Women (UNSRVAW 2009) argued that a state that does not act against crimes of violence against women is as guilty as the perpetrators. Because of this innovation, CEDAW and subsequent human rights instruments helped to transform domestic violence from a family matter to a violation of women's fundamental human rights to equality, security, liberty, integrity, and dignity (Thomas and Beasley 1993).

The CEDAW process in Israel reveals the limitations of a dominant social group shaping the meaning of a new social problem, and demonstrates how difference matters when it comes to domestic violence. In Israel, for a time, Jewish feminists agreed not to "be political" (e.g., address the Israeli-Palestinian conflict or other forms of inequality) in order to maintain a broad consensus around conventionally construed "women's issues," like violence against women. In contrast, Palestinian women in Israel were not as willing or able to extract violence against women from the broader context of state violence against them as a national minority. Gaps inherent to working across this divide stymied the construction of domestic violence as a social problem fully informed by the experiences and needs of all women in Israel. This became more obvious when NGOs later engaged more robustly in the CEDAW process.

Universalist notions that domestic violence affected all women in the same way were challenged by the diversification of a growing movement's priorities, programming, and people in the social problem construction process. The emerging second generation of social problem claimsmakers framed domestic violence in several ways when demanding a response from the state. Opportunities within the political, legal, and media realms that opened up in the 1990s made this possible.

DOMESTIC VIOLENCE 2.0

The life of a social problem campaign changes over time, as does the makeup and ideological orientation of the social movement(s) or spokespeople who choose it as one of their priorities. Laurel Weldon, in her comparative chronicle of movements against violence against women, argues that when "dominant groups design institutional structures, they leave the imprint of their own perspective" (Weldon 2002, 190). This is both the success and the challenge delivered by the first generation of the Israeli movement to transform domestic violence from a family matter to a problem for which the entire society is responsible. By generation, I mean an age-cohort of activists, to some extent, and more so, paradigmatic waves of social problem ownership that diversify claims and offer alternative frames for new audiences to engage in the problem (Loseke 2003, 69; Spector and Kitsuse 1977; Whittier 1997). Feminists and other advocates for social change—whom I will call "first-generation experts"—effected a paradigmatic shift by helping the public "discover" domestic violence and by creating facts on the ground: language, infrastructure, strategic maps and tactics to pursue goals, and social capital to access and persuade new stakeholders to become claimsmakers themselves. By the 1990s the first generation had produced a cultural object of knowledge that achieved preliminary institutionalization.

Because so little space exists for new claims in the social-problem marketplace and because the impulse for making new claims about domestic violence in Israel and elsewhere stemmed from the feminist analysis that *any* woman could be a battered woman, it is not surprising that first-generation experts framed domestic violence as, or that their claims were consumed by audiences as, a universal problem for all women. The rhetoric used harmonized away complex differences among battered women. Some acknowledged the inherent multiplicity of women's experiences—early on, for example, the Hotline for Battered Women in Haifa recruited and trained Palestinian and Jewish women to ensure linguistic and cultural access. Other organizations touted their delivery of services to *all* battered women, without acknowledging much of a variation of priorities or needs.

Regardless of its origins or limitations, the streamlined message that domestic violence is a universal problem was, on its face, both accurate and effective, reaching a wide range of disaffected or moderately interested audiences (Best 2008). A convergence of political opportunities took place in the 1990s, and a dynamic tipping point emerged as the problem of domestic violence became institutionalized into policy and society, achieving a more secure place on the public agenda. A "second generation" of domestic violence activity developed that focused on cultural differentiation (Arnold and Ake 2013). Multiple and overlapping generations began to *share* ownership of domestic violence as a social problem.

I call the 1990s the "decade of domestic violence" because of the spike in policy and legal activity, the growth of media and cultural inclusion, and the uptick in organizational reach, all bolstered by Hillary Clinton's iconic speech declaring that "human rights are women's rights, and women's rights are human rights" at the Fourth Women's Conference in Beijing in 1995. It was a decade of extremes in Israel, bookended by the First Intifada (Dec. 1987 through Sept. 1993) and the Second Intifada (Oct. 2000 through Feb. 2005), both of which drew state resources and public attention away from domestic concerns. In between, the Oslo Agreement with the Palestinian Authority and the treaty with Jordan triggered a vision of a "peace dividend," which enabled the government and others to consider social problems that had been sidelined by security concerns (Ajzenstadt 1998, 4).

The decade was marked by massive immigration from the former Soviet Union and Ethiopia and was punctuated by the assassination of Prime Minister Yitzhak Rabin (Labor party) on November 4, 1995.[26] Both of these "events" affected the cultural and moral tone of the country and raised new questions about the place of violence within society. The anti-domestic violence movement was buoyed by the election of a then-record number of twelve women MKs in 1992, when Rabin (Labor) ended Likud's fifteen-year rule.[27] After the assassination, Likud retook the government in 1996, led by Benjamin Netanyahu, who oversaw a rise in the budget allocation for domestic violence services. Three years later, Ehud Barak returned Labor to power, accompanied by a record-breaking fourteen women MKs, half of whom had direct affiliation with the Israel Women's Network. A fortuitous and fought-for combination of heightened exposure and increased relevance made the 1990s a tipping point for domestic violence that had lasting cultural effects for the state.

Knesset and NGOs

An important component of the social problems toolkit is to secure buy-in from elected officials, who demonstrate their commitment, not only by passing legislation but also by showing up and speaking out against domestic violence in public fora. These are valuable public education moments, even if, for some, they only constitute a public relations strategy rather than a political priority. NGOs mobilize constituents in preparation for these events; newspapers and social media capture photos of the day's activities, and circulate statistics about domestic violence as well as tragic and triumphal stories of battered women and their children. Such post-event exposure can aid in subsequent fundraising by NGOs. Annual events dedicated to domestic violence such as IDEVAW also have been a critical element in keeping domestic violence on the government's agenda. The struggle for legal reform as well as the actual passage of relevant legislation is central to the ongoing social problem process.

Women's organizations outside the chamber and women MKs within it kept the parliament's attention on domestic violence through the 1990s. As a result, in June 1991 the Family Violence Prevention Law was passed. It was both a product of and a contributor to the fight to gain recognition for domestic violence as a social problem: the culmination of over a dozen years of political lobbying; a new identity, rights, and obligations for "battered women" (Merry 1996); and a legal foundation for future reform. Ellen Pence, a long-time battered woman's advocate in the United States, considered the American version of the law "on par with the right to divorce, sue for custody of children, use birth control and vote" (Arnold and Ake 2013, 566). In Israel, Yisraela Hirschberg, senior social worker at the Jerusalem shelter "praise[d] the symbolic importance of the new law: 'Before, we existed in a marginal way within the government's social services framework . . . this law is the first public recognition that the problem of battered women exists, and that the government gives legitimation to it'" (Fishkoff 1992).

The law does not define or refine domestic violence as a stand-alone crime; it references existing penal law, but it enables battered women to more easily obtain an injunction against a spouse, which could limit contact, bar him from the home, freeze family assets, and trigger removal of weapons. As the name of the new law implies, persons covered by the Family Violence Prevention law include those related by blood, marriage, or other dependency: (1) blood relations: grandfather, grandmother, father, mother, child, grandchild, brother, sister, uncle, aunt, nephew, niece; (2) marital relations: spouse, common-law spouse (*yedu'a b'tzibur*), stepfather, stepmother, stepchild, adoptive parents, adopted child; (3) all those who in the past were related in the preceding recognized familial ways: divorced spouse, former common-law spouse, ex-stepparents, ex-stepchild, former adoptive parents, or former adopted child. Notwithstanding the breadth of the law, its primary audience was battered women and their children.

Immediately upon its passage, NGOs began their translational work to bring the law to the public, developing posters and pamphlets to alert family members of their new rights and to guide frontline workers to help women navigate the application process. Na'amat (Lev Ari 1991a, 1991b) published a handout that described an abusive man and agency resources available to women and their families, as well as a glossy thirty-page booklet that outlined the legal and social service systems in place to intervene with men who batter and to support battered women. IWN (Weisman and Makayes 1992) distributed 5,000 copies of a forty-page pamphlet on the new law, including examples of how to fill out the forms, in Hebrew. Still, advocates realized it was not a perfect law. Pragmatically, it is difficult to submit the application, particularly for women whose first language is Arabic or another non-Hebrew language. In terms of solutions, it is but one tactic to create an expectation of safety among battered women; it does little to improve the safety of Palestinian women who live among their husbands' extended families. Social workers were less sanguine about the new legislation because of the increased workload it required without a parallel increase in funding.

Women MKs crossed party lines to form a bloc on domestic violence legislation, thereby becoming high-status claimsmakers for the new social problem. The newly formed Knesset Committee on the Status of Women (established in 1992 and known as "the Women's Committee") quickly became the institutional "address" for domestic violence. The committee was charged with the elimination of violence against women, among other issues related to discrimination against women. Within a decade of its formation, the committee helped to pass a number of significant legal reforms. The Family Courts Law of 1995 enabled adjudication of matters related to marriage and divorce within civil courts, for example. Other key changes included legislation against stalking and sexual harassment; protections for battered women within criminal law procedures, penal law, employment law, and victims' rights; and amendments to the Family Violence Prevention Law related to removal of weapons, frontline workers' obligation to inform victims of resources, and mandated treatment for injunction respondents. The committee later investigated acute questions such as the rise in domestic violence homicides, so-called "honor killings," and the shelter-funding crisis, and issued clarion calls about the urgency of the problems. Achievements like these would have been impossible without the Women's Committee. But, because it was the driver behind the fight against domestic violence within the Knesset, the problem remained framed as a "women's issue."

NGOs seeking to galvanize public awareness and lobby parliamentary members took advantage of two international annual days of action: International Women's Day on March 8 and International Day for the Elimination of Violence against Women (IDEVAW) on November 25. Official activities vary somewhat from year to year. As domestic violence has grown more engrained in the government calendar, these events have become an annual nonpartisan political ritual. Elected officials commonly visit a shelter for battered women, publicly denounce violence against women, and endorse the collective fight against it. In 1995, for example, the Knesset sponsored a plenary for IDEVAW, and MKs across the political spectrum—Anat Ma'or (Meretz), Dalia Itsik (Labor), Yael Dayan (Labor), Naomi Blumenthal (Likud), Esther Salamovitch (Ye'ud), and Avner Hai-Chaqui (NRP)—visited the Jerusalem shelter, whose staff noted, "The inevitable publicity generated by such visits is also an effective way of bringing the issue into the public spotlight" (Jerusalem Shelter, winter/spring 1994–1995).

The Women's Committee typically hosts a special session where NGOs and community members share compelling stories and outline priorities, a practice that continues today. The November 2014 session, for example, sought to expand the boundaries of the term "domestic violence" by revealing men's violence against children as a form of violence against women. Karen Levy, who stayed in the Jerusalem shelter in 2009 through 2010 with her children, Yishai and Sara, and then moved back to the United States after her divorce, returned to share her story as a self-defined "mother without children": her ex-husband stabbed them to death when they were sent to Israel for a legally mandated summer visit with him. Her appearance attracted media attention, and the shelter subsequently featured her story in its newsletter and website.

NGOs also sponsor an array of community events and distribute resources on days of action such as a neighborhood resource fair, performance art at a department store, a march, a demonstration at a grocery store, a social media campaign, and so on. The Women's Coalition of Haifa distributed a flyer for IDEVAW in 1998 that listed two sets of numbers: numbers describing violence against women and numbers to call for help: since 1990, 206 domestic violence homicides; between 1990 and 1997, 18,196 rape crisis hotline calls; between May 1997 and November 1998, 6,000 battered women hotline calls; and since

1990, 1,200 stayed in battered women's shelters in the north. On the occasion of IDEVAW in 2001, in a critique of legal and media frames for understanding domestic violence homicides, a march was held in Tel Aviv entitled "Murdered on a Romantic Background [referring to "crimes of passion"]," cosponsored by left-of-center grassroots organizations comprising Palestinian women, lesbian women, feminists, peace activists, and advocacy staff.[28] The flyer urged the public to "Come, We Will Shout 'Enough to Terror against Women!'" Considering that the march occurred about a year into the Second Intifada, invocation of "terror" here instantly politicized the event. Large public events such as this one earn media coverage, particularly if an entertainer or politician participates.

Mediated Violence

The absence of domestic violence discourse in the media makes it difficult for "many victims to identify what happened as abuse"; in contrast, media inclusion of domestic violence can raise public awareness and promote empathy for newly defined victims, depending on how the intended media messages are framed and received and then interpreted and applied by audience members (Kitzinger 2004, 39, 182). Increased or alternative media inclusion of domestic violence typically occurs because of social problem construction activity: legislative reform, public protests, and so on. Thus the construction of domestic violence as a social problem takes place in a mediated fashion as well as in "real life." The two are inextricable. The media turn "real violence into represented violence" and represented violence references real violence (Humphries 2009, xi). It is an iterative process of mimicry and critique. Media serve as a conduit of images and stories about domestic violence, packaged and delivered to the public (Loseke 2003). Media scholar Stephen Coleman argues further that "the media contribute to the creation of a public mood toward particular individuals, issues, and themes, which leads to them being thought about in terms of respect, derision, or suspicion (Coleman 2008, 99, in B. Klein 2011, 908). The very inclusion of domestic violence within media signals its cultural relevance. If a social movement's goal is to raise public awareness and mobilize decision makers, absent the media, it would be difficult to name the problem, demonstrate its effect on society, offer a viable solution, and persuade audiences why they should care enough to fix it. Affirmative inclusion of a new social problem in various media can increase the likelihood of its short-term adoption and long-term institutionalization.

Types of media-based–social-problem inclusion can be broken into several categories: earned media, when the news covers a social problem (press conference, protest, crime report); paid media, when commercial time or space is purchased (ad, TV show); and owned media, when an organization generates content (a blog, newsletter). Feminists quickly captured earned media, for example, which was critical to the successful launch of domestic violence as a social problem, when print media wrote about the first battered women's shelter in Haifa in 1977. During the 1990s domestic violence narratives showed up in paid, earned, and owned media in multiple and overlapping ways: NGO-packaged stories, publicly volunteered confessional accounts, both "live" and framed by producers, personal stories shared by help seekers with NGO volunteers, "ripped from the headlines" fictional accounts. Then reports about the narratives were circulated among radio, television, newspapers, and film. Mediated domestic violence is a strategy and an effect of the construction of domestic violence as a social problem, similar to legislative reform.

Newspapers were particularly instructive in the 1990s about domestic violence as being a lethal problem. Their coverage of domestic violence rose along with the rise in domestic violence homicides. News coverage adhered to the standards of the crime-reporting genre: voyeuristic, sensationalistic, and decontextualized (Altheide 2002; Meloy and Miller 2009). Explicit violence is not uncommon on the front pages of Israeli newspapers because they regularly report on political violence. Graphic images of dead women are thus not stylistically out of step, and similar to rape, domestic violence homicide helps "sell" newspapers (Korn and Efrat 2004). At the same time, the news serves as a town crier, reminding readers or viewers that the problem exists and describing its parameters. During this period, the newspapers cried about domestic violence homicide.

Commonly following news coverage of a gruesome domestic violence homicide, late-night radio talk shows would host thematic call-in programs, an Israeli tradition, where activists, self-defined battered women, and family members shared their stories. Soon the growth of cable television and the introduction of Israel's commercial Channel 2 in November 1993 created competition for audience share. Building on the radio call-in format and inspired by American talk shows made famous by Oprah, Israeli television shows created a visual space for victim disclosures. The Haifa Battered Women's Hotline wrote about the symbiotic relationship between media and the construction of domestic violence as a social problem in their semiannual report to the New Israel Fund, a source of their funding:

> In the first half of 1994 one course was given for eight Arab volunteers, eight lectures were presented in various community centers and student groups in Haifa and the north to 200 participants, three appearances were made on popular television programs on Channel 1 and 2, four appearances were made on radio programs, and two articles appeared in the Arab[ic-language] newspaper, *Kol HaArav*. After every program there was a significant increase in new callers. Following one radio appearance, calls were received from women from [Ga]za, East Jerusalem and the West Bank [because of] the lack of services for them in these areas.

Similarly, many of the women I interviewed were moved to contact a domestic violence organization after viewing a public service announcement or a special documentary on domestic violence broadcast on television. Israeli media coverage of the infamous OJ Simpson criminal case, itself an extended multipart media product, had people debating domestic violence during the mid-1990s as well.

The public learns about domestic violence—that it exists and its contours—through media coverage of what has been deemed "newsworthy." Newspapers traditionally cover noteworthy crimes one at a time, including domestic violence homicides. I have a folder labeled "murdered women" where I drop lists compiled by NGOs and news articles with headlines such as "Ex-boyfriend sought in widowed mother's slaying," "Ethiopian immigrant woman found dead in Kiryat Bialik: The suspect in the murder, her life companion, he tried to commit suicide by hanging," "Life imprisonment for Jaffa resident who murdered his wife and his sister," and so on. A staff member of the Jerusalem Shelter explains the media effects of such intermittent attention on domestic violence:

> The past few years have seen great changes in the Israeli public's response to the phenomenon of domestic abuse, which cuts across ethnic, economic, religious and all other distinctions. Unfortunately, public outrage often comes on the heels of a personal tragedy, which has propelled the issue into the headlines. Only far-reaching social, judicial, economic and educational reforms can eradicate the deep-set sources of the phenomenon. (Newsletter, winter 1995–1996, 4)

Media coverage primes audiences by exposing us to certain representations of domestic violence. When the public's primer for domestic violence is focused on the tip of the pyramid, i.e., the most extreme and least frequent kind of domestic violence, murder, it offers a narrow conceptualization of the problem. The long-lasting media effect is evident in a survey that found 80 percent of Jewish Israelis "believe that violence against women is carried out only physically" (Sinai 2006). A lethality frame of domestic violence also enables readers to distance themselves from identifying with the victim and minimize its more mundane forms they may be experiencing, an opposite effect from fear-inducing news of stranger crime and terrorism (Altheide 2002). Media studies research also suggests that such episodic rather than thematic and contextualized reporting induces viewer attribution of individual rather than collective responsibility for social problems (Iyengar 1991). Mediated coverage of domestic violence homicide typically retains an isolated and "out of the blue" frame (Dobash, Dobash, and Cavanaugh 2009).

In an unprecedented move, however, during the same week in 1994, two major Hebrew-language daily newspapers, *Ma'ariv* (Monday, Dec. 19) and *Yediot Ahronot* (Wednesday, Dec. 12), each published major stories on the overwhelming number of women killed by their (ex) husbands or partners. *Ma'ariv's* full-color front-page headline read simply "It must stop," while *Yediot* issued a special supplement based on Tali Rozen's research entitled "Enough!" on the ninety-four women killed in the prior four-year period. In retrospect, the *Yediot* catalog of death reminds me of the *New York Times* 9/11 victim profiles: a series of small photos (most of the women are smiling), and written underneath each are her name, age, how many children she had, relationship with the person who killed her (husband, ex-boyfriend, etc.), the date of the murder, the motive (e.g., because she left him) and the mode (knife, registered gun, hammer, etc.). The papers also published commentary from national figures such as Prime Minister Rabin; the Ministers of Welfare and Police; members of Knesset; representatives from the large women's organizations, including WIZO, Na'amat, and Israel Women's Network; and academics, social workers, and lawyers. Mediating the social problem in this way drew a relationship across discrete news "events" to demonstrate the extent and the patterns of domestic violence homicides and brought together professional claimsmakers to help readers make sense of the patterns. During this period as well, the increase in lethal domestic violence began to be associated chronologically and analytically with the Gulf War and Israeli securitism more broadly (see Chapter 4).

During the 1990s news headlines focused national attention on domestic violence and sexual assault with extensive coverage of high-profile court cases.[29] Media coverage of the Shomrot Kibbutz gang rape case shook the public out of its denial of sexual violence in Israel, brought attention to feminist frames on domestic violence and NGO domestic violence services, and documented the efficacy of mobilized community power. The case began in 1988 when a counselor at a regional kibbutz high school called the Haifa Rape Crisis Center in distress over the gang rape of a fourteen-year-old girl by seven teenage boys at Kibbutz Shomrat. As a result, two volunteers from the center presented a lecture to the school staff. The victim's parents subsequently filed a formal complaint at the local police station. The Haifa district attorney dropped the case based on "lack of evidence," and because the young girl was not capable of testifying in court. In response, the Haifa Rape Crisis Center and Isha L'Isha organized a series of protests. The regional response, combined with growing public pressure at the national level because of media coverage, inspired the district attorney to reopen the case. However, in November 1992 the judge released the defendants because he could not prove their guilt beyond a reasonable doubt. Public outrage escalated, and the Supreme Court reheard the case and reversed the verdict (Haifa Women's Coalition Newsletter 1994).

The media also closely followed the dramatic case of Carmela Buhbut, a woman from the border town of Kiryat Shmona, who was convicted of and sentenced to seven years imprisonment for killing her husband, a law enforcement officer, after enduring twenty-four years of his abuse, which extended to intimidating the entire town and family into silence. NGOs mobilized public opinion to rally behind Buhbut, and the Supreme Court decreased her sentence to three years upon appeal.[30] Extended media coverage portrayed her story as an extraordinary tragedy involving a sympathetic victim and villainous perpetrator whose sons and neighbors were too frightened to intervene (Morgan, Adelman, and Soli 2008). Feminist organizations used the media in these and other major court cases related to domestic violence in the 1990s to educate the public and the press, inform judicial decisions, mobilize for legal change, and reach out to donors (Herbst and Gez 2012).

Media inclusion of domestic violence was not limited to reactive reporting of crime. In 1991 the producer of the television show *Mabat Sheni* (i.e., *Second Look*) invited Nili Tal,[31] a veteran newspaper journalist, and television director and reporter, to make a film about Israeli battered women to be broadcast alongside an American program on women who had killed their abusers. At first Tal had no idea how to find "battered women," other than in a shelter. Plenty of radio and TV shows had interviewed women in shelters, changing their names and covering their faces; Tal didn't want to add to the stigmatization of battered women. Instead, she decided to have the producer share her phone number at the end of the American show and invite battered women to call her. Her phone became a hotline, she said, with more than 200 women responding from all over the country and from every profession. Tal met and listened to their stories to find women willing to be interviewed on camera. I learned about her film preparation in the newspaper column she published about it (Tal 1992). She subsequently produced the fifty-nine minute documentary *Till Death Do Us Part* commissioned by Israel Channel 8, which told the story of the infamous domestic violence homicide of nineteen-year-old Einav Rogel by her exboyfriend Gilad Shemen in 1991 (Tal 1998).

The Rogel-Shemen story received much exposure in the media and on the streets. During the trial phase (1991–1992), the press presented the murder as a dramatic story between two young and attractive kibbutznik soldiers whose love had gone bad, but "the verdict described the murder as the final link in a chain of violent acts" (Herbst and Gez 2012, 139). When the case got to its appeal phase (1996–1998), it turned into a "battle for victimhood"—Rogel's or Shemen's—and Na'amat and other NGOs mobilized members and political allies, including Rogel's mother, who made an appearance on IDEVAW in 1996 (142). Tal's film, which was shown multiple times on television, documented the feminist tone of the public's rejection of Shemen's legal argument, which was also reflected in the vociferous judicial denial of his appeal.

Shemen's murder of Rogel and the subsequent community organizing and media coverage of the extended trials advanced the public's understanding of domestic violence as an *Israeli* problem that could happen to anyone, regardless of age, ethnicity, nationality, or way of life. The procedural outcome and substantive content of the judicial decisions in both trials also is evidence of the legitimacy and institutionalization of domestic violence as a social problem as framed by two decades of feminist movement organizing against it. Because the story involved IDF (Israel Defense Forces) soldiers and because Shemen also had killed a Palestinian woman in his line of duty, it fell in line with the growing narrative claiming a connection between military and domestic violence.

Domestic violence stories were featured on Israeli narrative television as well. For example, I was hooked during the summer of 1999 on the popular television drama *Florentine* (1997–2000), which centered on a group of friends from Jerusalem who moved to the bohemian Tel Aviv neighborhood of the same name. It included a storyline based on the real-life story of Shuki Beso, a young paratrooper who killed his father using an IDF-issued rifle to protect his battered mother after two decades of abuse. Narrative television provides viewers a unique opportunity to consume mediated domestic violence and identify with the victim or family members in a way that brief news reporting cannot.

Mediated messages about domestic violence are less univocal than I have conveyed here. Cases involving celebrities or politicians (e.g., when a son of the deputy mayor of Nazareth shot and killed his wife in 2010) garner more coverage along with those cases considered "exotic" and that align with established culture-based explanations, for example, the disproportionate number of Ethiopian Israeli men who kill their ex-wives. The Arabic-language press virtually ignored so-called "honor killings" until the mid-1990s; Hebrew media took several years more to cover these crimes as something more than a problem with Palestinian Arab culture (Abou-Tabickh 2010; Faier 2002; Touma-Sliman 2005). Similarly, media audiences vary in how they consume and discard or integrate mediated frames of domestic violence.

Nevertheless, the 1990s saw a marked increase in the number and type of stories told about gender violence in earned, paid, and owned media. Media-circulated stories alerted the public that the social problem exists, that it could occur in any family, and that powerful stakeholders deemed it unacceptable. At the same time, the public was mostly exposed to graphic stories of vulnerable and desperate women (and children) murdered by family members, which may have left the impression that "lesser" forms of violence and abuse did not merit attention.

Third Sector Growth and Differentiation

The 1990s "decade of domestic violence" was a turning point in the process of social problem construction not only because of political opportunities and heightened media inclusion but also because of the infrastructure and resource availability of Israel's robust and independent civil society or "third sector"

(Abulafia n.d.). Beginning in the 1980s, guided by the new Law of Associations (1980), NGOs proliferated to compensate for the withdrawal of the welfare state and the transfer of provision of services to agencies or businesses. NGOs grew in their capacity to address an array of domestic concerns that had been sidelined until the 1990s but were unleashed by the glimmer of a "peace dividend" at the end of the First Intifada. By 1995 the Israeli third sector was one of the largest in the world, contributing nearly 13 percent of the state's GDP, while relying more on funding sources other than the state or the Jewish Agency, such as the New Israel Fund (Gidron, Bar, and Katz 2004, v, 106).

This greatly aided in the institutionalization of domestic violence as a social problem by amplifying and diversifying women's voices, multiplying the reach of local activism, and paying women employees to work against domestic violence. Palestinian NGOs, in particular, rose in number, type, and effectiveness (Payes 2005). The key during this second generation of social-problem construction was a critique of a one-size-fits-all approach to defining and unraveling domestic violence. Instead, claimsmakers placed domestic violence within a larger context of differential citizenship, mobilized culture as a solution rather than seeking to eradicate it as a source of the problem (Adelman, Haldane, and Wies 2012), and joined forces in identity-based coalition efforts.

Alongside NGOs that did not explicitly differentiate their services or work, new organizations placed domestic violence within a larger context of differential citizenship, especially Palestinian and haredi Jewish women.[32] Adela Bayyadi-Shaloun (2014) lists a dozen Palestinian feminist and women's organizations founded between 1990 and 2000, not all in urban locations such as Nazareth or Haifa or Jerusalem, and many of which explicitly addressed violence against women (see also Abdu 2009). These NGOs framed the problem of violence against women as stemming from a set of interlocking circles of oppression: as Palestinians, as Palestinian women, and as Palestinian women living in Israel. This translated pragmatically into establishing hotlines and shelters for Palestinian girls and women, staffed by Palestinian women, in Palestinian locales: for example, the Women Against Violence crisis center, Nazareth (1992), its other shelter for Palestinian battered women (1993), and Assiwar's hotline for Palestinian victims of sexual violence (1997).

Developed in parallel, the Haifa Hotline for Battered Women (established in 1990) and the Haifa Women's Crisis Shelter (established in 1995) were intentionally developed to serve multicultural needs.[33] These NGOs recruited volunteers who possessed the cultural and linguistic literacy needed to work with a range of residents or callers. This allowed staff, volunteers, and women seeking services to explore difficult conversations literally in their own languages that might otherwise be impossible if conducted with "outsiders." New Palestinian

NGOs, such as al-Fanar (established in 1991) and Kayan-Feminist Organization (established in 1998), advocated for issues that Jewish-led NGOs lacked capacity and legitimacy for or interest in, such as so-called "honor crimes" and personal status issues in sharia and ecclesiastical courts. Differentiation enabled advocates to take advantage of the cultural authenticity associated with "the local."

The second approach to the construction of domestic violence as a social problem was turning inward to "mobilize culture." This allowed NGOs to refine niche messages, try culturally relevant tactics and strategies, and form new collaborations. Whereas Israeli institutions, including the police, dismissed Palestinian women as victims of their culture, NGOs began to take advantage of available cultural discourses. Anthropologist Elizabeth Faier, whose early research in the Haifa region overlapped with some of mine, argues that "Palestinian feminist activists navigated nationalism and feminism focusing efforts on land rights and gender violence. Using key cultural concepts to subvert gender violence by reappropriating the notion of the family honor *sharaf* and the nation to infuse new meaning, so-called 'honor killings' emerge[d] as a fulcrum in activists' discourses of honor, gender and the nation" (Faier 2002, 191). In other words, groups like al-Fanar talked about the shame brought on the community because of its silent acquiescence to, if not endorsement of, violence against women. Kayan's community-organizing model focused on developing immersive relationships in order to identify issues that mattered to local women in new or already existing groups or in partnership with local town or village councils. The multiyear joint initiative "Women Demand Mobility" for intracity and intercity bus lines in a small town in the Galilee, for example, started from Kayan's three-month empowerment course with women in Maghar, which took place during 1999 and 2000 (Alahmad and El Taji 2008). In April 2015 Kayan collaborated with the National Jusur Forum of Arab Women Leaders to facilitate a discussion on femicide and to develop a plan for a regional media campaign against it.

A third approach used by the second generation in constructing domestic violence and other related issues as social problems was to draw on an identity politics strategy: coalitions based on unique needs stemming from a particular cultural location.[34] Palestinian women formed three coalitions in the 1990s made up of women's and human rights NGOs. The first coalition, formed in 1993, al-Badil, focused on the intrafamilial murder of women known as so-called "honor crimes." Its groundbreaking public event in the winter of 1994, although disappointing because it did not attract any public officials, contributed to growing interest among a wider audience in creating a shift in how Palestinian (and later Jewish) Israelis framed this and other forms of gender violence (Touma-Siman 2005). By February 2010 Women Against Violence, working with about thirty other women's and human rights NGOs, was able to mobilize a demonstration of about 1,000 women and men, including elected officials and community leaders, in Nazareth in opposition to violence against Palestinian women. Participating in the march was Druze Sheikh Amin Canaan, whose daughter Manar had been killed several months prior (allegedly) by her husband. Canaan declared, "There is no religion in the world that allows murder as such, no one has the right to take another person's life, it doesn't matter what the reasons. Anyone who doubts that should turn to his spiritual leader and will receive the answer" (Khoury 2010). Palestinian women continue to recruit "influencers" like the sheikh and to leverage the cultural legitimacy and resources available to single-issue, identity-based coalitions.

The second coalition, the Working Group for Equality in Personal Status Issues, was formed in 1995 to rectify discrimination within the Law of Family Courts passed the same year. The law reorganized the civil courts so that judges could address family-based legal concerns within a single court, but retained inequitable access to them based on religion. Namely, Christians and Muslims still had less access than Druze and Jewish families to bring personal status issues to the civil family court. Within six years, the coalition achieved their goal with reform of the law in 2001. Partner organizations then identified a list of priorities to address moving forward, including implementation of the court's reform law and fighting underage marriage and polygyny.[35]

Many of the same partners formed a third coalition called the Working Group on the Status of Palestinian Women (WGSPW) in June 1996 in order to author a shadow report to submit to the CEDAW Committee.[36] The intention was to supplement if not confront the lack of representation of their lives in the state's initial official report, which mentioned Palestinian women only twice in a cursory way, and to indicate how Palestinian women in Israel experience multiple forms of discrimination: as members of the Palestinian national minority in Israel, as women in Israel, and as women within the Palestinian society in Israel. When the state withdrew the initial official report, the WGSPW submitted its eighty-eight-page shadow report in 1996 to be considered alongside the state's combined initial and second report. Their reports are the largest collection of multi-issue data on Palestinian women in Israel. In the fourth shadow report, the coalition reiterated the frustration that inspired its formation:

> The State of Israel states in its response to this question that it has consulted a list of organizations, including one member of this Working Group. However, although, this is the fourth occasion on which the Working Group has submitted a shadow report to the UN CEDAW Committee (the first shadow report was submitted in 1996) regarding the status of Palestinian women citizens of Israel, and despite the fact

that the Working Group provides copies of its shadow report to the State authorities, neither the Working Group nor its member organizations were contacted by the State for information. (WGSPWCI 2010, 5)

Violence against women is one of the key problems analyzed within the WGSPW shadow reports. In its initial report, the lack of commensurate services for Palestinian women is outlined, along with the lack of systematic data collection by government ministries. The coalition also points to a problematic implementation of existing laws against violence against Palestinian women.

Shadow reports submitted by the WGSPW serve several purposes in the construction of domestic violence as a social problem. In addition to signaling to its international audience of the differential relationship of Palestinian women to the state in terms of their absence from the official report, and for domestic purposes incorporating the distinct experiences and needs of Palestinian women into the definitional parameters of the problem and its solution, the reports also counter the state's tendency to diminish subordinate groups' political power by dividing up non-Jewish citizens by religion or ethnicity, by illustrating the unified, national voice of Palestinian NGOs in their opposition to a wide range of forms of violence against women.

Identity- and issue-based coalitions can more easily secure buy-in from "local" stakeholders by leveraging the collective power of a large, more diverse but still insider group of partners and constituents and by drawing international attention to a shared experience. For Palestinian women in Israel, the transnational network made up of NGOs using CEDAW within the supranational body of the UN created a "boomerang effect" where synergy of domestic and international activism informed state reform (Keck and Sikkink 1998). NGOs sought to effect change in terms of resource allocation (inclusion within the state), but also in terms of the very configuration of the political system—the meaning and structure of the state (Payes 2005, 4).

That such rapid growth in the construction and institutionalization of domestic violence as a social problem emerged in the 1990s reflects a combination of political opportunity with establishment of a Labor Party government in 1992 and global synergy with the UN's passage of the Declaration against Violence against Women (DVAW) in December 1993. The globalization of domestic violence discourse resulted in activists considering domestic violence as a violation of women's human rights, and Israel wanted to be part of that conversation (Adelman 2005a; Bunch and Reilly 1994; Merry 2001).

By the end of the 1990s, domestic violence services were entrenched in the Israel social-welfare landscape. The NGO developmental shift from grassroots organizations to professionalized and service-oriented agencies had already begun. At the time, researchers discovered surprisingly that emotional burnout among shelter staff was lower than expected. Rachel Dekel and Einat Peled (2000) explain that may be because

> Israeli battered women shelters are, for the most part, public social service agencies funded and supervised by the Labor and Welfare Ministry. Hence, unlike many feminist grass-root shelters in Britain and North America, Israeli shelter workers devote most of their time to delivery of direct services and are rarely involved in advocacy work. . . . The non-political and less complex job description of Israeli shelter workers may explain the relatively low levels of reported burnout. Further, paid personnel in Israeli battered women's shelters typically are professional workers, who are not victims/survivors themselves. This may imply greater emotional distance from clients' lives and problems and, as a result, less emotional burnout.

At the end of the twentieth century, the institutionalization of domestic violence was observed as a social problem. Its frame had shifted from one based within a universal notion of women's equality to a more culturally differentiated and politicized approach among Palestinian, haredi Jewish, and multicultural NGOs. Meanwhile, mainstream domestic violence resources grew along a narrower frame with low-paid staff delivering crisis and counseling services to victims and their families, and doing so under the supervision and regulation of the state.

LOOKING BACK, LOOKING FORWARD

The twenty-first century saw a continual growth of both universal and differentiated constructions of domestic violence as a social problem, set within a political context that included the wrenching violence and repression of the Second Intifada, and its associated economic downturn, and a growing reliance on a global human rights framework for delineating the aspirational boundaries of the movement against violence against women. The construction of domestic violence as a social problem went into a mature phase where its reception into the state deepened while its domain of meaning expanded. Domestic violence became the signal issue for the expression of state feminism and a unifying target for financial support from abroad.

Feminists had selected gender violence—defined broadly to include domestic violence and trafficking of women for sex work, for example—as *the* international women's issue and harnessed human rights rhetoric to strategize across international borders (Montoya 2013). Consider the contrast in attention paid to women's status as examined through a human rights lens. Israel's first CEDAW report, a fourteen-page document, was so incomplete and unprofessional that it was subsequently withdrawn and resubmitted as a combined First and Second Report in 1997. Today, in its external-facing communications, the State of Israel now embraces the international women's human rights framework and presents itself as a leader in the fight against violence against women. When Ambassador Prosor addressed the UN Commission on the Status of Women on March 11, 2013, his remarks, woven through with Jewish symbolism and texts, highlighted how domestic violence and its victims have been incorporated within the cultural politics of the state. Violence against women, he said, is a threat to the nation-state: "The Jewish tradition tells us [according to Psalm 144:12] 'Our daughters are the cornerstones of society.' Women hold together families, build strong communities, and serve as the foundation of thriving nations. A society that disempowers its women is destined to crumble. And today, we gather to discuss an issue that threatens to erode our societies from within."

Prosor then sketched a profile of a battered woman:

Today my mind is with women like Efrat Golden, an Israeli woman who was abused by her father as a child—and beaten by her husband as an adult. Fearing for her safety, she took her two children to a government-sponsored shelter, where she found a mentor to help her rebuild her shattered life. She came to the shelter with nothing but hope and a passion for music. Eventually, with the support of her mentor, she developed her love for music. Today, she supports herself and her children by singing professionally in venues across the country. All abused women have a song to sing. (Prosor 2013)

It is a triumphant story of a tragic figure saved by a generous volunteer or staff member at a (government) shelter, able to overcome her damaged past to live independently, a story similar to ones found in NGO newsletters and websites. It is a mainstream social-problem story template: a reference to a deviant father, a crisis intervention, and a rebirth. That domestic violence services exist and that a state ambassador proudly details them and his state's interest in the global movement against gender violence in official remarks to a UN body is remarkable, and it demonstrates the growth of domestic violence as an institutionalized social problem in Israel: integrated not only into feminist activism and civil society but also into the cultural politics of the state. At the same time, Prosor's remarks indicate the direction and limitations of that growth.

How a state defines the parameters of and its responsibility toward domestic violence results from a combination of local and global conditions. "Unless pressured by local activists, governments may ratify CEDAW merely to look good internationally and even to substitute for serious domestic policy action. This suggests that autonomous feminist movements are not merely helpful but necessary to implement international treaties and that without them, global norms create perverse incentives for governments" (Htun and Weldon 2012a, 563). In the Israeli case, the state does "look good," at least on paper, as a result of its recognition of and participation in the fight against domestic violence. Rhetorically, its leaders seek identification with modern democratic transparency that an embrace of CEDAW and human rights can offer. And the quality of service and scholarship Israeli legal experts such as Carmel Shalev and Ruth Halperin-Kaddari have contributed to the UN CEDAW Committee and its domestic implementation may have produced a positive impression of the state. However, I am less sure if there is a direct payoff in the international arena for the government, given the deeply negative perceptions within the UN attached to the Israeli-Palestinian conflict.

At the domestic level, advocates have been able to use the CEDAW blueprint, with its data-gathering and its process for submitting reports, as a centrifugal force. Within Israel, a central focus of activists has been to persuade the public that domestic violence is a pervasive social problem and that solving this entrenched exploitation within intimate relationships will require long-term social transformation. In the meantime, victims deserve empathy, resources, and resolution, and perpetrators should be held accountable. According to organizational leaders, pursuing this dual short- and long-term goal would require a multipronged approach to transform not only people's attitudes but also their encounters with the state. Thus the movement sought to have the state recognize domestic violence as a problem and then to make the state responsible for helping to solve it.

Over time, the state has carved out several entry points to domestic violence services. The Knesset's Committee on the Status of Women helps to set and advance the legislative and policy agenda on domestic violence for the state, with expert guidance (and pressure) from a range of NGOs. The Ministry of Welfare regulates battered women's shelters around the country as well as counseling at regional Centers for the Prevention and Treatment of Family Violence. The National Insurance Institute handles payment of income supplements, child allowances, and pensions for solo mothers and women. The Ministry of Public Security oversees policing of domestic violence and prisons for incarcerated offenders. The Ministry of Justice manages the courts where women can petition for orders of protection, where personal status matters other than divorce can be heard, and where batterers are prosecuted or cases appealed. The Ministry of Religious Services funds communal courts where personal status matters including divorce are adjudicated. The Ministry of Education serves as a gatekeeper for family life and sex education curricula in schools. The Ministry of Immigrant Absorption facilitates adjustment of new citizens who face high levels of domestic violence. The Ministry of the Interior determines citizenship status and thus who qualifies for which state services and benefits. The Ministry of Finance lays out the state's budget priorities that relate to the funding of the rest of the ministries. Each entry point represents a bundle of goals, policies, and monetary investments, which newcomers will come to expect as the natural order of state affairs. In essence, it is difficult to identify a division of the government that does not directly work with women struggling with men's violence against them or affect the policies that guide that work.

The state, however, is not a neutral site or mechanism for social change. Israel's CEDAW expert and legal scholar Ruth Halperin-Kaddari (2004, 187) applauds the movement against violence against women because its "relative success in raising awareness and consciousness of the problem has led to government and leadership involvement in treating it," but she laments the unintended consequence thereof that has "translated [this success] into an overall impasse in this area." The state took up domestic violence as a social problem, and expectedly, it was subjected to various levels of bureaucratization, professionalization, and depoliticization, what can be called the governmentalization of domestic violence (Bush 1992). And, yet, lamentations about the cooptation of the battered women's movement or feminism more generally may be misplaced (Arnold and Ake 2013). An expansion of the categories of women who identify themselves as victims of domestic violence and who have become new victims of domestic violence continues to grow. The expectations these "new victims" articulate echo the second-generation experts' vision for culturally resonant responses to domestic violence, inflected by their differentiated relationship to the state as citizens and noncitizens.

Here is one brief example to illustrate the development of an even wider array of claimsmakers who are trying to integrate domestic violence as a social problem within their community and to responsibilize the state (and see Chapter 5 for a discussion of Eritrean women's community organizing). Bedouin women in the south have come together to address issues that matter to them, and domestic violence is one of these issues. Left out of public consideration because of their marginality, such as language, which is Arabic; population size of about 200,000; geographic location (the least dense, most rural region, whose anchor city is Be'er Sheva); housing, which is spread out across recognized and unrecognized villages, with the latter lacking basic services; and pervasive poverty and unemployment, Bedouin people are the recipient of few state resources, and women get the least of them. In response, Bedouin women have developed a number of organizations related to women's legal, economic, and physical security, as well as an umbrella network: Ma'an—Forum for Arab Bedouin Women's Organizations of the Negev, established in 1999.

One of the organizations, Itach-Maaki Women Lawyers for Social Justice, founded in 2001, has supported the Center for Arab-Bedouin Women's Rights in the Negev since 2006. In 2010 the center's director, Insaf Abu Shareb, working with Henriette Dahan-Kalav (Ben Gurion University) conducted research on Bedouin women's experiences and needs related to domestic violence. Their stories and the center's advocacy are helping to expand the domain of what constitutes domestic violence, which contrasts with how the state has defined the problem and framed how women should respond to it.[37] Bedouin women reported high levels of multiple forms of violence because of their nested status as Bedouin women within a patriarchal society, reliance on sharia courts that favor men's custody of children and retention of marital property, and Israeli law that discriminates against Bedouins in terms of forced settlement and of distribution of and access to state resources, services, and benefits.

Bedouin women shared their experiences with poverty, violence, and polygyny, a common practice in the south. Nearly nine out of ten women do not work outside the home and rely on their husband's income and/or social insurance to live. In addition to the absence of the state (e.g., no police stations in unrecognized villages), the widespread practice of polygyny among Bedouins is largely ignored by the police and only accommodated partially by other government agencies. On the ground, the National Insurance Institute recognizes the cultural practice of polygyny (despite it being a crime). Women described, however, that when a husband takes a second wife, he often economically abandons the first wife and her children. If they stay married, she is ineligible for social insurance as a solo parent. If he divorces her, she will live the life of a solo parent, but remain residentially within the husband's domicile in order not to lose access to her children; in that case, the National Insurance Institute considers her part of the household and thus ineligible for solo parent benefits.

Abu Shareb explained that the state addressed plural marriage among Yemenite immigrants in the 1950s and the 1960s, but that Prime Minister Ben Gurion "said he didn't want to open another front with the Bedouins. With all the battles they had already, he couldn't have another front to fight on. And that is where [Bedouin] women were abandoned" (Lidman 2016). Abu Shareb further argued that the state does not exhibit cultural sensitivity when it comes to demolishing Bedouin homes, so why be sensitive to "Bedouin culture" when it comes to polygamy and domestic violence? "The state must decide if it wants to invest time and money [in stopping polygamy] the same way the state is investing in house demolitions [of Bedouins living in unrecognized villages]—an incredible amount of money each year," she said (ibid.). A complex and sometimes competing set of concerns frame what domestic violence means for Bedouin women.

Bedouin women's stories of their everyday experiences of intimate violence and violent encounters with the state are a valuable component of the process to expand the category of "domestic violence" as a social problem. The stories themselves are shaped by multiple generations of organizing against violence against women, and for national and communal security and protection from the state. NGOs will circulate the statistics and stories to lobby for policy changes, attract media coverage, solicit donations, and help other women navigate the gap between how things are and how they ought to be.

Looking back, what domestic violence means has changed substantially over time—that is, who cares about it, how people organize against it, and the role of the state in taking responsibility for addressing it. However, acknowledging the desire to uproot domestic violence, but continuing to decontextualize domestic violence from its roots will only allow it to return. Looking forward to the development of the third generation of social problemization, I anticipate a shift from urging the state to take responsibility for addressing the *symptoms* of domestic violence toward coalitions of networks joining forces to address how statecraft constitutes a major *source* of the problem. Ultimately, if successful, this change in perspective will necessitate a wider set of stakeholders to adopt a less individualistic and more structural way of thinking about domestic violence.

In May 2015 Aida Touma-Sliman (Hadash Party, representing the Joint Arab List) was elected to her first term as a Member of Knesset. Among other positions of leadership, she is the fourth Palestinian woman to serve in the Knesset and the first to chair a parliamentary committee. Touma-Sliman is a fifty-one-year-old widow and mother of two children; a student leader; founder of the largest Palestinian women's NGO in the state, Women Against Violence; and editor of the Arab daily newspaper *Al-Ittihad.* Touma-Sliman was appointed as chair of the Knesset Committee on the Advancement of the Status of Women and Gender, the most visible "address" for domestic violence within the government. Already she has expanded the priorities of the committee to focus, for example, on underpaid ultra-Orthodox women who are kindergarten teachers and on Bedouin women in unrecognized villages whose homes the state is demolishing, "those women who don't have the knowledge and power to articulate their problems or to resist oppression" (Maltz 2015a). Perhaps she will be help lead the third generation that catalyzes public attention to the sources rather than the symptoms of the problem of domestic violence, or inspire those who will be.

CONCLUSION

Historian Linda Gordon became interested in conducting historical research on family violence in the United States because she noticed "that most who discussed it—experts, journalists, friends—assumed they were discussing a new problem" (1988, 2). Each transformation of domestic violence from personal injury to public concern is unique but contains similar elements. The condition is named, although its definition may remain ambiguous or contested, or morph over time. Its victims and perpetrators are identified and offered new subjectivities (Merry 1996). The extent and effects of the problem are detailed, solutions are proposed, and the urgent need for the public to address domestic violence is communicated to constituents and stakeholders, if effective, using culturally persuasive messages. Solutions typically include legislative and policy reform, which require buy-in from elected officials and bureaucratic staff. The media, broadly defined, play both a documentary and a constitutive role in constructing a social problem by covering its advancement through movement activities and, in doing so, becoming a conduit for a movement framing the problem. However, opposition will likely emerge to deny the existence of the problem or to critique the underlying goals of its advocates.

Institutionalization of a new social problem is both a goal and a trap, leading to moderation of passion, professionalization of labor, and bureaucratization of resources. Yet long-term tenure of a social problem is contingent on maintaining public interest and investment, which results in reframing to adapt to newly identified needs internal to the problem and to social trends relevant to decision makers and funders.

Domestic violence, similar to other new social problems, has advanced and receded over time. When it emerges within a particular period and place, the category is refashioned and invested with new cultural meaning. In terms of this study, the successful transformation of domestic violence in Israel is reflected not only in the amount of time and money spent by the academy, government and NGOs, the number of shelters, and annual arrest rates but also in the common-sense manner that domestic violence is discussed and managed (Yanay 2005). Advocates no longer have to persuade the public of the very existence of the problem, and elected officials have internalized the statistics and stories offered to them by various claimsmakers. A movement that began from the social margins made the case that domestic violence is worthy of its fair share of scarce public attention and limited state resources (Htun and Weldon 2012a, 564). It rapidly developed organizations, mobilized the media, produced and harnessed research, pushed for legislative and policy changes, sought to hold frontline workers accountable, leveraged the power of international pressure, and even fielded a party in the national elections. Advocates against domestic violence in Israel have successfully birthed a new social problem. Domestic violence researchers Eli Buchbinder and Zvi Eisikovits matter-of-factly refer to "the transformation of violence against woman from a personal and interpersonal problem to a social problem in Israel, like other Western countries" (2008a, 1).

However well-coordinated and linear the collective efforts exercised in the process may appear to be, the success of the transformation process cannot be described as continuous, easily attained, or even predictable (Taylor 1989). Public recognition of domestic violence, and therefore its very cultural existence, emerged as a result of social movement activities set within a constellation of political conditions and stakeholders that changed over time. Because new social problems require constant tending if they are to stay in the public eye, domestic violence in Israel will continue to be the target of an iterative process of incomplete awareness and discovery, leading to both critique and institutionalization of new categories of injury, new identities, and new interventions, and ultimately changing the relationship between domestic violence and cultural politics of the state. This chapter traced how the new problem of domestic violence altered the life of the state and how the state shaped the construction of domestic violence as a social problem. In the next several chapters, I examine three different spheres of cultural production and statecraft that, at first glance, may appear unrelated to the production of domestic violence.

3 | The Domestic Politics of Just Leaving

"AND WHO ARE YOU?" the rabbinical court judge intones, staring down at me from the elevated dark wooden judicial bench. The judge's two colleagues flanking him have their heads down while they read the file for the upcoming case. "I'm a volunteer from the emergency hotline for battered women here in Haifa," I reply, naively not anticipating any further questioning. "Well, we'll call you if there is an emergency," the judge responds dismissively. Out of the corner of my eye, I notice an older man who is standing at the door of this renovated schoolroom, now a hearing room in the regional rabbinical courthouse. He serves as clerk and security guard—shuttling paperwork, announcing cases to be heard to the crowd of people milling outside in the hallway, and generally maintaining order. The clerk begins to walk toward me, motioning for me to step away from the diminutive woman whose hand I am holding. Flabbergasted, I say firmly, "but I just want to sit here with this woman." I promise him I will not say anything; I will sit and be quiet. The judge repeats his order for me to leave the room. I try one more strategy, gesturing to the woman at my side: "But she wants me to stay with her." The judge cuts me off in mid-sentence with a wave of his hand, and I leave the room.

Esther is the woman whose hand I was holding before being removed by the judge, making me leave her in the courtroom to handle the divorce hearing on her own. Through my association as a volunteer with a local NGO, I earlier had arranged to meet her at the rabbinical court in order to provide some moral support. Esther is an older Jewish woman, an immigrant from Ethiopia, whose husband batters her. Given her limited economic resources and the centrality of marriage within her community, the violence likely is quite severe for her to seek this marital dissolution. I get to the courthouse early, but she is already there, surrounded by a group of relatives, including her husband. None of them speak much Hebrew; Esther and I communicate mainly through a young man, a student from the University of Haifa, who happens to be serving as a volunteer Amharic interpreter this morning at the courthouse. We recognize each other from time spent at the university library, and he agrees to help us out. Esther's family is occupying one of the wooden benches lining the hallway; they move over a bit so I can sit next to her as she clasps a bundle of folded papers in her hands. The papers represent the lengthy legal struggle she has faced trying to obtain a divorce from her husband, who refuses to release her from the marriage. Esther thinks that today he may agree to divorce her because relatives have been talking with him, trying to persuade him to do so.

Sitting alone outside the courtroom, as I wait impatiently for the hearing to end, the sun begins to filter into the high windows in the hallway. Esther's was the last case called for the day, and I worry that the panel of judges will not complete the hearing before they end their workday, typically in the early afternoon. Before I have a chance to worry much longer, Esther exits the courtroom surrounded by family and tells me through the interpreter that this court lacks jurisdiction over the case. She will have to reschedule the hearing and arrange to travel to the rabbinical court located near her husband's apartment, without knowing whether he is prepared to release Esther from the marriage. I am deflated by the additional delay that Esther must now endure, but I am not surprised by the bureaucratic mistake. I have seen how the court's records are managed and how understaffed its front office is. I also have heard stories from other battered women of canceled, postponed, and rescheduled hearings that prolong the divorce process.

A few weeks after being ejected from Esther's hearing, I return once again to the neighborhood that houses the drab Haifa rabbinical court building and stand near its entrance, imagining what is happening inside the dark, square courtrooms. I observe more than one man being escorted in handcuffs into the building by law enforcement officers. Religious and secular Jewish women, trailing small children, enter and exit, their faces reflecting their busy lives and the stressful and intimate contexts of their visit: disputes over child support or custody, alimony, marital dissolution, and family inheritance. Harried looking lawyers dragging overstuffed briefcases, or stacks of folders, conduct business on cellphones, always in a rush. Inside the front vestibule, I notice a sign announcing that everyone entering the courthouse must check their gun; the warning does not reassure me, given the combustible intersections between domestic violence and divorce. Tension permeates this building where people go either to negotiate the terms of their relationships or to terminate them.

In this chapter I focus on the intersection between domestic violence and Israel's pluralistic personal status law system in order to analyze why and how divorce—the very solution to domestic violence offered by many friends, family members, social workers, law enforcement officers, and judges—can be so difficult and dangerous for battered women.[1] I illustrate how an overburdened legal system tasked with enforcing social boundaries within a fractured, multicultural state compromises battered women's safety and dignity. Namely, women describe how the state's regulation of marital life, and in particular how a couple legally ends their intimate relationship, constitutes a continuation or even an intensification of the domestic violence that originally motivated their desire to divorce. Battered women's and frontline workers' encounters with the constraints and opportunities found within this complex and confusing personal status law system captures how the cultural politics of state-building legally institutionalizes domestic violence. The analysis accounts for "divorce-related domestic violence" and a range of creative strategies that women deploy to subvert the personal status law system (Adelman 2000).

ISRAEL'S PLURALISTIC PERSONAL STATUS LAW SYSTEM

Israelis are governed by an array of legal codes. Within the realm of personal status, some laws are universally applied to all citizens, while others pertain only to a specific religion-defined community (Merry 2006). Personal status law secures a person's identity, belonging, and position within the state by determining who is able to marry whom and how marital relationships can be terminated (Sezgin 2013). It also regulates family matters associated with marriage and divorce, such as inheritance, child custody, spousal maintenance, child support, and property division. The pluralistic personal status law system in Israel can be described through its contradictions: at once multicultural and integrated yet segregated by religion; jointly sacred and secular; and semi-independent as legal institutions, but maintained by political bargains and state funding.

The current arrangement of legal pluralism was set in place by the "status quo agreement," adopted by conflicting Jewish groups in 1947, as a promise to limit jurisdiction over marriage and divorce to Jewish rabbinical courts in the aspirational State of Israel (thereby defaulting to separate communal courts for non-Jewish citizens). The status quo agreement enabled Zionist leaders to present a unified front to and secure approval of a new state from the UN. The status quo agreement's resulting personal status law system is thus part of the state's origin story and is considered central to the state's existence and self-definition as a Jewish state, similar to how autonomous control over communal courts has been incorporated into Palestinian nationalism. Political party adherence to the status quo has forged government coalitions, and threats to the status quo have caused their downfall. Despite expansion of the concurrent civil family court system and growing support for religious pluralism, exclusive religious governance of family formation and dissolution persists in Israel. The Knesset consistently rejects proposals for civil marriage and divorce, and personal status law has been exempted from reform attempts related to gender equality, religious pluralism, and human rights (Halperin-Kaddari 2004; Raday 2012).

Personal status law is managed across two types of courts: civil and religious. The civil family courts serve all citizens,[2] but they jurisprudentially incorporate some religious law, based on the religion identity of the litigants.[3] Religious courts are actually a collection of distinct courts, funded and regulated by the state, each of which serves one of the four major religion groups: Jewish, Muslim, Druze, and Christian.[4]

Religious and civil courts share concurrent jurisdiction for personal status matters, except for marriage and divorce, which religious courts manage exclusively. Separate religious courts determine lineage, and thus membership, according to each community's kinship rules. For example, as defined by Orthodox interpretations, Jewish identity is reckoned through matrilineal descent, so that individuals are considered Jewish if their mothers are considered Jewish. In contrast, Muslim identity is reckoned through patrilineal descent so that individuals are considered Muslim if their fathers are considered Muslim. When couples wish to begin or end their relationship, they must turn to the religious court that aligns with their religion identity. Boundaries between the courts are porous; the state's bureaucratic requirements, judicial decisions, and funding inform the administration and rulings of the religious courts, and civil family courts incorporate interpretations of community members' religious law in matters pertaining to marriage and divorce.[5] While in some countries communal courts possess legal and financial autonomy, religious courts in Israel are under the ultimate authority of the High Court of Justice and are financially supported by the state.

The pluralistic personal status law system results in the sociolegal phenomenon of "forum shopping," what some Israelis call the "race to the courts" (Rosen-Zvi 1989; O'Leary 2013, 24). Couples may agree to assign all legal matters attached to a divorce (other than the divorce) to either the religious or family court. If, however, the couple does not agree or has not communicated their legal goal, the race begins. The court where the first petitioner initiates a divorce or requests a hearing—for example, related to spousal or child maintenance—determines which venue possesses jurisdiction over the full panoply of legal issues. Women typically obtain better outcomes in family courts. Family court judges follow a "tender years" doctrine for child custody,[6] award higher spousal maintenance judgments, and practice a more equitable division of property, despite the High Court of Justice *Bavli* decision that requires religious courts to do the same. Nevertheless, a woman may not be aware of the distinctions between venues, or she may be pressured or prefer handling family issues in a religious venue, where she may have an established relationship with the qadi, for example, who can speak her mother tongue without resorting to a translator, if available. Others may be attracted to lower costs associated with most religious courts (Kopf 2011). The tug of war between religious and civil courts continues with the High Court of Justice and Knesset reframing some issues or circumstances as requiring (or open to) civil adjudication or interpretation, while religious courts scramble to retain their authority if not relevance for the Israeli public still required to engage their services to begin and end their intimate relationships (Triger 2012).

The state has had to grow its bureaucratic and legal capacity primarily to accommodate the thousands and thousands of immigrants to Israel in the 1990s from the former Soviet Union who qualified for citizenship based on the Ministry of the Interior's administration of the Law of Return, but who are not recognized as Jewish by the rabbinical courts. Nor are their children. As a result, these "persons without a religion" could not marry or divorce in Israel. In 2010, the Law on Spousal Agreements for Persons Without a Religion sought to fill this legal gap. It did so by assigning jurisdiction over these couples to regional family courts, if no religious court or member of the public objected. Lacking objection, the family court can register and dissolve such marriages, as they do in cases of "mixed" and same-gender marriages.[7] That this anomalous model has not been adopted as pathways to marriage and divorce for those declared ineligible to marry, or for those preferring a civil option for marriage and divorce, reflects the role that the pluralistic personal status law system has been assigned to play in constructing national identity and belonging. At the very least, persistence of the religiously segregated marriage and divorce system reflects the power of religious parties, which demand a promise to protect the status quo in exchange for joining the ruling coalition-based government. Regardless of motivation, as I discuss in the remainder of the chapter, such kinship-based membership within "the political family" produces unique forms of domestic violence (Stevens 1999, 6; Adelman 2000; O. Cohen and Savaya 2003; Meler 2013).

DIVORCE LAW

Marriage and divorce are handled exclusively by religious courts, whose judges serve as community gatekeepers by policing its boundaries and ensuring the public's compliance to their interpretation of relevant law. A comparative view of Jewish and Muslim divorce,[8] echoed in Druze and Christian divorce law,[9] reveals unexpected commonalities as well as differences among intertwined ideas animating divorce law: an ideology of gender complementarity and a focus on marital reconciliation.

An ideology of gender complementarity underlies Jewish and Muslim ideas about family life, mirroring classic functionalism in which parts of a mechanism work in sync with each other.[10] In this way husband and wife are likened to a map with clearly marked boundaries: men and women possess distinct traits, skills, and responsibilities, which are explained through biological and theological frameworks. When brought together through marriage, men and women complement each other to create a complete system. Viewed from within, this interdependent system can be a fairly harmonious one in which men and women contribute in their own way to the family economy, and derive purpose and meaning from their respective, valued positions within the family and community. According to Muslim and Jewish law, as long as a wife fulfills her marital duties, a husband must provide for her. Being a wife within this sociolegal context is a protected and privileged status.

Moreover, societal concern for men's abandonment of women and children inspired the construction of legal barriers to thwart impulsive marital dissolution, such as mandatory maintenance of Muslim wives for a period of time, and the removal of legal barriers to enable a Muslim woman to secure support from her natal family or to remarry and start a new family (e.g., judicial dissolution of the marriage, Eisenman 1978, 35). Jewish law allows for the greatest leniency of evidentiary laws for the presumption of death, and thus dissolution of marriage, for those women deserted by their husbands, for example, during times of war (Tedeschi 1966); and Jewish law requires that divorce be conducted by mutual consent (Elon 1974). The requirement of mutuality within Jewish divorce was developed to protect women from abandonment; mutuality, however, differentially affects men and women, particularly in the event of domestic violence. Ironically, the very legal codes built to encourage men to fulfill their marital duties, over time also have provided legal avenues for men to thwart or manipulate those duties in perverse ways.

The same legal codes that propel men to protect women and children through marriage also reinforce their vulnerability and "institutionalized powerlessness" when it comes to divorce (Kaufman 1991). For example, in contrast to sharia court judges, rabbinical court judges cannot dissolve a Jewish marriage. A marriage may be dissolved under one of two conditions: one spouse dies or both husband and wife agree of their own free will to divorce. Under the latter condition, a husband "writes her a bill of divorcement, hands it to her, and sends her away from his house" (Deuteronomy 24:1 cited in Biale 1984, 70). By accepting it, she is released from the marriage (Breitowitz 1993). However, if one spouse wants to end the marriage but the other does not, there is no divorce. The rabbinical court may determine if there is a basis for obliging and then further compelling the husband to give—or the wife to receive—the divorce. If formally obliging and then compelling fails to produce a divorce, rabbinical courts in Israel can turn to the attorney general to request incarceration of the recalcitrant spouse for a period up to five years, which can then be extended as needed. Rabbinical courts also may employ strategies (e.g., sending abroad a private detective to track down a recalcitrant spouse) or sanctions to persuade men (and some women) to divorce, ranging from driver's license revocation to blocking bank accounts (Rabbinical Courts 2007).[11] Usage and effectiveness of such sanctions is disputed among judges, NGOs, and women seeking divorce (Founier et al. 2012, 351).

Similar to Jewish divorce law, for Muslims, a marriage is automatically dissolved upon the death of one of the spouses. Additionally, however, a husband can unilaterally end the marriage by orally repudiating the wife, known as *talaq*. There are two main types of repudiation: *talaq al-raj'i* and *talaq al-ba'in*; the former is revocable, the latter irrevocable. Unlike Jewish divorce law, no witnesses or institutional oversight are required under Islamic law. Despite its existence within Islamic jurisprudence, unilateral divorce was criminalized as part of the Women's Equal Rights Law, foundational legislation passed by the Knesset in 1951, which, after great debate, otherwise exempted personal status law from its purview. When adhered to, these reforms may provide women with some insurance against a non-mutual divorce or against the future withdrawal of an oral pronouncement of divorce. However, if a sharia court subsequently approves a "forced divorce," the dissolution remains valid. Beyond the unilateral divorce of repudiation, mutual consent divorce, *khul'*, is also available to Muslims: a woman initiates separation, and if her husband consents, the marriage is terminated, but the wife surrenders her right to *mahr mu'akkhar* (delayed dower), property, maintenance, and for some, child custody. Also unique to Islamic law, when compared to Jewish law, is the possibility of judicial dissolution (*tafriq*), as I will soon describe.

While there is great concern for abandoned women within Jewish and Muslim divorce law, no such parallel concern exists for women desiring to end the marital relationship or leave the family home. According to interpretations of Muslim (and Greek Catholic) law, a wife can lose spousal maintenance if found to be a disobedient or rebellious woman, a *nashiza* (Shalhoub-Kevorkian and Khsheiboun 2015). Jewish law similarly can find a woman as rebellious, as a *moredet*, "when she persistently refuses to cohabit with her husband" (Elon 1974, 382). Technically, a battered woman, for example, who flees the family home to stay with extended family or in a shelter may be considered rebellious and lose her right to maintenance (in Hebrew: *mezonot*; in Arabic: *nafaqa*); property rights and child custody decisions depend on the individual responses of the husband, extended family, and judges. Additional mechanisms exist within rabbinical and sharia courts to attempt to return a woman to or reconcile a family: "*shalom bayit*"—peace in the home—is practiced among some Jewish families, and "*bayt al-ta'a*"—house of obedience—is practiced among some Muslim families (Graetz 1998; Batshon 2010). The aim of reconciliation is to avoid divorce, if at all possible. Of course, religious court judges are neither monolithic in their treatment of women nor do they accept litigants' tactics without question (Shehada 2009).

Ultimately, a religious court is where marriages are legally terminated. When a couple mutually agrees to divorce and can compromise on decisions about property, children, and support, the process can be streamlined. When spouses do not agree about either the divorce or matters related to it, however, the twin ideologies of gender complementarity and reconciliation embedded within divorce law grants men (as judges and husbands) control over women (as wives). The detrimental effect of the personal status law system, and how women make sense of it, becomes more visible through an analysis of divorce law in practice, as seen from the perspective of the litigants. Divorce-related domestic violence comprises two main types: first, men's escalation of physical violence associated with separation and divorce, observed throughout the world; second, a set of legal tactics men use during the divorce process to control or punish their wives.

DIVORCE-RELATED DOMESTIC VIOLENCE

Domestic violence does not commonly begin when a divorce is initiated. On the contrary, a long history of domestic violence is often a key motivation for divorce. Muslim women in Israel, for example, report that extreme forms of physical and sexual abuse are among the primary reasons they pursued and obtained a divorce (O. Cohen, Savaya, and Natour 1997; Rabho 2013). Not surprisingly, divorce is widely understood as a possible solution to domestic violence. Well-intentioned friends, family members, law enforcement officers, and social service staff who urge battered women to leave the intimate partner anticipate that divorce will bring an end to the misery and violence. Yet the suggestion, "Why doesn't she just leave?" fails to take into account the phenomenon of divorce-related domestic violence (Adelman 2000). Divorcing couples do "bargain in the shadow of the law" (Mnookin and Kornhauser 1979), but in contrast to the assumption that domestic violence ends simply because one spouse seeks or even obtains a separation or divorce, scholars and advocates have pointed to the termination of an intimate relationship as a potentially lethal time period for a battered woman (Beck et al. 2011; Campbell et al. 2003). Here I elaborate on this pattern by documenting physical violence, including domestic violence homicide, and its collateral victims, before I turn to an analysis of other forms of divorce-related domestic violence unique to the personal status law system in Israel.

Escalation of Physical Violence

Men commonly target or terrorize women when they seek to end the relationship or after a separation or divorce. Battered women report a range of violence and intimidation in response to their quest to leave. In an early Israeli study, 39 percent of women who had stayed in a shelter reported that, upon exiting the shelter, they continued to be beaten by their husbands; more than one-quarter of these women were living apart from their husbands at the time (Epstein and Marder 1986). In another Israeli study, two-thirds of women who had fled their husbands to stay in a shelter were either in the middle of divorce proceedings or were already divorced (Burgansky 1989). Research focused on post-divorce domestic violence in Israel profiled several battered women: Gila lost an eye during one such post-divorce assault; Dalia's husband hired a private investigator to find and return her home from a shelter; Tova was threatened by her ex-husband by phone and assaulted in person; and Maya's ex-husband raped her (Eldar-Avidan 1998, 1999). In a newspaper story reported to mark the International Day for the Elimination of Violence against Women, Yafa recounted while sitting in a shelter for battered women: "I got horrible beatings when I was pregnant and three times I miscarried because of the beatings. Two days before I came to the shelter, my husband kicked me in the head and I lost consciousness. [In three days] I have an appointment [at the rabbinical court] for the divorce and my husband threatens that the day . . . won't pass quietly" (*Davar* 1991).

Some women are threatened with physical harm even before they initiate a divorce. A man from the former Soviet Union explained to an Israeli judge: "I told her that if she went to the rabbinical court to get divorced, she would be hurt. I told her that I would kill myself but that, before that, I would kill her" (*Haaretz*, Feb. 8, 1995). While theories range as to why men use lethal violence against family members (e.g., Campbell et al. 2003; DeKeseredy and Schwartz 2009), it is commonplace to read a newspaper article reporting on such an "incident" and find a precipitating separation or divorce.

Numerous such stories were reported in newspapers over the course of my research, which illustrates a link between escalated physical forms of domestic violence and divorce or separation.[12] Here are several that demonstrate how domestic violence homicide involves people from various sectors of society. A homicide took place in the working-class city of Holon, located just south of Tel Aviv-Yafo, where Ra'anan Shafik murdered his estranged wife, Sarah Granit, after she threatened to leave him for good. She repeatedly told him that they no longer had anything in common, hung up the phone when he called, and would not answer the door when he knocked. Finally, she had to leave the house to get to work. As she went down to the street to get into her car, her husband confronted her. An argument ensued. It prompted the neighbors to call the police. Before the police arrived, Shafik pulled out a lug wrench, and struck Granit repeatedly in the head, beating her to death (Mar. 24, 1994). A second homicide involved immigrants from the United States, who were members of Kibbutz Mashabi Sde, located in the Negev Desert. Thirty-five-year-old Eric Dillard killed his twenty-eight-year-old wife, Molly Dillard, a decade after they had moved to Israel together. They had three children. It appears that after a stormy fight with his wife, Dillard pulled out a hammer and beat her over the head. They had had an appointment with a social worker that day to discuss Molly's desire to leave him and to get divorced (Dec. 18, 1994).

Another homicide involved two young people, both from the small town of Mazkeret Batya: twenty-two-year-old IDF airman Shai Maimon murdered his twenty-one-year-old ex-girlfriend, Dorit Hakim, a Tel Aviv University student. The regional police commander cited Shai's motivation as Dorit's pronouncement several days prior to his lethal violence that the relationship was over. He was trying to convince Dorit to return to him. Failing to do so, he used his brother's pistol to shoot and kill her before he turned the weapon on himself (Mar. 3, 1995). A fourth homicide reported in December 2011 was said to be the first in the Jewish settlement in the West Bank (near Hebron) "not committed out of nationalistic motives," according to Malachi Levinger, head of the settlement's council. Gabi Twito shot and killed his ex-wife Mazal Twito four years post-divorce. After he pressed her to reconcile at dinner in her home, "he took an M16 rifle that belonged to his son, who is in the army, and shot his ex-wife and then killed himself" (Levinson 2011, A2). Jewish men from different ethnic, religious, and political backgrounds, who hailed from a variety of social locations, committed each of these homicides, and did so using a variety of weapons. The common thread among them is separation or divorce. Divorce may be a successful strategy for some women to pursue safety, but initiating separation may prompt an increase, change, or intensification in some men's violence.

Men's target for divorce-related domestic violence is not limited to intimate partners but also includes "collateral victims," when children serve as a proxy for or punishment of the intimate partner (Dobash and Dobash 2012). The newspaper of record, for example, noted that Asaf Goldring murdered his daughter Noa "as a form of revenge against his ex-wife" (*Haaretz* Service 2009). In an earlier case, Etti Tivoni left her husband, Erez, and sought protection from him in a shelter. During her stay, she secured a divorce. One week later, her ex-husband was allowed a supervised visit with their children, Eden, aged four, and Avital, aged two, at a WIZO Child Education Center. After he requested to have a few moments alone with them, Erez doused the children with gasoline and set them on fire. Avital died on the spot. It took her older brother nearly a month to succumb to his injuries. According to subsequent reports, Erez confessed that he had also intended to kill his ex-wife (Milner 1999). Notably, in the Tivoni case, the mother took the very steps encouraged by social services: she left her home, entered a shelter, got divorced, and entrusted her children to their care for a legally mandated visit with the father.

In another case of collateral damage, Palestinian mother Abir Dandis complained about her husband's threats to the Israeli police in Ma'aleh Adumim, a Jewish settlement in the West Bank, at least five times. After being told they do not handle complaints from (non-Jewish) residents of the territories, she was directed to the Israeli police in Arad, a town within the Green Line near her husband's home in the Negev. She complained in Arad to no effect, a day before he killed their children in May 2013 (Curiel 2013; *Times of Israel* 2013). In the midst of a "strenuous custody battle" Dandis had brought the children to live with her and her family in a part of the West Bank under the Palestinian

Authority. Her husband, Ali Amtirat, a 40-year-old Bedouin man from al-Fora'a, a village in Israel, continued to threaten her and the children, and told her he would not divorce her. She returned the girls to Amtirat only after his brothers kidnapped her brother and threatened to hurt him unless she complied. The Arad police in the Negev failed to respond to her final, prescient complaint (Raved 2013). The next day, Amtirat strangled their two daughters, four-year-old Asinad and two-year-old Rimas. For these battered women, leaving did not end the violence; instead, estranged husbands disciplined the mothers of Noa, Avital, and Erez, and Asinad and Rimas for ending the intimate relationship by targeting their children. Maddeningly, these children were made even more vulnerable by ineffective responses from social services and policing: the state's first responders to domestic violence.

Men's intensification and escalation of physical, sometimes lethal, violence against (ex-) wives, children, extended family and friends, social workers, or lawyers is well documented during the period leading up to or following a separation or divorce. Men's violent efforts to block the actual or metaphoric exit from the family home are evidence of the difficulties some women encounter when trying to terminate an intimate relationship. However, men's threats and physical violence are only one kind of divorce-related domestic violence.

The Process Is the Punishment

I turn now to consider another kind of divorce-related domestic violence: the divorce process itself, when women endure a Kafkaesque journey in an effort to dissolve their marriage (Weiss and Gross-Horowitz 2012), particularly when domestic violence is a central part of it. In Israel the divorce "process is the punishment" for a battered woman, who seeks to end her marriage as a legal pathway to a life separate from her husband (Feeley 1979). The punishment is meted out during an extended divorce process, by judges who interpret and administer legal codes and by husbands who take advantage of their legal entitlement to determine if, when, and under what circumstances a marriage will end. One battered woman explained,

> [W]hen I began the legal process, he was very agitated. He said everything was his, and beat the small children. . . . He said it is his house, his furniture, he said that he will not give me the divorce, but should leave if I wanted to. He [said] he would not divide up the property and no rabbinical court and no court of law would be able to take anything from him. He would stand there and yell and scare the girls and me too but I would not show him [that I was scared]. (Mor 1995, 158)

Separation and divorce processes that entail ongoing violence, time-consuming and costly legal processes, protracted and inequitable negotiations over child custody or maintenance, the legal impossibility of ending the relationship, or paradoxically, the legal impossibility of staying married, endanger battered women. Battered women seeking to divorce (or remain married to) their husbands encounter an array of legal codes and competing courts, which confound not only those who study the personal status law system but also those who find themselves subject to it. Battered women's stories of their experience with divorce demonstrate how the process itself constitutes a form of punitive domestic violence.

The most visible form of this unique type of divorce-related domestic violence is the denial of divorce, when women desiring to end a marriage are legally unable to do so because men simply will not release them from the relationship. Additional legal tools include institutionalized or forced reconciliation, extortion and blackmail, and control of women's sexuality and reproduction. Additionally, men use divorce—and the social and economic marginalization associated with it—as a threat against battered women. Yet battered women find ways to resist men's mobilization of divorce law within as well as outside of the complex court system. Women's partial victories over divorce-related domestic violence take several forms, ranging from forming alliances with religious court judges to rejecting divorce as the sole determinant of the status of their relationship or selfhood. I analyze each divorce-related domestic violence strategy separately, although they are related and often overlap within one woman's experience of the divorce process. Along the way, I point to how belonging to one or another national or religious community presents legal opportunities and barriers to battered women.

Divorce Denial

In an all too accurate parody of Israeli law, writer Amos Kolleck suggests, "You want to make marriage last. Because the divorce process is much more complicated" (*Hadassah Magazine*, Dec. 1994). Although he likely was referring only to Jewish families, the complexity of the divorce process for families in Israel is shared across religion and nationality. Each year about half of the couples filing for divorce do so in a timely manner by agreement; this means another 8,000 couples face potentially intractable divorce processes (Ettinger 2013b).

Missing from this statistic are families who lack any access to divorce: Latin (Roman) and Greek Catholic Israelis are the two largest Christian denominations that allow only dissolution (i.e., unconsummated marriage disestablished), annulment (i.e., post-consummation marriage disestablished), or separation (i.e., spouses live apart but remain legally married). The prospect of securing a positive outcome when pursuing one of these options is low, and the process is long (Batshon 2012), especially in cases of dissolution and annulment, which must be processed by the Vatican.

Divorce denial occurs when divorce proceedings are avoided or initiated but then delayed, continually prevented from advancing, or terminated against the will of one of the spouses. Women I spoke with understood the delay, denial, and associated threats as another form of abuse; more than one described it as being "held hostage." One woman was too afraid to meet me for an interview about her experience with divorce because her husband had started beating her up when she arrived home from attending a support group for women denied divorce. Although women, in general, are harmed by divorce denial for biological, social, economic, and legal reasons, battered women are particularly vulnerable to this tactic because divorce denial is a legal way for men to build an additional barrier against women exiting the relationship. Denying a divorce offers a husband who batters a practical and legal tactic to continue the relationship, control access to family property, or punish his wife for trying to leave.

A language exists within Judaism to explain the denial of divorce, although the legal institution that manages divorce in Israel (the rabbinate) differs from women's advocacy groups as to its meaning. According to the rabbinate, an *agunah* is the legal status of a woman whose husband is either physically or mentally unable to divorce her. The term is derived from the word *agun* (anchor) and "refers to parties who are literally 'chained' to their former spouses" (Breitowitz 1993, 1n1). The rabbinical court defines an agunah only as a woman whose husband is missing and thus unable to execute a divorce. The court uses the term *"mesoravet get"*—a woman denied a *get* (writ of divorce)—to refer to a woman whose husband defies a rabbinic court order of compulsion to execute a *get* (and see Chigier 1967; 1985, 260). These narrower conceptualizations differ from the broader understanding of the terms used by NGOs, which were developed to pursue justice for women denied divorce, raise public awareness about the issue, and advocate for substantive and procedural legal changes (e.g., Mevoi Satum; Center for Women's Justice; Yad L'Isha, Helping Hand for Women/Power to Women; Center for Women in Jewish Law; and the International Coalition for Aguna Rights, ICAR).

Advocacy groups claim men deny divorces to upward of 15,000 women, including but over and above the small number who have been officially compelled to do so by the rabbinate. This broader understanding of the problem has gained significant community awareness, demonstrated by its empathetic representation within popular culture in Israel with two multi-award-winning films capturing the public's attention: a documentary entitled *Sentenced to Marriage* (2004) that follows the lives of women and their advocates as they negotiate and wait for men to release them from marriage; and a second, feature film,

Gett: The Trial of Vivian Amsalem (2014), which tracks one woman's multiyear quest for divorce in a suffocating rabbinical court hearing room. Ruth Halperin-Kaddari and the Rackman Center, legal advocates for Jewish family law reform, were consultants on the film, and it was screened at a Rackman conference to help mark the International Day for the Elimination of Violence against Women in November 2014. The film was to be screened in February 2015 during the annual rabbinical conference in Israel as well.

The rising profile of divorce denial or "*get* abuse," and the higher volume of women's criticism of it, has put people like Rabbi Eli Ben-Dahan, director-general of the rabbinical courts between 1984 and 2010, in a defensive stance. He argued "the claims by women's organizations of thousands of women whose husbands refuse to give them divorces have no basis in reality" (Fendel 2007).[13] The Chief Rabbinate reports that they obtained a *get* for 159 agunot in 2013 and for another 184 in 2014, and then for 180 women in 2015 (Chief Rabbinate 2015; JTA, 2016a). The rabbinical court system recognizes, on their own terms, the legal phenomenon of divorce denial as a problem in need of remedies. The courts have had the option to recommend imprisonment of those who continue to deny the *get* after officially being compelled to do so; and since 1995 the courts have the discretion to order civil sanctions, when they deem it appropriate, against those compelled.[14] The courts are now tasked to handle difficult cases via a special unit that tracks down recalcitrant men, whether located inside the state or beyond its borders; their website posts pictures and descriptions of a small handful of such "wanted men." Ultimately, the rabbinate's goal is not to render the resulting *get* as "coerced" (*meuseh*), and thus invalid. At the same time, the rabbinate seeks to prevent a woman denied divorce from engaging in extramarital relations (see upcoming section where I discuss sexuality and reproduction).

Early on rabbinical court judges hesitated before approving an order to compel a husband to produce a *get*. Between 1953 and 1977, only twelve men received compulsion orders (Chigier 1985, 271). Nearly four decades later, the number of recalcitrant spouses sanctioned or imprisoned budged, but not by much, given the increased population size and divorce rate (Kaplan 2012). According to their records, rabbinical courts handed down 165 decisions for sanctions against forty-seven recalcitrant men in 2015, plus twenty-three orders for incarceration (Chief Rabbinate 2015; Ettinger 2016).[15] Nevertheless, persuading a rabbinical court to have a recalcitrant spouse compelled, sanctioned, and incarcerated requires an extended period of time, and none of these options guarantees a divorce.[16]

Shai Cohen, for example, lived with his wife for two years, and they had two children together before they socially ended the relationship. From the time of the breakup, it took six years for the rabbinical court to incarcerate Cohen for refusing to give his wife a divorce. It took nearly six more years for Cohen, then sitting in Ela Prison, to seriously consider the divorce. At the age of forty, he was escorted by prison guards to the Rabbinical Court of Appeals in Jerusalem for a hearing. "The hearing ended on an upbeat with the attorneys set to draft an agreement leading to the divorce" (Ettinger 2013a). With the hearing about to end, Cohen went to the bathroom, jumped to the ground from its second-floor window, and subsequently disappeared, likely to the West Bank. Shai Cohen added "fugitive" to his status as a "refusenik" that day. Meanwhile, his wife remains a married *mesorevet get*, a woman denied a divorce by her recalcitrant husband. The guards and officers accompanying Cohen were later sanctioned for their liability in his escape.

Divorce denial transcends state borders, too, because recalcitrant husbands can cross them in an effort to escape sanctions. Men abandon their wives by leaving Israel; others flee to Israel to avoid executing a divorce. On January 22, 1997, the US Department of State issued an unprecedented travel warning to its Jewish citizens that "they may be subject to involuntary and prolonged stays in Israel if a [divorce] case is filed against them in a Rabbinical Court." The particular case that prompted the announcement involved Seymour Klagsbrun, an Orthodox Jewish-American man from Monsey, New York, who had refused to grant his wife a *get* for over twelve years. Eventually, Klagsbrun claimed that he had obtained rabbinic permission to marry a second wife (without divorcing his first wife), and had done so in May 1996. The Monsey community rejected his claim and local rabbis prohibited him from worshiping in any area synagogue. According to the *Jewish Advocate* (Boston) report, in an attempt to find a more welcoming atmosphere, Klagsbrun traveled to Israel. When the Israeli rabbinical court learned of the divorce case, they initiated an injunction against Klagsbrun prohibiting him from leaving the country, ostensibly until he granted his wife the *get*. Such sanctions may convince handfuls of men whom the rabbinate recognizes as recalcitrant to legally end the relationship, but not those individuals who either go unrecognized as deniers or who are immune to civil sanctions or incarceration.

Battered women denied divorce are not limited to problems inherent in Jewish law. Christian, Muslim, and Druze women can be faced with an unending marriage as well. For example, a Catholic woman reported to the feminist Palestinian NGO Kayan that her request for separation lasted fifteen years; another's application for separation was denied, despite her reports of "domestic violence and the fact that she and her husband had been living separately for years" (Batshon 2012, 7). When I spoke with Nahida, a twenty-four-year-old Palestinian Muslim citizen of Israel in 1995, she was a high school graduate who had fled her abusive husband and marital home, leaving behind four children. She was living with her parents in their modest home when we met at midday during Ramadan. Nahida was unemployed because of her lack of job skills and a physical impairment that made it painful for her to stand up for long periods of time, thereby disqualifying her from unskilled factory labor or cleaning jobs, common employment options for Arab women lacking formal education. Her parents were supportive of Nahida's decision to move out of her marital home because they wished to protect her from further physical harm. Nahida was mostly concerned that she could not see her young children and that her husband's new wife, who now raised them, was turning them against Nahida. She was further troubled that because of laws regarding married couples' assets and liabilities, Nahida unknowingly financed her husband's illegal second marriage to a Palestinian woman from the West Bank, when he obtained a loan using both their names. At the age of twenty-four, Nahida was left without an income or access to her children, but remains married because her husband refuses to divorce her. She has been unsuccessful in efforts to persuade the qadi to dissolve the marriage. In some cases, regardless of the written legal codes, as a Palestinian lawyer in Israel remarked to me: "If the husband does not agree, there is no divorce. Even if there is a [valid] reason, if he does not agree, there is no divorce."

In contrast to Jewish divorce law in Israel, which locks a woman within an unwanted marriage when the husband refuses to grant the divorce, Islamic law as practiced in Israel is open to judicial dissolution of marriage. Sharia court judges (qadis) can and do dissolve a marriage after a husband abandons his wife or has been incarcerated for an extended period of time. When the husband is present but does not wish to divorce, the qadi determines whether the divorce is required, basing his decision on a report submitted by two arbitrators from the community. The judge may then compel the wife to return home, compel the husband to repudiate the wife, or judicially dissolve the marriage (*tafriq*). If the marriage is to be terminated, the qadi apportions blame for the dissolution (akin to a fault divorce) and determines the amount of dower the wife deserves to receive.

Yet, in any particular case, abstract legal options may not translate into reality when relying on a qadi's or a husband's discretionary power built into the divorce process. A Muslim woman who had fled to the shelter for Palestinian battered women in Israel, run by Palestinian women, desperately sought a divorce from her husband. Her lawyer narrated the woman's story to me when we met in 1999, a period during which sharia courts were becoming more attuned to women's demands for justice. Despite these qadi-driven developments, her client was unable to secure a divorce:

The husband who used drugs [demanded:] "if you want the divorce then give me the kids. . . ." A year and a half of meetings and threats [followed]. . . . At the [most recent meeting], I noticed that he was very quiet. I thought that he was planning something . . . he began to threaten [her]—"If you don't give me the children and return home I will kill you!" I sat there thinking [his threats] were of no merit, just talk! But when we went [inside] to the qadi, he began the threats again. So, I requested from the qadi to record [the threats] in the protocol, and to call the police. The qadi refused [both requests]. That's the way it is!

So, when we left [the courtroom] . . . the father of her husband began to talk to [my client]: "Come home and I will be responsible for you and the children. I won't allow him to continue in this way." I noticed that the husband came by and took something out of his pocket . . . he began to try to kill her, stabbing her with the knife. What I noticed was that none of the people who were around there got involved! That was the blow for me! He stabbed her many times; she was taken to Rambam Hospital by ambulance. I returned to the courtroom and screamed at them: "Look, you didn't call the police and look what happened!" He didn't give her the divorce. She almost died. . . . [Then] he began looking for me: "Where is the lawyer? I will kill her also!" People didn't let me leave [the courtroom]. . . . Two days later I got a call: "I am still looking for you; I will give you what is coming to you; I will find you." So, I went to the police to complain. . . . He is in jail [on account of the] stabbing, and threatening me, and the social worker, [but] they are still married.

Although this lawyer's client did not benefit from it, sharia courts have reformed the practice of marital dissolution in Israel based on the flexibility encoded within its inherited Ottoman Family Rights Law (1917),[17] which draws on more than one school of thought for handling marital disputes. For example, Hanafi jurisprudence, the main school of thought followed in the region, typically considered the most lenient, is the most rigid when it comes to divorce: it "allows a Muslim man to divorce his wife easily . . . [and] makes it difficult for a woman to divorce her husband" (Abou Ramadan 2006, 250). In contrast, Ottoman Family Law's Article 130 articulates a more robust Maliki jurisprudential framework from which qadis can trigger a judicial dissolution process (255). Despite the growing recognition within rabbinical and sharia courts of the need to assist women when they wish to end their relationship, all communal courts in Israel prefer that couples undergo marital reconciliation rather than divorce.

Institutionalized and Forced Reconciliation

Twenty years ago, when Israeli smoking policies were being reformed, the well-known comedian Uzi Baron joked on a popular Friday evening talk show: "If you put out a cigarette on the road, the police will receive a fine of 225 shekels (about $75), but if you put it out on your wife, the police will just request that you do *shalom bayit*." Although policing of domestic violence has improved somewhat over time, the joke points to the enduring culture of institutionalized reconciliation embedded within the divorce process, even in the face of domestic violence (Lazarus-Black 2007; London 1997). In essence, persuading men to grant a divorce is a job assigned to wives (and their lawyers or extended family), and the task of persuading women to stay married is the responsibility of their husbands, and the religious courts, or extended family. Religious court judges see reconciliation as being in their community's best interest. A respected Islamic leader declared that the purity and stability of the Muslim family creates the future of the *ummah*, the Muslim people (Layish 1975). Two decades later, Taibe mayor Rafik Haji Yehiye echoed a similar position in his public opposition to a government-funded battered women's shelter—only the second intended for Palestinian Arab women in Israel—slated to open in his town: "In the Arab sector there are sharia courts and those with skills who are able to establish shalom bayit within families in conflict" (Elgazi 1995, 7a). Reconciliation strategies, including formal arbitration, informal communal conflict resolution, and familial pressure that help a couple to avoid divorce, are intended to help not only the nuclear family but also the stability and unity of the community as a whole. The health of a family stands in for and contributes to the enduring strength of the nation. The corollary: families should be cared for by kinsmen, rather than by strangers.

The Hebrew term "shalom bayit" translates directly as "peace of the house" and articulates the concept of reconciliation to keep the family harmonized as a whole. It also points to the labor expended by women as wives and mothers to maintain family unity whether authentically or as a façade. This hidden labor may include remaining silent with regard to men's violence and agreeing to reconcile with a husband. Shalom bayit is institutionalized in the ideology of reconciliation practiced in religious courts. Callers that I listened to on the hotline for battered women, and others that I interviewed in the 1990s frequently complained that their husbands play a game with them by requesting reconciliation to delay or cancel divorce proceedings. The director of services for Arab women at the Haifa antiviolence hotline argued, "Among us, it is not so acceptable for women to leave; there are those who do and they go to their parents' home. Then, they do a *sulha* [reconciliation, i.e., with their husband] with some respected community member presiding" (and see Haj-Yahia 1995). Reconciliation aims to effect an agreement among spouses to live well together despite one spouse's initial or enduring interest in ending the relationship. Nahida, for example, explained that she would often flee to her father's home only to have her husband go to the qadi and demand reconciliation and obedience from his wife (*bayt al-ta'a*), that is, that she return home: "I felt like a cow [being herded around and told to] come." She remembers being beaten the day after they signed one such reconciliation agreement. Although police cannot officially enforce these orders, women's responses to these religious court judicial orders or recommendations are taken into consideration when judges evaluate a divorce petition.

Some battered women go to great lengths to get divorced and then are thwarted by a husband's request of reconciliation. Rima is a Latin Catholic Palestinian Israeli who has three children under the age of eleven. She lives in one of the poorest neighborhoods in Haifa. During our interview in her home, she related that she is alternately beaten and abandoned by her husband and left with no money or food; the electricity and water services at Rima's house have been cut off for months at a time, including when we met. We sat near the front door of the house in order to take advantage of the quickly setting sun as a source of light. In the past, her priest repeatedly encouraged her to reconcile with her husband. But, after working with hotline volunteers for more than a year, Rima sought a way to divorce. She convinced her husband to convert with her to Eastern Greek Orthodox Catholicism, a denomination that allows divorce, and charges "an extraordinarily high fee" for the conversion and divorce (Batshon 2012, 8). Two weeks later, her husband halted the process, citing his interest in reconciliation. As a result, Rima remained married, subject to Canonic law.

Spouses like Rima who seek divorce within the Greek Orthodox church, including those who convert to gain access to divorce, face a significantly longer process when one party dissents. An analysis conducted by Kayan reports that a mutually desired divorce required an average of just 1.5 hearings per case, which increased to an average of 6.3 hearings (and a high point of 11 hearings) when one spouse dissents (Batshon 2012, 6). No rules regulate the minimum or maximum time between these hearings: "For divorces where no accord was ever reached, the proceedings took between two and ten years" (6). Mira, a Jewish Ashkenazi woman, was similarly forced into a spiral of reconciliations with her husband. When we met, she had been married for eight years, during three of which Mira had been trying to get a divorce. Each time the couple was scheduled to advance toward a divorce, her husband requested reconciliation, to which the rabbinical court judges quickly agreed, sending the couple home, where the beatings continued. Mira then scheduled another hearing, and the cycle repeated. At any point in the divorce process, a husband may use this technique to delay or even terminate divorce proceedings. Men know that reconciliation gains them social legitimacy in the eyes of religious court judges and, very likely, control over their wives. Because religious court fees are typically lower than family court fees, it is also a relatively cheap mechanism for men who wish to stay married.

Over time, however, the Chief Rabbinate has become more responsive to feminist criticism of shalom bayit. Prior to 2006 the rabbinical courts would report only the number of petitions submitted annually for shalom bayit, along with all other types of petitions, focusing attention on the level of activity rather than legal outcomes. Beginning in 2006 they began to report the number submitted (*n*=1032), as well as the percentage approved (5 percent). Less than a decade later, they report that only 2.6 percent of petitions for shalom bayit (*n*=969) filed in 2014 were approved. Other than the number of divorces finalized each year, shalom bayit is the only legal activity provided with a disposition rate, indicating an institutional interest in communicating this information to the public, likely inspired by exposure to clients of Talem and Bat Melech, two NGOs delivering services for religious Jewish battered women.

Extortion and Blackmail

One of the more common techniques for abusing women during the divorce process is conditioning the execution of the divorce on acceptance of unreasonable settlements, including demand of a sum of money or property. Payment for divorce has roots in both the Jewish and the Islamic marital traditions in which the arrangement is partly an economic one. In this traditional scenario, women, when initiating a divorce, are required to surrender all or part of the dowry. I am referring to the contemporary manipulation of this practice whereby men intentionally extort large sums of money or demand that their wives forfeit rights to marital property, child support, or child custody to obtain a divorce. Some do this to try to dissuade their wives from seeking the divorce or to punish them for doing so.

Extortion or blackmail may include physical threats or harm before, during, or after formal negotiations in a lawyer's office or courtroom. It may be in the form of lump-sum payments, extremely low or no child support, personal property such as a family's apartment, car, or business, or child custody. A volunteer from the Haifa hotline escorted Deborah to the rabbinical court to be divorced because she was too scared of her husband to leave the house by herself. When the proceedings began, her husband demanded an additional NIS 40,000 (approximately $14,000 at the time) in exchange for the divorce. According to lawyers, social workers, and other experts, this level of blackmail is quite common. Women take out loans or borrow money from parents to pay divorce bribes.

There are also men who abuse their wives by suddenly or periodically deserting them to live with another woman, or disappearing by fleeing the country or living marginal, untraceable lives. This may leave women with no means of support and full responsibility for children, but still legally tied to the husband. Susan Weiss and Netty Gross-Horowitz (2012, 41–59) witnessed the effect of this phenomenon as advocates for such women: Eitan took advantage of his "clueless" secular but traditional Mizrahi wife Shira's desire to end their marriage and live a normal life away from her husband, who had unpredictable mood swings; when he physically assaulted her, she called law enforcement to have him removed from the home. Despite living apart from Eitan over the course of ten years, he provided no economic support for their three children, and appeared only to negotiate or failed to show up at nineteen rabbinical court hearings related to her request for a divorce. Eitan pushed and pushed Shira to compromise—as did the *dayyanim*—even while he stood in shackles in the rabbinical court, until she conceded, again and again, to less and less, in exchange for his execution of the divorce. Ultimately, Shira's lawyer advised her to agree to all his demands in order to "set herself free" (52), although her concessions still proved insufficient. Husbands like Shira's can gradually up the ante over time to force the wife to either concede to his demands or remain his wife, or both.

Frontline workers are accustomed to the explicit blackmail associated with divorce. A social worker at a Haifa shelter for battered women explained to me in the mid-1990s that the husband of a young religious Jewish woman who had spent time there gradually increased his demands in return for his agreement to divorce—first, the family home, then their bank accounts, next the car—until relinquishing custody of their five children was his final condition. Kayan's legal department coordinator Shiri Batshon (2012) found in her research on divorce in Christian ecclesiastical courts that "Many women complained that unless and until their husband consented to the divorce, they were 'imprisoned' in the marriage, and this gave their husbands leverage to extort huge financial and material concessions from them" (6). A lawyer I interviewed advises battered women: "if you give in and give up some of your rights, perhaps he will agree." A perverse perception of this extortion or condition-based divorce has emerged within rabbinical courts, where husbands who offer such conditions are perceived by judges as willing to give the divorce, but women who reject unreasonable demands are labeled as divorce refusers (Wilmovsky and Tamir 2012, 110). The blackmail need not occur within a specific marriage to intimidate a woman seeking divorce. Common knowledge and local stories, whether appropriate to a particular husband, are powerful cultural messages. As one veteran volunteer at the Haifa hotline explained: "The message that women get from everywhere is that they will lose the apartment, that the kids will be taken away. They don't know their rights, and battered women are especially living with a huge threat, a physical threat, so they decide the apartment or my life; it's like robbery on the street, he points a gun at you and says your money or your life and of course, you give him everything you have." Divorce thus becomes a market commodity, where there is a "price" for ending a relationship: whatever a wife is willing or able to pay.

Recent attempts to reform the divorce economy have produced two possible avenues for battered women. The first is the reform to the Spousal Property Relations Law instituted in 2008, which aims to undercut the price of a divorce by allowing a family court to settle the property division decision prior to execution of the divorce, under certain conditions, including evidence of domestic violence. Nevertheless, pre-divorce division of property may still be subject to men's threats and intimidation and can still leave a woman married to her divorce-denying husband. In the same year, lawyer and family law advocate Susan Weiss established a groundbreaking precedent in civil tort law adjudicated within the Family Court, whereby a woman was awarded compensation in the amount of NIS 550,000 ($137,500) for emotional suffering because of the husband's decade-long denial of divorce, even after the rabbinical court compelled him to do so (Weiss 2013). These and other legal innovations, both civil and religious, may help ease the burden of or at least balance the number and kind of tactics available when navigating this legally pluralistic and highly competitive personal status law system. Although legal pluralism, per se, does not necessitate women's vulnerability to extortion and blackmail, in this instance, it is commonplace for battered women in the midst of divorce to be threatened economically by their husbands because of this particular configuration of legal pluralism. Moreover, at least within rabbinical courts, husbands can be aided by court judges who narrowly interpret divorce law when pressing men to divorce their wives but broadly when they are pressuring women to agree to the husband's terms (Weiss and Gross-Horowitz 2012, 8). Pursuing a divorce when the couple disagrees to its terms demands extended amounts of time and money, resources that the majority of women do not possess (Dagan-Buzaglo, Hasson, and Ophir 2014). Leaving a relationship may require a battered woman's capitulation to terms that would render her impoverished, without a home or assets, or leave her as a noncustodial parent. Economically intangible assets such as one's sexuality or reproductive future also may be part of a battered woman's bargain to secure a divorce.

Control of Sexuality and Reproduction

A brief look at the legal codes that regulate marital sexuality and reproduction reveal how unpredictable contradictions between religion and state produce battered women's vulnerability while enhancing men's social and legal power. Rabbinical court legal advocate Gitit Nahliel argues that Jewish women seek divorce more than men do because their need for divorce is gendered (Israel Women's Network 1998). Women's biological capacity for pregnancy is limited by age, as is their social capacity for finding a new husband, should they so desire. If a married Jewish woman consorts or lives with a man other than her husband, she will lose her right to spousal maintenance; if she has a sexual relationship with a man who is not her husband, she is barred from marrying the lover subsequent to dissolution of the original marriage. If she becomes pregnant by a man other than her legal husband, any child resulting from this forbidden relationship is considered a *mamzer* and unable to participate in religious life rituals, including marriage, for up to ten generations henceforth. In contrast, married Jewish men may live with and impregnate single women with rare biological or legal implications. Thus, in cases of a lengthy divorce denial, a woman's intimate life, including her sexuality and reproduction, can be seriously compromised.

Struggle over the definition and regulation of *mamzerut*, colloquially defined as "bastardy," continues to plague women's personal lives, and the struggle between religion and statecraft. An infamous case involving two siblings barred from marriage due to their mamzer status nearly cost Golda Meir her government in 1972 in a battle between those advocating for a solution based in civil marriage and divorce and those seeking a resolution through Jewish law. The first chief rabbi of the IDF, and Ashkanazi chief rabbi from 1972 to 1982, Shlomo Goren (of the Religious Zionist camp) reversed the Langer siblings' mamzer status, which had been declared and confirmed by several rabbinical courts (JTA, 1973). Since then, the attorney general's office has urged rabbinical courts to reject paternity claims by a woman against a man who is not her husband so as to avoid possible determination of mamzer status (Dayan 2006). Still, Attorney General Aharon Barak affirmed in 1976 that rabbinical courts have jurisdiction to determine a person's eligibility to marry, but advocated that no one be added to the "blacklist" unless and until they submitted a request to register a marriage (Dayan 2006). Yet, rabbinical court judges in Tiberias retrospectively annulled the twelve-year marriage of Shoshana Haddad because one of her ancestors, a Cohen, might have married a divorcee 2,500 years ago (Shapiro 1994). At the time, Jerusalem city council member Anat Hoffman claimed that the secret computerized list contained the names of 10,000 persons, although then Chief Rabbi Elihu Bakshi-Doron said it included only 4,000 names (Shapiro 1994). By August 2012, the blacklist grew to number 5,397 persons barred from marriage whether because of mamzerut or inadequate proof of Jewish identity, regardless of their age or request for approval to marry (S. Weiss 2013, 264). The Ministry of Religious Services continues to maintain and actively consult the blacklist. Today between 300,000 and 400,000 people, mostly from the former Soviet Union, are unable to marry in Israel because of the suspect nature of their Jewish identity.

Women undergo extraordinary efforts to prevent tainting their children with the label of mamzer or tainting themselves as an adulterer. Fear of these religious rules keeps women married and keeps women, no matter their religiosity, from ignoring or rejecting the jurisdiction of the rabbinical courts and maintaining sexual lives apart from their husbands without obtaining a legal divorce. All but one of the Jewish battered women I interviewed articulated that producing mamzerim would cause great distress in their family and the larger Israeli community. The lone dissenter suggested conspiratorially that every Jewish woman should have a baby with a man other than her husband to break the hold of religious control over personal status law. For decades various NGOs have lobbied for civil marriage or for alternatives to marriage. The most extreme and recent rejection of Israel's approach to personal status was expressed at TEDxJaffa, by Member of Knesset, media personality, and activist Merav Michaeli (2012), who urged all Israelis to "cancel marriage," both religious and civil.

Other women are simply unaware of how they are personally implicated in the bifurcated court system. The "clueless" agunah mentioned previously, Shira, is a secular woman who was surprised by the religious rituals in which she was required to participate in order to get married; later on she was again taken aback not only by the mandate to secure a religious divorce but also by how it worked:

> "Can't a rabbinic court just declare my marriage over?" Shira wondered, thinking about some of the divorce trials she had seen staged on the imported soaps aired on Israeli T.V. . . . "No [her lawyer Pazit responded]. It doesn't work that way. We need Eitan. The halakha is that a marriage is over only when a husband delivers a bill of divorce, physically, to his wife." "Well, I don't care about halakha. I am not religious. Let's just go to family court," Shira suggested. "That's a civil court, and they don't have to decide things according to halakha, no?" "No," Pazit answered testily. . . . It does not matter if you are the Baba Sali [a holy Moroccan rabbi] or Dana International [a famous Israeli transvestite (sic) pop singer]. The family courts have no say in the matter." (Weiss and Gross-Horowitz 2012, 51)

Shira waited over ten years for her husband to agree to divorce her, during which time she lost more than one opportunity to have an intimate partner. One boyfriend wanted to have a "kosher wedding and a kosher relationship" with Shira, but she was not free to do so (53). Similarly, the ultra-Orthodox Tikvah, married to Ze'ev for 20 years (and still counting) said she "dreamed of having more kids, but it's not my fate" (99), even though the couple lived as husband and wife for only three months before Tikvah decided that his brutal violence, which only escalated when she became pregnant, including withholding money from her to purchase food, was simply too much to bear. Advocates explained, "What happened is fairly simple. Tikvah cannot marry and have more children, or even go out for coffee with a man, because she does not have a *get*" (99).

While focusing on steps to end domestic violence, battered women also have concerns about their future intimate and family lives; men need not worry. Under specific circumstances, Jewish men, like Muslim men, are allowed to marry more than one wife under their respective religion's law. Originally, Jewish law allowed for polygyny (i.e., plural wives for one husband). It was banned for Ashkenazi Jews approximately 1,000 years ago through a *takkanah* (legal decree) by Rabbi Gershom ben Judah Me'or (960–1028). Soon after the establishment of the State of Israel in 1950, the Israeli Rabbinate extended this ban to all Jewish communities (Edelman 1994). The ban was adopted into Israeli law in 1959 in the form of universal criminalized bigamy. As a result, Muslim men have no legal defense to the state's charge of bigamy, despite it being allowed religiously (see Chapter 5 for a discussion of accommodated polygyny among Bedouins in the Negev). However, a Jewish man retains a positive religious defense against such a charge if his wife refuses to accept the divorce and he is granted marital "relief" with permission by rabbinical court judges to marry a second wife (*hetter nissu'in*). Notwithstanding the official low number, according to research conducted by the Rackman Center, forty-two such permits were awarded between 2004 and 2007, and permission to marry a second wife has gained the power of urban myth among Jews and is used by husbands to threaten their divorce-desiring wives to delay proceedings or to extort favorable settlements.

Similarly, sharaf politics, whereby a man's social standing depends on his own actions as well as "the sexual behavior of the women under his charge" (Lang 2005, 37) informs how Palestinian women navigate their intimate lives prior to, during, and after marriage. Unlike Jewish women, Muslim and Druze women cannot be denied divorce if a qadi agrees to dissolve the marriage. However, a marital practice originally intended to protect women may instead entrap them when they wish to end the relationship. During the engagement or premarital period, the marriage contract is signed (*kabt al-kitab*), and the couple is socially and legally considered married. Therefore the couple is able to get to know each other better while being "protected" against gossip about or discovery of premarital social or sexual contact (or an "early" pregnancy). This arrangement may protect women who otherwise risk social stigma or physical harm from family members who disapprove of premarital socializing. However, in return for this short-term protection, the couple will be required to legally dissolve the "unactualized marriage" if a spouse wishes to discontinue the relationship (Savaya and Cohen 2004; Abu-Rabia-Queder 2007). The dissolution of an unactualized marriage may subsequently affect a woman's social standing and ability to marry again. A cruel and unanticipated result of this practice is illustrated by Nawal's story, a young woman from an Arab town in the north of Israel whom I interviewed in 1999. Upon engagement and signing of the protective marital contract, her fiancé[18] began to exhibit controlling behaviors such as extreme jealousy, physical violence, and emotional abuse. Nawal found herself in limbo, doubly threatened: too scared to initiate a divorce but fearful about actualizing the marriage with a wedding. Although a considerable number of couples do formally dissolve unactualized marriages in sharia courts, for some women, the need to divorce not only gives men permission to continue or escalate their use of violence, it also can constrain battered women's sexuality and reproductive futures.

The women's stories detailed thus far have focused on the struggle of and for battered women to secure a divorce. This struggle continues, with individual women, aided primarily by NGOs, seeking to "just leave" if not "leave justly" by socially, legally, and economically ending their relationship. Yet not all battered women, despite their desire for the violence to end, want their marriage and all it affords them to end. For these women, divorce is another threat to their well-being. Remaining married is their goal, or at least a strategy battered women employ to accommodate their conflicting needs.

Divorce as Threat

Men also use divorce law as a tactic to keep women in line by threatening to end the marriage. Indeed, Muslim women who initiate divorce do so primarily because of their husbands' violent threats to their life; these divorcees have a higher level of education and paid employment than married women who remain in stressful marriages but who also experienced violence (Kulik and Klein 2010). Similarly, among dual-earner Jewish couples, women who earn as much as or more than their spouse have a higher rate of divorce (Raz-Yurovich 2012). In this family-centered state, divorce can marginalize women whose salient identity is based on motherhood and the marital home (Adelman 2005b, 120; Abu-Rabia-Queder and Weiner-Levy 2013; Kanaaneh 2002).

Divorce rates vary, depending on nationality, religion, social class/education, and geography. Overall, based on Israel's Central Bureau of Statistics (2014), Jewish Israelis have the highest divorce rate (1.9, calculated per 1,000 people), followed by Muslims (1.3), Druze (1.1), and Christians (0.8). The social stigma associated with divorce varies accordingly. Middle-aged Palestinian Arab women in Israel whom Muhammad Haj-Yahia (2000b) interviewed preferred that women address their concerns with domestic violence within the family: "If my daughter told me that her husband beats her, I would be very angry. First of all, I would advise her to try talking with him directly without involving people from the outside. She must not remain silent about the violence, yet she also should not let others know what is happening in her family" (247). If, however, the violence persisted for an extended length of time or rose to a "particularly severe level" (247), and the extended family was unable to intervene successfully, women stated they would encourage their daughter to seek outside assistance. Nevertheless, only 6 percent of the women Haj-Yahia interviewed advocated divorce as a solution to domestic violence: "I will do everything I can to help her—and so will her father and brothers. I would only encourage her to divorce her husband if I am convinced that there is absolutely no other choice" (248). Haj-Yahia argues that women's resistance to men's domestic violence, for example, by pursuing formal interventions including social services or law enforcement, can alienate the husband and his family against the wife and her family, thereby precluding reconciliation and leading to pressure on the husband to divorce the wife.

Munira's story represents women who feel so physically threatened by their husbands that they live apart from but remain legally married to their husbands, because of a mix of sociolegal barriers to divorce. An Arab Catholic woman, Munira and her young child live with her family in a middle-class home overlooking a lush valley. Munira seemed excited to have a guest, guiding me through her home and around the immediate neighborhood. During our interview, she spoke openly about her decision to leave her husband and the satisfaction she derives from living in her parents' home, relatively free from the threat of violence, raising her child with her mother's assistance. When asked about the terms of their separation and the possibility of obtaining an annulment from Rome, Munira exclaimed suddenly: "What good would [an annulment] do for me? I am 'used goods' according to the men here." Despite her young age of twenty-three, she figured that a publicly known intimate relationship was out of the question, and she remained focused on the well-being of her child and the peaceful atmosphere of her family's home. Munira's family supports her decision, and although her marital status provides a relatively respected social status, she spoke about constraints on her social and physical mobility, circumscribed by extended family members, including child relatives, neighbors, and religious leaders, who impose a heavy burden of surveillance in her village.

Palestinian Muslim battered women are especially vulnerable to the threat of divorce because Islamic law allows for men to execute unilateral divorce; the criminal sanction for performing such a divorce (i.e., without the wife's consent) does not annul its legal validity. Moreover, Muslim women who adjudicate a divorce in sharia court often have child custody assigned to the father, according to Muslim custom, rather than the tender years doctrine practiced in family court. Fouzieh Abou Ramadan, who objected to losing guardianship of her children in the sharia court to her husband, appealed its decision to the High Court of Justice, which has reversed several similar sharia court decisions (Kopf 2011). She also called off a post-divorce engagement because she "didn't feel strong enough to fight . . . and didn't want to take a risk" of losing her children (ibid.). Kayan's (2014) study of five Muslim women's experience of post-divorce remarriage demonstrated the burden placed on the mother to rebut the presumption that the father should have custody of the children. Barring a protracted and costly legal fight, this means that once divorced, most Muslim women will not remarry (al-Krenawi and Graham 1998). A case of a divorced Muslim woman remarrying, and thus losing the custody of her three daughters, was so exceptional that she was featured in television and radio reports.

Divorce can socially devalue a woman, economically penalize her, result in a mother's loss of child custody, or mean that she returns to live with her parents. Under these circumstances, threat of divorce is a particularly effective technique for men to use to intimidate or punish a woman. Because of these constraints, battered women may strategize to stay married in order to avoid the multiple costs associated with divorce.

RESISTANCE AND PARTIAL VICTORIES

Divorced, single women face significant economic barriers and social dislocation in Israel, to the point that unmarried Palestinian women have articulated a preference for single life over that of a divorcee (Sa'ar 2004). Seen from this angle, battered women in particular must navigate conflicting needs and wants. While the chapter thus far has focused on the victimization of battered women through divorce law, battered women do succeed in obtaining a divorce or eschew its power to determine their lives. So here I turn to stories of women who sought an exit from their relationships in ways that both reinforce and counter dominant cultural stereotypes or scripts about women who are victimized by their intimate partners.

Fighting Your Way Out

On February 18, 1994, forty-year-old Carmela Buhbut shot her husband, Yehuda, following an incident in which he had stabbed her. She used an army rifle belonging to one of her four sons. The family lived in Kiryat Shmona, a small development town on the northern border where news reports of violence and shooting usually refer to katuysha rockets and bomb shelters. Shortly thereafter, on September 12, 1994, Carmela was convicted of manslaughter and sentenced by the District Court in Nazareth to a seven-year prison sentence. In response feminists demonstrated in Jerusalem, Tel Aviv, and Haifa, protesting that Carmela Buhbut had suffered enough at the hands of her husband. During the demonstration in Haifa, I observed a placard that read, "Prison or the cemetery: Is this the fate of women beaten in Israel?" Feminist legal scholar Frances Raday (2009) quoted extensively from subsequent court testimony on Buhbut's appeal in an essay on "Law in Israel." In the words of Supreme Court Justice Dalia Dorner's decision, Buhbut killed her husband after exhausting every possible (unhelpful) resource:

> Carmela Buhbut was a battered woman. For twenty-four years her
> husband treated her brutally. In the village where she lived, this was
> an open secret. Her husband's parents, his brother, his sisters and the
> community all knew of it and all kept silent. She wandered around
> like a shadow, carrying on her face and body signs of her injuries, and
> she did not smile. Her sons grew up in the atmosphere of the beating
> of their mother, and even when they were grown up did not intervene.
> In November 1993, she was hospitalized after her husband had beaten
> her on the head with a clog. Serious injuries had been detected, and

accordingly, it was clear that she had been beaten. She explained to the hospital staff that she had beaten herself, and amazingly, her explanation was accepted.

Local law enforcement officers were complicit in the community's silence; they, too, feared Yehuda Buhbut and considered him vicious and dangerous. Given the lack of legal protection, reinforced by community-wide collusion, the Supreme Court agreed that she decided to "kill or be killed," and reduced her sentence from seven to three years.

When tactics such as appeasement, negotiation, or other forms of family-based resistance prove ineffective to cope with or manage men's violence and when conditions constrain the possibility of mobilizing external resources, battered women may use violence to defend themselves, resist, or otherwise escape from men who batter (Pence and Dasgupta 2006). Women who use such "resistive violence" (Pence 2012) are adjudicated in a criminal justice system that distinguishes them as either a victim or an offender (Ferraro 2006). Those women who fit the cultural image of the innocent and powerless victim tend to gain sympathy from the judiciary (and the public) for their use of violence. Introduction of testimony related to the so-called "battered woman syndrome," or the more accurately termed "expert testimony of the effects of battering on survivors," during the sentencing stage of prosecution of battered women convicted of killing their batterers has helped legal professionals understand how, why, and when battered women use violence (Ferraro 2003, 2006; Maguigan 1991; Richie 2012; Schneider 2000). This evolving perspective was not integrated into Israeli legal culture to mitigate the original sentence of Carmela Buhbut who killed her husband as the only viable exit she saw from the relationship. Upon appeal, Buhbut's case reinforced the "good victim" narrative of the helpless and passive battered woman driven to violence only as a last resort after enduring a reign of terror. Her case captured significant attention and ultimately resulted in legal reform intended to help women like her.[19] Women whose profiles do not align with this constructed victim typology risk removing themselves from home imprisonment to being incarcerated by the state for using resistive violence, rather than a combination of family and criminal law as mechanisms to terminate their intimate relationships.

Professional Persuasion

Divorce stories are full of compromise. No one seems to end a marriage getting everything they need or want. In terms of battered women, some give in and give up maintenance, property, or child custody in order to end the relationship. Other women benefit from persuasive arbiters, informal or formal, who successfully influence men using legal as well as illegal means to get them to consent to divorce their wives. The office of the Chief Rabbinate, for example, tries to locate husbands whom they have officially deemed recalcitrant around the world in order to persuade them to execute a divorce, which can include coordination among the Interior Ministry, Foreign Ministry, and domestic law enforcement and security services, as well as foreign judicial authorities. A small minority of rabbis act more akin to bounty hunters. It is unclear by what means some men are "persuaded," whether this implies the use of moral suasion, intimidation, violence, or a quid pro quo exchange of money. In a well-publicized case in 1994, two Israeli rabbis flew to France and spent two days "persuading" a husband who had denied his wife a divorce for twenty-seven years; more recently, Rabbi Mendel Epstein and his co-conspirators were indicted on a series of recalcitrant husband-related kidnapping charges in New Jersey (Jones 2015). Although relief granted to individual women's lives is celebrated, critics claim that discretionary reliance on self-help or institutionalized divorce squads does not offer a systemic solution to or prevention of women denied divorce.

Charismatic, social pressure can be an effective tool. A feminist Palestinian Israeli lawyer coaxed a man who batters his wife to release her from the marriage by appealing to his sense of morality, while simultaneously engaging the qadi's support. The husband was willing to divorce his wife only if she would promise to return home:

> I obtained a divorce for a woman. . . . The woman is a Christian Orthodox [who had converted and] married a Muslim. He was always a known criminal, in and out of jail. . . . Two months ago when he was released from jail, he [returned home and] began to beat her. She came to the shelter, and sued for maintenance and divorce [in the sharia court]. . . . In the hallway of the sharia court the husband came and threatened us: "you will not leave here, you will go directly to the hospital." I sat there quietly not wanting to answer him . . . but soon he saw that I was relaxed and [we began to talk]. I persuaded him that it would best for him to get divorced. "I will agree," he said, and we went into the court. Once there, he said, "I will divorce her but I will not give her the divorce today, return home, and in a week I will give her the divorce." I said, fine, she will return home. He signed the agreement. [But] she . . . stayed in the shelter.
>
> The court date came [for finalizing the divorce]. I thought all day, how can I convince him to give the divorce? I got to the court early . . . and saw that he was waiting. "Why didn't she return home? Don't think that today I will agree to divorce her," he said. No, I replied, it is okay, we have a shelter, it is a very nice place. At our place it is forbidden that the women leave and we watch to make sure that they don't do

bad things. "But I want her to return home!" Fine, I said, give her the [divorce] and she will return home. At that point I was so tired!

We entered the court. He did not agree and began [to get so agitated and angry] that I thought he would beat her [right there]. The judge . . . noticed that something wasn't right and called the police, [who] warned him. . . . The Qadi asked again [if he would divorce her] "If she doesn't return [home], I don't want [the divorce]," he said. The Qadi gave us ten minutes . . . for me to convince him. I convinced him somehow. He began to recite according to sharia law . . . and [the wife] began to laugh! I was sitting between them. It all went [smoothly]. He gave her the children, the house, maintenance! Everything! All of the marital property.

Perhaps the husband capitulated because of the law enforcement warning, because of fear of being reincarcerated. He may have held the qadi's moral and religious status in great regard. The lawyer's expression of empathy about his concerns for his wife's whereabouts and behavior may have placated him. Multiple ambassadors operated here, where the powers of persuasion derived from a combination of professional insight, cultural values, and mobilization of allies.

Quid Pro Quo

Women often rely on professionals and religious community leaders to help push their husbands toward divorce. This requires a relationship of trust and a tolerance for taking risks. I observed a hearing held in the qadi's anteroom in a sharia court, for example, in which a battered woman initially forfeited custody of her children in order to persuade her husband to agree to pronounce the divorce. During our post-hearing conversation, she explained to me how she gave up custody in order to appease her husband and obtain the divorce, relying on her knowledge that, ultimately, the qadi would not assign custody to the father. She predicted correctly: the judge immediately awarded custody to her after the husband pronounced the divorce.

Other women operate more in a do-it-yourself mode and maneuver their husbands without legal or religious council. One such woman is Nina, an attractive Mizrahi (formerly battered) woman who wears youthful clothing: jeans, high-heeled sandals, and a flattering T-shirt. The news is blaring in Nina's salon while her two children do homework and we talk. She giggles remembering how she convinced her husband that in exchange for the *get*, she would allow him to move back into the house. After he executed the divorce, she promptly denied his request. He still comes around her house, trying to convince her to take him back, but so far Nina is relishing both her solitude and solo parenting experience. I met several times in the mid-1990s with a group of Ethiopian Israeli women in an activity and support group taking place in a community center in the Galilee. Besides wanting to know why I was not married, they were intrigued by my research. One of the women, Nama, was unemployed when we spoke at a mutual friend's apartment. She spoke quickly and quietly while she told her story of being married at the age of thirteen (prior to immigrating to Israel) to an older man. The last time her now ex-husband beat her, Nama almost lost an eye. The severity of the violence scared her, and she decided to leave her husband. In exchange for the divorce, Nama said, "I agreed to pay a large fine that he owed the authorities" because of a prior criminal offense. When asked what her lawyer thought of the settlement, Nama explained that she had decided neither to hire a lawyer—the proceedings all took place in the rabbinical court where no lawyer is required—nor to request a temporary restraining order against her husband, because she judged that these steps would only provoke her husband to deny her the divorce.

Nina and Nama used creative as well as straightforward quid-pro-quo strategies to get divorced as did other women I interviewed: one promised a post-divorce relationship and then reneged, others paid the husband's legal fees and fines or demanded a sum of money, another agreed not to press criminal charges for prior assaults, still another relinquished child custody, while yet another woman conceded rights to family property. Interpersonal persuasion based on insider knowledge of the batterer achieved through material transactions can be an effective mechanism to terminate a relationship within the context of legal vulnerability.

Resilience in the Face of Sociolegal Dilemmas

Not all women have the ability to use violence, tap into professional help, or effect a material transaction in exchange for (or to prevent) a divorce. Time, coupled with resilience, has enabled women to craft new lives that incorporate safety and dignity, alongside an unwanted legal status. Munira, for example, separated from her husband and lives peacefully in her family's home with her child. Chana's life trajectory was similar to Munira's until one day, out of sheer luck rather than any sort of active strategizing, suddenly, she found herself divorced. We spoke shortly after the divorce was executed, when Chana was in her early fifties with two grown children who had no relationship with their father. She told me that one of the most remarkable violent incidents in her memory was when her husband beat her with one of his prized possessions, a switch used to control horses. Typically, after noisy episodes like that one, a neighbor would come and check to see that Chana was okay. Chana and her husband lived apart for more than a decade before he decided to release her from the marriage—only when his girlfriend's pressure to get married became unbearable. In the divorce settlement, Chana was able to remain in the family's modest apartment. According to Chana, it was only the pressure the husband felt from his girlfriend that produced this favorable outcome.

Publically exposing one's family troubles including domestic violence and divorce can cause women to feel socially isolated, particularly if they live in a face-to-face community such as Druze, Bedouin, haredi, or kibbutz communities, where everyone knows one another (Abu-Rabia-Queder 2007; Shechory-Bitton 2014; Shoham 2005). To fight the stigma, counter isolation, and maintain their spiritual lives, a group of ultra-orthodox haredi battered women participate in a support group for religious divorced women called "Mother of Sons." Mother of Sons is an organization where "women join together to celebrate the holidays at a hotel with all sorts of programs and activities" (Danan 2009, 65). Peer support gives women otherwise dislocated from their communities through divorce a mechanism to retain or reinvent their religious identity as observant women while physically distancing them, at least temporarily during holidays, from the judgment of their neighbors.

Some Palestinian Muslim women express a preference to stay married but live separately rather than risk social stigma and the loss of maintenance or child custody (Rabho 2013, 268). Other battered women refuse to accept the bill for divorce from their husbands, when it is against their economic interests. Without a divorce, a married woman is entitled to her husband's maintenance. If he does not pay it, the National Insurance Institute will cover at least a percentage of it. Masha, a Russian immigrant woman, explained to me that if she had accepted the divorce along with the husband's conditions for it, she would have nowhere to live. Masha's husband is an alcoholic involved in questionable, borderline criminal activities who beats her and attacks her grown son (but not her daughter) who still lives in the family flat. The family immigrated to Israel about two years prior to our conversation in the 1990s along with a massive contingent of new immigrants from the former Soviet Union. Their home, although nearly empty of food and located in a run-down working-class neighborhood, retains the feeling of a well-appointed European apartment because of the furnishings the family brought over from Russia: upholstered couches, hand-worked furniture, and the china cup in which Masha served me coffee. She explained, "My husband will only give me the divorce if I give up my rights to this apartment," which is the family's one asset. Both children work and study in an effort to help make payments on the home. Logically, women with few assets strategize to ensure they can at least have a place to live.

Women who come from middle-class or elite families may decide to wait out the divorce storm. Shulamit, an Ashkenazi Jewish woman in her middle forties, recently left a battered women's shelter to live alone in a subsidized, modest one-bedroom apartment where we spoke. This new residence is a stark contrast to the family villa, but she loves the peace and quiet of living alone. More importantly, Shulamit told me that she is inspired by the knowledge that she will gain access to a large sum of marital money if she can just have patience while refusing her husband's unfair divorce settlement offer. I sit in her tiny kitchen while she chain-smokes and washes a few dishes in the sink; otherwise, the place is spotless. I can tell that she enjoys having control over her own space since she has left her husband and transitioned out of the crowded and noisy shelter. Several other women who were also in the shelter live close by, and they constitute an informal support group for each other. Shulamit argued that her circumstances are unique in comparison to the others she met in the shelter and that, given her social status, refusing to accept the divorce was in her long-term economic interest.

Obtaining a legal divorce is not fundamental to the everyday lives and self-identities of these women. They resist the cultural pressure to conform to religious law and instead create an alternative status for themselves: independent woman. As one formerly battered woman, who is also a volunteer on the hotline, wrote in a poem that she shared with me: "I live alone and it is good for me." Refusing the divorce and crafting a new life is a viable survival strategy from their perspective. While Munira and Shulamit were able to secure alternative housing and remain married to their husbands, for Masha housing is the key issue that keeps her tied to her husband. Chana was prepared to live out her life legally tied to her husband; but for the new woman in her husband's life, she would still be married today. Participants in the new social group Mothers of Sons commiserate at the same time that they invent a welcoming space for divorced haredi (formerly battered) women. Stories of how battered women survive, resist, and obtain partial victories are as important as cataloging new and hidden forms of violence such as divorce-related domestic violence.

CONCLUSION

In this chapter I analyzed how a set of contingent political conditions and socio-legal realities embedded within Israel's pluralistic personal status law system intensify battered women's vulnerabilities while simultaneously offering men who batter perfectly legal tools to control women's lives. Battered women face two related risks when deploying separation or divorce as a survival tactic: men's escalation of physical violence, and a legal process that feels more like a punishment. Although this chapter focused on the vulnerabilities of battered women produced by and institutionalized within the state's hybrid civil-religious regulation of family life, I pointed as well to how women desperately and creatively navigate this complex system to maintain or terminate their marriages. I also have intentionally organized women's and frontline workers' stories in a way to highlight commonalities as well as meaningful differences among women.

Women's domestic lives encounter the state in myriad and overlapping ways. For analytic purposes here, I unpack them one at a time, noting that they operate simultaneously. The first encounter is in terms of religion. Battered women seeking to end the violence in their intimate relationships by ending the marriage are required by the state to manage the divorce process within a court segregated by religion, staffed exclusively by religious men, where reconciliation overrides exit, regardless of a couple's religiosity. Citizens lack legal mobility when it comes to the divorce itself, although they can opt into semi-civil courts for other family matters. Moreover, divorce stigma—the pressure to get married and stay married—permeates the exit process, despite the presence of domestic violence. For Jewish women, even if a termination of the relationship is judicially supported, the husband may never execute a divorce. For Palestinian women, exit options vary by religion and may not include a legal divorce. Because of the way divorce is processed in communal courts, women are subject to men's violence, divorce denial, financial extortion, control of sexuality and reproduction, and perhaps surprisingly, the threat of divorce. Inspired by the growing debate over women being denied divorce, rabbinical courts have made gestures to ameliorate women's lives, yet legal innovations developed according to religious practice that might prevent the barriers battered women frequently face have been largely rejected. Sharia courts have begun to respond to feminist critiques, while still balancing the interests of the Islamic Movement (Shahar 2006). Rabbinical courts, too, have felt the public sting of vociferous criticism of how women are treated during divorce processes that can be endless.

The very state system that splits jurisdiction in two ways—among religions and between family and religious courts—yet still retains a monopoly over divorce for religious courts has created an opportunity for some leverage. This leverage may reside, for example, within an individual qadi's commitment to securing economic protection and social dignity for a woman seeking to live apart from her husband (Rabho 2015), or it may reside in the collective sense when more and more people vote with their feet in an effort to avoid contact with the system, or when legal innovations become institutionalized. A combination of critique and competition has raised judicial awareness resulting for some in a defensive posture, and for others, efforts to improve women's experiences and outcomes.

Battered women's second encounter with the state is in terms of gender. Supporters and critics agree that the religious and civil family courts treat men and women differently when it comes to matters associated with divorce. Lawyers, social workers, and other advocates and professionals on the frontlines of domestic violence work note that men typically prefer the treatment and outcomes produced in religious courts, whereas women tend to prefer family courts because of the standards used and judgments made regarding child custody and maintenance, division of property, and spousal maintenance. Yet even divorce procedures that are prima facie gender-neutral (e.g., Jewish divorce must be mutual, or certain Catholics have no access to divorce) or women-protective (e.g., revocable divorce, marriage-like engagement and plural marriage for Muslims, or no social contact between a divorced Druze couple) entail gendered opportunities and costs, with battered women in particular paying the higher price.

Yet citizens are not similarly situated when it comes to the possibility of forum shopping. Whether the husband or wife wins the race to the courts matters. Not all women are aware of the potential gendered benefits of family courts nor do they all find family courts welcoming or accessible. Judges in family courts are disproportionately Jewish, and they are not trained systematically in Muslim, Christian, and Druze personal status law, which they apply with interpretive discretion in matters related to divorce. The dominant language of the family court is Hebrew, with Arabic, the other official state language, relegated to a secondary position at best. Civil family courts, which handle family matters associated with divorce, offer women a more gender egalitarian courtroom, but present a host of constraints as well, ranging from costly lawyers and court fees to drawn-out legal processes, varying interpretations of religious law and escalating conflicts with religious courts, all of which can affect the outcomes of their cases (Bogoch and Halperin-Kaddari 2006; Batshon 2010). Again, even battered women who secure the best terms for legal matters associated with divorce, whether in a family or a religious court, must still finalize the divorce or separation itself.

The third encounter that battered women have with the state is in terms of nation. The status quo agreement that created Israel's pluralistic personal status law system launched the new state's Jewish cultural identity by linking a particular version of it to the regulation of marriage and divorce solely in rabbinical courts. At the same time, it divided jurisdictional control over family life among Palestinians to communal religious authorities, within their respective courts. Family law and nation are mutually constitutive so that the management of personal status law takes on symbolic significance and becomes a key arbiter of identity and belonging. Ongoing political and legal decisions to sustain the status quo associate Palestinian and Jewish identity with religion-based definitions of family, nation, and state formation (Lerner 2009). As a result, jurisdictional tensions between civil and religious courts over personal status law have been present since pro-state and antistate Jewry signed the *status quo ante* agreement giving religious meaning to the Jewish nation's new state, and highlighting Palestinian political autonomy within the family realm. At the time, some regretted the status quo agreement, although few anticipated the agreement would endure.

Today those who culturally value religious control over marriage and divorce lament how the agreement has not been kept as robustly as promised. Changes within personal status law applauded by those on the frontlines of domestic violence have escalated competition and conflict between the concurrent courts—those changes include, for example, the reorganization and widening jurisdiction of the family courts to all citizens, judicial decisions that demand imposition of civil law in religious courts, innovative civil remedies to address personal status law dilemmas, persistent public and transnational critiques of the treatment of women in religious courts, and the rising numbers of citizens who support civil marriage and divorce or who bypass domestic courts entirely. From the perspective of religious courts, challenges to the status quo are framed as a threat to the collective, and affirmations of the status quo are framed as communal loyalty.

Religious court judges and community leaders, who balk at their eroding authority within their respective national collectives, may play out this resentment in a proxy war on the backs of battered women. They do so by denying or ignoring the jurisdiction of family courts, rejecting legal innovations, or branding the turn to family courts as betrayal to the community. Because both Jewish and Palestinian nationalism rely on the state's retention of the religious management of marriage and divorce, battered women's hopes for divorce relief depend in large part on a cultural reimagining of what it means to be Israeli.

Political scientist Martin Edelman suggests in his analysis of the Israeli legal system that the civil courts "have taken the lead in promoting a democratic national culture based on the rule of law [while t]he other [religious] court systems have emphasized group identity and solidarity at the expense of a unifying political culture" (Edelman 1994, 5). I would argue further that this pluralistic configuration is indicative of an unsettled and contested polity, where tensions among feminism, religion, and nationalism pull the state in a tug of war between fundamentalisms, secular and religious. In the meantime, the current configuration of Israel's pluralistic personal status law system also reflects how the state produces domestic life within a contentious multiculturalism by determining who can marry whom, what constitutes a family, and how an intimate relationship can be terminated. The resulting marriage between family and state formation reorders not only the public life of the state but also its so-called private life, whether through intention or omission.

In the next chapter, I continue to explore the cultural politics of the state and domestic violence by analyzing the conventional responsibilities of a modern polity: securing its boundaries and the well-being of its citizens within them. From this vantage point, the politics of domestic violence reveal various states of insecurity.

4 | States of Insecurity

IN NOVEMBER 2011, in honor of the United Nation's International Day for the Elimination of Violence against Women (IDEVAW), a sixty-second public service announcement (PSA) by Gun Free Kitchen Tables was released in Israel. The PSA begins with a security guard returning home at the end of his shift and matter-of-factly dropping his keys and gun onto the kitchen table. Three women respond on camera saying, "A gun in the house does not enhance security. On the contrary, we know what is liable to happen. . . ." The PSA continues with Alamnesh Zalaka, an Ethiopian Israeli woman,[1] describing how she survived being shot eight times at close range by her intimate partner who, at the time, was an off-duty security guard. Reflecting the campaign's stance against the proliferation of weapons in the name of national security, she says, "A gun at home does not protect me."

The Gun Free Kitchen Tables campaign urges the Israeli public to realize that "security weapons surely do not belong at home." It visualizes this sentiment with a graphic of a gun on a dinner plate, flanked by a fork and knife, with a red "X" painted over it. In addition to developing the PSA, campaign participants lobby Knesset members and government agency leaders, circulate calls to action on social media, hold public demonstrations and marches, present community lectures, and earn mainstream media coverage. They call on the Minister of Public Security to enforce, and private security agencies to uphold, legal reforms requiring security guards to leave their weapons at work at the end of the shift. Campaign partners lead groundbreaking civil lawsuits against the state and security guard agencies for failing to uphold gun regulations, such as the suit against the agency that employed Avi Radai, the off-duty security guard who tried to kill Alamnesh Zalaka. The need for the grassroots campaign was underscored days after the PSA's premiere by the killing of forty-five-year-old Aviva Makesh on December 11, 2011, in the Haifa suburb of Kiryat Motzkin, by her ex-husband, Moshe Jambar, an off-duty security guard using his work-issued weapon (Hovel 2011).

Gun Free Kitchen Tables was cofounded in 2010 by Mazali and Smadar Ben Natan as a project of Isha L'Isha Haifa Feminist Center to address the "normalization of firearms and their proliferation throughout civilian space" (Mazali 2016b).[2] A coalition of over a dozen feminist, peace, and civil rights organizations soon joined the campaign.[3] The project stems from concerns with gun-related domestic violence, ranging from intimidation to homicide, sometimes referred to as "armed domestic violence" (IANSA 2009). The campaign, funded mainly by monies from the United States, Sweden, and the Netherlands, is grounded in Rela Mazali's research on the privatized security industry in Israel (e.g., Mazali 2009). As a first step, the campaign directs public attention to the gendered costs of the increasing proliferation—particularly since the outbreak of the Second Intifada in September 2000—of armed security guards stationed at bus stations, restaurants, cafes, shops and malls, government agencies, and schools (Ben Natan and Mazali 2014).

The campaign is unique in two ways. It is the first gun control campaign in Israel, a state where existential fears drive weapons policy, and it explicitly links routinized national security arrangements with women's lack of safety at home. The grassroots campaign has begun to raise public awareness and advocate for relief from the domestic price that women (and men) pay in the name of national security.

The Gun Free Kitchen Tables campaign serves as an entry point into this chapter's analysis of the complex relationship between domestic violence and the cultural politics of everyday life in a security state such as Israel. The first part of the chapter defines and illustrates the term "securitism," where ongoing political conflict renders crisis as normative, borders unsettled, and putative lines between military and civilian life obfuscated. The second part of the chapter explores how the dominance of political violence culturally displaces domestic violence. In the third part, I outline the slow and partial recognition of possible relationships between national security and domestic violence. In the fourth and final part, I turn to consider how police preferences to protect against national rather than domestic violence produces differential policing and dilemmas for battered women. I conclude the chapter with a look at recent efforts to integrate domestic security into notions of national security in Israel through the UN Security Council Resolution #1325 framework, which calls on states to incorporate women into conflict resolution and prevention processes. This analysis of the security state reveals the continued weakness of individual and pathological explanations of domestic violence and requires a renewed perspective on how foundational areas of statecraft such as defense are central to understanding domestic violence.

THE CULTURAL LOGIC OF SECURITISM

Early on, security studies (part of international relations and strategic studies) focused on a state's use of military force to defend its borders, either as a means to prevent a conventional or nuclear war or to win one: the ultimate arena of statecraft. Analyses that centered on state-level resources and decision making, however, not only assumed clear distinctions among the state, military, and society, and the measurability of national security threats, but these analyses also typically excluded "nonmilitary" threats. Consideration of such nonmilitary threats, ranging from domestic politics to global warming to non-state actors, has been joined explicitly to the study of war and political conflict within "critical security studies."

Critical security studies additionally serve as a corrective to security studies' largely apolitical stance toward its subject and epistemological reliance on political science's positivism and rational actor orientation. The notion of "human security" expands the number and type of preconditions for enjoying national security beyond mere survival of the polity and refines what it means to live securely in the world: the "impact of insecurities on people, not just their consequences for the state" (Tripp 2013, 7). In turn, feminist security studies deconstruct the public-private distinction and infuse phenomenologically gendered perspectives into the study of international relations and human security (Sa'ar, Sachs, and Aharoni 2011). Thus I use an integrated approach to security studies to talk about the gender- and nation-based effects of both the cultural logic of securitization—that is, the framing and processes by which risk to the state is defined, assessed and protected against—and securitism, by which I mean the ideological underpinnings and cultural manifestations of this risk to the state.

Security Logic in Israel

In Israel securitization coupled with securitism is an overarching form of statecraft. The term "security"—*bitahon*—refers to the existential life of the state, and its protection is implicated in every facet of the lifecycle, from the demographic war over birthrates to disputes over the uniformity of gravestones of fallen soldiers. Securitism's ubiquity can obscure its constructed nature:

> Israel has never had one, systematic, written and/or oral security doctrine. From the early days of the Yishuv [the pre-1948 Jewish community in Palestine] to the present, there has been disagreement on the scope of the danger facing Israel and on how best to achieve and ensure national security. Not only the general public, but political leaders and military experts are unable to reach a definitive conclusion on the subject. (H. Herzog 1998, 63–64)

Here is a seemingly mundane example of how securitism is developed and culturally embedded. The most popular radio network among Jewish Israelis, the state-run *Galei Tzahal* (Army Radio), was designed as a means to communicate with troops and the public about fast-changing national security conditions, and to help fashion a melting pot out of new immigrants; it continues to launch the careers of Israeli journalists (Soffer 2012; Estrin 2015). The Kol Yisrael-Arabic radio station, initiated by the Israel Broadcasting Authority in the early 1950s, was to contribute as well to state-building and national security by forging an Israeli identity among Arabs newly living within the burgeoning state; it dominated the airwaves until Radio Ashams (Sun Radio) was established in 2003 (Jamal 2009, 109; Torstrick 2004, 74).

A lesser-known illustration of securitism is found in the regulation of intimacy and marriage. In the name of national security, two laws passed in 1952 having to do with guarding the state's borders (i.e., the Citizenship Law in 1952 and the Entry to Israel Law in 1952) were amended since the outbreak of the Second Intifada to bar family reunification between Palestinian citizens in Israel married to Palestinian residents of the West Bank or Gaza, who are more recently referred to as citizens of an "enemy state." Upon appeal, the High Court of Justice determined that "In the security situation Israel is currently facing, Palestinians from the Territories who reside in Israel are dangerous because their loyalty might be to the country or entity currently in military confrontation with Israel" (Ajzenstadt and Barak 2008, 360). Various cultural (Goodman 1989, 1998), social (M. Weiss 2002), political (H. Herzog 1996; Lissak 2001), and economic (Rivlin 2011) phenomena are central partners in the state's assessment of risk to and management of national security.

Israel's securitism is guided by its self-defined exceptionality as a state under siege. Since May 14, 1948, when David Ben Gurion proclaimed the state, it has operated using a bundle of "overlapping and complementary emergency legal sources," including the British Mandate's Defence (Emergency) Regulations, which give the state legitimized yet expansive discretionary power that can be easily abused politically (Mehozay 2012, 141). Recognizing the contradiction between such emergency powers and the goal of a democratic state, the first Knesset directed the Constitution, Law, and Justice Committee to fashion a proper and permanent law regarding state security (N. Safran 1981, 134). The Knesset has failed to do so. Instead, it has edited the regulations in a piecemeal fashion and repeatedly extended the application of Article 38 of Basic Law: The Government, each time for a period of up to a year (Harkov 2013).

In a recent unanimous decision, the High Court of Justice rejected a petition—thirteen years after it was filed—to void the remaining emergency regulations. Justice Elyakim Rubenstein noted in the judicial opinion that "Israel is a normal country that is not normal"; it is a normal state because it is a democracy, but not normal "because the threats to its existence still remain" (Paraszczuk 2012). The premised abnormality and constant striving for normality legitimize the state's sense of purpose (Campbell 1998, 12, in Forte 2003, 215). This securitism is not limited to bureaucratic declarations; they affect the daily operations of the state, from censorship of the media to land use rights to budgetary matters to gun control policies to policing of crime.

A significant component of the cultural logic of securitism is an ambiguity between military and civilian life (Barak and Sheffer 2006, 2007). The term militarism has been used to refer to a society that has been militarized—that is, mobilized by the military. Militarism is a mixture of relations that may range from a military regime (i.e., praetorianism) to the institutionalized expression of military traits (e.g., order, discipline, and hierarchy) and values (e.g., use of force, courage, and self-sacrifice) throughout society that leads to militaristic political decision making—that is, cultural militarism (Ben-Eliezer 1998). Militarism influences people's values and beliefs regarding the legitimacy of the army and its use of force, and creates a naturalized hierarchy of belonging to or distance from the state (Lutz 2002).

Israel is referred to as a "nation of soldiers" or a "people in uniform," where "everybody serves in the army." The ambiguity among spheres of influence was amplified during the First Intifada when an increasing number of reserve duty soldiers were sent into the occupied territories for longer periods of service to quell the Palestinian uprising, working more akin to militarized police. According to some, Israelis retain the ability to shift between crisis (wartime) and "routine time"; during routine times, when the Israeli army performs "nonmilitary" work, it constitutes a civil institution (Kimmerling 1985). Others dispute whether civilians are in control of the military (Horowitz and Lissak 1989; S. Cohen 2006) or whether Israel is an "army that has a state" (Sheffer and Barak 2010). The debate can be partially resolved with the concept of "militarism" or the militarization of society, where society accepts or even encourages military use of force as a legitimate mechanism of statecraft (Gavriely-Nuri 2013; Lomsky-Feder and Ben-Ari 1999; Levy 2012, 2014).

However, Israel is a state where boundaries between the military and society are highly permeable, perhaps even nonexistent. Critics argue that Israel does not experience military coups; rather, Israelis democratically elect their military commanders (Shalvi 2002); they refer to Israel as a "government of generals" and scorn that the offices of the president and prime minister, cabinet ministry, and political party leadership are dominated by former chiefs of staff, generals, and other retired officers who seek military solutions to political problems and grant military leaders disproportionate access to and influence on government matters (Benn 2002; British Broadcasting Corporation News 2001; Broza and Geffen 1978). Since 1948 twelve unique individuals have been elected to the position of prime minister; each was an Ashkenazi Jewish man (excepting Golda Meir, an Ashkenazi Jewish woman) with significant military leadership experience. Six of them also simultaneously held the defense portfolio or were the minister of

defense prior or subsequent to being elected as a prime minister. Supporters celebrate the appearance of military heroes in top government positions, arguing
that only such battle-tested warriors can effectively represent the state's interests
to obtain a "secure peace" for Israel, or are "strong enough to make decisions"
to resolve the Palestinian conflict (Lynfield 1999). It is not easy to determine
whether ongoing political conflict is a cause or effect of the military's role in
governance.[4]

This chicken-or-egg perspective reflects the long-term confluence between
the "military" and "society," which inspires the concept of "security network."
Israel's security network comprises the defense establishment, namely, active
and retired security officials, the latter "integrated into various political, socioeconomic, and cultural spheres, as well as a host of civilian politicians, bureau-
crats, private entrepreneurs, and journalists on the national and local levels"
(Barak and Sheffer 2006, 235). The results:

> A high level of continuous mutual penetration and interdependency,
> where security officials require mainly the formal approval of their civilian
> partners, who occupy key positions in the cabinet, the Knesset, and other
> institutions, and in return legitimize the latter's actions. The persistence
> of this state of affairs renders [irrelevant] the notion . . . of a 'crisis' in civil-
> military relations in Israel . . . because these terms suggest the existence of
> two clearly delineated and stable subsystems that are more or less equal in
> strength and interact voluntarily. (Barak and Sheffer 2006, 238)

The security network was an integral and intentional component of Israel's state
formation process, and it has grown over time (238, 249).

Thus what I am calling securitism is an even broader capture of society than
militarism where intermingling between military and civilian life, even the domination of the military within civilian life, constitutes just one of many arenas
in and mechanisms by which the state manages national security, and makes
security the "project of all" (Ben-Eliezer 1998; Robbins and Ben-Eliezer 2000).
Securitism means that people are always, already on the defense, obfuscating
any presumed distinction between being at war and not at war. This state of
constant readiness is reflected in the oxymoron "*shigrat herum*" (emergency routine), which I first heard about during the 1991 Gulf War, when Israelis inter-
mittently retreated to and emerged from interior sealed rooms and bomb shelters
to avoid harm from Iraqi Scud missiles, all the while carrying on with life as it
was. Yossi Beilin, at the time a central figure in the peace process, noted in his
memoir, "We have become accustomed to the 'emergency routine.' . . . People
are born into it . . . [and] have never known a routine other than the emergency

routine" (Beilin 1992, 266). Living on a crisis footing means proceeding with school and work as well as basketball games in the midst of rocket strikes (Zilber 2012; Kershner 2014). The dominant Israeli cultural stance toward such threats against national security is aligned with the state's retention of its emergency regulations. Despite the outward-facing presentation of normative behavior, Israeli researchers have become experts in how "national trauma" (i.e., exposure to political violence, both war and terrorism) affects mental and physical health (Saar, Sachs, and Aharoni 2011; Farrell and Cobain 2002; Kezwer 2002; Neria, Bravova, and Halper 2010; Solomon 1995).

Differential Relationship to the State

Given their shared legal citizenship but differential relationship to the state (Shafir and Peled 2002), Palestinian and Jewish Israelis experience securitism and securitization in both similar and distinct ways. The Israeli Jewish public, for example, is educated through a variety of rites (e.g., war memorials) and sites (e.g., heritage museums) to value sacrifices made by compatriots who established the state, to protect the state through military service, to be vigilant against enemies of the state, and to silence criticism of the state during peak moments of insecurity (Dominguez 1989; Handelman and Katz 1995; Handelman and Shamgar-Handelman 1997). For Jewish Israelis, national strength and sacrifice for the state is encoded in existential fears that predominate everyday life and political decision making.

The desire for self-reliance can be traced in large part to "pre-state" modern Jewish European history, reinforced by ongoing international conflict over the Israeli state. For hundreds of years, Jews faced fluctuating periods of political tolerance and subjugation, its worst period in recent memory being the genocidal Holocaust. In response, European Jews desired cultural assimilation or political autonomy. In the late nineteenth and early twentieth centuries, those who favored a national polity for Jews in Palestine encouraged immigration and assembled into various and sometimes competing militaries (e.g., Haganah, Irgun, Palmach, Lehi) to advance their particular vision for the Zionist movement.

Ultimately, their efforts secured an independent Jewish state, construed as a muscular post-Holocaust counter to both British resistance and Arab opposition (Ben-Eliezer 1998; Boyarin 1997; Shapira 1992). The new State of Israel forged a unified standing army that it named the Israel Defense Forces (IDF), made up originally of conscripted Jewish citizens, and developed a robust Ministry of Defense and related security industries in order to protect its boundaries from internal and external threats. Once established, the state encouraged Jews in the Middle East (Iraq, Morocco, etc.) to participate in the "ingathering of the exiles" and populate the new state; the majority were sent to live in new development towns designed to help secure the state's borders as well.

Living in a security state is predicated on a combination of national sacrifice and existential fear for Palestinian Israelis as well. However, for Palestinians, securitism refers to their status as a "trapped minority" within the state (Rabinovitz 2001) and efforts required to retain the memory and ensure the future of the Palestinian nation (Kassem 2011; Sa'di and Abu-Lughod 2007). This is achieved, paradoxically, by gaining recognition and resources from the same entity that produces their vulnerability. Palestinians, opposed to the establishment of a Jewish state, and classified as enemies leading up its declaration, have been treated with suspicion by the state.

The creation of the State of Israel was effected through military occupation and dispossession of Palestinian life and land; Palestinians refer to the war that defended the newly declared state as *al-Nakba*, the catastrophe. From its creation in 1948 and up until 1966, Palestinians who remained living within the armistice line—citizens of the new state—were governed under the jurisdiction of a military administration. This limited their physical mobility and economic viability, as well as their ability to negotiate with the Israeli state regarding the management of Islamic institutions and holy sites (Ghanem 2001; Lustick 1980). After 1966, Palestinian citizens became subject to domestic law exclusively, although emergency regulations frequently are invoked rather than penal law as a means of social control (Ajzenstadt and Barak 2008; Hofnung 1996). Palestinians in the occupied territories, many with familial and economic ties to Palestinian citizens in Israel, came under military rule after the 1967 War. In response, many Jewish citizens question the minority "Arab sector's" loyalty to the state. This concern is reflected in survey data that indicate the divide among Jewish Israelis whether "Arabs should be expelled or transferred from Israel" with 48 percent strongly agreeing or agreeing and another 46 percent strongly disagreeing or disagreeing (Pew Research Center 2016). From a top-down perspective, the government avoids relying on Arab-identified political parties to form a ruling coalition.

Incidents during the Second Intifada provide painful evidence of Palestinians' differential citizenship within the security state. During one week in October 2000, police killed thirteen Palestinian men in Israel—twelve were citizens—who were protesting against the state's killing of Palestinians in the occupied territories. The subsequent Orr Commission found no justification for the use of lethal force, disclosing that snipers had been used against those unarmed protesters. Public airing of anti-Arab positions by elected representatives is reinforced by political and economic marginalization of Palestinian citizens who, it has been argued, experience "citizenship lite" (Sikkuy 2004). Not surprisingly, Palestinian citizens doubt that Israel's securitism can protect their national interests.

Palestinian and Jewish Israelis are part of the "war story," which fixes men as warriors and women as peacemakers, and frames the enemy as inferior or unsavory (cooke, 1996). In the security state, dominant men do masculinity and earn martial citizenship through military sacrifice for the nation, while women do femininity and enact marital citizenship through the demographic security strategy of marriage and motherhood: nurturing husband soldiers and children who will become soldiers (Berkovitch 1999; El Or and Atran 1997).[5] Yuval-Davis (1987) developed a term to describe this gendered ideological and a spatial division of labor, "*womenandchildren*," meaning those who occupy the home-front and constitute the rationale for men who literally "man" the warfront.

Mandatory conscription into the IDF enables eligible men to earn martial citizenship, which grants them rights and resources distributed by the state. When Benjamin Netanyahu was elected prime minister in June 1996, following Rabin's assassination, he lauded the securitization of citizenship within section nine of his government's coalition platform. Referring to minority citizens who are either conscripted (e.g., Druze men) or volunteer to serve in the IDF (e.g., Bedouin men), he promised that

> The government will act toward the full integration of minorities into every area. Special efforts will be made for the advancement of minorities, which have joined their fate with that of the Jewish people and the State of Israel, and have served in the security forces. . . . Efforts will be made to absorb minority academics, particularly those who have completed military duties in the service of the state, in public institutions, in order to continue their participation in public and official responsibility for the state they served in the security services. (Israel Foreign Affairs 2015)

Because the obligation of military service in Israel is based on one's nationality, religion, and religiosity, not all Israelis have equal access to the risks and rewards of martial and marital citizenship accorded by the state (Hofnung 1994, Sa'ar and Yahia-Younis 2008).[6]

Jewish, Druze, and Circassian men are obliged to serve for thirty-two months in the IDF, in addition to annual reserve duty. Bedouin men are encouraged to serve, and Muslim and Christian men may volunteer to serve, although few do. Most ultra-Orthodox Jewish men receive continual deferment from conscription (their national service, so to speak, is to study Judaism), although debate over the morality and economic effects of these exemptions has led to controversial legislative reform mandating them to share an "equal burden" and capping the number of future exemptions.[7] Muslim and Christian women are exempt from army service, although national civil service is an option for Palestinian citizens. Jewish women are conscripted for twenty-four months. Despite the perception that all women serve in the army, the IDF exempts Jewish women from service when they are married, pregnant, or mothers; they also are eligible for an exemption based on conscience or religiosity, with a national service option.[8] Nevertheless, the IDF champions the army's gender equality and its zero tolerance for sexual harassment, despite headline-grabbing reports of both sexual assault and harassment perpetrated by high-ranking officials in the military, the police, and the Knesset (Roth 2016).[9]

Those exempted from military service serve their nation in other ways. Muslim and Christian women are not conscripted and can neither marry nor birth soldiers for the state. Ghadir, for example, a twenty-five-year-old woman from an elite family in Nazareth, who was described in a news magazine as "look[ing] and talk[ing] Israeli," when "asked where her Israeliness ends, she immediately points to the army. 'When I register for university and they ask me on the form about my army service, I stop cold. Do I write "Exempt"? I'm not a cripple. So I leave it blank. This whole business of the army creates a feeling of impotence and vulnerability'" (*Jerusalem Report*, 1995). Women ineligible for military conscription enact their belonging to the national collective through marriage and mothering (Kanaaneh 2002).

A person's relationship to the IDF determines their relationship to securitism: not serving indicates rejection of the state, but an embrace of the national Jewish or Palestinian collective. On the other hand, military service is a rite of passage to a securitized identity of soldier/veteran available only to those willing to sacrifice themselves or their children for the state (Ben-Ari 1998; Berkovitch 1999; Hajjar 1996).

Overall, military service is not close to universal in practice, but the notion of a "people's army" persists culturally and politically; conscientious objectors are vilified as traitors, and two decades of calls for a formal shift from a mass to a professional military have yet to be realized (Sasson-Levy 2010; Levy 2008). The uniformed soldier with a gun slung over his shoulder remains an iconic Israeli image of heroic masculinity, trumped only by memorials held in honor of fallen soldiers.

SECURITISM DISPLACES DOMESTIC VIOLENCE

Securitism manifests as a gap if not a competition between victims of political violence and domestic violence: as problematic losses addressed by the state, and as people valued, remembered, or protected by the state. Domestic violence has been sidelined as a social problem, for example, because the state has orchestrated a hierarchy of victims of violence, constructed through the ritualized "present absence" of the political dead. The political dead, who shore up national security, are construed as a collective loss, in contrast to the domestic dead, who are framed as an individual family's loss as a result of pathology or criminality. The hierarchy of suffering and loss is found again in the deference given to defense over domestic violence.

The Political Dead

On December 29, 2014, President Reuven Rivlin and First Lady Nechama Rivlin hosted a day of bar and bat mitzvah celebratory activities for fifty children who have themselves survived or whose family members were injured by or killed in "hostile actions," that is, terrorist attacks. Cosponsored by Almagor, the Terror Victims Association, it was the twelfth year of the annual ceremony that invoked the Jewish transition of childhood to adulthood. The day started at the Western Wall—a symbol of the state's Jewish identity and its unification of the city of Jerusalem in the War of 1967—and closed with a ceremony at the President's House in West Jerusalem, where Rivlin commented to the assembled guests, "There is a price to our being Jewish, to our independence, sometimes the price is too high, and almost always the price we pay is unbearable. An unbearable price that each one of you knows firsthand, but there is also a lot of power and strength which should be remembered" (JTA, 2014). This annual event is just one among numerous efforts to memorialize or remember victims of national security-based violence, what I have termed "the political dead."

The Ministry of Defense's Bereaved Families department is the official source of recognition, economic compensation, and social benefits allocated to widows, siblings, and children whose family members have fallen during military battle or accidents. After vociferous public debate regarding the commensurability of military and civilian death, which pitted bereaved military families against families of victims of terrorism, the National Insurance Institute now supports those affected by terrorist attacks (Lebel 2014). As a result, civilian casualties are treated more similarly to soldiers injured or killed in action so that injured citizens—whether soldier or civilians—will not bear a disproportionate cost of the collective's national defense, especially when the traditional location of a military's frontline is either obscured or no longer relevant (Sommer 2003, 338).

The cultural logic of securitism underlies state traditions, such as a bar and bat mitzvah celebration for youth survivors of political violence, invented to memorialize the political dead. A set of three annual ceremonial days linked to honor the political dead and celebrate the establishment of the state is an "artifact of deliberate design" that tells the story of how "[th]e destruction of European Jewry was followed by the War of Independence, during which the State of Israel was created, and through which the state kept its freedom, as it has ever since through the mortal sacrifices of its citizenry" (Handelman and Katz 1995, 78, 82).

The narrative told by these three days of "national reckoning" echo that of the state holiday for Passover, which they follow: enslavement, loss, and redemption (Handelman and Katz 1995, 83). *Yom HaShoah*, Holocaust Day, marks the anniversary of the Warsaw Ghetto uprising, its opening ritual held at Yad Vashem, Israel's Holocaust memorial.[10] A week later, the length of the Jewish mourning period of *shiva*, the country turns its attention across the street to Mt. Herzl, Israel's national cemetery and those killed in defense of the state (and since the Second Intifada, victims of terror as well) with an official twenty-four hours of mourning on *Yom HaZikaron*, Day of Remembrance.[11] Newspaper photos capture the country at a standstill: people standing outside of their cars on a highway, for example, while the state's emergency alert siren is sounded for a moment. The day of mourning ends symbolically at sundown and transitions to the celebratory holiday *Yom HaAtzmaut*, Independence Day, when the birth of the state is feted with barbeques, boisterous parades, and hiking (Dominguez 1986, Handelman 1998, 2003).

Public time and space are officially dedicated to the political dead, from military cemeteries to commemorative battle sites and museums—for example, Ammunition Hill in Jerusalem (Azaryahu 1992; Ben-Ze'ev and Ben-Ari 1999; Handelman and Shamgar-Handelman 1997). The Central Memorial for the Victims of Hostile Acts and Terrorism, established in 2000,[12] joins numerous geographically sited municipal memorials to the political dead (Shay 2005). The state further securitizes the political dead by creating a new social category of "war widow" administered within the state's bureaucracy (Shamgar-Handelman 1981, 1986), by sending high-ranking representatives to attend funerals for citizens who have fallen during military service or hostile actions, and since early 2016, by awarding decorations of valor for those who die protecting others from political violence (Eichner 2016).

These memory projects prepare and remember individuals for their physical sacrifice to the state by establishing the presence of their absence caused by political death (Handelman and Shamgar-Handelman 1997). With the inclusion of "martyrs and heroes" of the Holocaust, and the addition of civilian casualties of terrorism, the category of the political dead has expanded. Victims of political violence have been made by the state into tangible, cultural objects: visible, accessible, and valued. Surviving victims and victims' family members of political violence dominate news reports of terrorist incidents, as well as subsequent coverage of memorial projects developed in remembrance of them. Yet other than fleeting media mention and incomplete lists managed by a few NGOs, no such parallel mechanism exists to produce knowledge or hold memories of the domestic dead.[13]

Deference to Defense

National security policies venerated by the public appear differently when viewed from a domestic violence perspective. Securitism explains the oft-repeated call for more security guards and the easing of gun control policies in the face of political attacks on civilians, and concomitant delayed response to battered women's calls for domestic security *from* these protections (G. Cohen 2014; G. Cohen, Hasson, and Arad 2014). Deference to defense and displacement of domestic violence by securitism can be seen, for example, in the evolution and subsequent devolution of Israel's gun control policies.

The National Rifle Association's (NRA) CEO Wayne LaPierre recently pointed to Israel as the embodiment of his lobby's anti–gun control position (*Times of Israel*, 2012). He is correct in the sense that layers of armed security forces and civilians populate public space. Streets, bus stops, and cafes host uniformed IDF soldiers with M16s slung over their shoulders or 9mm pistols holstered at their hips. Similarly armed border guards patrol high-conflict border areas, including in and around Jerusalem. Police officers—armed with rifles and handguns—look after public safety, assisted by twice their number of armed volunteers in the Civil Guard. Privately hired and armed security guards stand at the entrances of schools, hospitals, and restaurants, screening anyone who approaches. Some civilians, including but not limited to Jewish Israelis who live in the occupied territories or near still-contested borders, drive or walk around armed as well, for example, at the grocery store or while doing business. However, it is not a "gun utopia" in the way the NRA has claimed (Rosenbaum 2012), and gun possession is oriented toward protection against political rather than criminal violence. Nonetheless, in addition to privately licensed firearms, an unknown number of unlicensed weapons circulate, and security forces typically carry their weapons between work and home, turning the homefront into a potential domestic battlefield.

Feminist NGOs have repeatedly articulated concern with inadequate state oversight of security weapons because of women being killed by their intimate partners with those weapons. Early opposition to limiting access to weapons of those convicted of domestic violence was based on national security concerns; although prohibition of weapons possession was included as an option in the foundational domestic violence legislation in 1991, it also allowed for exceptions. Then two non-domestic violence incidents with firearms took place. In September 1992 a former mental health patient shot and killed several women at a clinic in Jerusalem; Prime Minister Yitzhak Rabin was later assassinated by a Jewish man during a peace rally in Tel Aviv in November 1995. In both incidents, which subsequently resulted in a reconfiguration and significant tightening up of gun licensing, the shooter's license to possess a weapon inadvertently had not been withdrawn.

Next it was soldier suicide that drew attention to the unintended consequences of the unfettered movement of military weapons between the so-called public and private spheres (Alon 2005). During the height of the Second Intifada in 2003, forty-three soldiers died by suicide. When researchers documented that use of firearms was the primary means of suicide among soldiers, the IDF quickly altered its policy, mandating that "soldiers should leave their weapons on base when headed home for weekend leave"; one year later the number of gun-related suicides among soldiers declined from an average of 28 to 16.5, mostly because of a decrease in weekend deaths (Lubin et al. 2010, 422, and see Shelef et al. 2016). Outrage over unnecessary sacrifice of IDF soldiers, combined with the immediacy of policy changes within a centralized institution such as the IDF, resulted in swift cultural changes, albeit narrow in scope.

In contrast, efforts to limit guns from the home or the movement of guns from work to home with the goal of decreasing *domestic violence homicide* have been debated for years. The gendered cost primarily for Jewish and Druze women of such easy access to weapons was officially noted in a special report on family violence submitted in 1998 to then minister of public security, Avigdor Kahalani (Shapiro 1998), but efforts to restrict guards from bringing their guns home were met with official responses such as this one from then deputy police commander, Ido Gutman, speaking in January 1998:

> Everyone is very sensitive about this issue. It isn't just the women's groups who are concerned. But there are limitations regarding restrictions. Let's assume that some 20 women are killed each year by people who hold gun permits. What are we going to do? Stop giving permits? Then we'd have an absurd situation where you'd have unarmed guards at schools and a terrorist could come in and kill a whole classroom. Then what would Ms. [Ofra] Friedman [chairwoman of Na'amat, the women's branch of the Histadrut Labor Organization, and high-profile advocate for battered women] say? (Sered 2000, 99)

Here a high-ranking law enforcement officer speaking to the press presents a hierarchy of victims, pitting past and prospective victims of political violence—the most innocent of victims, a classroom of children—against the average number of seemingly disposable battered women.

Ample evidence of the need to address the domestic deployment of security-issued weapons continued to be readily available. In April 1998, for example, a thirty-two-year-old Jerusalem resident was suspected of shooting his ex-wife and her parents in their home located in Carmiel, a town in northern Israel. According to the newspaper account, "The rampage occurred . . . during an argument over [whether he could take] the couple's 4-year-old daughter [for an outing] (*Haaretz* 1998)." The ex-husband worked as a security guard in Jerusalem and had brought his work-issued pistol with him when he traveled north. He allegedly shot his ex-wife, who survived, seven times, wounded his former mother-in-law, and killed his former father-in-law. Three additional women were killed and one injured in December 1998 by men using legally licensed firearms (Sered 2000, 99). Five years later, the problem with security weapons continued, unabated. Twenty-six-year-old Hailu Taiku-Keren from Ashdod, for example, was shot to death by her boyfriend, Lisan Gola, from Tirat HaCarmel, on April 10, 2003. He worked as a security guard at the Ramat Aviv Mall. They had been a couple for about three years and did not live together. According to her parents, for the last few months of her life, she and her boyfriend had broken up and gotten back together several times.

Jewish and Druze men have access to and use firearms, including their IDF and private security work-issued weapons, to not only kill their (former) intimate partner but also to intimidate and injure them. During an interview with a now-divorced formerly battered woman in the summer of 1999, I spent several hours sitting at her kitchen table. It was a modest room, dominated by a four-person table. The heaviness of the conversation about domestic violence was illuminated if not lightened somewhat by the sun streaming into the room. We drank tea and ate sugar cookies that are commonly offered to me when I visit someone's home. Eventually, a friend of hers joined us, helping me to prompt her with questions about the relationship and the abuse she had endured over the years. Toward the end of the conversation, the friend inquired, "Did you tell Madelaine about the gun?" She had not yet. The ubiquity of guns in the home can make them recede into the background, yet they hold a prominent place in the statistics about known domestic violence homicides.

Knowledge about domestic violence homicides is sporadic and incomplete. The police keep monthly and annual records of the total number of homicides, now broken down to include the total number of domestic violence homicides. They rely on the variable of "marital status" to determine whether the murder is counted as a domestic violence homicide; only married couples are included in this official tally. Based on these government statistics, between 1994 and 2010, the number of women killed each year by a spouse hovered between six and eighteen, an average of about thirteen each year. However, a recent internal comptroller report presented to the Ministry of Public Security revealed that the police have neither properly implemented domestic violence policies, particularly related to the prevention of domestic violence homicide, nor kept comprehensive records thereof (Kubovich 2014). So official statistics from the Ministry of Public Security neither jibe with newspaper-based reports nor do they readily indicate the weapon used. NGOs have been the most reliable repository for domestic violence homicide reports.

Gun Free Kitchen Tables maintains a "memoriam" list of those people killed by using private security weapons in the domestic sphere, noting: "At least 18 women and 15 men were killed between 2002 and 2013 with the firearms of private security firms stored in guards' homes. After 11 consecutive years each of which witnessed one or more of these murders, 2014 was the first without a single murder in homes or families with a security guard's off-duty gun"; an additional seven people died by suicide using these weapons (GFKT 2015). My analysis of NGO databases indicates that between 1990 and 1999, former or current husbands/boyfriends killed 139 women. Of these 139 women, 50 (35.9 percent) were shot to death; 46 (33.0 percent) were stabbed; 28 (20.1 percent) were strangled or beaten; 9 (6.4 percent) were killed by other means, such as poison or burning; and seven (5.0 percent) were killed by unknown causes. Other researchers report that between January 2000 and April 2005 thirty-eight women were killed by intimate partners using a firearm, eighteen of them licensed weapons, including security guards who killed eight women and soldiers or law enforcement officers who killed six women, all using their work-issued and licensed weapons (Sachs, Sa'ar and Aharoni 2005a, 22). According to researcher Revital Sela-Shayovitz (2010a, 150), in the first decade of the new century, men perpetrated all but one of the reported armed–domestic violence homicides using a legally licensed weapon.

The GFKT campaign has accumulated evidence and increased the visibility of the need for domestic security *from* national security agents. By 2008 security guards were banned from taking their work-issued weapons home with them at the end of a shift, although security agencies were given discretion to authorize exemptions for guards. Unfortunately, the ban lacked implementation. Fifteen years after submission of the special report in 1998 on family violence, the Knesset held a committee discussion on the growing problem of widespread gun possession, and the head of the Israel Police presented a plan to help prevent security guards from using their work-issued guns to kill their family members: sixteen women, they noted, were killed by security guards between 2002 and 2013 (G. Cohen, Kubovich, and Lis 2013; Mizrahi 2013).

In April 2013, in an attempt to implement the earlier measure through a compromise, security guards were mandated to have a gun safe installed at home. Security agencies appeared to support the reform, which shifted responsibility and cost (about NIS 500, or $135 in US dollars, for hardware and its installation) from them to individual security guards (Israel Social TV 2013). In contrast, lawyer Smadar Ben Natan, cofounder of the Gun Free Kitchen Tables coalition, rejected the compromise on the basis that it would not protect intimate partners and others from security guards who do not install the safe or do not house the gun in a safe at the end of the shift; or if the gun is safeguarded, it can be easily retrieved (E. M. Segal 2013).

Then the next month, on May 20, 2013, in an unusual incident of neighborhood violent crime, a former border guard and security guard shot and killed four people in a bank in Be'er Sheva. The next day Minister of Public Security Yitzhak Abramovich announced, "Limited gun ownership is at the top of our agenda"; he also announced new gun control measures (G. Cohen and Kubovich 2013). Domestic violence advocates supported the new directives issued in July 2013 that limit eligibility for a gun license and where and how licensees can possess a gun. Research conducted by GFKT in honor of the International Women's Day in March 2014 indicated that private security firms were implementing old and new directives. However, according to the Israel Comptroller's May 2014 report "Firearms Permits and Regulation," government ministries failed to properly enforce the new regulations related to gun license screening (Hartman 2014).

Still, the number of security guards bringing their weapons home decreased significantly, and by July 2014, GFKT noted a full twelve months had passed with no women killed by a security guard using his work weapon. A congratulatory headline in a special issue of *La'Isha* magazine (enjoyed by over a million, mainly women, readers) announced, "The gun came down from the kitchen table." But calls were soon issued to ease gun control measures in light of incidents of political violence, such as the brutal attack in a Jerusalem synagogue in West Jerusalem where five Jewish worshippers were murdered by two Palestinian assailants from East Jerusalem wielding knives, axes, and guns; a police officer later died of wounds sustained during the attack (G. Cohen 2014; G. Cohen, Hasson, and Arad 2014). The effective gun control measures that GFKT had helped to pass and implement were partially rescinded. This time around, media coverage brought a critical perspective to the proliferation of small arms, despite the official framing as a national security.

Although feminist critiques of how national security measures made women insecure at home were ignored or marginalized for years, and most gun-control policy reforms came on the heels of non–domestic violence incidents, the targeted GFKT campaign and its affirmative media coverage mobilized the state to reform its policies. It now looks to hold onto its policy reform successes related to security guards while trying to "crack open the military monopoly over security issues (GFKT 2015, 4). Their aspiration seemed impossible thirty-five years ago when feminists across the country gathered to network, share ideas, and strategize for the future.

AN AWAKENING TO SECURITIZED DOMESTIC VIOLENCE

The GFKT's thus far savvy campaign linking national and domestic security is the result of decades of feminist organizing. But not all feminists have made this connection, and some outright reject what they perceive as the politicization of feminism in general and violence against women in particular. Indeed, one of the reasons why violence against women became Israeli feminism's most enduring and widely accepted social problem was its presentation as a neutral issue affecting all women, disconnected from the traditional meaning of "politics." This allowed the movement to gain support without engaging in the entrenched political dispute over Israel's borders. Feminists and anti-domestic violence advocates had to fight against the domination of security to get domestic violence on the national agenda; some did so by avoiding "politics," while others did so by embracing and subverting securitism. Over time, a slow awakening to the securitization of domestic violence developed.

Domestic Violence Is Not About Security?
The Third National Feminist Conference was held at the Jerusalem YMCA in May 1980, and its 500 or so participants met under the theme: "A Decade of Feminism in Israel." Representatives from twenty-five organizations introduced themselves and their work, and eighteen workshops and panels were presented (H. Safran 2006, 104). Topics included "Women against Violence against Women," "Feminism and Socialism," "The World of Mizrahi Women," "The World of the Arab Woman," "Psychology of Women," and "A Vision for the Future" (A Decade of Women 1981). The workshop on violence against women produced practical recommendations (ibid.). During the final session of the conference, a representative from the Haifa shelter shared a lawyer's recommendation to reform the penal code to better address family violence. At the end of the session, when many of the participants had already left, conference hosts led an open format. A woman stood up and proposed a resolution, addressing the then thirteen-year occupation of territories taken in 1967:[14]

> We express solidarity for our Palestinian sisters in the occupied territories in their struggle as women for social equality and as Palestinian women against the occupying force. The end of the occupation must precede a joint struggle for Arab and Jewish women's liberation (24).

A fierce debate broke out among the women remaining in the room about the link, if any, between feminism and the occupation. Marcia Freedman tried to amend the resolution to read "We feminist women in Israel express our identification with Palestinian women in particular and Arab women in the Middle East in general, in our shared struggle for self-definition and liberation," but it went nowhere. Freedman described the feeling in the room:

> And then all hell broke loose, mostly from the Tel Aviv women, leaders of the movement in Tel Aviv. The struggle was amazing. At some point, someone cut off the microphone . . . at the end, a large group of women got up and walked out, all of the Tel Aviv women simply got up and walked out, and the conference dispersed and ended . . . an ending like

that was very painful for everyone, for me it was one of the most painful moments of all the time I spent in Israel. And also, it seems, for the other women. (H. Safran 2006, 104)

A counter resolution had been made to the effect that the issue of Palestine had no relevance at all to feminism and no place at the conference (A Decade of Feminism 1981, 55). But, in the end, the room was too chaotic for a vote to be held on any resolution. Newspapers covering the event referred to the cadre of women who offered the resolution as being "from an extreme left wing organization."

It was inevitable that the Palestine question would be raised sooner or later because the agreement to keep feminist politics "pure" was no longer tenable (H. Safran 2006, 105). The 1980 conference was a turning point, with radical feminism's desire for cultural transformation giving way in two directions: to liberal feminism's direct services for women victims of violence, and women peace activists organizing against the Lebanon War that broke out in 1982 (106). From that period, politicizing domestic violence by linking it in any way to Palestinian liberation, the immorality of the occupation, or national security concerns was eschewed by liberal activists and mainstream advocates who carved out a nonpolitical space for domestic violence by framing their labor as social welfare work or assistance to women as an undifferentiated class. Neutralizing domestic violence made it an accessible issue, acceptable to a wide array of allies, but this also contained the fight against domestic violence to moments when decision makers and lay people alike were not distracted by national security concerns.

Waiting for a Peace Dividend

The lower profile held by violence against women because of its framing as a domestic issue, relevant to women and families but not the state at large, becomes most visible when national security is overtly threatened. Paradoxically, it is during these periods of heightened securitism that battered women often have sought assistance at higher than normal rates. Helpseeking notwithstanding, public concern for domestic violence is tempered when the state defines itself as at war or under siege. During Israel's military actions in the Gaza Strip during the summer of 2014, for example, a spike occurred in hotline calls as well as in the number of battered women seeking shelter. Daniella Kehat, then executive director of NO2Violence, which delivers services for battered women, reported that she sought "to add the NGO's phone number to the other emergency numbers appearing in the media"; however, one media outlet refused to do so, she was told, because it "would weaken national morale" (Kashti 2014).

During the same period, far-right MK Moshe Feiglin,[15] who has never considered himself a feminist, chastised his colleague MK Aliza Lavie (Yesh Atid), chairwoman of the Knesset Committee for the Status of Women and Gender

Equality, for discussing a proposed law against sexual violence during wartime, when it was not appropriate to talk about things "like flowers and sexual assault" (Sztokman 2014). The same rhetoric pitting national against domestic security had been used more than once in the past to dismiss or delay discussion of domestic violence at the Knesset. When securing the homeland takes precedence over security at home, which it does under a cultural logic of securitism, it is difficult to sustain emotional engagement and economic support for victims of domestic violence, or even to circulate crisis intervention information.

It is easy to be distracted when focal cultural attention on national security facilitated by the mediated "theatre of terror" (Weimann 1983) kicks in an involuntary or overworked fight-or-flight response, even among women who have dedicated their lives to dismantling domestic violence. This happened in stark relief in 1993 and 1994, when I was in Haifa doing fieldwork while volunteering at the hotline. It was a year of contrasts: in September 1993, the Rabin-Arafat-Clinton handshake took place in Washington, DC, followed several months later by Israeli Jewish settler Baruch Goldstein's murder spree of twenty-nine Palestinians gathered during Ramadan for Friday morning prayers on February 25, 1994, in a mosque in Hebron, West Bank. Both events captured significant media coverage and filled public conversations.

Then, on April 6, a car bomb attack on a bus in the center of Afula, located about twenty miles southeast of Haifa, left eight people dead. A week later, a suicide bomber killed five people in the central bus station in Hadera, about twenty-five miles south of Haifa.[16] Radio stations reported hourly on the events and set the tone by replacing their usual playlist with somber music. Televised news, which I could hear and see through people's windows in the evening when I walked around the neighborhood, was dominated by dramatic, personalized stories of each victim and what their loss meant to family and friends (Wolfsfeld, Frosh, and Awabdy 2008; Sella 2014). Conversations on transportation, at the university, and in domestic violence advocacy organizations shifted almost exclusively to the bombings. The women—staff and volunteers, representing nearly the national, religious, and ethnic diversity of the state—and I shared outrage, fear, uncertainty, and sadness. We gleaned rumors about whether Haifa, the largest city in the region, would be the next target. We tried to calculate our own safety: Should I take this or that bus? Shop in the open-air market? We began to edit our movements similar to a battered woman walking on eggshells, not knowing what would precipitate the next violent event. Distracted by *these* victims' stories, domestic violence seemed at best mundane or at worst irrelevant to the very public loss of life to political violence.

Domesticated issues such as violence against women are commonly placed on hold during periods of heightened political violence (H. Herzog 1996). A subversion of the rule coming from a former MK from the Labor party is instructive. In November 2000, just a month into the Second Intifada, Yael Dayan reminded a crowd commemorating International Day for the Elimination of Violence against Women, "The current political turmoil and terror attacks are no reason to abandon the efforts to prevent violence against women. . . . Murder is murder and violence is violence. . . . We will not halt the war against the terror against us" (Gleit 2000, 2). In contrast, MK Limor Livnat, a leader within the Likud party who supports the political goal of a "Greater Israel," insisted that it is the *peace process* that has drained resources away from domestic violence and matters pertaining to the development of civil society.

An earlier rare break from talk of national *insecurity* enabled at least temporary consideration of domestic concerns. Sharing my observation of excitement as well as continued pessimism regarding the peace accord between the PLO and Israel in September 1993, I articulated the growing anticipation of a new era in Israeli life in an October letter I sent to the United States:

> The biggest issue of all this year is the peace process. You cannot enter any store, restaurant, or conversation without discussing the pros and cons, the fears and the elation, the cynicism and the guarded optimism. The business communities [seeking new markets] are paving the way. Interestingly, it is the women's groups and the artist/writers who have been responsible for the majority of the earliest on-the-ground and grassroots communications [between Palestinians and Jews]. There are a number of [NGO] conferences organized around the topic of "after the peace" or the "effect of peace on fill-in-the-blank." A feminist conference this year will be entitled something like "Women in the New Age of Peace." People are anticipating many social and economic changes from what they call the "peace dividend." Meanwhile, the problem of domestic violence continues. Just last Friday a woman was nearly burned to death by her husband who said "If I can't have you, no one will."

The sense permeating that period was the possibility that Israelis might be able to shift their gaze from defense of national security to development of civil society. Environmentalists, feminists, and Palestinian rights activists readied themselves for the arrival of a peace dividend that would inspire investment in domestic sectors that had been put on hold, pending resolution of the national conflict between the Palestinians and the State of Israel. Others predicted that the shift would be from national security to a civil war between religious and secular Jewish Israelis, or between Jewish and Palestinian Israelis, simmering tensions that had been held off in the face of an externalized enemy of the Jewish people. Still others were concerned that any benefits reaped from resolution of the Palestinian-Israeli crisis would remain with those already at the top economically and politically. The now-infamous handshake revealed how long domestic priorities had been submerged under concerns for national security.

Any possible "peace dividend" was quickly overcome by the officially pronounced failure of the peace process, the Second Intifada (2000–2005), the walling off of the West Bank by Israel's security wall, increased anti-Palestinian rhetoric and violence within the Green Line, and ongoing political conflict involving Lebanon and Gaza. Existential concerns continue to enhance Israeli securitism, rendering domestic violence less worthy of public attention or investment. However, some kind of relationship between securitism and domestic violence had begun to emerge.

Securitism Produces Domestic Violence

Feminists across the globe have posited a relationship between gender violence and war, equating its gender hierarchies and inequalities with men's violence against women, whether within the general population or military families or by soldiers against communities designated by the state as the enemy, during "peace time" as well as during declared and undeclared wartime.[17] Lucille Mair, the United Nations secretary general for the Women's Conference held in Copenhagen in 1980, for example, noted, "Economic distress and political instability in the third world exist in a climate of mounting violence and militarism. . . . Violence follows an ideological continuum, starting from the domestic sphere where it is tolerated, if not positively accepted. It then moves to the public, political arena where it is glamorized and even celebrated. . . . Women and children are the prime victims of this cult of aggression" (Moghadam 2001, 60, in Bunch and Carillo 1991). Others argue that violence travels in the opposite direction: political violence is carried home on the backs of soldiers who redeploy it against family members. A more nuanced argument points to how shared norms—for example, regarding masculinity, sexuality, violence, and women, rather than the mere accumulation of decontextualized skills—are conducive to gender violence at home (Morris 1996, 655, 720; Enloe 2000; Rabrenovic and Roskos 2001, 50).

In Israel, claims about a relationship between state security strategies and domestic violence emerged during periods of intense political violence. Here I consider the emergence of various versions of this claim during the First Intifada, the Gulf War 1991, the Second Intifada, and the Gaza War 2014. The notion that military service and the occupation were related to the prevalence of domestic violence grew along with the critique of the state's treatment of Palestinians in the West Bank and the Gaza Strip during the First Intifada. Several important cultural changes converged at this historical moment: Palestinians were organizing collectively to express their opposition to the Israeli state's control over their lives in the West Bank and Gaza Strip, and Israelis were talking about domestic violence in public, on the radio, and on television shows, while politicians were debating how to address domestic violence legislatively. The promises of the peace dividend encouraged Israelis to consider the negative effects of occupation on civil life in Israel.

During the Intifada (1987 to 1993), the link between soldiering and domestic violence garnered supporters among those who critiqued the increase in days men spent in *milluim*, annual reserve duty, and their shift in orientation from soldier to police officer in the occupied territories. According to this explanation, and echoing Ben-Ari's (1998) notion of "combat schema," men serving in the occupied territories and along contested borders not only learn how to behave violently but also are encouraged to do so to solve problems, suppress emotions, and demand compliance to their wishes. Soldiers trained to deploy violence to maintain order and protect the integrity of the nation's borders cannot easily become civilianized. Instead they bring home military norms of domination and violence to enforce control over, protect the integrity of, and quash women's resistance to their regime of domestic power.

Soon after the outbreak of the (First) Intifada in December 1987, I learned from a friend also studying abroad that winter at Hebrew University about a silent vigil against the occupation being held for one hour early on Friday afternoons in a main square in downtown West Jerusalem. The vigils were organized informally by a loose network, which came to call themselves Women in Black (WIB). Women gathered at the same time each week, wearing black, and silently held signs with the slogan "End the Occupation." The practice spread to close to forty locations around the country. WIB was an unusual phenomenon: a public statement against state policy, made solely by a decentralized and diverse group of women (H. Safran 1994). The public responded to WIB's subversive message with sexual harassment and threats of sexual violence. Men (and some women) pedestrians and drivers screamed at participants, threw produce at them, and denounced them as traitors who needed to be fucked (Ferree and Hess, 105, in Safran 1994, 17). *Jerusalem Post* editors condemned Women in Black for hijacking the women's movement in Israel as "super-dovish, ultra-leftist activists on behalf of Israeli withdrawal and a PLO [Palestine Liberation Organization] state" ("Killing Women's Liberation," March 10, 1995).

In contrast to those who eschewed any link, feminist peace activists, both Jewish and Palestinian, claimed a connection among "the situation of women, the ongoing conflict, and the gradual militarization of Israeli society" (Chazan 1991, 156). More specifically, they were concerned with the construction of masculinity that codifies the use of violence to resolve conflict. During the annual march celebrating International Women's Day organized by the Movement of Democratic Women in Israel a placard read: "Equality Between Jews and Arabs and Between Women and Men." One of the organizers explained: "Equal rights for women are included in peace. We will not obtain equality until the peace process is completed" (*Jerusalem Post*, Mar. 9, 1995). Such activists were denounced for linking feminism (which, for most Israelis, meant violence against women) and state violence.

Allied antimilitarist organizations built on the WIB model argued that men's military service in the occupied territories during the Intifada had normalized violence to the point that violence had crossed the Green Line and infiltrated domestic life within Israel. Erella Shadmi, for example, a former senior police officer who spoke at the Conference on Women and Peace in 1993, explained domestic violence in Israel in this way: "Occupation is, first of all, the symptom of a sick society; a society in which violence is legitimate and accepted from the social standpoint as a mechanism for personal expression and for solving conflict situations as well as for gaining rights and benefits" (Deutsch 1994, 95).

Later, a few months after the start of what became known as the Second Intifada, the Coalition of Women for Peace sponsored a mass WIB vigil on December 27, 2002, whose theme was "The Occupation Is Killing All of Us. Women Say: Enough!" The flyer advertising the vigil and other organizational materials emphasized that their opposition to the Occupation, all forms of racism and oppression, and the "militarism that permeates Israeli society" is linked to their daily experience of "discrimination and violence against women." Other groups such as New Profile, an antimilitarist organization dedicated to developing civil society, and Black Laundry, a group of lesbian feminists and gay men who coined the slogan "No Pride in Occupation," also identified the convergence between nationalist securitism and the normalization of violence in Israel. This integrated stance against the logic of national security and domestic forms of violence has resulted in the severe political marginalization of these groups, particularly during periods of national crisis when external threats forge unity of the body politic and censor internal criticisms and differences (M. Weiss 2002).

It became more common during and after the Gulf War—the first war in which IDF soldiers were forced to remain at home—for advocates and academics to claim a link between domestic violence and the security of the state. The Gulf War began on August 2, 1990, when Iraq invaded Kuwait. Nearly six months later, on January 18, 1991, the first of thirty-nine Scud missiles was fired at Israel, which, in a coalition with the United States, agreed to stand down in spite of these attacks. It was unusual that the IDF had not been fully mobilized to preempt or respond to the attack. Notably, the reported rate of domestic violence homicide rose during this and subsequent Scud missile attacks. In 1990 it was reported that current or former husbands or boyfriends killed twenty-seven women. In 1991, the year of the Gulf War, forty-two women were murdered. In 1992, the year following the war, the number dropped back to a more "normal" rate of eighteen.

Overall, women's advocacy groups generally agree that the number of women killed by intimate partners increased during the Gulf War and then subsequently decreased. Advocates interpreted this sharp increase, along with a rise in calls to victim hotlines during the Gulf War, as a direct result of noncompliance with the logic of securitism, which typically mobilized men to the traditional war-front. Ruth Rasnic, founder of one of the first battered women's shelters in Israel, suggested, "There was an emasculation of the Israeli [Jewish] male. They felt fear and helplessness. Their anger built up" (Greenberg and Stanger 1991, 15). Similarly, in 1998, another period when Israelis feared missile attacks from Iraq, Neta Yitzhaki, coordinator of the Women's International Zionist Organization's (WIZO) hotline for women, reported, "Women have been calling to say their husbands are tense, and they fear this will lead to an outbreak of violence [against them]. Some have expressed apprehension at being in the sealed room with their husbands. . . . They do not want to leave their homes in this time of national tension or to complain to police, so instead they call the helplines in order to discharge their anxieties" (Shevi 1998).[18]

Political scientist Gad Barzalai (1996, 156–68) wrote about the uniqueness of the Gulf War for Israeli soldiers. His reflections relate to the atypical war-related "masculinity stress" theory of domestic violence offered by advocates in the field:

> The militaristic characteristic of the Israeli society came to light despite the military passivity. Hence, the experience of the Israeli society in the course of the Gulf War is another indicator of the blurred boundaries between the international system and domestic politics, as well as a manifestation of the militaristic propensity in a society in wartime. . . . [Scud missiles began to fall on January 18, 1991, and a] special state of emergency was declared, and civilian life became subordinated to the army and the security establishment. . . . For six weeks the home front found itself subjected, with no real air defense, to a cruel regimen of ballistic missile attacks. . . . Usually, an Israeli's "patriotism" was measured in terms of whether he or she either mobilized or volunteered for war work. In the Gulf War, by contrast, the criterion was survivorship, assimilation into the collective mind-set of being reconciled to military passivism, staying put throughout the missile attacks on the home front.

Much was made in the popular press of the purported damage to the male psyche as a result of this passivity. Zahava Solomon, who conducted research for the IDF on combat stress and soldiers' coping mechanisms in times of war, reported:

> The Gulf War was challenging to [Jewish] masculine identity and
> perhaps strengthened the need to be macho, because [he] wasn't located
> at the front. . . . The polarization between the roles of women and
> men was broken . . . there was no difference between the front and the
> rear. It stripped the men of their masculinity. It took away their active
> coping mechanisms, which provide them power and security. . . . It was
> compulsory passivity—men couldn't wear uniforms, leave the house,
> or defend [it]. . . . [I]t removed the ground from beneath their feet.
> (T. Cohen 1995, 4–5)

At the time, Solomon (1995) called for additional research, noting that there are "few [systematic] studies of the impact of war itself on the family unit" (59) in Israel or elsewhere.

Solomon (1995) confirmed that during the Gulf War, calls to hotlines increased, with areas of concern centered on the abuse of children, elderly parents, and spouses; however, one large emergency room in the central area saw a radical decrease in the number of women presenting domestic violence–related injuries, down from 60 percent to 5.7 percent (Solomon 1995). This is not surprising, given the directive and interest to stay close to home. Dr. Reuven Gal, head of the Israel Institute for Military Studies and a former IDF chief psychologist, offered a similar analysis, but he did not comment on the gendered nature of the Gulf War experience he described: "We're really somewhat ashamed and embarrassed by it . . . we sat like fools in our sealed rooms . . . we were passive and we've tried to suppress our collective memory of it" (*Jerusalem Post*, Jan. 28, 1996). Other scholars, too, posited that macro stressors such as war, immigration and poverty have a strong effect on domestic violence homicide in Israel (Edelstein 2013; Landau 2003; Landau and Hattis Rolef 1998).[19]

Ties between securitism and domestic violence were evident again during the Second Intifada, when the rate of domestic violence homicides (particularly among immigrants from the FSU and Ethiopia) and reported domestic violence increased simultaneous to a sharp spike in human suicide bombings: women's requests for restraining orders increased 57 percent (Nagar 2006, in Sela-Shayovitz 2010a, 138). A survey designed to measure the effect of armed conflict during the Second Intifada on women's personal and political sense of security and well-being found that Palestinian women in Israel faced "increasingly violent state policing and public Jewish hostility"; women directly exposed to both political and gender-based violence (overrepresented by national and ethnic minority women) reported the highest levels of stress (Sachs, Sa'ar, and Aharoni 2007, 594, 604). During the same period, the overall economy suffered, and the state also made budgetary cuts to social welfare, among other government programs, in order to fund enhanced security measures, including the Security Wall.

A pattern emerges where the security state becomes the larger cultural context within which domestic violence is produced.[20]

During the Gaza military incursion (Operation Protective Edge) in summer 2014, 55,000 reservists were mobilized to respond to over 2,000 rockets launched from Gaza into the southern region of Israel, and "banners appeared at main junctions around the country proclaiming 'A strong home front means victory on the battle field'" (Kershner 2014). At the time, advocates noted an increase in calls to hotlines and requests for shelter. A battered woman explained that, "We were afraid to go outside since there were so many red alerts. We all sat at home or in the bomb shelter all day. My problems with my husband started earlier, but now he was stressed, taking it out on the children, yelling and hitting them. I was afraid, but finally realized I had no choice but to leave" (Kashti 2014). Maslan, the Negev's Center for Victims of Sexual Assault and Domestic Violence in Be'er Sheva, which serves the region most vulnerable to rockets, reported a 60 percent increase in requests for support in July as compared to June; a network of shelters reported a 20 percent increase in the number of first-time callers and a 30 percent increase in the number of battered women seeking shelter (ibid.). Thus, twenty years after feminist peace activists were dismissed for linking the occupation and state violence with violence against women, the Israel Police in a presentation at a special hearing on domestic violence in the Knesset attributed the increase in reports of domestic violence to the macro-level conditions of living in a war zone: the increase, he argued, "by dozens of percent" in complaints to law enforcement and calls to hotlines (37 percent year-over-year) was due to the fifty-day conflict with Hamas in Gaza because of the "high-stress environment and the sustained amount of time the couples spent in fortified rooms" (Newman 2014).

Most interestingly, political rhetoric used by elected officials who lead the security state, has changed over time when taking a public position against domestic violence. It morphs from generic opposition to domestic violence and an offer of government help, to comparing domestic violence to terrorism, to calling domestic violence a threat to society and promising to eliminate the infiltrator, and then calling for an end to domestic violence in order to secure the Israeli brand abroad. On Women's Day in March 1992, Bat-Adam, a coalition of women's organizations, sponsored "Operation Testimony" to encourage women to share their stories of violence and abuse in public, and President Chaim Herzog "expressed his deep concern at the increase in violence against women and pledged his help in attempting to eradicate it" (Weisman and Makayes 1992, 6).

Five years later, in 1997, Prime Minister Netanyahu (Likud) launched a campaign against domestic violence, boldly comparing it to terrorism "saying that the only difference between the battle against family violence and terror is that the former is hidden and fought within the home" (JTA, 1997; N. Gross 1997). During a visit to a battered women's shelter in Haifa in July, 1999, Prime Minister Ehud Barak (Labor) told reporters, "The government views violence in the schools, the streets and in homes as a central threat to Israeli society. . . . We will do everything possible to uproot this scourge" (Rudge 1999, 2). In 2001 in Jerusalem, Prime Minister Ariel Sharon (Likud) called the struggle against violence to women "an important battle for the image of Israeli society." He said his government had allocated NIS 12.5 million for this purpose (about $3.125 million in US dollars), including NIS 3.6 million (about $900,000 in US dollars) toward shelters for battered women. Additional funds would be allocated next year, he promised (Shehori 2001). Although no politician here is arguing that the state's assessment of risk and management of national security produces domestic violence, they have adopted the cultural idiom of securitism to frame their stance against domestic violence.

For some, the security state holds a prominent place in their thinking, particularly when it comes to the normalization of violence based on living in a country at war, where force is deployed to defend against or overpower the enemy. The directionality of violence remains unresolved: does violence begin at home and move outward in ever-greater spheres of influence until it informs national security strategies, or does intimate partner abuse stem from soldiers' saturation with state-sanctioned violence? Others note that living in a security state exacerbates domestic violence. Finally, the language of war is integrated into the movement against domestic violence. Securitism may be embedded metaphorically in the fight against domestic violence—like having a "terrorist at home"—but conventional meanings of securitism continue to trump the needs of battered women, particularly when it comes to the policing of domestic violence.

SECURITY VERSUS SECURITY

The Israel Police, as well as the people they are charged to protect, construct the securitization of domestic violence, pitting national security against domestic security in a hierarchical struggle, rather than considering them as mutually constituted. For example, consider arguments built on a cultural logic of securitism, which are made by police to explain their handling of domestic violence complaints. In the mid-1970s, when MK Marcia Freedman searched for information about domestic violence, this is what she reported: "'Arabs beat their wives, not Jews,' I was told by Haifa's Chief of Police. 'They say that even if they don't know what she's done wrong, she'll know,' he finished, smiling at me from across his desk, inviting me to share the joke" (Freedman 1990, 102).

In the same conversation, the chief explained that they keep no statistics on domestic violence complaints, and only arrest a man if they see "blood or broken bones." Otherwise, it is a "private family affair." In essence, if only Arab men beat their wives, and the police do not consider domestic violence within their purview (unless it reaches a threshold they have set), then Arab women do not deserve the state's protection. This approach to policing has persisted in an apposition: Police blame domestic violence on Palestinian culture, absolving themselves of inaction; or they collude with Palestinian men in order to show respect for and protect "culture" (Adelman, Erez, and Shalhoub-Kevorkian 2003; Erez and Shalhoub-Kevorkian 2004; Shalhoub-Kevorkian 2004; Shalhoub-Kevorkian and Erez 2002). Police posit their lack of response as a culturally informed way to protect women:

> I am an experienced police officer and I know that by ignoring her actual physical abuse today, I will help her live tomorrow. You need to understand . . . their culture allows men [to] kill women on the basis of family honor. When she comes and asks my help I explain to her that she might be killed, and that it is better to go back home and [we] won't inform anybody about her visit to the police. She belongs to Arab mentality, and they know nothing about respecting women—first the mentality should be changed and only then we could work according to Israeli norms of Kvod Ha'adam Ve Heroto [Basic Law of Human Dignity and Freedom 1992]. (Shalhoub-Kevorkian and Erez 2002, 123, in Erez, Ibarra, and Gur 2015, 945)

In earlier analyses, my colleagues and I named such differential policing as the "culturalization of violence against women" (Adelman, Erez, and Shalhoub-Kevorkian 2003), and the "militarization of domestic violence" (Adelman 2003). Today both analyses are better subsumed within the broader frame of securitism, for several related reasons.

First, police value and prefer engaging in the technologized and professionalized fight against terrorism to protect national security. This is reflected in budgeting, work assignments, the status and emotional urgency associated with this type of "high policing," as well as the diminished attention to crimes perpetrated by Jews (but not those by Arabs) during periods of high-terrorism threat (Jonathan 2010; Jonathan and Weisburd 2010; Sela-Shayovitz 2014; Weisburd et al. 2010). Moreover, and similar to other states, the Israel National Police had to be legislatively directed and organizationally mandated to internalize domestic violence as a legitimately criminalized behavior that was within their jurisdiction to regulate.

The transformation has been slow and remains incomplete. Law enforcement officers would prefer if social workers took more responsibility for handling domestic violence (Buchbinder and Eisikovits 2008a). Besides diminishing the confusion and sense of ineffectiveness engendered when policing domestic violence, handing domestic violence over to other frontline workers also would enable them to attend to what they label as more important law enforcement activities:

> When we learn that a suicide bomber is planning to attack or that we need to prevent a terrorist attack, we stop thinking and functioning. I can tell you this because it happened to me two weeks ago when I learned that someone was planning to blow himself up in the area where my parents live . . . so you think I was able to work, help raped women, or address other issues . . . all I had on my mind was preventing such a terrorist attack from happening." (Shalhoub-Kevorkian 2004, 184, in Erez, Ibarra, and Gur 2015, 948)

This dynamic, common to policing in regions with ongoing political conflict, further subverts policy reforms aimed at creating a new social problem ideal of universal state protection for domestic violence victims, whether desirable or effective (Adelman, Erez, and Shalhoub-Kevorkian 2003; Ben-Porat and Yuval 2012; Korn 2000, 2003; Shoham 2000; Rattner and Fishman 1998). The resulting hierarchy is reinforced by the devotion of state resources to defense concerns, reflected similarly in the "clear priority" given to "national security over domestic security" by law enforcement officers officially charged with a dual purpose since 1974 of preventing and fighting terrorism and crime (Sa'ar, Sachs, and Aharoni 2011, 57; Shalhoub-Kevorkian 2004).[21]

Second, Jewish police view Arab citizens as a "suspect population" (Cole and Lynch 2006) and treat non-Jewish citizens as such, "governing through crime" in the name of fighting terrorism (Jonathan and Weisburd 2010; Simon 2007). The Israel National Police force is administered by the Ministry of Public Security, as is the Israel Prison Service. The police are responsible for maintenance of social order and crime prevention related to terrorism, organized crime, drugs, property crime, cybercrime, and personal security. Regardless of the subtleties of jurisdiction, the police are part of the larger "security sector" that includes not only the military but also "border guards and coast guard, the intelligence and internal security services, and military industries" (Barak and Sheffer 2007, 24n2).

Being part of the state's security sector has implications for the targets or recipients of police work as well. Palestinians in Lod, for example, lump the police in with General Security Services (Shin Bet), Mossad, and the IDF, not only deeming them as untrustworthy but also living in deep fear of them (Pasquetti 2013). For most Palestinians, police are the local face of the national security sector, a proxy for the state that, upon its establishment, dispossessed their homes and land and criminalized their mobility, under a military administration between 1948 and 1966. From 1967 onward, the police and its security sector partners prevented family members from the West Bank and Gaza from visiting and working without authorization within the Green Line, or arrested and incarcerated them when they crossed into Israel. It was the police who fired into a crowd of Palestinian protesters, killing thirteen men, in October 2000, and it is the police who invoke emergency regulations to handle routine criminal activity but with fewer civil protections for the accused.

Third, the very composition of the security sector as a whole, and the police in particular, does not reflect the demography of the state. This is both a result and a cause of the national security divide between the police and Palestinian citizens. The ratio of policemen to policewomen, for example, is 3:1, although this varies by region. The percentage of women drops from the national average of 25 percent to 18.7 percent women in the north; the breakdown among police in terms of nationality and religion is Jewish 88 percent, Druze 5.8 percent, Christian 1.7 percent, Muslim 1.3 percent, Bedouin 1.0 percent, and Circassian 0.3 percent. (Israel Police 2015, 121, 123, 125). To help drive down the prevalence of illegal weapons, domestic violence, and murder, among other crimes in the Arab community, the Israel Police appointed Jamal Hakrush, a Muslim man from Kfar Kanna in the Galilee, as its deputy commissioner in April 2016; second-in-command Hakrush will oversee a new division aimed at improving policing in the Arab community, aided by the recruitment of 1,300 law enforcement officers, and the creation of dozens of new police stations in Arab regions (*Times of Israel*, 2016a). The initiative has been received with mixed responses, with establishment Arab leaders cautiously supportive.

According to a report commissioned by the Knesset on the policing of domestic violence against Arab women (2010), the police have 220 investigators assigned throughout the country who are trained to handle domestic violence complaints. Seventy of the domestic violence investigators are women: two Christian women, one Muslim woman, one Druze woman, and sixty-six Jewish women. Thirty-three of the investigators speak Arabic, and ten of the Arabic speakers are women. Thus, despite the espoused community-policing model, the police do not mirror the communities they serve.

Fourth, police assessments of Arab men's domestic violence as a cultural problem and of women as its passive victim stem from the national security context in which domestic violence and its policing co-occur. Whereas the police characterize other men in Israel as uncivilized, immoral, and violent toward women (e.g., Mizrahim, Russians, and Ethiopians), it is only Palestinians who are labeled as enemies of the state. Palestinian women activists in Israel argue that the criminalization of domestic violence presents dilemmas for many citizens who already were averse to inviting the state to regulate their family and nation (Shalhoub-Kevorkian 1999). Each woman must determine if, when, and how to report domestic violence to the police within this security dilemma: on the one hand, being targeted with "safety advice" from social workers and police that reifies Palestinian culture and, on the other hand, being encouraged by family and community not to place their nation's dirty laundry into the hands of Jewish Israelis who "will use it to discriminate against us further" (Shalhoub-Kevorkian 1999, 203, in Erez, Ibarra, and Gur 2015, 941).

A high level of rejection of police as a suitable or effective step is reflected in reporting levels. The Knesset's commissioned report on the policing of domestic violence against Arab women from 2010 indicates that the number of complaints to the police (projected to be 13.5 percent in 2010) is not proportionate to the population (20 percent). When Arab women do submit a complaint to the police, they report physical assault (69.5 percent) more frequently than Jewish women (51.6 percent), and threats and intimidation less frequently (26.9 percent) than Jewish women (45.9 percent). Given the distinction in types of crimes reported, it makes sense that, in terms of processing Arab women's cases, fewer were closed, and about twice as many were prosecuted than those of Jewish women. Not surprisingly as well, this has led to a disproportionately higher percentage of Arab men imprisoned (36 percent) than Jewish men (although the bulk of these sentences were for violence against children). Women who report typically do so when the violence has become intolerable and she has family support (Erez, Ibarra, and Gur 2015, 943). Notably, ultra-Orthodox (many of whom are either against or neutral regarding the State of Israel) and Palestinian Israelis share a negative orientation toward the police, and women in both communities grapple with tensions between the desire to rely on communal modes of justice and the limited protection and risks involved when they turn to the police.

CONCLUSION

I opened this chapter with a story about the grassroots coalition Gun Free Kitchen Tables' campaign to prevent at-home, post-shift access to work-issued weapons by security guards—who protect the public from violence aimed at national security—in order to increase domestic security. It began as a focused initiative aimed at a particular policy that was based on a narrow conceptualization of security that ignored a contradiction between protecting the state and protecting women's safety, which was visible only by applying a gendered perspective. I will close the chapter with a brief look at some of the efforts to break the ideological distinction between personal and political by integrating the notion of "domestic security" into the state's overarching rubric of national security through UN Security Council Resolution 1325.

Resolution 1325 was adopted on October 31, 2000. It focuses on two main themes: protecting women and girls against violence during and after armed conflict, and including women in conflict resolution and peacemaking processes. Israel was the first member state to commit to the resolution, but it took an additional nine years of grassroots organizing and professional lobbying for the government to agree to develop an action plan to implement it. The Jerusalem Link's International Women's Commission for a Just and Sustainable Israeli–Palestinian Peace (IWC) member Anat Saragusti (2009, 7) calls 1325 "a revolution" because it "urges member states to ensure increased representation of women at all decision-making levels of conflict resolution . . . and in the reconciliation and peacemaking processes which follow."

Indeed, a number of grassroots NGOs seized the advocacy opportunities presented by 1325 and its sister resolutions that soon followed, which sought gender security–related norms (Aharoni 2014). Isha L'Isha in Haifa, for example, developed a "Women, Peace and Security Project" made up of several components. They hosted a series of lectures to discuss feminist perspectives on citizenship and the meaning of security. To preempt the claim that there are no women qualified to participate in state-level decision making, Isha also researched and produced a guidebook listing 200 women ready for negotiation teams in 2005. Isha, in partnership with the Kayan-Feminist Organization, hosted the first national conference on 1325 in Israel in April 2004 to raise awareness about the absence of women from national security discourse (Aharoni and Deeb 2004), to measure the effect of political and personal insecurity on women (Myrtenbaum 2005; Sachs, Sa'ar, and Aharoni 2005b), and to learn what insecurity means to women (Sachs, Sa'ar, and Aharoni, 2007; Women's Security Index 2013). Along with other feminist and peace NGOs, they coordinated "alternative to Herzliya" conferences to protest the lack of women participating and to question "whose security and strength" was being discussed in this key national security gathering focused narrowly on economic and military issues.[22] Isha also participated in lobbying efforts that resulted in groundbreaking reform to the Women's Equal Rights Law in 2005 to reflect the requirement to include women in all decision-making bodies.

Despite the potential that 1325 offers for reshaping the statecraft of national security to reflect women's comprehensive security needs, it has been the target of criticism for substantive and procedural reasons. The language of the resolution relies on a rigid gender binary that assumes women are either victims of armed conflict or peace-loving opponents of it. Resolution 1325 also does not formulate how many or which women possessing what kind of outlook on security should be incorporated into decision-making bodies by the state, or even how women should be incorporated. Procedurally, similar to other United Nations instruments built on "soft power," it lacks an explicit accountability mechanism, instead relying internally on NGOs and scorecard diplomacy exercised externally by international influencers (Shalhoub-Kevorkian 2010; Chazan 2004).

A series of public discussions designed by the UNIFEM-funded International Women's Commission that sought to elicit input on 1325 found that the majority of Jewish women participants honed closely to the "cultural stereotypes, unfamiliarity with the 'other,' denial of the asymmetry between the sides, and frustration at the political process" (Limor 2009, 27). Another IWC member, reflecting on the public discussions, observed, "We set out to hear 'the woman's viewpoint' as if it was something just sitting there waiting for us to pick it up. We had forgotten that most of us had been urged to leave off women's issues for now until better times arrived, for when the occupation or exploitation or recession would come to an end. We made motherhood into our most important aspect of uniqueness as women, but motherhood, too, has its nationalist and local aspects" (Haghagh 2009, 48–49). Palestinian women's NGOs and participants in public hearings on and research for 1325 spoke about their fear of state violence along with personal security. Distinct experiences and opposing viewpoints on Israel's military actions in Gaza during winter 2008–2009 exacerbated existing tensions between Jewish and Palestinian women; this and other flashpoints made it too difficult by 2011 for the IWC to continue.

The challenge of incorporating conflicting political orientations continued with the two-year development of an Israeli Comprehensive Action Plan to implement 1325, released in October 2013. Led by Itach-Maaki, its partners, and a coalition of thirty NGOs, the final document articulated five objectives with indicators. Not surprisingly, given the central role it has played in Israeli state feminism, the objective related to protecting women from violence in the public and private sector was its most elaborated section. However, participants were unable to agree on the status of the territories, and so security issues associated with the occupation are absent from the document. Nevertheless, the document was part of a multiyear effort to convince the government to integrate 1325 within its own National Action Plan. On December 14, 2014, Knesset Decision #2331 assigned the renamed "National Authority for Gender Equality" in the Prime Minister's office responsibility to lead an interministerial committee to develop such a plan (Chazan 2014). Although the Ministries of Welfare, Justice, and Public Security have been familiar faces attending Knesset sessions on women's status and violence against women, because of 1325, this time around the Ministry of Defense would be in the room as well (Sztokman 2015).

The physical boundaries of the Israeli state remain contested—politically, legally, militarily, religiously, and ethically—along with who belongs to its body politic. Whether this arrangement is desired, defended, or derided, Israel constitutes a prime example of a security state where protecting the nation is a taken-for-granted priority that affects every aspect of life. Palestinian and Jewish Israelis participate in this security project in overlapping and very distinct ways, which informs their understanding of domestic violence, its manifestation in their everyday lives, and the constrained choices they make to manage it. Statecraft guided by securitism means that the state, normatively centered on preventing and punishing political violence through national security measures, will elide domestic violence from being considered a threat to the future of the polity unless the very definition of security is subverted from within.

5 | A Political Economy of Domestic Violence

WHAT DOES THE COST OF COTTAGE CHEESE have to do with domestic violence? In June 2011 twenty-five-year-old Itzik Alrov from Bnei Brak posted a call on Facebook to boycott cottage cheese, a daily staple for many Israelis. He called for the boycott because a small tub of cottage cheese had recently doubled in price as a result of the state's deregulation of the dairy market (Magnezi 2011). Indeed, the cost of dairy products had risen from 5 percent higher than OECD averages in 2005 to 51 percent higher in 2011 (Taub Center 2015, 6). Israelis, fed up with a surge in food prices and the overall increase in the cost of living, swarmed his Facebook page, which quickly attracted more than 100,000 friends. The grassroots cottage cheese boycott greatly diminished sales, pushing the near-monopoly Tnuva and smaller other domestic corporations that dominate Israel's dairy market to lower prices on key items, and the government promised to reinstate market regulations (Sikular 2012). Cottage cheese resumed its normative place in the Israeli diet.

Within a month of the cottage cheese boycott, another twenty-five-year-old, Daphne Leef, set up a tent on the pedestrian promenade on Rothschild Boulevard in the center of Tel Aviv to protest the rapid rise in housing costs for both owners and renters (Frankel and Crystal 2011). She, too, invited the public to join her via Facebook. Tens of thousands of like-minded Israelis, some inspired by the collective power exhibited during the Arab Spring and protests in Spain and Chile, and others mobilized by NGOs and student or trade unions, joined her tent encampment along the boulevard or held encampments in their own towns and cities (Rosenhek and Shalev 2014). Hundreds of thousands participated in mass demonstrations, some of the largest in Israeli history. Under the umbrella slogan "the people demand social justice," Israelis protested a host of concerns: lack of affordable housing, retrenchment of social services, and growth of economic inequality (Kershner 2011). In other words, young Israelis sought *government* relief from the rising cost of domestic life.

With protests quickly gaining in size, scope, volume, and public support—a YNET poll conducted on August 2, 2011, indicated that 85 percent of the population endorsed the protests (Grinberg 2014, 252)—Prime Minister Benjamin Netanyahu announced a set of housing initiatives and formed the Trajtenberg Committee. Committee members were to investigate ways to address public concerns over the structural conditions that, since the mid-1980s, had brought Israeli society to an unprecedented level of poverty, inequality, and social alienation (Trajtenberg 2012). By early September, the summer protests peaked with nearly half a million people participating in marches and rallies across the country. However, within a few days, the encampment on Rothschild Boulevard was mostly dismantled, its momentum for social justice soon muted, but not erased entirely.

So what does the cost of cottage cheese (or housing) have to do with domestic violence in Israel? In this chapter I propose an answer by exploring what I have termed "a political economy of domestic violence" (Adelman 2004a). Researchers have documented how a lack of economic autonomy constrains women's power or leverage in an intimate relationship, limiting her resource-based options while enhancing her vulnerability and entrapment (Ptacek 1999). However, analyses of the mutually constitutive relationship between social class and domestic violence often rely—implicitly or explicitly—on a culture of violence thesis, which presumes that poor people are inured to domestic violence or are naturally at risk for it. This leads to policy recommendations for women to become economically independent (i.e., end the poverty) or to stop making poor choices when it comes to relationships (i.e., end the relationship) rather than an examination of the policies that produced the nonrandom distribution of poverty and domestic violence in the first place, or the policies that allow the ongoing impoverishment of battered women.

Few scholars explore how financial dislocation induced or exacerbated by the arrangement of the political economy increases domestic violence and derails women's economic mobility, or how "downward mobility and economic inequality weaken social capital and thus erode community norms that may prevent domestic violence" (Weissman 2013, 234, and see Weissman 2007; Alcade 2010b). Instead, attention has been focused on the "symptoms of oppression rather than the sources of oppression" (Weissman 2013, 237). These analyses lead to policies and interventions which suggest that "changing people's behavior . . . [solves] their problems, [so] . . . people's behavior [i]s the source of their problems" (Chadburn 2015). The political economy of domestic violence approach that I outline here complements individual-level explanations and effects by accounting for state-induced sources of the problem.

A political economy of domestic violence in this era of globalized inequality requires new ways of interrogating "mechanisms of capitalist governance" that shape women's vulnerability to violence and their possibilities for safety and well-being (Blim 2000, 33). In Israel, as in other places, a political economy of domestic violence is neither a ratio of haves to have-nots nor a measurement of the prevalence of domestic violence among poor families. A political economy of domestic violence moves beyond documentation of various forms of economic abuse. Instead, it is a reckoning of how the political arrangement of the economy—a key area of statecraft—favors some over others to feed structural inequality, and how this structural inequality renders women vulnerable to domestic violence. This approach reveals articulations between domestic violence and statecraft from several perspectives: the priorities, policies, and practices of the polity; the dominant familial and national ideologies embedded within the state's economic priorities; the resulting arrangement of a stratified economy; and manifest and latent distances between the state and its citizens (and noncitizens). For example, elected officials may express a demographic desire for large families, but few advocate for the financial reinforcements necessary to ensure their well-being. This duality is captured in a contradiction: Israel funds the highest rate of assisted reproductive technology usage in the world, nearly twice that of the next highest, while at the same time, it hosts one of the highest levels of family poverty among OECD countries (Birenbaum-Carmeli and Carmeli 2010; Bowers 2014; Kahn 2000). Such a contradictory materialist stance toward the family found within the logic of Israeli state-economy relations can easily be ignored or hidden when the public focuses on individual-based explanations of domestic violence that require no social transformations, offers solutions to domestic violence that are part of the problem, or prioritizes political violence over other forms of victimization. In this chapter I draw attention to how Israel's political economy engenders and exacerbates domestic violence.

Next I explain further what I mean by "political economy" and what is known about the relationship between economics and domestic violence. I then offer four entry points into the political economy of domestic violence: (1) legacies of Israel's political economic priorities that structure domestic violence; (2) ambivalent familism that leaves battered women and their families behind; (3) global flows of labor and political violence that lead to new victims of domestic violence; and (4) budgetary tensions between national security and social justice. The chapter concludes with a reflection on shelters and possible contributions a political economy of domestic violence might make.

POLITICAL ECONOMY

The area of intellectual inquiry termed "political economy" or "political economics" is central to the history of economic thought. Simply put, political economy describes the study of the relationship between the state and the economy, and debates focus on determining the most opportune relationship between the two. The fundamental tension within political economy is between those who advocate state investment into the welfare of the body politic and those who prefer minimalist state interference in the economy. Underlying this tension is a clash of values over whether or how to use politics to advance either self-interest or the common good (Segal 2016). Classical liberal economics argues largely against government interference in the individual pursuit of wealth within the capitalist "free market," yet its adherents often forget that one of its architects, Adam Smith, felt that the state in the eighteenth century had an obligation to provide public infrastructure. Karl Polanyi maintained that the state gives form to the economy and that it remains a political question whether its regulation of the market will aid citizens or corporations. Marx argued in his trenchant critique of political economy in the nineteenth century that the capitalist state as a governing body expresses the will and interests of the ruling class to the exclusion of the working class. Under a system of centralized socialism, the state actually owns and controls the economy, although to whose benefit remains under dispute. According to its adherents, the Keynesian welfare state "intervenes within the processes of economic reproduction and distribution to reallocate life chances between individuals and/or classes"—e.g., President Obama's stimulus bill in 2009 to counter the Great Recession or the Nordic economic model (Pierson 1998, 7). Politicians and legislators continue to disagree about the ultimate goal of political economy and the best route to achieving it.

Postwar Britain, with its organized labor, public education and healthcare, and state provisioning of a safety net, embodied the ideals of the welfare state.[1] Sociologist David Brady remarks, "Poverty is lower and equality is more likely to be established when welfare states are generous" (2008, 6). However, when elected in 1979, Prime Minister Margaret Thatcher dismantled the British welfare state and replaced it with much of Milton Friedman's neoclassical laissez faire economics.[2] Thatcher sought to reduce the state's high inflation, balance its budget and encourage growth by lowering taxes, marginalizing unions, opening markets, and privatizing enterprise. Since the 1980s similar policies have been implemented in Latin America and other developing countries through structural adjustment programs (SAPs), when the United States "exported neoliberal capitalist logic as riders on loans through the World Bank and the IMF" (Kingsolver 2002, 24, and see Gibson-Graham 1996). These macroeconomic changes resulted in the downsizing of government purview, lessening of social expenditures, and the privatization of the public sphere around the globe (Jurik 2004). The poor felt the penalizing economic effects so swiftly that by 1987 critics such as UNICEF called for "adjustment with a human face" (Jolly 1991). At the end of the Cold War in 1989, the Washington Consensus emerged on the topic of worldwide economic liberalization. The Washington Consensus was a set of policies among the US federal legislative and executive branches, and international financial institutions on "what the developing countries should do"; the approach originally included public investment into education and health, but also encouraged fiscal discipline, deregulation of commerce, and privatization (Williamson 2004, 18).

Today's neoliberalism is an even more business-centric and sped-up version of this approach to political economy, and it has produced a new logic of state/economy relations (Carrier and Miller 1998; Goode and Masovsky 2001; Munger 2002; Pierson 1998). In this era of swiftly moving capital, corporations exist that trump the economic and even political power of some governments, whose own policies, as a result, become more market-like or oriented toward the interests of global capital. Israel has experienced this form of neoliberalism, and the debates surrounding it as well. Yakir Plessner (1994), former deputy governor of the Bank of Israel, construes this form of globalization as a positive development in political economy because it opens new markets, allows for competitive innovation, and encourages entrepreneurialism.

Critics lament that the resulting dominance of the transnational market undermines state commitment to the welfare of the body politic, if not its very authority (Okongwu and Mencher 2000). They further argue that contraction of the welfare state expands the gap between the many who subsist and the few who rapidly accumulate (Rifkin 2000). Legal scholar Ruth Colker bluntly concludes that this hypercapitalism "is overly enamored with laissez faire economics and insufficiently concerned with our health and well-being" (Colker 1998, xi). Sharing this perspective, Israel's social justice protests in the summer of 2011 sought once again to put a human face on the punishing effects of a neoliberal political economy.

ECONOMICS AND DOMESTIC VIOLENCE

Research has demonstrated that money is a core issue of marital conflict "resolved" by domestic violence, because of differing expectations about household earnings and autonomy (e.g., who should earn how much by doing what kind of work, where and with whom; how and when money should be spent and on what). Economic abuse can look like refusal to relinquish a paycheck or pay household bills, prohibitions against wage labor, subversion of educational or vocational development, failure to secure employment, impediments to job security such as threats or harassment at work, or controlling access to household assets (Dobash et al. 2000; Moe and Bell 2004). For some women, it is their access to resources or employment that increases their risk for domestic violence (Brush 2011). For others, domestic violence contributes to or exacerbates unemployment, or otherwise negatively affects women's economic stability or health (Sanders 2015).

A woman's economic status can be made precarious when she attempts to leave via a physical separation or legal divorce. Her exit from the relationship may result in impoverishment and social dislocation, homelessness or a stay in shelter, a loss of childcare or transportation, all of which may in turn lead to loss of employment and other means of support, including in-kind resources from extended family and community members. In the event that the state forces a batterer to leave the family home, whether through civil or criminal mechanisms, the result may be the loss of his income or others' contributions to the household economy. The community as a whole pays opportunity costs associated with domestic violence as well, such as lower educational outcomes, employee productivity, and earning capacity over time, as well as ever-increasing budgets for criminal justice, health care, and social service systems.

Domestic violence cuts across social class lines, but poor women at the margins publicly present concerns with it at higher rates in many states. Domestic violence within the economic periphery might be documented disproportionately because people at the margins more frequently get caught up in systems of surveillance and social control, and women with requisite economic means and other forms of capital are able to bypass these same systems while managing their safety. The combined stigma of domestic violence and poverty (and racism, ethnocentrism, heterosexism, etc.) means that resilient women who may lack the right combination of social, cultural, and human capital because of structural inequality are commonly understood as pathological or irresponsible, and unworthy of public investment (Brush 2011; Quadagno 1994; Richie 2015). Underlying these perceptions is the assumption that, if a battered woman would "just leave," then the violence she endures would end, and she and her children could survive or even thrive economically. These perceptions do not account for the politics of respectability attached to women striving to present a peaceful domestic life to their own community as well as to outsiders (Weis et al. 1998). Nor do they understand how socioeconomic survival leads at least some women "to choose between danger and destitution" (Edin and Lein 1997, 158).

DOMESTIC VIOLENCE LEGACIES OF ISRAEL'S POLITICAL ECONOMY

Policy legacies of Israel's political economy (Orloff 2002) that structure domestic violence—social stratification based on nation, religion, ethnicity, and gender—originate in layers of competing interests that span multiple continents, predating the establishment of the state.[3] Prior to waves of Zionist-inspired immigration initiated at the end of the nineteenth century, Palestinian Arabs labored primarily in subsistence agriculture and developed urban centers of commerce; Jewish residents were semi-dependent on funds distributed by coreligionists from abroad. Zionist leaders envisioned the state-in-the-making as a political-economic mechanism to return the Jewish people to and refashion them as laborers within their national homeland.[4] Mutual support based on Jewish nationalism helped to absorb a rapidly growing immigrant population, but inequality was central to its proto-state–building institutions. The Histadrut, for example, the Labor Party–dominated workers union federation established in 1920, which controlled much employment, wage bargaining, and social services, organized "Hebrew labor" and instituted a family wage policy, which assumed a male breadwinner family model (Plessner 1994, 107; G. Ben-Porat 2008). It also gave preference to Jewish over Palestinian workers (Gozansky 2015). Similarly, the Jewish Agency (established in 1929) funneled foreign capital solely to support the growing Jewish community. In contrast, Palestinians lacked a parallel source of either external investment or population growth, reinforcing their economic marginalization. Social stratification, already embedded within the region, intensified with the rise of Zionist nationalism.

Although sovereignty for the Israeli state in 1948 brought with it a mix of progressive social welfare and liberal economic legislation, its leaders continued to direct the collectivist yet exclusivist economy as a mechanism of state-building and used US aid and philanthropic and business investment from abroad as well as West German reparations to do so (Ben-Porat 2008). The Israeli state ran the economy: it was "a major employer, the main owner of land, and the main investor in all branches of the economy" (Carmi and Rosenfeld 2010, 385). The 156,000 Palestinians who remained in Israel after the war, including internal refugees, lived under military rule in under-resourced separate villages, a couple of larger towns, and distinct neighborhoods within "mixed cities" such as Haifa. The Palestinian economy had to shift from farming to wage labor because much of the land formerly owned and used by Palestinians was transferred by the state to house the rising population of Jewish immigrants (Daoud 2012).[5] Mizrahi immigrants, who numbered close to 750,000 in the state's first years, which is about the same number of Palestinians who became external refugees in 1948, were sent to live in formerly Arab towns and neighborhoods, undeveloped camps, settlements, and new "development towns" sited in politically strategic but socially and economically isolated rural locations (Carmi and Rosenfeld 2010; Yiftachel 2000).

Policies, particularly those related to military service, social insurance, and housing, helped improve the economic standing of some while holding back others through restrictions related to land ownership and use, inequitable protection from the market, and differential access to social benefits because of uneven infrastructure and policy implementation (Rosenhek 2011). Maternity benefits in the 1950s, for example, were partially tied to hospital births, but Palestinian women had limited access to hospitals, and higher childcare subsidies were allocated in the 1970s to women who worked fewer hours, and thus earned less (Ajzenstadt and Gal 2001, 305). Druze men (but not women) were conscripted by the IDF, and Muslims and Christians were not. Planning and development monies that continued to reward Jewish over Palestinian Arab locales, and Ashkenazi over Mizrahi residential areas, reinforced the splintering of the state into segregated and stratified spaces. Speaking to the problem of racist housing policies and practices in the United States, Ta-Nehisi Coates (2014) said, "If you sought to advantage one group . . . and disadvantage another, you could scarcely choose a more graceful method than housing discrimination. Housing determines access to transportation, green spaces, decent schools, decent food, decent jobs, and decent services. . . . Housing segregation is the weapon that mortally injures, but does not bruise." This formal inducement of disadvantage, what has been called "nation-state privilege" (Carmi and Rosefeld 2010, 382) has long-term implications for domestic violence.

Residential patterns in Israel are tightly linked to social class, access to employment and services, and mobility. So where a battered woman lives helps to structure the domestic violence against her and resources available to her. I learned this explicitly when I began volunteering for the Hotline for Battered Women in Haifa in the mid-1990s and spoke with Rana, its Arab coordinator. I asked her what she thought were some of the unique problems that Palestinian battered women face. She answered me back with a question, "Like what?" I anticipated that she might talk about the possible reluctance of women to call police, or to turn to Jewish-majority advocacy organizations. Instead, she sat across from me and outlined the spatial arrangement of an Arab village in Israel. She then explained how traditional family living patterns and land inheritance practices, in combination with discriminatory land scarcity and building permit bureaucracy, produced a residential pattern that resembled to me Jeremy Bentham's Panopticon. "An extended family lives in a group of homes constructed in a circle," she explained. Parents give their sons land to build their houses—or more likely, because of restrictions on land use, the right to build another level on top of already existing family homes. Some wives relocate from their childhood home in one village, town, or city and move elsewhere to live with their husbands, while men enjoy residential stability, and the power of kinship that comes with it.[6] She continued:

> Brothers live together near each other; it takes maybe ten years to finish building [the new home]. In the end, they get married, and the house is finished and [registered] under his name. If a woman wants to call the police, and she has no telephone—the telephone is at the brother-in-law's house.[7] [He will ask], why are you calling? The brother-in-law will

convince her to go home. Maybe he [also] beats her or also her father-in-law or mother-in-law [does]. . . . [And] if the woman wants to leave? The in-laws will threaten her, drive her crazy! All of the brothers are there, and will make her leave without her things, or her children.

She then described barriers to helpseeking based on housing and residential patterns and offered one example of how these patterns *could* enable helpseeking:

There are no rental homes [in the Arab sector]. [If she leaves the house], she must return to her parents' house. In the city it is a little different. No one knows [who is] married or divorced! But in the village, everyone is a relative, everyone watches. It is not just that I live with his cousins, and his family, but my father is there, too, and the brother of my father, and cousins of mine here: all mixed together! If there is a family problem everyone knows. Everyone is a relative. It could be that this housing situation provides support for each other. It depends. But if there is no system of support, you go and tell one person and they say, what do you want, my mother-in-law also beats me or my husband beats me also. This is very meaningful. There is one example I know of where the parents-in-law, when they hear he is beating her, they come immediately and protect her.

The effect of residential location and housing on domestic violence remains relevant today (Rabho 2013, 2015). When the Galilee Society recently conducted research on violence in the family and in the community among Palestinians in Israel, they asked whether married women lived in the same, natal village or town where their parents resided as well. Those who did reported a slightly lower rate of domestic violence (28.6 percent) than those living away from their parents in another village or town (33.2 percent) (Galilee Society 2014, 6). Although the statistical difference may not be significant, it is instructive that the survey question was worthwhile to ask. Whether in a Palestinian town, a Druze village, Bedouin encampment, or Jewish kibbutz or a *moshav* where kin ties are intense and multilayered, monitoring of people's whereabouts is common. Population density may be lower in a rural region than in an urban neighborhood, but the physical arrangement of living space and the social networks among residents in either can be a conduit for safety or for endangerment of women, depending on how people use the space and the meaning they give to the relationships within it.

To the physical layout of a village, Rana then added entrenched forms of government-based economic discrimination against "the Arab sector" as another factor for me to consider. Economic discrimination exacerbates unemployment, poverty, and an already weak infrastructure, and perpetuates a lack of services ranging from government offices to health care to transportation to playgrounds. Such underdevelopment is a policy legacy, which began in the early state period, and its effects have accumulated over time, she explained.

Palestinian Arab villages and towns are still not allocated a proportionate level of public resources, despite needing a disproportionate level to match need, or to approach a level playing field with Jewish towns and cities (Lewin-Epstein and Semyonov 1993, 31; Haider 2010). The state's Orr Commission reported a systemic pattern of "distress, deprivation and discrimination" experienced by Palestinian citizens in terms of education, employment opportunities, land, housing, infrastructure, religious assets, and local government budgets (Orr Commission of Inquiry 2003, chap. 1, sec. 32).[8] Over time, these policies have maintained a hierarchy of inequality and distance from the state, which can too easily contribute to gender violence. In Shalhoub-Kevorkian and Daher-Nashif's (2013, 305) examination of the dual flames of state exclusion and patriarchal control that they argue feed femicide, they quote a social worker from the Palestinian Israeli NGO Women Against Violence, speaking at a conference on "Women and Girls in Ramleh and Lydda":

> Palestinian Arab society is a patriarchal society, but violence is a worldwide phenomenon, and we are living in a state of which the military and militarization are a fundamental part. . . . In mixed cities such as Ramleh, we witness the state's constant efforts to weaken and exclude the Arab community. . . . The Israeli state doesn't invest in it in the same manner as it invests in other places. It does not allocate the same budgetary funds, build infrastructure or run awareness-raising programs in schools as it does for the Jewish population . . . the socioeconomic situation of the Arabs in Ramleh is very difficult . . . Israelis have tightened the stranglehold around them, which has minimized their ability to develop and learn. All this leads to a maximization of violence, as is well known all over the world . . . The man knows that he is expected to build a home and to finance a family, and when he can't do so he feels inadequate as a man.

The gender frustration thesis, that is, men unable to actualize their masculine destinies resort to controlling intimate partners, has its critics. Nevertheless, it frames local discourse and helps explain why Palestinian women in Israel face constrained choices: stay silent, and endure and endorse gender violence; entrust one's safety to family members or communal leaders, who may not support the violence but also may assign responsibility for its cessation on women's behavior;

seek assistance from NGOs, which may offer only short-term solutions; or turn to the state for protection, which also may not deliver effective support, and risk rejection or blame from police and social workers, collusion between the state and community, and stigma from the community for doing so (Touma-Sliman 2005). In short, when a Palestinian woman turns to the state, she putatively endorses not only its legitimacy but also its agents' culturalized justifications for Palestinian men's violence against women—police dismiss domestic violence as part of "the Arab mentality" and fail to take it seriously (Adelman, Erez, and Shalhoub-Kevorkian 2003; Erez and Shalhoub-Kevorkian 2004)—in exchange for unreliable resources and services. None of the available options ameliorate the very conditions that thwart the mobility of a family's economic status and that inspire Palestinians to so carefully guard national boundaries by controlling women's bodies (Daoud 2012).

The Policy Legacies of Immigration

Although Palestinian and Ethiopian Israelis have distinct histories and very different relationships with the state, a similar combination of culturalized justifications and political economic explanations have been made regarding the disproportionate number of domestic violence homicides perpetrated by Ethiopian immigrant men in Israel, whose patriarchal control has been displaced by the state. Despite a persistent controversy over the authenticity of their non-Talmudic Judaism, Israel welcomed over 90,000 Ethiopian Jewish immigrants during the government's clandestine Operation Moses (1984), emergency Operation Solomon (1991), and recent Operation Dove's Wing (2013); in April 2016 the Knesset approved funding for the final wave of Ethiopian immigrants, totaling just over 9,000 people, as part of the Zionist vision to continue the "ingathering of exiles" (Efraim 2015; JTA, 2016b; Weil 1997). New immigrants are a critical lifeblood of Israel's political economy.

Like waves of immigrants before them, government policies intended for Ethiopians to assimilate into Israeli culture (Dominguez 1989). Ethiopian immigrants were labeled early on as a docile if not primitive ethnic minority and were subjected to official as well as unofficial expressions of xenophobia and racism (Shoham 2013a). For years the state, represented by the Chief Rabbinate, rejected the authority of their spiritual leaders (*kessim*, as rendered in Hebrew), and the police and social services replaced extended family and communal elders (*shmagaleh*), who had mediated family disputes (Geiger 2013).[9] After time spent segregated in immigrant absorption centers, many Ethiopian immigrants have been sent to live in peripheral towns and cities, where they struggle with social isolation and severe poverty and unemployment or underemployment.

Indeed, representatives of welfare services have suggested that men's violence against women in the Ethiopian community is because of their terrible economic situation, exacerbated by lower educational achievement, and because of the distinct contrast between family structures found in Ethiopia and Israel. Researchers, too, attribute higher rates of domestic violence, including homicide, among Ethiopians to several factors: cultural chasm and economic problems (Sela-Shayovitz 2010b); men's acculturation stress and psychological disorders (Edelstein 2013); reversal of rigid gender complementarity because of women's relative success in securing low-wage employment (Weil 2004); and the breakdown in communal-based forms of social control and dispute resolution (Shoham 2013a). Michal Mizrahi, coordinator of the NGO Maslan's hotline for victims of sexual assault and domestic violence in the Negev, explained in a newspaper interview that in 2007 only six out of 400 calls to the hotline were from Ethiopian women, not because of a lack of violence but because of their "culture and mentality": a public complaint, she elaborated, would lose a woman the support of her community (Bronofsky 2007). In turn, community members criticized the lack of public services available to the Ethiopian community. "Tzipi Nachshon Glick, the welfare ministry's national coordinator for the treatment of domestic violence, says the government understands the need for Amharic-speaking social workers, but there is an acute shortage of funding for social services across the board in Israel" (Kraft 2007).

Yet, during a period when the total number of complaints to the police about domestic violence decreased slightly, the percentage of newly reported cases of domestic violence against Ethiopian women increased. Between 2005 and 2009 domestic violence complaints by Ethiopian women ranged from 2.3 to 2.6 percent, exceeding the community's size at about 1.5 percent of the population; Ethiopian Israelis also were disproportionately represented in Center for the Prevention and Treatment of Family Violence records during the same time period (ranging from a low of 3.8 percent to a high of 6.3 percent) (Ben Natan 2011; Myers-JDC-Brookdale 2012). Ethiopian Israeli women also have been disproportionately represented in shelters for battered women. Battered Ethiopian Israeli women are taking advantage of limited welfare and policing resources available to them as part of their overall faster integration into mainstream society, perhaps risking further alienation from their husbands and community (Geiger 2013, 235). Referring to women's speedier absorption, the Ministry of Immigrant Absorption has sought to facilitate this transformation in a new program that asks women "to advance at a pace that doesn't 'break' her husband" (Blumenfeld 2012).

The state continues to bank on future generations of Ethiopian immigrants improving their educational and employment outcomes and growing less tolerant of domestic violence as they assimilate from their "traditional society" of origin to what they call Israeli egalitarianism (Wallach, Weingram, and Avitan 2010, 1287). Some research supports the state's forecast of transformation.

When asked to explain how it is for men today in Israel, Ethiopian men share perspectives that track generational differences. A younger, more educated man said: "I do not believe that men have lost their status. Once men decided and women remained at home. In Israel, there is equality between men and women. If my woman goes out to work and helps in the finances of the family, it does not mean that I have lost my status. We should explain to some men that this is not an offense to their status and respect" (Geiger 2013, 239). An older and less educated man, who took part in the same research project, described the transition he has navigated: "Women did not know anything else other than to serve men. Here women go to work and support their family. In the beginning it was hard to live with it. She is blooming. She learns the language and she has friends. I came to accept it even though it is hard because I was used to see men at the highest status" (239). Yet the men Geiger interviewed also lamented the deadly effect of the state's destruction of Ethiopian communal dispute resolution methods, the tearing apart of their extended family kin structure, and their lack of economic mobility.

The state continues to invest its monies in the hope that new generations of Ethiopians and Palestinians will adopt what they name as Israel's modern and western culture of gender egalitarianism. Unfortunately, the official push for cultural assimilation combined with entrenched stratification has created an undertow pulling for cultural retrenchment. Domestic violence remains a cultural matter, rather than a political and economic problem for the state. However, targets of racism have become more vocal in their rejection of discrimination and their lack of economic advancement in a state where about half of their families live below the poverty line. In the meantime, positioned on the lowest rungs of the employment and income scale, Palestinian and Ethiopian battered women are affected severely by state budget cuts to the social safety net in terms of unemployment benefits, income support, and child allowances. Mizrahi battered women also are affected severely by any changes to social welfare legislation. A pattern of differential accumulation based on nation, ethnicity, religion, and gender persists today because of a host of state decisions that leave some families behind.

AMBIVALENT FAMILISM: NEOLIBERALISM AND IMPOVERISHED BATTERED WOMEN

Israel's political economy underwent a massive transformation in the 1980s, when its leaders began a shift from social welfare investment as a means of national formation and state-building to one more explicitly aligned with global capital interests centered on individual success (Grinberg 2014). The neoliberal transformation in Israel echoed structural changes around the globe, led largely by American economists. The new economic logic found expression in the state budget, which reflects the values and priorities of its elected officials and those who influence their decision making. Similar to other states, the fight over Israel's revenues and expenditures mirrors cultural tensions over what it means to be an Israeli and who deserves a share of the state's resources. The resulting distribution of wealth and poverty reflects an "ambivalent familism," where the state continues to develop a wide range of family-based welfare supports and has increasingly incorporated "battered women in shelter" as a target of such support, but has discerned ever more harshly between "legitimate social dependency" and "bad dependency" by repeatedly cutting state benefits (Saraceno 1994). This has left solo mothers—many (formerly) battered Mizrahi women—destitute and desperate.

In contrast to the incredible growth the state oversaw in its first quarter century, economists in Israel consider the period of 1974–1985 its "lost years," when the viability of the state was in balance (Ben-Porat 2008, 96). The 1967 War had provided Israeli employers access to cheap Palestinian labor from and a new market for Israeli products in the West Bank and Gaza. This "drove up competition for unskilled work" (Daoud 2012, 85). Rapid economic growth, however unevenly distributed because of increased market segmentation and social stratification, contributed to a maturing state with a developing social safety net. That is, until the 1970s, when inflation and recessionary conditions manifested around the globe, which were further complicated in Israel by its military-dominated state-run economy. Not even the Likud party, elected in 1977 to replace Labor's political and economic failures, was able to reorganize the economy and privatize state-owned companies (Ben-Porat 2008, 97). Prime Minister Begin (Likud) oversaw major deficit spending and inflation that ultimately spiked to 450 percent by 1984 as Israel's war "Operation Peace of the Galilee" in Lebanon festered.

Under guidance of a Labor-Likud centrist national unity government and with pressure from US President Reagan,[10] the "liberalization" of Israel's political economy began with the Emergency Economic Stabilization Plan on July 1, 1985, "the day Israeli capitalism was born" (Arlosoroff 2015). Among other measures taken to stabilize the economy, the state made severe budget cuts, forced up interest rates, and issued new currency called the New Israel Shekel (NIS) valued at 1/1000th of the old shekel. Today the state describes itself as "a diverse open market economy" (Ministry of Finance 2011, 5). Its political economy is characterized by "deregulation of the labor market, liberalization of financial markets, lifting of restrictions on movement of capital and goods, heightened involvement of foreign capital, privatization of public assets, and restrictive fiscal and monetary policies" (Maman and Rosenhek 2012, 343). In contrast to conventional changes that neoliberal economics impose on most states, Israeli neoliberalism has not resulted in the withdrawal or weakening of the state vis-à-vis the economy; instead, state and capital remain "symbiotic, coalescent and often fused" (Nitzan and Bichler 2002, 13).

Macroeconomic changes in the state's economy have rewarded a small number of "winners" and exacerbated existing inequalities. Welfare policies incorporated "lower levels of benefits, a relatively intensive use of selective programmes based on means tests" and "formal and informal exclusionary practices toward subordinate social groups" (Rosenhek 2011, 63). The consequence: the level of income inequality—the distribution of household income across the population—is severe. The state's Gini coefficient, measured at 0.38, marks it with the "second highest level of income inequality after government taxes and transfers among OECD countries" (OECD 2013a; World Bank 2014a; UNHDP 2013).[11] According to Israel's Central Bureau of Statistics, "the average CEO salary [of about NIS 375,000 a month] . . . was forty-two times greater than the average [monthly] wage in Israel in 2012 (NIS 9,018) and eighty-seven times greater than the minimum [monthly] wage that year (NIS 4,300) (Swirski, Konor-Attias, and Ophir 2014, 15). Israel and the United States vie for first place when it comes to income inequality, while the cost of living in Israel—housing and food in particular—has climbed sharply in the first decade and a half of the twenty-first century.

At the same time, Israel has one of the highest rates of relative poverty among "high income" countries. Two decades ago, one out of ten Israelis lived in poverty; today it is one out of five Israelis, and one out of three children (OECD 2014; Barkali et al. 2013).[12] Among forty-one state members of the OECD and the European Union, Israel ranks thirty-seventh in terms of child poverty, with only Greece, Mexico, Bulgaria, and Romania filling in the remaining four worst positions (UNICEF Office of Research 2016). The poverty rate among the most marginalized in the country—concentrated in development towns and Jerusalem—is even higher. At least one-half of Palestinian Arab families live in poverty (Hesketh et al. 2011; Barkali et al. 2013). Israel's National Insurance Institute estimates conservatively that 66 percent of ultra-Orthodox Jewish families live in poverty (Grave-Lazi 2014). Over one-third of single (or solo) mothers live below the poverty line; most are Mizrahi women (Lavie 2014). The relative poverty level remains high, particularly for those already situated at the peripheries of society (Bank of Israel 2014). Yet the Bank of Israel notes that the state does significantly less than the OECD average to alleviate the market poverty rate (i.e., household income prior to taxes and transfers) or the market inequality rate (i.e., household income after taxes and transfers) (Bank of Israel 2014, 242). Because of this stratification, even families with two workers in Israel struggle within the new neoliberal economy.

Families in Israel have changed over time. The age of first marriages has gone up, along with the divorce rate, although the latter varies greatly by religion and ethnicity, and overall remains low, when compared to the United States. Similar to other countries, the number of women raising children on their own, known as solo mothers in Israel, has increased.[13] Israel has seen a rise in single mothers as a percentage of all families with children, from 4.5 percent in 1975 to 9.9 percent in 2001. The rate in 2012 stands at 12.6 percent, and about 8 percent of children under eighteen live in a single-parent household (CBS 2013, 12). Over time, how women become solo mothers also has shifted. Unique to Israel is the infusion of solo mother-headed families because of mass immigration waves in the 1990s from the former Soviet Union and Ethiopia; it was a not uncommon family form in the FSU, but an unintended outcome of immigration policies and the difficult journey to Israel for Ethiopian immigrants (S. Swirski et al. 2003, 2–3; CBS 2013).

It is less common for women to have children outside the framework of marriage,[14] so solo mothers are primarily the result of widowhood and divorce, notwithstanding the previously noted exceptions, and elite women choosing or lesbians counted as single parents (Lavie 2014). Early in the state's history, war widows comprised, if not the largest percentage of solo mothers, certainly the most visible and culturally venerated category because of their national sacrifice (Shamgar-Handelman 1981). MKs expressed this viewpoint during discussions of widows' social benefits in 1950: "We are not giving these families charity, we are duty-bound to pay them ransom for our own souls"; and again in 1967: "We must compensate them in the only way we are capable of, award them maximum financial compensation . . . as a sacred debt" (*Divrei Haknesset*, in Katz 1993, 52). Women who lose their husbands through a car or workplace accident or lethal disease joined war widows but as "no-choice" solo mothers. In contrast, divorced women today comprise the largest proportion of solo mothers, viewed as a discretionary choice, and perhaps even selfish (S. Swirski et al. 2003, 3). From 1985 to 2005, widows went from making up 40 percent of single parent families to 12 percent, and the number of divorced women shifted from just over half to nearly three-quarters of single parents in Israel (Stier 2011, 213).

Like so many other states, the logic of Israel's political economy has relied on a normative nuclear family formation. Namely, policies have been predicated upon a "two-parent family in which the man is considered the head of household and the chief breadwinner. This model is reflected in the considerable gender and national wage gap, and enshrined in social norms and laws that regulate family patterns including marriage, procreation, parenting, inheritance, taxation, social security, and the like" (S. Swirski et al. 2003, 4). Still, the state has tried through affirmative and punitive policies to encourage women to enter the workforce, particularly Mizrahi Jewish, Palestinian, and haredi Jewish women, whose workforce participation rates have been lower than Ashkenazi Jewish women (Ajzenstadt and Gal 2001). Haredi and Palestinian Israeli women's unemployment is often called out as a drain on the economy (Lahav 2015). Nevertheless, in the idealized family formation, horizontal and vertical care is feminized (Saraceno 1994). The presumption is that women will care for their husbands, children, and elder parents, along with any wage labor they generate.

Not all solo mothers are impoverished battered Mizrahi women. However, the highest divorce rate is found among Jewish Israelis, and a conservative estimate is that at least one-third of Jewish women getting divorced have faced threats of violence and extortion. The majority of solo mothers are divorced or separated (75 percent). More than a third of solo mothers live under the official poverty line (Stier 2011). Mizrahi families have an overall higher rate of poverty than Ashkenazi families. Logically, Mizrahi solo mothers who have been battered are disproportionately represented among the ranks of the poor. The increasing number of solo mothers, the dominant reason for their status (separation or divorce), and their lack of exercised political power informs the development and implementation of the state's welfare policies. Because of their precarious economic status, solo mothers and battered women among them are affected by even slight shifts in unemployment trends, paid labor wages, and state welfare policies.

Social welfare policy changes have paralleled changes in demographics and family formation. Notably, in a contradictory trajectory, the state has gradually expanded the categories of eligible recipients but has simultaneously cut social benefits. A series of legislative reforms oblige the state to support one- and two-parent families through allocations such as maternity benefits, child allowances, daycare subsidies, mandated child support, payment of child support in lieu of deadbeat dads, income support, unemployment, and old age benefits.[15] However, "only widows were entitled to the highest levels of assistance" until 1992, when the Knesset passed the Single Parent Family Law, "which equalized the level of payments across different categories of eligible women—i.e., widows, unmarried women, divorced women (S. Swirski et al. 2003, 8). The law also changed the terms of the income maintenance employment test: a solo mother could now raise her children until they reached seven years of age without being required to search for or secure wage labor (9) and tied payments to the cost of living (Lavie 2014, 117). These reforms acknowledged women's mothering responsibilities, regardless of how they came to be single parents.

Subsequent antipoverty measures have targeted battered women either explicitly or implicitly. The state expanded who qualified for a solo parent level of benefits to include separated women and women denied divorce, many who are battered women, although women in common-law marriages (i.e., a type of cohabitation among Jewish couples) were then excluded. Then, in 2001, the definition of solo parent was expanded again to include battered women staying in shelters (S. Swirski et al. 2003, 9). Later the state added benefits to help support battered women's transition from shelters to independent living: the Eighteenth Knesset passed a bill allocating a one-time grant to a woman upon leaving a shelter (NIS 8,000, plus NIS 1,000 for each child up to two); because a two-month bureaucratic delay in its delivery was not unusual, a year later, legislative reform required that she receive the money literally upon exiting. Otherwise, the chair of the Knesset Committee on the Status of Women MK Aliza Lavie (Yesh Atid) explained, "The consequences of a lack of money at this initial time are severe; when women leave they have nowhere to go, and often they return to their violent partner. In this way the investment in the rehabilitation goes to waste" (Lis 2013b). The state responded quickly to ensure return on its investment—the procedure was revamped just weeks after the committee had visited a shelter as part of the International Day for the Elimination of Violence against Women when women and shelter staff shared the problem with government representatives.

The extension of welfare benefits to separated women, women denied divorce, and battered women in shelters acknowledged their economic insecurity and ongoing obligation to care for their children, particularly while in marital status transition. However, welfare benefits targeting only women currently in or exiting shelters meant that the overwhelming majority of battered women were not eligible for such supports. (Even if every battered woman wanted to leave home and stay in a shelter, capacity is limited to about 250 women at any one time.) This signaled a growth in the state's recognition that battered women were deserving state dependents, but only a narrow percentage of "successful" battered women who left their homes, and their husbands, were rewarded as such. In essence, this punished the remaining tens of thousands of battered women who remained at home (for numerous reasons, including fear of losing the right to public housing), who did not end the relationship, or who left home or ended the relationship without the consent or facilitation of a shelter stay. Shelters became the de facto bureaucratic arbiter to categorize a woman as deserving state assistance. Battered women who bypassed the social services' chosen pathway to independence were lumped in with other solo mothers, all of whom faced cuts to their welfare benefits.

Despite the extension of who "counts" as a solo parent, the safety net for the poor has been subverted by cuts to benefits, starting with the neoliberal revolution in 1985 and echoed in subsequent slashes. The Knesset approved a massive round of cuts at the end of June 2003:

"Netanyahu cut everything—rent subsidies, assistance to low-income families, child allowances, income maintenance, sharp cuts" recalled Leah Achdut, an economist who was then deputy head of the National Insurance Institute, which oversees many of Israel's public welfare programs. By 2003 . . . public spending had already fallen substantially from the unsustainable levels of the mid-1980s—from roughly 70 to 50 percent of GDP—but the country's economic leaders were not satisfied. "People said it's not enough, we have to reduce taxes and government more to encourage the private sector," said Achdut. "Bibi [Netanyahu] very much believes this—in this respect, he is entirely American." (E. Press 2011)

As she recalls the period of severe economic reform, the former deputy head of the NII considered these cuts as counter to Israeli values. This round of cuts ignored women's unpaid work of mothering care and the paucity of wage work accessible to women, particularly Mizrahi women living in the geographic periphery, and focused on paid wage labor as required "economic activity," which reformers argued would ameliorate family poverty (Bank of Israel 2014, 244).

Women did not stay silent. As a protest against welfare policy reform, Vicki Knafo, a forty-three-year-old Mizrahi divorced mother of three, and one of many single mothers whose family was deeply affected by the cuts, began to walk with an Israeli flag in her hand by herself on July 2, 2003—in the midst of the Second Intifada, but during a brief ceasefire period—nearly 200 kilometers from her home in the development town Mitzpe Ramon in the Negev Desert to Jerusalem (Herbst 2013, 129).[16] Her one-woman march quickly attracted other single mothers like Smadar Lavie, a fellow protestor, single mother, and anthropologist, who explained, "Vicky marched because she could no longer pay her bills. On June 29, 2003, the New Israeli Shekel (NIS) was worth about twenty-three cents in US currency. Her half-time job paid her about 1,217 NIS (about $280) a month. The amendment cut 1,304 NIS (about $300) from Vicky's monthly income welfare supplement of 1,983 NIS (about $456), reducing it to 679 NIS (about $156), an amount swallowed up by her retroactive debt, reducing her welfare to nothing" (Lavie 2012, 301).[17] Together, single mothers pitched a tent in front of the Knesset building and stayed for over two months. Most left only after a Palestinian suicide bomber targeted a bus in Jerusalem, breaking the ceasefire between the State of Israel and Hamas that had been brokered to go into effect June 29, 2003.[18] According to Lavie, "The plight of the single mothers was completely off the public agenda in favor of the Palestine-Israel conflict. Most mothers left the encampment within a few days of the bombing" (Lavie 2012, 311).

Before they decamped, the public had received Vicki Knafo and her fellow protestors as "warrior mothers," heroines of the state or an example of "beautiful Israel" (Herbst 2013, 136; Lis and Sinai 2003). Soon, however, the Israeli government triggered a moral panic about single mothers by reframing protestors as selfish parasites (Ajzenstadt 2009; Herbst 2013). Then Finance Minister Benjamin Netanyahu commented:

> The women who receive allowances get used to not working and their children get used to the fact that their mothers do not work. It is a dependence trap, a thick-jam trap from which they cannot escape. In such an environment, children learn from their parents to reach out and receive support. . . . I must release those children from this culture of dependence on government welfare. They must not join the chain. (Flotzer, July18, 2003, quoted in Herbst 2013, 139–40)

Others blamed single mothers for their economic circumstances because they "chose to dump their husbands" (140). Echoing concerns in the United States with the growing number and kind of women recipients of state-based economic support and the absence of men in poor households, the state framed welfare recipients as irresponsible drains on the moral economy and used welfare policy "to reproduce two-parent families by stigmatizing and denigrating mother-only families for being the cause of their own problems" (Curtis 2001, 63; Abramovitz 1996; Kilty and Vidal de Haynes 2000; Mink 1995). Welfare reform was a central part of the state's efforts to move the country from a social compact of mutual responsibility undergirded by a "state-based risk management system" to one based on individual risk and responsibility (Sa'ar 2016). Few talked, however, about how among these solo mothers were women who had left their homes or ended a relationship in a bid to remove men's intimate partner violence from their children's lives or their own.

Over the next decade, the neoliberal presumption that marriage or work would relieve women and families of crushing poverty grew stronger. Finance Minister Yair Lapid (Yesh Atid) defended another round of cuts to family benefits arguing in a Facebook post, "It has been proven repeatedly that child allowances do not get people out of poverty. They perpetuate poverty. There is only one thing that allows families to get out of poverty—that is work" (*Ynet* 2013). Lowering child allowances was the policy stick the Ministry of Welfare chose to use to encourage poor people to have fewer children—a future-oriented decision to be sure, but one that did not help to house, feed, and clothe the children already brought into the world.

The tremendous shift in fiscal policy over time from a state with social welfare supports to a winner-takes-all market-based global economy, layered onto a still uneven domestic infrastructure, and rising cost of living, has trapped women at home, and limited women's mobility within and outside of intimate relationships at the economic margins, particularly Mizrahi women, among others. Stratification structures the lives of separated or divorced (formerly) battered women living in poverty. Echoing how battered women talk about walking on eggshells around men who batter them, Smadar Lavie argues, "The state welfare bureaucracy [is] a system of torture for its single Mizrahi mother clients. . . . The success [a Mizrahi single mother] finds as she moves through bureaucratic time-space is dependent upon the Divinity of Chance, the serendipity overseeing any bureaucratic encounter. If she accomplishes any of her goals at a bureau, it is akin to a miracle. The mother does not know, and has no way of knowing, which actions correlate with success or failure" (Lavie 2014, 18, 82). Indeed, social welfare policies are typically fashioned by those whose lives will not be affected by their outcome, while the experiences and needs of those affected most dearly by such policies are left out of the policy-making process (Segal 2016).

The contraction of the Israeli social welfare state includes the intentional shift of responsibility for human security away from the state to those at the economic margins. In the economic context of neoliberalism, single mothers have been demonized targets of social welfare policy reforms (Schneider and Ingram 2005) that are based on assumptions that all able-bodied individuals should have a job, and that moving them from "welfare to work" would alleviate poverty. However, Israel has a mixed record when it comes to valuing solo mothers and the battered women among them.

GLOBAL LABOR FLOWS OF NEW VULNERABILITIES

The political decision to turn away from a more robust safety net and shift toward a "Startup Nation" with a globally desirable homegrown Silicon Wadi (Ministry of Finance 2011, 6; Senor and Singer 2009) has been a success from the point of view of the "roughly 20 families [who] control companies that account for half the total value of Israel's stock market," but not from the perspective of those still waiting for a trickle-down effect from this success (Krugman 2015). Longtime investor and entrepreneur Yossi Vardi observes that only nine percent of the Israeli public "is enjoying the fruits of the high-tech party" (Orpaz 2015). The earning power of entrepreneurs and the reach of corporations have been improved by Israel's embrace of neoliberalism, but the global flow of capital requires and enables people to cross borders as well. Despite how well Israel guards its physical borders, the nearly borderless market of the global economy has proven quite powerful.

Israel is now home to tens of thousands of noncitizens who have come to live and work, and their legal statuses range from authorized and unauthorized to juridical limbo (Oksenberg 2009). The state invited some of these noncitizen migrants as authorized guest workers. Others have crashed the party, so to speak, in pursuit of marriage (i.e., non-Jewish spouses); money is what attracts most unauthorized laborers who have been criminally trafficked or recruited via employment brokers, who have overstayed their tourist visa or work permit, or who have arrived independently. Still others arrive in the pursuit of physical survival (i.e., refugees and asylum seekers). The state encourages the labor contribution of migrant workers when it fits business sector needs, and invests heavily in recruiting Jewish immigrants to become citizens.

At the same time, Israel also seeks to prevent the permanent settlement of both authorized and unauthorized guest workers, as well as refugees, in order to protect the Jewish character of the state (Rosenhek 2000). Israel's Minister of Interior in 2010, Eli Yishai, argued: "Absorption of foreign and dangerous non-Jews, infiltrators and other asylum seekers is what will bring havoc on us all" (Shoham 2013a, 191). MK Miri Regev (Likud) in May 2012 referred to asylum seekers as a "cancer in the body" of the country. Their antagonistic attitude toward non-Jewish residents as part of the new fabric of society is not exceptional in Israel or elsewhere (Raijman and Semyonov 2004; Kamin 2013). Caught within these contradictions are noncitizen migrant women, whose border crossing engenders new forms of vulnerability to domestic violence. Because of policies associated with their noncitizenship status, migrant women in Israel uniquely contend with domestic violence, among other forms of exploitation and violence they may have endured before they arrived and while they live or work in Israel.

Authorized/Unauthorized Foreign Workers

Foreign workers have sustained Israel's economy for decades, and state policies, reinforced by public sentiment, expect them to be guests who do not overstay their welcome. Palestinians from the West Bank and Gaza were the state's first "guest workers" after the 1967 War: noncitizens crossing a border to do short-term labor, as both authorized and unauthorized workers (Bartram 1998). Palestinian women also labored in Israel, mostly as domestic workers or in informal micro-businesses. Notably during this period, domestic violence was not yet considered a social problem. When the Intifada started two decades later in December 1987, Palestinian labor became intermittingly unreliable because of Israeli checkpoints and border closures and Palestinian worker strikes.

The post–Intifada Oslo Agreement closure of the border prevented most Palestinian laborers from working in Israel, so employers demanded an alternative source of workers from the government (Rosenhek 2000).[19] The government acquiesced and authorized worker permits, mostly in agriculture and construction. According to official figures, the combined number of authorized and unauthorized foreign workers rose from 110,000 in 1995 to a high of 243,000 in 2001, at the start of the Second Intifada (Drori 2009, 53). Periodically, the government commits to reducing the number of foreign workers to help low-skilled Israelis find work. Yet, the state has acquiesced more than once to employers' demands for cheap labor, and continues issuing work permits (Amir 2002; Winer 2014). Today, unauthorized foreign workers who originally entered on a tourist visa number about 91,000 (about 60 percent from the FSU), and 101,000 permitted foreign workers from 100 countries live in Israel, about 70 percent from Asia and 27 percent from Europe (primarily the FSU); their average age is just over thirty-eight (CBS 2015). These permitted workers include domestic caregivers, a job title dominated by noncitizen migrant women.[20]

The public face of the 60,000 or so guest worker–domestic caregivers in Israel is the winner of Israel's inaugural *X Factor* television music competition, Rose Fostanes, who had already worked for six years when she won the first season of the most popular Israeli television show in 2014 (*Haaretz* 2014). An out lesbian from the Philippines, she was given special dispensation to end her caregiving work and stay in the country to pursue a singing career (*Haaretz* 2014; Stern 2015; *Times of Israel*, 2014). Unfortunately, her stage life was a nonstarter, and Fostanes now faces possible deportation, although as of April 2016, she remains in Israel (Stern 2015; Esmaquel 2016).

Encouraged by progressive welfare policies that cover in-home care for people with disabilities and the elderly (Drori 2009, 90), caregivers are the largest contingent of foreign workers in Israel. They are part of the growing globalization of domestic work and the overall feminization of migration (Hondagneu-Sotelo 2003). Women pushed out of their home countries by IMF-structured austerity budgets, recessionary conditions, or low wages are pulled to Israel's higher wages by its labor recruitment efforts or word-of-mouth (Raijman, Schammah-Gesser, and Kemp 2003). Filipina caregivers replace higher paid public employees or unpaid labor formerly provided by wives and adult children who have entered the workforce (Kolker 2015).

Several policies that seek to prevent noncitizen migrant workers from "taking root" in Israel directly inform domestic violence: prohibition of mothering and marriage, and the "binding" nature of the contract.[21] The binding nature of the work permit means that a caregiver is tied to a specific employer, which creates a dependency of the worker on that employer, who can hold passports, withhold pay, or threaten a caregiver with violence. Should a caregiver arrive or become pregnant during her work permit in Israel, the child has limited rights, and the worker's stay in Israel is capped at sixty-three months (Kav LaOved 2010, 2015; Shkolnik 2015). This is an improvement over the original policy, mandating that caregivers who gave birth while in Israel must either leave the country with their baby within three months or send the baby home to be cared for by someone else; otherwise, their work permit would have been revoked (Kav LaOved 2010).[22]

The marriage and family policy aspires as well to prevent noncitizen mothers from settling down in Israel. Foreign workers in Israel cannot bring first-degree family members with them, nor can family visit them; family members cannot secure work permits at the same time, to avoid family reunification. Additionally,

> The Interior Ministry's reading of the procedure prohibiting family members from immigrating together into Israel is very broad and flexible, and is extended to any intimate relationships between migrant workers formed in Israel. This means that when two migrant workers meet in Israel and enter a relationship, they too become, in the eyes of the Interior Ministry, "first degree family members" in violation of their visa conditions, and hence legitimate targets for detention and deportation. (Kav LaOved 2010, 13)

The broad and flexible application of this policy makes foreign workers even more vulnerable to gender violence. Being physically removed from a spouse or partner back home does not preclude long-distance intimidation and abuse, particularly related to remittances and child rearing. Caregivers who work in the homes of their employers are vulnerable to sexual harassment and assault, and/or they may form intimate relationships with an employer or a member of the employer's family. Prohibition against relationships with another migrant worker or the structure of the workplace or work hours may unintentionally make an intimate relationship with an Israeli more attractive.

Noncitizen/Non-Jewish Spouse

The Ministry of Aliyah and Immigrant Absorption welcomes Jewish immigrants from around the world, who are encouraged to "make aliyah" with the help of a *sal klita*, or basket of absorption benefits. Benefits include cash, rent subsidy, health coverage, language study, mortgage discount, and tax and customs relief (Ministry of Aliyah and Immigrant Absorption 2016). Non-Jewish people can migrate to Israel as spouses of Jewish Israelis. They are considered noncitizens until their legal status has been finalized, which can take up to five years. But there is a group of noncitizen spouses of Israelis who have no opportunity to apply for citizenship. Because of fear of establishing a back-door pathway to a de facto "right of return," Palestinians from the West Bank and Gaza have been barred since 2002 from legally (re)unifying with Israeli spouses. These unauthorized Palestinians married to Israelis lack the social and political rights otherwise accorded to citizens, forming what is known as a "mixed status family." Mixed status is a notoriously fertile context for domestic violence because of the risks involved in reporting and seeking resources (Salcido and Adelman 2004; Erez, Adelman, and Gregory 2009). According to Shahar Shoham of Physicians for Human Rights, an estimated 20,000 Palestinian women currently live in Israel, who are all the more vulnerable to domestic violence because of their permanent unauthorized status, which constrains their geographic mobility and interactions with agents of the state (Moshe 2013). Palestinian women citizens married to unauthorized spouses face similar vulnerabilities.[23]

The story of a noncitizen migrant named Isabella who entered the country legally as the spouse of an Israeli demonstrates another domestic violence effect on women of the borderless marketplace.[24] Isabella is an Orthodox Christian woman from Romania who worked in her home country in a factory owned by an Israeli.[25] The factory owner's brother met Isabella when he was visiting in Romania. They wed there in 2004 and then moved to Jaffa, near Tel Aviv. Isabella did not realize that her new husband was a heroin addict. After he agreed to treatment, she became pregnant, which is when his physical abuse began, resulting in her going to the ER repeatedly. When she was ready, she reported him to the police. The husband was placed on house arrest; Isabella was sent to a battered women's shelter in Haifa. "She was alone in Israel, speaking little Hebrew and illiterate, in a city far from the area where she had lived, pregnant, and covered with bruises left on her body by her husband" (Vilnai 2009). Despite having secured a divorce and wanting to return to her family in Romania, Isabella cannot: her baby has no passport, the baby's father will not give his approval, and his family took out a restraining order barring her from leaving the country. Although Isabella has sole custody, she fears being deported without her daughter. In the meantime, as a noncitizen, she has limited social rights and no political rights.

Isabella's story is not unique in that men who travel abroad for business or family visits may meet someone they wish to marry, or the couple will meet on the Internet. When the prospective spouse is not Jewish, however, marriage laws combined with domestic violence bring with it additional challenges to a woman's mobility, livelihood, and motherhood. The Ministry of Social Affairs reports that "eight percent of women staying in shelters for battered women in 2013 and 2014 lacked residency permits"; according to Yael Gold, executive director of a shelter run by No to Violence, "most women without residency permits never make it to the shelters because they are locked up and don't know how to reach them. . . ." and the ones who do, have "no identity card, no ability to work, no money, no medical insurance" (Rozovsky 2016). The Interior Ministry is aware of these challenges, as is the inter-ministerial committee that hears humanitarian requests for citizenship, the Knesset's Public Petitions Committee, along with municipal social services, law enforcement, lawyers, and shelter staff, all of whom hear, too, from noncitizen battered women whose marriages (and mothering) cross the border.

Some frontline workers refer to women who were b(r)ought from Eastern Europe, Africa, or the Far East by Israeli men for marriage as "mail-order brides."[26] In "dozens of these cases, husbands registered cautionary notes at the Interior Ministry, stating that they are not certain that the women married them out of love but rather out of interest in obtaining Israeli citizenship" (Lis 2013a). Haifa District Court Judge Ron Shapiro argues against monitoring the relationship to be sure it is sincere before granting the wife legal status; doing so, "the Interior Ministry's policy becomes an instrument in the hands of violent husbands who impose their wishes on their wives, who depend on them in order to remain here" (Lis 2013a). Jewish immigrants to Israel from the FSU also threaten to expel from the country their non-Jewish wives from the FSU (Tartakovsky and Mezhibovsky 2012). Because marriage does not automatically confer legal status to a non-Jewish immigrant, and because the spouse who holds Israeli citizenship must submit a request for a change in status for the new spouse, non-Jewish women who cross state borders for love or work, or both, face an enhanced risk of domestic violence and decreased access to state-based resources or personal mobility.

Trafficked Women

Another group of women made vulnerable to gender violence, including domestic violence, are those involved in the global sex trade. The movement of women that commonly involves smuggling across or illegal crossing of state borders for the purpose of sexual labor is considered as a type of "human trafficking." It is a worldwide phenomenon exacerbated by fast-growing economic inequality and increased ease of communication and mobility. Trafficking reflects international labor migration patterns where individuals facing impoverishment and discrimination seek out economic opportunities elsewhere. This illicit trade of sexual labor is navigated primarily by criminal networks in originating countries that coordinate transit through mediating countries on the way to destination countries (Bertone 2000). It was recognized as a social problem as early as 1949 in the UN Convention on the Suppression of the Traffic in Persons and the Exploitation of the Prostitution of Others, which was revised in 1994 to define trafficking as a criminal enterprise. Motivated by the possibility of moral and material sanctions, Israel signed the UN Convention against Transnational Organized Crime Palermo Protocol in 2001 and ratified it in 2008.

Israel gained worldwide notoriety in 2001 when the United States categorized it as a Tier 3 destination country that inadequately addressed human trafficking—based on a three-tier system, where Tier 3 is the least desirable.[27] Its ranking aligns with Israel's position within the global economy, which opened its borders not only to high-tech innovations and angel investors but also to sexual laborers from around the world. Along with stigma, placement in the third tier carries the potential of economic sanctions from the United States. Thus, under pressure to clear its name (Kelley and Simmons 2015), within a year Israel took steps necessary for promotion in 2002 to Tier 2, including establishment of a Parliamentary Inquiry Committee on the Trafficking of Women.[28] Within a decade, Israel joined Tier 1, the most desirable rating.

Yet, when attention was drawn domestically to the problem, state representatives claimed the state was victimized by the illegal workers and blamed prostitution on other foreign workers (S. Herzog 2008).[29] For example, "At a conference held at Beit Berl College in 2001, Israel Police Commander Yossi Sidbon, head of the Tel Aviv police district, explained why trafficking in women had grown: 'In the Tel Aviv area today there are about 200,000 foreign workers and tens of thousands of Palestinians who come from the [Palestinian] Authority. What can you do?—They just need sex services'" (Dayan in Levenkron and Dahan 2003, 36). This perspective contradicts the state's policy of welcoming authorized, noncitizen workers, mostly an all-men labor force in construction and agriculture from Thailand, Romania, and the West Bank; it ignores the existence of prostitution in Israel since its establishment as a state; and it downplays Israel's open door to immigrants from FSU, which made it a prospective target for Israeli and European traffickers. Although many women were brought to Israel under false pretenses (e.g., guaranteed employment as au pairs), women from the FSU, who were motivated to leave by the economic disruption, gendered unemployment, and loss of a safety net associated with the fall of state socialism and the turn to global capitalism, also were pulled by the high demand of and access to Israel's sex industry (Bridger, Kay, and Pinnick 1996; Levenkron and Dahan 2003; Weisz-Rind 2000; USAID 1999; Vandenberg 1997). The "scorecard diplomacy" embedded within the anti-trafficking law to impose moral sanctions on states by assessing and ranking their comparative behavior worked well in the Israeli case in that the numbers of women trafficked for the sex industry diminished greatly (Kelley and Simmons 2015).

Trafficked women face issues related to domestic violence similar to those associated with women immigrants with unauthorized or ambiguous legal status. Women trafficked from the FSU often experience domestic violence in their country of origin and various forms of sexual abuse during their journey to Israel (Hacker and Cohen 2012, 61). Women travel on forged papers, are smuggled into the country, and overstay tourist visas. Once they arrive, some have identity and travel documents held by pimps. Some women work in brothels and most in "discreet apartments." Led by the chair of the Knesset Committee for the Advancement of the Status of Women, MK Zahava Galon (Meretz), a component of Israel's response to human trafficking was the establishment in 2004 of Ma'agan Shelter by the Ministry of Social Services and Ministry of Internal Security.[30] It was to serve as a rehabilitative space to house women exiting prostitution after being trafficked, rather than being detained and before being deported, settled, or remaining unauthorized in Israel. The gatekeeping mechanism for admission to Ma'agan shelter is referral from the police.

Women working and living without authorization have sex, develop short- and long-term intimate relationships, and are sexually assaulted. This means that some will have children and simultaneously struggle with domestic violence, possible loss of motherhood, and work-related violence, before, during, and after participating in prostitution. A woman who stayed in the Ma'agan shelter experienced this triad of pain. Roslana entered Israel on a passport forged by Ukrainian traffickers.[31] She lacked legal residency status and worked without a permit as a prostitute without a pimp. "She describes the [Israeli father of her child] as violent, probably a drug user, who enjoys partying. He has four children from different women, two of whom live with him," but he refused to acknowledge paternity of Roslana's son for four years, until the boy urgently needed medical care (Hacker and Cohen 2012, 135). At that point, so that the boy could receive treatment, he agreed to a paternity test in exchange for custody of the child. The local welfare service office did not help her visit her son.

Trafficked women's experiences of constrained motherhood and domestic violence is related to a myriad of legal and economic limitations. A research report prepared for submission to the US Department of State by the Hotline for Refugees and Migrants noted the complications of multiple layers of law and policy that were involved for women facing personal status issues along with their legal status:

> The [shelter's] attorneys also provide representation in alimony claims for children born to a victim of trafficking and an Israeli man. . . . Personal status claims are not covered by the legal aid eligibility of trafficking victims, and assistance is provided for the residents of Ma'agan Shelter under the terms of the regulations enacted following the UN Convention on Civil Proceedings in Civil and Commercial Matters between Citizens of Different Countries. (Hacker and Cohen 2012, 41)

Though the number of women traveling to Israel as trafficked sex workers may be lower, those who have remained, with or without permission of the state, reflect the political economy of domestic violence.

Over time, the anti-trafficking campaign appears to have been successful. Israel has maintained its Tier 1 status. Yet prostitution continues.[32] Perhaps policing or prosecution of prostitution has been pulled back. More likely, either the number of women trafficked for or working without legal status in prostitution has diminished or they have learned to be less detectable by the authorities. An investigation argues the latter:

> Sexual escort sites suggest there may be an upgrading of trafficked prostitution into better quality of service, merging with local call-girls and using better facilities, and the decentralization of these women in many locations in the affluent northern urban area of Tel Aviv with less visible "delivery" outdoor (outcall) services. Therefore, [it] is more plausible that the "pretty Russia whores" have not vanished from Israel but "VIP discrete ladies" have simply disappeared from the streets. (Cavaglion 2010, 208)

Without knowing the exact figures or whereabouts of trafficked women, since it was opened in 2004, the population of Ma'agan shelter observed a shift in its residents, from mainly hosting trafficked sex workers from the FSU to more recently serving as a temporary home for women trafficked for slavery: women foreign workers who arrive on a tourist visa and then are exploited by employers, as well as African refugees (Hacker and Cohen 2012, 62–65). The distinction between a trafficked person and a refugee is porous; for example, some asylum seekers from Africa were trafficked into Israel after surviving Bedouin-run torture camps in the Sinai Desert (Rozen and Kuttner 2016).

Refugees and Asylum Seekers

A new category of noncitizen migrant emerged in Israel when Muslim and Orthodox Christian African refugees began to arrive in their flight from state and paramilitary violence in Darfur and the southern Sudan region, and Eritrea. Catapulted by new European restrictions on immigration, they walked from East Africa to the Sinai Desert by paying smugglers or being trafficked, and then crossed into Israel at its border with Egypt. Migration rates peaked in 2010 when approximately 1,000 asylum seekers arrived each month (Nakash et al. 2014). By March 2015, according to the Ministry of the Interior, 45,711 African refugees (73 percent Eritrean and 19 percent Sudanese) were living in Israel (Rozen 2015a, 7).

When they arrive, refugees, or infiltrators, as the state officially refers to them,[33] face a bewildering array of wrenching poverty, detention, confusing policies, and official pressure to leave. As a whole, Israelis exhibit xenophobia toward these noncitizens as well and scoff at the transformation of south Tel Aviv into what they call "south Sudan." However, in contrast to trafficked women, whose visibility and stigma the state took steps to avoid, the government has treated migrants seeking asylum from Sudan and Eritrea more like criminals, releasing some to physically live in the state, but with a temporary visa that requires bureaucratic quarterly renewal and does not permit them to work, attend school, or receive medical care or social services (Kamin 2015).

Unauthorized foreign nationals can be detained in one of four facilities: Saharonim Prison (built in 2007 expressly to hold African detainees, with a holding capacity in 2015 up to 3,000), Holot Detention Center (opened in 2013 across from Saharonim to house African detainees), Givon Prison, and Yahalom Detention Facility at Ben Gurion Airport, where detainees are housed prior to their deportation (Rozen and Kuttner 2016, 13–14). Holot, the largest facility, reached its capacity of 3,360 male refugees in December 2015 (14). Refugee requests for relief or asylum are mostly ignored. "More than 90 percent of [asylum claims] come from Eritrea, Sudan and the Congo, but Israel has recognized fewer than 1 percent of [them], and since 2009, less than 0.15 percent—the lowest rate in the Western world" (Pileggi 2015). Those who wish to leave have the choice to "self-deport" to Rwanda or Uganda, or suffer indeterminate imprisonment.[34] Israel reports that 6,400 such "infiltrators" left of their own accord in 2014 (CBS 2015). Refugees living in town can be summoned to Holot, "excluding those who have a wife and/or children they provide for in Israel" (Rozen 2015a, 11).[35] Because of the protracted and controversial legal dispute over the harsh conditions of their detention, the global face of the African refugee community may be male, but upward of 7,000 women refugees live in Israel, too.

African refugees who live in juridical limbo—couples, singles, families, and children—have settled into enclaves mostly near the bus station in south Tel Aviv. Like many women immigrants, African women refugees work in the lowest of low-skilled jobs and share resources while juggling childcare and a new language (Kav LaOved 2014). Refugee women in Tel Aviv can now turn to the grassroots Eritrean Women's Community Center, which opened in July 2012 in partnership with its sister organization Release Eritrea.[36] It doubles as a child daycare center, and brings women together for peer support and celebratory activities, self-development and skill-building classes, and sessions on workers' rights and family planning. Founding director Zebib Sultan was inspired to open the center because of what she experienced in her own life.[37] Sultan and her husband shared a two-bedroom apartment with another couple and four other people. "I always saw her crying," Zebib said. 'She told me it was because she missed her family, because of her financial problems, but I got the sense that there was something else, that she was afraid of her husband" (Lazareva 2013). It took some time for Sultan to discover the husband of the other couple beat his wife every day.

Despite the impossibility of tracking the "actual" rate of domestic violence in any community, local activists selected this issue as their first priority among so many other harsh living conditions worthy of attention, even when few were originally willing to discuss it. Volunteer Habtum Mehari, also an Eritrean refugee, explained, "It's the most pressing issue in the community today" (ibid.). Cofounder Sanait Kidana estimates that 70 percent of Eritrean husbands batter their wives and that she "couldn't listen to any more stories about murdered women, domestic violence, threats and harassment" (Lee 2012). Sultan informed the Knesset Special Committee on Problems Facing Foreign Workers and the Committee for Public Petitions that domestic violence is a critical problem facing refugee women, along with pressure and threats from husbands' family and friends not to report to authorities or withdraw complaints to the police, sometimes communicated via phone calls from relatives in Eritrea (Moshe 2013). Although this kind of pressure is not uncommon, the high stakes involved are unique to asylum seekers: men arrested or jailed for domestic violence risk long-term detention or deportation.

Not unlike Ethiopian immigrants in Israel, Eritrean and Sudanese women refugees who are battered must contend with the violence they endured when traveling to Israel, changes to the family's gendered division of labor, loss of intervention from extended family and communal resources, poverty, social discrimination, and generational gaps between parents and children. Refugee battered women also grapple with the uncertainty of their asylum claims, threats of deportation, lack of access to health care or other social rights, workplace exploitation, and the unknown future for themselves and their families.

NATIONAL SECURITY VERSUS SOCIAL JUSTICE

Government leaders take much pride in the state's official endorsement of the equality of all its citizens, but the reality behind the rhetoric is, as always, more complex (Ajzenstadt 2002). The roots of this stratification are located not in a "war economy" but in the political economy of a state "that has a high, continuous stake in militarism" (Carmi and Rosenfeld 2010, 389). This is reflected in the state's budget. Management of public revenues and expenditures is a central mandate of any state. And, like many states boasting advanced economies, the overall size of Israel's budget has grown over time. "Unlike most other welfare states," however, this growth "has taken place alongside an ongoing political and military conflict" (Gal and Bar 2000, 577). Israel's war footing existed both before and after the state's turn to economic liberalization in the mid-1980s. Defense spending may have diminished from a high point of one-third of government expenditures after the 1973 War, but in macroeconomic terms, national security has remained a significant outlay of the state budget (Bassock 2013a and 2013b).

Figures for defense spending are not completely transparent, supplements are added after the official budget has been passed or are assigned partially to the subsequent year's budget, ministries and media present conflicting numbers, and nomenclature can make comparisons difficult. Nevertheless, raw budget numbers make sense only when they are contextualized within a larger spending framework. The OECD reports that Israel—a member since September 2010—allocated 14.7 percent of its government expenditures on defense and 25.9 percent on social protection in 2011, in contrast to OECD averages of 3.6 percent and 35.6 percent, respectively (OECD 2013a, and see World Bank 2014b, 2014c).[38] Said another way, Israeli spending "on defense in 2013 amounted to 5.6 percent of GDP, or $2,037 per person (Bassock 2015). In comparison, according to a senior researcher at the Institute for National Security Studies, "only the United States approached those figures, spending 3.8 percent of GDP on its military, or $20,023 per capita," (ibid.). Israel's overall defense budget would occupy an even greater proportion of state expenditures if the United States were not underwriting about one-fifth of it (CIA 2016).

The security-centric economy includes supplementary appropriations directed to handle multiyear military campaigns, such as the First and Second Intifada, and three significant military actions in the Gaza Strip between 2008 and 2014. According to the Adva Center's analysis, "Between 1989 and 2010, the Ministry of Defense received special appropriations totaling NIS 45 billion," a sum larger than the state's investment in K-16 education in 2009 (Swirsky 2010, 20). For example, Israel's Operation Cast Lead, fought for three weeks during the winter of 2008–2009, cost about NIS 5 billion (over $1 billion in US dollars)—not including the loss of tourism dollars, investment monies, economic activity, and workplace productivity—and an additional NIS 1 billion to fortify buildings in the adjacent region (Swirsky 2010). The Israel Central Bank explained that the NIS 7 billion Operation Protective Edge, the state's fifty-day war with Gaza in the summer of 2014, was paid for without exceeding the budget deficit target "but only by cutting public spending," and noted that if the state wishes to stay within its budget deficit targets while still meeting defense costs, the government will have to raise tax revenues in the next few years by about 13 billion NIS, which is equivalent to $3.6 billion in US dollars (Reuters 2015).

According to the Public Knowledge Workshop (2016) and the Adva Center's most recent analysis (Swirski and Hoffmann-Dishon 2015), the total Ministry of Defense budget was close to NIS 61 billion in 2012, the budget for 2013 began at NIS 52.6 billion but ended up closer to NIS 62.2 billion because of an approved supplement, and the defense budget for 2014 grew from an original allocation of NIS 51 to nearly NIS 70 billion; the draft budget for 2015 was a request for close to NIS 57 billion, although elections were called before it was approved, so the two-year budget agreed upon by the ministries of defense and finance in November 2015 allocated NIS 60.1 billion for 2016 (about USD $15.5 billion). The Defense Ministry noted that, out of the total defense budget in 2014, the IDF budget was NIS 26.05 billion, and was to have decreased to NIS 22.4 billion in the draft budget for 2015. In 2015, IDF Chief of Staff, Gadi Eisenkot, proposed a five-year budget for the military at an annual level of NIS 30 billion (about $7.8 billion in US dollars), the IDF's largest ever (G. Cohen 2015). Multiyear planning may provide a patina of predictability, but the defense budget remains entitled to multiple forms of growth over time.

The state's political economy priorities are based not only on explicit outlays to the ministry of defense, but also to indirect costs associated with Israel's military control over Palestinians in the territories. In addition to funds allocated to the IDF, for example, the state invests monies in the development of infrastructure (local administration, roads, water, electricity, industrial zones, etc.), tax incentives, subsidies, and basic services for Israel's settlements over the Green Line—e.g., housing, health, education, and security (Bornstein 2002). It also expends funds to build and maintain the Separation Wall and to withdraw, resettle, and compensate Israeli residents displaced from territories such as Sinai and Gaza. It is estimated that, between 1970 and 2008, the state invested NIS 381 billion in the occupied territories (Hever 2010, 68). In turn, however, development towns, established to secure Israel's pre-1967 borders, have remained on the economic periphery, lacking infrastructure and economic activity, thereby exacerbating the vulnerability of geographically marginal communities.[39]

The security economy also has a multiplier effect for individuals, families, and businesses that benefit from their service in or financial association with the military or defense-related industries (see Chapter 4 for a breakdown of who serves in the IDF). Early on, the state looked to the IDF as a national education institution that would facilitate cultural assimilation; it also is touted as a pathway to economic security for those on the margins. The Ministry of Defense provides generous bridge pensions to its retirees and benefits to veterans with disabilities (Gal and Bar 2000). IDF experience leads to employment opportunities, including public or private work earmarked as requiring security clearance (Swirski, Konur-Attias, and Etkin 2002; S. Swirski 2010, 2015). Until recent reforms, only families with military veterans qualified for various education and housing subsidies, and child allowances (Rosenhek 2011). As a result of economic liberalization, newly privatized for-profit companies and start-ups now own defense-driven research and development whose innovations, including expertise in security services, are then offered back to both global and domestic markets, including the Ministry of Defense (Bichler and Nitzan 1996; Hever 2010, 53). More than just government allocations to manage defense efforts, security plays multiple roles in Israel: as a centrifugal ideological force for national unity, as a cultural tool for socialization, and as an economic engine and career builder.

Until recently, dominant public discourse has rarely included criticism of the central place of defense in the state's economy, the number and length of its wars and military action, or the loss of life incurred through military service. Constituent groups such as Palestinians or feminist peace activists who *do* point to their moral and economic costs are dismissed as disloyal citizens. In contrast, social justice groups seeking to ameliorate economic inequality, and to attract the widest audience for their message, intentionally do *not* link the effects of the security economy on the growing cost of their everyday lives (e.g., the summer 2003 solo mothers protest, and the Summer 2011 tent protest) (Lavie 2014).

Political success generally hinges on a party's orientation to national security, with consideration of basic needs and quality of life coming up short: a classic butter versus guns scenario. A "graduate" of the social protests in 2011, and then political up-and-comer MK Stav Shaffir (Labor) has garnered a mix of opprobrium and approbation for criticizing from the inside of the government how the state allocates its resources: favoring settlements over social justice, she claims, both in terms of the amount of funds and in the process used to transfer them. After securing a Knesset seat in 2013, she argued, "In the end, it all comes down to the budget. . . . How the budget is allocated determines whether there is equality and social justice in this country" (Maltz 2015b). Taking note of opaque transfers to settlements, she has called not only for transparency but also for these resources to be returned to Israel: "The government keeps this overfunding a secret from the public, because what will they think in Be'er Sheva, Haifa or Jerusalem when they find out that across the Green Line they get houses, summer camps and public buildings for free, at the expense of the rest of Israel's citizens?" (Lis 2014). Despite the limited number of colleagues who were present to hear her "Real Zionism" Knesset speech on January 21, 2015, in response to a discussion on raising the minimum wage, its YouTube video went viral within and beyond Israel's contested borders:

> Don't preach to us about Zionism, because real Zionism means dividing the budget equally among all the citizens of the country. Real Zionism is taking care of the weak. Real Zionism is solidarity, not only in battle, but in everyday life. To keep each other safe. That's what it is to be an Israeli, that is Zionism. To be concerned about the future of the citizens

of this country . . . and you are taking it and destroying it. . . . You forget about the Negev and the Galil [economic peripheries in the south and the north] in order to transfer NIS 1.2 billion to the settlements in bonuses.

Outsiders, too, such as the OECD, have noticed problems with the macroeconomic model of smaller government and lower public spending, without either adjusting allocations to defense or addressing the high levels of poverty and income inequality:

> For many years, [Israeli] governments had prioritised not only debt reduction and income-tax cuts but also reduced public spending by combining deficit targets with a very tight lid on outlays. . . . However, the sizeable debt-servicing costs . . . plus the large defence budget . . . still have to be accommodated by some combination of greater taxation and lower civilian spending . . . [but] civilian public spending has long been parsimonious and is currently among the lowest levels in the OECD area as a share of GDP. . . . Recognising that public spending could not be reasonably pushed much lower, a slightly softer version of the expenditure ceiling has applied to budgets since 2011. . . . And, in 2011 the authorities abandoned multi-year schedules of cuts in rates of corporate and personal income tax (the latter concentrated in the upper rates of tax). In part this was a response to political pressure arising from the tent protests for "capital" to carry a greater share of the tax burden, but it also reflected recognition that the benefits of tax-rate cuts (principally second-round effects on private investment and consumption) had diminished over time. (OECD 2013b, 14)

Said plainly, the OECD argues that the state's "parsimonious" commitment to public health, education, and welfare and its continued large investment into security are undermining its economic functioning and stability. Although the glass ceiling curtails middle class women's economic advancement, the state's political economic stance is the "sticky floor that keeps so many women glued to poverty" (Rosen 1994; Berheide 1992).

Yet Prime Minister Netanyahu in his bid for reelection in 2015 argued that guns still must be prioritized over butter: "We're talking about housing prices and cost of living. I do not forget about life itself, living," he said in a tweet. "The greatest challenge standing before us and our lives as Israeli citizens and of this state is the threat of Iran being armed with a nuclear weapon" (*Times of Israel*, 2015a).

In the lead up to the national election on May 17, 2015, called early by Netanyahu himself, the Likud candidate focused public attention on Iran as its number one threat. Then, on election morning, with polls predicting a close finish between political party rivals Likud and Zionist Union, and in a last ditch effort to get out his base to vote, Netanyahu publicly accused his political rivals—the left—of tainting the election outcome by bussing Arabs "in droves" to the polls, thereby reinforcing the notion that a fifth of Israel's citizens constitute a dangerous fifth column. However, a member of the prime minister's voter base, Yossi Levy, a Sephardi fifty-year-old lifelong Likudnik, who works as a fruit and vegetable market shopkeeper in Haifa, explained why he planned to abandon the party in the election: "War is something we live with all the time, now all that interests me is keeping the refrigerator full" (Fisher-Ilan 2015). Echoing the shopkeeper's sentiments was a Channel 10 poll, reported in *Haaretz*, which found that 56 percent of voters identified cost of living and social welfare while only 27 percent identified security as the primary influence on their upcoming vote; the report was published under the headline "Nice Iran speech, Bibi, but what about the price of cottage cheese?" (Rosenberg 2015).[40]

CONCLUSION

Usually, only the most desperate, economically marginalized women seek protection from intimate partner violence in a shelter. Living in a shelter provides a woman (and her children) the most basic of survival needs: food and housing and temporary safety from physical danger. Shelters can be crowded, noisy, and stressful places. Most are located in repurposed spaces not intended to handle multiple families in crisis, living far from home. New buildings designed as shelters for battered women in Hadera (Sept. 2015) and planned for Rishon LeZion (2016) and Herzilya (2016) are notable exceptions.

Shelters are not always a welcome addition to a town or neighborhood. It took some time for the shelter's neighbors in Jerusalem, for example, to adjust to the new institution. WIZO's shelter in Ashdod was originally intended for Be'ersheva, the largest city in the southern part of the country, but its mayor rejected it outright. A shelter that had been slated to open in toney Maoz Aviv in northern Tel Aviv faced organized opposition from neighbors. In their legal bid to halt its construction, they complained about how the shelter would ruin the peace and quiet that characterized the neighborhood. Similarly, Taibe mayor Rafik Haj-Yehia rejected Minister of Welfare Ora Namir's shelter proposal because he felt it didn't fit the culture of his Arab town (the shelter didn't open, but he lost a chance to be appointed ambassador to Finland because of it). Yet, in other neighborhoods, I have seen how neighbors become protective of the building and its residents.

In the mid-1990s I volunteered weekly at a shelter in Haifa. I joined a cadre of mostly social work and psychology university students who provided after-school care for children. We played with them, helped with homework, and tried to ensure that they did not hurt themselves or others; a paid staff person supervised us. The shelter, an old, rambling building located in a working class neighborhood, had a dark staircase that led to the gated entrance. On my designated days, I would buzz at the steel gate. Often a child appeared demanding to know who I was, alternately smiling and yelling at me. I would wait until an adult unlocked the gate with the key that hung beyond my reach. When I closed the heavy gate behind me, the clanging noise reverberated in the empty hallway. Slamming shut, and locking automatically, it sounded like a dungeon door.

Inside the shelter, the cacophony continued. Women inside yelled back and forth to each other while cleaning the kitchen and main room, which doubled as dining room and lounge. When the weather was nice, we took the children to the museum or the park, but mostly we stayed inside, coloring, building blocks, or playing a modified game of soccer or basketball, which often turned into a mean game of dodgeball, bringing back gym-class nightmares. The children were devoted to the Power Rangers and practiced their martial artistry in front of the TV; with my luck, it was broadcast during my regular shift on Tuesday afternoons at four o'clock. (We often resorted to shutting off the television as a threat to impose order.) Afterward, the children were usually prepared to fight with anything that moved. The shelter was always full of mothers and their children.

The very existence of shelters and the changes they have undergone offer a window into the political economy of domestic violence. The contemporary shelter for battered women is a reincarnation of refuges built in the early modern period in Europe to rescue prostitutes and prevent "at risk" women from falling into immoral labor (S. Cohen 1992). This model aligns with the Israeli social work approach of removing at-risk youth (usually from impoverished families who have yet to culturally assimilate into Israeli standards) and placing them in residential group homes.

Today's shelters are where battered women find temporary asylum from domestic violence. Feminists in Israel borrowed the shelter model from the United Kingdom and the United States, countries with strong ties to Israel, where activists, academics, and government authorities have lived, studied, traveled, done business, and networked. Activists opened the first shelters because they found unacceptable the notion that a woman should have to live with an abusive man. The assumption was that shelters would be a short-term "time-out" for women to have "a quiet head" to regroup, experience a violence-free period of time, and decide their next steps. The number of shelters in Israel at first grew slowly, relying on volunteers, supplemented by local and international donations. Back in 1992, when the few existing shelters were turning away women every week, the Israel State Comptroller noted that Norway, a country with a comparable population of four million at the time, had forty-seven shelters (Fishkoff 1992).

Israel now has a total of fourteen shelters, depending on how you count: some claim thirteen; it could be fifteen if you include Ma'agan shelter, all of which serve a population numbering 8.3 million. Save for one exception, shelters are located in either primary or secondary urban locations where social services, work opportunities, and schools are most robust. Indeed, many women leaving shelter create new lives in the vicinity. Each shelter has its own history and personality, based on the ideological orientation of its staff and the demographics of its residents. While several shelters retain a feminist egalitarian-empowerment orientation, most others operate within a bureaucratic social services model (Rodriguez 1988). Once independent, all shelters are now regulated by the Ministry of Welfare and other government authorities. The demographic profile of shelter residents has shifted along with changes in who crosses Israel's border, with or without authorization.

What has not changed since the establishment of the first shelter in Israel nearly four decades ago is the need for some women to seek shelter from intimate partners. Shelter demographics have never proportionately aligned with population statistics in terms of age, nationality, ethnicity, religion, or immigration status, but they do reflect larger trends in the movement of people in Israeli society. Shelter has always been a last-ditch resource for women who have no other options: impoverished and dislocated women, regardless of their country of origin or religion.

During a visit to the battered women's crisis shelter in Haifa in December 2011, I noticed a decorated Christmas tree in the communal area of the house adjacent to the kitchen. Given the low percentage of Christians in the country, I was surprised to hear from shelter staff that many of the women and children residents celebrated the holiday. When I asked, a staff member described the current shelter residents and shared their annual report from 2010: about a third (34 percent) of the adult women residents were "native-born Israeli Jews," about a third (36 percent) were "Israeli Arabs," and about a third (30 percent) were "immigrants." The third designation "immigrants" (the Central Bureau of Statistics has used the phrase "immigrants since 1990") refers to women from the FSU (including a substantial number of Christians or women designated by the state as having no religion) and Ethiopia, and non-Jewish women who were foreign workers—authorized, unauthorized, in legal limbo, or trafficked—who have found their way to battered women's shelters.[41] Each woman in the shelter is situated within the political-economic context of differential citizenship. For other women not counted among shelter residents, this differential citizenship lessens shelter as an option.

A political economy of domestic violence reveals the accessibility, suitability, and usefulness of a shelter, depending on a community's encounters with the state. First, shelters were not developed from the ground up in ways that meet the needs of a diverse set of residents who have very different relationships to the state (although the exceptional Haifa Women's Crisis Shelter was from its origins designated as multicultural). This could be parsed as "culturally responsive" in terms of location, language, food, culturally knowledgeable or "insider" staff, and programming. Because shelters in Israel (or most anywhere) have not been designed by and for a range of women and because normative residential life is segregated, advocates have opened new shelters specifically targeting members of their own community: for example, shelters in Jerusalem and Bnei Brak for ultra-Orthodox Jewish women who would otherwise not have left their home or who feel more at ease doing so now with the blessing of religious authorities. Palestinian women, too, have created their own hotlines and shelters to ensure their fit.

Second, since their establishment, shelters for battered women have been labeled as foreign and dangerous entities associated with Western feminism and/or the Israeli state. This perception is parsed by men whose communities have the most contentious or marginal relationship with the state as threatening the family and men's power within it, including Palestinian Israelis, Ethiopian Israelis, and ultra-Orthodox Jewish Israelis (Faier 2013). Thus the niche or targeted approach also enhances the utility of shelters by countering their being framed as inappropriate or immoral resources for women.

Third, a sharp illustration further clarifies the ironies of differential citizenship and domestic violence. The Ministry of Social Services established an alternate, yet ineffective, shelter for Bedouin women in Be'er Sheva. Despite it being the largest city in the Negev, the city remained inaccessible to many rural Bedouins. The minister installed a male Bedouin sheikh as head of the shelter, which may have accorded it legitimacy but also likely deterred many women from using the shelter. The ministry staffed the shelter with a Jewish social worker who did not speak Arabic, which further alienated its target constituents. Research conducted by the NGO Itach-Maaki Women Lawyers for Social Justice on violence against Bedouin women in the south found that "95 percent of abused women expressed a lack of willingness to enter a shelter for battered women because of their shame and fear of the community's action toward them and their children for seeking shelter . . . for fear of their lives in absence of an effective system adapted to their culture that prevents the risk to their lives" (Itach-Maaki 2014, 8, 14). The state also is partly responsible for a Bedouin woman's contemporary domestic entrapment and her family's economic and social dislocation through forced settlement of her tribe, nonrecognition, or threatened demolition of her village or unwillingness to enforce anti-polygyny laws (Abu-Rabia-Queder 2007; Dahan-Kalev and LeFebvre, with El-Sana-Alh'jooj 2012). Differential citizenship has not only been a *producer* of the problem but also undermines the *solution* to the problem proffered by the state, constructing shelters as unsustainable for many women who live in the state's political economic margins. Rather than revealing connections between the state and domestic violence against Bedouin women, the problem is instead explained as a weakness of battered Bedouin women because of their lack of willingness to seek help from the state.

Fourth, because shelters have been integrated into the life of the state, they are subject to its surveillance and funding formulas. And timing is everything. Neoliberalization of the economy intensified just as the state began to heed calls from civil society (and pressure from within the government) to take on the social problem of domestic violence—in part, by investing through social welfare reforms in domestic violence services such as hotlines, shelters, transitional housing, and centers for the treatment and prevention of family violence, previously initiated and led by NGOs. Successive governments rhetorically have denounced domestic violence and, over the years, have increased funding that underwrites a large percentage of shelters' most basic needs, while requiring shelter staff to raise monies to "complete" the basic budget plus more funding (often from abroad) to provide any unanticipated, unapproved, or desired additional programing or materials (Konur 2000). This has led to the governmentalizing of domestic violence (Omanit 2003, 140); the state does not always deliver on even its promises of limited funds, and has shelter staff spending significant time raising funds and accounting for its revenues and expenses, as would any business. For example, on International Day for the Elimination of Violence against Women in 2009, Prime Minister Netanyahu visited a shelter for battered women and promised to allocate NIS 5 million to build new shelters and renovate existing shelters and to subsidize rent for women leaving shelters. However, even though that would have been an insufficient amount to fulfill those stated goals, a year later, none of the money had materialized (Weiler-Polak 2010).

The government has committed funds to the shelter system and to battered women who have spent time in and intend to exit from them and set up an independent life. However, once she begins that independent life ostensibly as a solo mother, she joins the rank and file of poor women who face a bleak job market, a rising cost of living, and state cuts to social supports. Among other marginalized groups, Mizrahi women have questioned the priorities of NGOs and state leaders who choose to isolate domestic violence from the web of inequality in which they exist (Dahan-Kalev 2001). Helping women victims of domestic violence, one at a time, has become a normative part of policing and social services. This is the embodiment of a political economy of domestic violence in Israel: understanding domestic violence as either an individual deviance based on poor communication skills and "bad choices," or a problem stemming from a culture of poverty, defined as either the inability to support oneself economically, or unwillingness to assimilate from one's so-called primitive heritage, all of which require treatment of the victim (and a recent government campaign urges men who batter to get individual treatment as well) (McDonald 2005).

Embedded prominently within the state's restructuring of the economy is an emphasis on individual responsibility and privatization of social services. Rarely discussed are the decisions to increase defense funding to protect the body politic while shrinking the size of social reinforcements that nourish the domestic body. The political economy of domestic violence that I have sketched here uncovers the dilemmas and contradictions experienced by battered women inherent within twenty-first century global capitalism.

6 | Reframing Domestic Violence and the State

As I NOTED IN CHAPTER 1, twenty-five years ago, I noticed a sticker for a rape crisis hotline on a bathroom stall door in the library at the Hebrew University of Jerusalem. The encounter resonated with me as an anthropologist-in-the-making. At the time, however, minimal fieldwork had been conducted intentionally on the topic of gender-based violence (Adelman 2010). Rather than change disciplines, I developed an interdisciplinary framework to study domestic violence that would retain the intellectual holism and attention to the construction of difference that attracted me to anthropology in the first place. Ultimately, it has led to this ethnographic analysis of the relationship between the state and domestic violence, where I have explored how domestic violence—its meaning, manifestations, and management—is mediated through central arenas of statecraft: the construction of national identity through the configuration of family law; the secure establishment and protection of domestic borders; and the prioritized allocation of state resources. In other words, I have illustrated how domestic violence intentionally or unintentionally "shows up" in the everyday life of the state, and vice versa.

The book is intended as a counter-narrative to troubling trends I have found within the research literature and within the framing and treatment of domestic violence in the field (Messing, Adelman, and Durfee 2012). First, this book balances the weaknesses endemic to large-scale survey research by rendering visible the everyday, phenomenological aspects of domestic violence as well as the nuanced ways people connect their experiences of intimate partner violence to other sociocultural institutions. Second, it avoids the constraints of legal or social service–based research—and victim blaming—by studying a broadly diverse population in a contextualized manner that incorporates rather than ignores their salient identities and material circumstances. Finally, rather than debate whether the state is a suitable solution for domestic violence, it considers how the cultural politics of the state itself shape domestic violence.

The case study reveals how domestic violence can be, unexpectedly, the product of and informed by what are typically labeled as political concerns: how a state defines itself and its status among other states, establishes sovereignty and defends its borders, forges its economy, and organizes its governance and legal systems. Thus, while I welcome the growing critique of our overreliance

on the state to solve the problem of domestic violence—because of the dele-
terious effects of state violence on already marginalized communities, among
other reasons—with this research, I want to shift the focus onto the culture of
the state itself and its role in producing domestic violence: how the very construction of the nation and the state is implicated in vulnerability and victimization, and even the emergence of new categories of victims. The approach I take
in *Battering States* demands a reorientation that shifts attention away from individuals isolated within intimate relationships toward a dynamic and multiscalar
analysis of what I have termed the "politics of domestic violence," where cultural
difference and context matter, and the political is indeed personal.

From an integrated academic and advocacy position, the relationship
between the state and domestic violence has changed over time. We have moved
from documenting what domestic violence is, and proving that it exists, to
demanding that our local communities and the state take some responsibility to
intervening into or preventing such violence, often by drawing on the symbolic
and sustaining resources of transnational networks (Adelman 2005a). My hope
with this book is to add more stories from people and places and perspectives
that are not commonly considered as relevant to domestic violence studies, those
associated with the multifaceted lifework of the state.

This politics of domestic violence approach allows for a series of novel entry
points to intimate partner violence. *Battering States* asks cultural questions, such
as how familial relationships are shaped by the construction and configuration of the state, how certain groups of battered women are constituted and
differentiated as vulnerable by encounters with the state, and how states navigate their global identity by referencing the regulation of domestic violence. At
the same time, I do not assume that all citizens and residents have access to,
desire, or enact the same kind of belonging to the state. The contested nature of
belonging means that people develop a range of cross-cutting positions based on
their gender, nationality, ethnicity, religion and religiosity, and socioeconomic
and geographic locations. Notably, gender matters in this study of the politics
of domestic violence, along with other markers of identity, place, and power.
In lieu of a homogenous or static understanding of the state, I pursued a more
subtle line of inquiry by embracing the notion of a multivalent state with many
moving parts that are sometimes in conflict with one another. The book illustrates how there is no one unified "state" that acts; instead, there is a plurality of
peopled arenas, fields, and networks, some deemed illegal, some informal, some
awarded the imprimatur of the state, and some inside the official halls of government business. Taken together these form a dynamic and unwieldy "state" that
sometimes works on a similar issue in a coordinated fashion, but mostly not.
What I have examined here from a domestic violence perspective are three sets of

activities integral to "doing states": the classification of belonging, determination, and protection of borders and social order, and management of resources. As each chapter shows, my study is fundamentally about revealing the cultural work and contingent histories that forge the state along with domestic violence. The result is an innovative and interdisciplinary approach to the politics of domestic violence, which I hope will engender new studies that reveal how statecraft and domestic violence are linked and that will contribute to finding just pathways out of this entrenched, global problem.

THE NEXT TWENTY-FIVE YEARS

The book focuses on Israel as an exemplar of the politics of domestic violence, so here I reflect on several implications of the case study, as well as a series of possible comparative or parallel lines of inquiry, which I hope will be useful to other scholars and justice provocateurs who push the movement against domestic violence forward on the frontline. Disciplinary boundaries and professional specializations notwithstanding, thinking about domestic violence as always about more than the violence has been a productive stance in my experience. By this I mean that domestic violence is not only about the violence, per se, or even about making violence unacceptable. Taking several analytic steps back enabled me to notice how domestic violence may be embedded within a state's election laws and political configuration, its war footing and military engagement, its application of neoliberal economic principles and who is deemed deserving of its resources within a hierarchy of population categories, the rigidity of its borders and its policy responses to large-scale migration or labor shortages, and the policing of what constitutes a family. Israel was a rich research site in part because I had the opportunity to observe and learn from activists who articulated these connections and critiqued the mainstream disconnection between domestic violence and the state.

Because each state has its own cultural history, intrastate inequalities, and unique international relations, domestic violence is likely related to competing national narratives that explain who "we" are and who are the enemies, as well as why things are the way they are today, or the vision of how they ought to be. From just this preliminary list of possible starting points, the politics of domestic violence clearly require a more holistic standpoint toward a problem that has been too often contained more narrowly to sex, emotions, or marriage. Taking a more holistic posture may necessitate collaborations with people who have never before considered their work from a domestic violence perspective, but I would argue that domestic violence can be more effectively studied and pragmatically addressed if it is not treated as a phenomenon separate and apart from key areas of statecraft.

Historians provide significant insight into this holistic approach to a politics of domestic violence, documenting how it has surfaced and receded from public view as a recognizable breach of cultural norms requiring intervention within and beyond the family. Linda Gordon (1988), for example, corrects the common presentist orientation by demonstrating how multiple waves of feminists, social workers, and women victims transformed domestic violence from an expected yet privatized injury to a claim for state protection in the United States. They did so through sustained political campaigns, most often associated with nineteenth-century social movements fighting for temperance, child saving, and moral purity in the United States. Within these reform movements, only certain categories of women were considered victims worthy of public concern. Elizabeth Pleck (1987) further reveals that in the nineteenth century, Americans were actually *rediscovering* domestic violence. During the colonial period in Massachusetts, between 1640 and 1680, the Puritans had formulated and enforced laws against wife beating. These historical studies offer templates or at least guidance in how to identify connections between domestic violence and state-building within contemporary research.

Next, in terms of comparative implications, the Israeli case suggests several areas of inquiry. Starting with the development of domestic violence as a social problem, it would be helpful to better understand how certain frames are constructed (moral behavior, women's health, strengthening families, human rights, cultural mobilization, and so on), why they are more or less persuasive within certain historical and cultural contexts, and what it takes to sustain public interest in domestic violence. Given the growth of culturally relevant and constituent-based services and activism in Israel, which I analyzed in Chapter 2, I also am curious how identity-based networks compete, coexist, cooperate, or collaborate. In addition, rather than stick with a unitary state approach and track changes over time, as I have done here, others may wish to trace how various strategies have traveled around the globe, such as how Kayan-Feminist Organization locally organized their "16 Days of Activism Against Gender-Based Violence Campaign" drive among Palestinian women and girls in Israel in November 2015.

Turning to family law, a relatively well-researched area, which has been the focal point of much reform effort, it remains a question as to how frequently these efforts are inspired or tied explicitly to concerns about domestic violence. Similar to other states that maintain a legally pluralistic system of family law, particularly as related to religious-based marriage and divorce codes, Israel continues to exempt religious courts from domestic antidiscrimination legislation or international human rights conventions, as noted in Chapter 3. The associated drive to privatize legal remedies or create "multicultural accommodations" (Shachar 2001, 2009) continues to grow, which has direct implications for domestic violence research and advocacy as well, ranging from Jewish families in the United States to newly arriving Muslim families in Germany.

This raises, too, the related theoretical and pragmatic issue of when and how women are asked in any number of states to prioritize culture or nation or religion over security and dignity. Thus an area ripe for study is the role of religious and cultural leaders in the struggle against domestic violence. Whereas, earlier, religion often was identified as a cause of domestic violence and secularism as at least a partial solution, domestic violence and family law activists in Israel have had some success in engaging with religious court judges and other communal leaders: Jewish women are now trained and accepted as pleaders who participate in rabbinical court hearings; the Bat Melech organization oversees two shelters for ultra-Orthodox battered women. In a precedent-setting event, Jewish, Druze, Muslim, and Christian religious leaders met at the Van Leer Jerusalem Institute in May 2013 for a day-long conference called "Leading Toward Safe Families: Religious Leaders Deal with Domestic Violence." At the event, among other comments, Islamic legal scholar and chief Qadi of Jerusalem, Iyad Zahalka, denounced violence against women. The rarity of these men meeting together further amplified their remarks.

Efforts to mobilize religion or religious leaders are not barrier-free, however, because women seeking to reform family law can get caught in state affairs as well. For example, Bedouin women organizing against polygyny in the Negev face an Israeli state that infrequently enforces its criminal law against plural marriage, and community leaders who denounce the women for serving state interests. Even when change is pursued within one religious group, it may have a negative spillover effect on another. This happened when two ultra-Orthodox political parties who signed coalition agreements with Prime Minister Netanyahu in May 2015 guaranteeing their authority to "safeguard the status quo" then opposed the bill sponsored by the political parties Meretz, Zionist Union, and Joint Arab List to require at least one woman qadi to serve as a sharia court judge, because they "fear that tomorrow it will serve as a precedent in the rabbinical courts" (Ettinger 2015b). Indeed, as the Jewish demand grows for civil family law and religious pluralism, the status quo gets chipped away at legislatively and judicially.[1] This dynamic between law and politics in Israel is surely familiar to those who study other multicultural states (Sezgin 2013).

A brief look at securitism suggests an unfortunately robust area for future research and activism, whether it is to examine in a more linear fashion the effects of soldiering or battle experience on the perpetration of domestic violence, or to explore more contextually how being "at war," facing political violence or living in either a short- or long-term existential crisis informs how people define, relate to, and regulate domestic violence. Nascent efforts have emerged to integrate domestic violence and broader notions of human security into international relations and security studies, as well as into the practice of conflict resolution. Yet the increasing militarization and privatization of law enforcement, along with the ubiquity of counterterrorism activities and anti-immigrant ideology around the world, may have direct consequences on the policing of domestic violence, both in terms of the interest and availability of officers to respond to individual reports and of the interest and willingness of communities under political surveillance, that may already be subject to either under- or over-policing, to call the police and report domestic violence. This phenomenon is currently growing worse in Israel among Palestinians and migrant workers, for example. Still, might the call to the general population to "say something" if they "see something" also apply to observations of domestic violence? If so, this may provide victims with some protection while perhaps further embedding domestic violence within the punitive state, or at least those most vulnerable to it.

How states balance (or not) the classic need to protect its borders with the newer desire to protect its families is a question relevant to most states today. Research indicates that the presence of a gun in the home greatly multiplies the risk of domestic violence homicide, no matter what state you live in.[2] Thus the Israeli model of gun control may be instructive. Since passage of the state's first arms law in 1949, citizens have not possessed a right to bear arms. Nor does a meaningful gun lobby exist. Israel maintains a relatively low ratio of weapons to adults (1:19) (G. Cohen, Kubovich, and Lis 2013), and lawful weapon possession is highly regulated by the state.[3] Over time, the state has developed fairly restrictive gun control policies, considering the persistent legitimacy of weapons.[4]

It was the increased proliferation of guns due to the ubiquity of (low-paid, privatized) armed security guards during the Second Intifada that motivated the development of the surprisingly successful Gun Free Kitchen Tables campaign, as described in Chapter 4. But in October 2015, gun license applications increased 5000 percent after Minister of Internal Security Gilad Erdan announced, "In light of the security situation I've decided to make it easier to obtain a permit for owning a weapon. In recent weeks many civilians have assisted the police in stopping terrorists who were carrying out attacks. Civilians who are skilled at using firearms are a multiplier force in our struggle against terrorists, so I've taken steps to make obtaining guns easier for now" (Kubovich 2015; Dovrat-Mezrich 2015; Gross 2016; Gross and Davidovich 2016). When political violence increases, eligibility requirements tend to be loosened, which translates into more homes with more guns, and thus more risk for battered women and their children. Because activism and research has focused on the proliferation of security weapons, however, what has received limited analysis are the experiences of the logic of securitism within Palestinian families, either on an everyday basis or during moments deemed a national crisis. One area of inquiry to consider is the gendered effects of Muslim and Christian Palestinian men's and women's inaccessibility to firearms, exclusion from military service, or possible lack of identification with external threats to the state on domestic violence (Sa'ar and Yahia-Younis 2008; Sachs, Sa'ar, and Aharoni 2007).

The Israeli case may constitute a particularly pronounced example of the interaction between domestic violence and the cultural politics of a security state. However, it represents a point on a map of varying modes of the security state, inviting researchers to document how it operates in other societies and analyze how universal or voluntary conscription, militarized masculinity, political violence, postcolonialism, or the shifting tectonics of world powers and proxy wars may shape domestic violence discourse. The politics of domestic violence in Israel may also provide direction to those who conduct research in locales that currently experience or who have experienced protracted armed conflicts in the past but have not yet fully considered either their effect or the effect of post-conflict transitions on domestic violence. The application of this framework to the study of domestic violence in nations where the security state is less robust or plays a relatively more subdued role in the culture and economy could be considered as well.

The political economy of a state has rarely been considered within domestic violence studies as I explain in Chapter 5. Yet entrepreneurs and third-sector leaders, including antiviolence, feminist, environmental justice, and peace NGOs, among others, have envisioned the possible social and economic benefits of a post-conflict transition in Israel. The short-lived success of the Oslo Accords and the peace agreement with Jordan drew foreign capital investment and attracted new buyers for Israeli goods in the mid-1990s, for example. This led Palestinian and Israeli business and civil society leaders in continued pursuit of the elusive peace dividend to form a coalition in July 2012 operating under the auspices of the World Economic Forum called "Breaking the Impasse" (BTI) to encourage elected officials and public support for a political solution to end the conflict with a two-state solution. On the morning of the May 2015 national elections, BTI member and high-tech businessman Dov Moran explained his opposition to Likud candidate Netanyahu's exclusive focus on security and lack of attention to economic concerns: "No doubt that if we go towards a peace process, security spending should go down and this would clearly allow dividing the pie differently, and even make the pie bigger" (T. Cohen and Scheer 2015).

Whether motivated by social justice or profit maximization, and regardless of the specific policy outcome, relatively new critical commentary about Israel's political economy focused on security-based constraints on economic growth articulated by mainstream voices has begun. A concern remains about who will benefit from business-driven reform of Israel's political economy, when it is tied so closely to a small number of elite private investors, on the one hand, and the sprawling security network on the other hand. Shifting from guns to butter, as imagined by the BTI, may be possible in the future, but will Mizrahi solo mothers, Ethiopian, ultra-Orthodox, and Palestinian family households living in poverty have any bread to spread it on? A more (neo)liberal economy that is good for business may not necessarily be good for battered women, or a state's citizens and residents more generally. In the meantime, it behooves domestic violence scholars and activists alike to follow the money—the state's financial policies, its national budget, its reliance on civil society to fill in gaps in basic needs (and raise funds to do so), and its Gini coefficient.

The political economy is one of the primary means that decision makers, whether inside or outside the government, "do states." It is a central component of the life of the state. Advocates argue that domestic violence policies be determined by prioritizing the material resource needs of the most marginalized battered women in a particular society (Coker 2000; Richie 2015). Although I agree with the premise, I have tried here to build on it by taking another analytic step back in order to unpack the relationship between political economy and domestic violence by looking at the macro-level production of stratification and differential citizenship—in the name of state-building. In other words, economic stress alone does not entirely explain domestic violence either as a cause or as an effect (WHO and PAHO 2012). One-size-fits-all policies predicated on the false generalization that low-income women experience the highest level or most severe forms of domestic violence (Kiss et al. 2012) or that treat battered women as a homogenous category, unfortunately, will likely ameliorate some and cause harm to others (Hidrobo and Fernald 2013).

MOBILIZING THE CULTURAL POLITICS OF THE STATE FOR JUSTICE?

I return, finally, to the debate about contradictions embedded within the relationship between the state and domestic violence. Among others, Wendy Brown trenchantly critiques the state as a vehicle not simply of inequality but of domination; she urges liberals and progressives to rethink their "appeals to expand state benefits, and ever-increasing reliance on the state for adjudication of social injury" at the very moment when state power is being consolidated "through regulation and privatization" (Brown 1995, 18). Katherine Franke (2012, 46) similarly warns against the seduction of "winning" state-conferred rights because of how "those very rights end up quite easily requisitioned by the state to advance its own larger interests." Yet the state is neither a monolithic entity nor an unnecessary partner in the pursuit of social change. More critically, because of its multidimensional relationship to domestic violence, engagement with the cultural politics of the state will be an effective and strategic, if still partial and cautionary, route for pursuing social justice.

Notes

CHAPTER 1

1. Rape Crisis of Durham merged with the Orange-Durham Coalition for Battered Women in 2001 to create the Durham Crisis Response Center.
2. Kelly, Burton, and Regan (1996, 94–96) complicate the binary categories of "victim" and "survivor" that associate the former with negative and the latter with positive characteristics. Instead, individuals who have been victimized are already, always survivors; a simplistic linear model ignores dynamic experiences of injury and survival.
3. About a year into these conversations, I became so full of stories about sexual violence that I became too scared to keep the windows down in my car when I stopped at a red light in town, despite the fact that known assailants rather than strangers are largely the problem when it comes to rape (Madriz 1997).
4. Because I was profiled by security guards to be a Jewish student, the search was perfunctory (smile, pat, pat, go ahead) rather than a time-intensive and more invasive ritual of humiliation endured by those identified as Palestinians or other suspected groups.
5. There are nine rape crisis centers operating in Israel (including Women Against Violence). All are associated with the Israel Association of Rape Crisis Centers. They operate hotlines for women, men, religious women, and Arabic-speaking women.
6. Anthropologist Rebecca Torstick at Indiana University crafted the evocative phrase "the battering state" during a conversation about my research in 1998 at the Annual Congress of the International Union of Anthropological and Ethnological Sciences hosted by William and Mary College, Williamsburg, Virginia. I thank her for generously sharing it with me. The title of the book also echoes Begoña Aretxaga's (2003) essay "Maddening States," in which she outlines the enduring place of the state in people's everyday lives.
7. Anthropologists have both ignored and studied domestic violence over the years. I place my own work within the "intentional" stage of ethnographic research on domestic violence, which "brings domestic violence to the center of analytic, methodological, and theoretical concerns for the ethnographer" (Adelman 2010, 188).
8. Nomenclature referring to the intentional killing of women includes terms such as domestic homicide (Websdale 1999), femicide (Russell and Radford 1992; WHO and PAHO 2012), feminicide (Lagarde y de los Ríos 2010), intimate partner murder (Dobash and Dobash 2015), spousal homicide (Wilson and Daly 1993), and uxoricide (Adinkrah 1999). Among them, femicide and feminicide

are umbrella terms, referring to the gender-based killing of women of either an intimate or a nonintimate nature (Carey and Torres 2010; Taylor and Jasinski 2011; WHO and PAHO 2012). These terms are analytically useful, especially when considering links between gender violence and political violence or poverty, but too broad for my purposes here. Instead, I chose the term "domestic violence homicide" because it aligns with my selection of the term "domestic violence." Furthermore, "domestic violence homicide" ties the murder of women to either a pattern of battering or to husbands' proprietary behavior embedded within the domestic sphere (as reflected in family law, for example). Finally, Israelis do not use the term "domestic." Instead, they use phrases such as "violence against women in the family," or the problem of "battered women," among others. I do use the term "intimate partner violence" or homicide to avoid distracting repetition.

9. I am less interested here in the distinction between narrative and story, and more interested in using the term "story" as a heuristic device.

10. The first lesbian and gay organization in Israel, the Society for the Protection of Personal Rights, was established in Haifa in 1976. A lesbian-feminist organization (KLAF) was formed in 1977.

11. Early thinking focused on why women stay in relationships with men who batter (few were asking why men were violent). Walker's "learned helplessness" (1979) proposed a cycle of violence that over time caused women to develop a mental disorder. In contrast, feminist research has emphasized women's helpseeking strategies and the learned helplessness of institutions (Maguigan 1991; Schneider 2000).

12. Of course, not all families have equal access to privacy rights; uneven, politicized state interference into some families but not others is addressed in Chapter 4.

13. Theda Skocpol's (1985) classic analysis "Bringing the State Back In" was a response to the disappearance of the state within political theory.

14. The British possessed legislative authority through the promulgation of Orders in Council by the King and Ordinances by the High Commissioner.

15. The British continued the Jewish tradition of having a Sephardi Hakham Bakshi but instituted a new custom of electing an Ashkenazi chief rabbi, which reinforced distinctions between the two communities.

16. This broad statement does not reflect shifting alliances, such as how the Israeli-Palestinian conflict was used as a proxy to fight the Cold War.

CHAPTER 2

1. A 1926 ordinance recognized additional religious communities: Roman Catholic, Greek Orthodox, Georgian Armenian Community, Armenian (Catholic), Syrian (Catholic), Chaldean (Uniate), Greek Catholic Melkite, Maronite, and Syrian Orthodox Community, according each "autonomy for the internal affairs of [the] Community, subject to the [Mandatory] provisions" (Abramov 1976, 109).

2. It is beyond the scope of this chapter to discuss all reforms made to personal status laws.

3. The distinction being that "a women's movement is a social movement comprised primarily of women, led primarily by women; it may be a conservative movement, a labor movement or any other movement of women. . . . Feminist movements identify the status quo as being disadvantageous to women as compared to men" (Htun and Weldon 2012b).

4. This was not a new attitude. The New Yishuv sought to "correct" Old Yishuv lifeways and their dependency on distributive *halukkah* and *kollelim* systems of economic support from abroad as well. Ashkenazi Jews sought to civilize Mizrahi Jews during the Mandate period (Loewenberg 1991).

5. In between these periods, women's organizations went into "an abeyance phase," which is "a holding pattern of a group which continues to mount some type of challenge even in a nonreceptive political environment" (Taylor 1989, 772). In Israel, this meant mainly provisioning social services (B. Swirski 1991b, 294).

6. This is not to say that family regulation remained confidential. On the contrary, each transaction serves as a lesson to the community about what is possible or impossible to achieve in one's family life.

7. Notably, within days of the new state's declaration of independence, on the afternoon of Friday, May 23, 1948, thirty-five-year-old former police officer Michael Cohen shot and killed his twenty-seven-year-old wife, Yaffa, on the second floor of their apartment in Tel Aviv (Meron 1993).

8. During a two-year period, he had served as the state's defense minister.

9. Not all overtly nonpolitical forms of violence were pushed aside. Mimi Ajzenstadt (2002) explains how juvenile delinquency and neglect of children were central concerns of the new state's leaders, who desired that the next generation grow to be strong citizens. State intervention into (mostly Mizrahi) families was accepted as a means to induce cultural assimilation of new immigrants.

10. During her four years in the Knesset, Freedman's party affiliation shifted to Ya'ad, then to the Independent Socialists, and finally to the Women's Party (Freedman 1990, 141).

11. Olmert was elected mayor of Jerusalem in 1993. A decade later, he was elected to the Knesset and was named Prime Minister in 2006 when Ariel Sharon became comatose and never recovered. Olmert resigned in 2009 due to corruption charges; he began serving a nineteen-month sentence in February 2016.

12. Shlomo Hillel was born in Baghdad, immigrated to Israel in 1923, and became one of the founders of Kibbutz Maagan Michael. Between 1946 and 1951, he was a Mossad attaché for "Aliyah Bet," which helped Jews from Iraq, Iran, Syria, and Egypt illegally migrate to Israel. Among other government roles, he went on to serve as speaker of the 11th Knesset (*Knesset.gov.il*).

13. Marcia Freedman (1990, 202) revealed that the women's organization Na'amat was registered as owner of the building in Wadi Nisnas, but that its president Nava Arad refused to rent it to the shelter. Soon after media exposure of the conditions in which victimized women and children were living, the government purchased the building from Na'amat and allowed the shelter to use it.

14. Marcia Freedman (1990, 202–03) reports that Carmela Nakash was one of the original residents of the Haifa shelter and had stayed there "for almost a year" but "during that year there had been no sign of the husband"; the collective decided "it was right to make her move on" in what Freedman describes as "one of the last decisions we made as a group . . . and the first time we violated our own cardinal rule—that we did not make decisions for the women, did not presume to know what was good for them, and did not limit their stay at the shelter."

15. Opposition to the "magic number" of 200,000 was articulated during an April 2013 conference at Ariel University cosponsored by The Familists, an antifeminist NGO established in 2005.

16. Mor later published her findings (Eisikovits, Buchbinder, and Mor 1998).

17. Avni (1990, 1991a, 1991b, 1991c, 1991d) and Burgansky (1989) published some of the first academic research on domestic violence in Israel. Zvi Eisikovits and his colleagues at the University of Haifa published the first national survey on domestic violence in Israel (Eisikovits, Winstock, and Fishman 2004), among other related topics. See also Ben-Porat and Itzhaky (2008); Dahan and Levi (2011); Daher-Nashef (2014); Edelstein (2013); Eisikovits, Buchbinder, and Bshara (2008); Erez, Ibarra, and Gur (2015); Goldblatt and Granot (2005); Haj-Yahia (1998, 2000a, 2003); Kacen (2006); Shechory-Bitton (2014); Shoham (2005, 2013a, 2013b); Tartakovsky and Mezhibovsky (2012); and Vignansky and Timor (2015).

18. Ora Namir served as the Secretary General of Na'amat Tel Aviv 1967–1979. She was the Minister of Labor and Social Welfare, during Rabin's Labor government, 1992–1996.

19. Interventions for men who batter developed into a continuum of care model. In 1980 Herzliya shelter director Ruth Rasnic, borrowing concepts such as self-help group treatment from the United States, established the first program for men who batter. Soon after passage of the 1991 Law for the Prevention of Family Violence, the need for services for men who batter was addressed by the Ministry of Welfare, which developed Treatment and Prevention of Family Violence municipal centers, some in partnership with women's organizations, offering counseling and groups to self-referred men (Zohar 1995); in the mid-1990s they started offering court-mandated presentencing therapeutic groups through the Adult Probation Division (Buchbinder and Eisikovits 2008b; Enosh 2008). *Beit Noam* (House of Tenderness), a residential educational pilot program for men who batter was opened in 1997 with temporary government funds (Hartaf and Bar-On 2000; Keynan, et al. 2003). *Beit Hatikva* (House of Hope), a rehabilitative program for men incarcerated because of domestic violence launched at Hermon prison in 2000 (Shteltzer-Pier 2003). The newest program, *Maftahot* (Keys), is a community-based residential unit to ease transition from prison to home for men who have completed their sentences for domestic violence (Hamai, Buchbinder, Enosh, Dotan, and Barzilai 2009).

20. Police data are culled from IWN (2004), Konur (2000), Israel Police (2015) and Sinai (2002).

21. Leah Rabin, the Prime Minister's wife, represented Israel at the first UN Conference on Women in Mexico City in 1975. Political insider Tamar Eshel was appointed to represent Israel in Copenhagen in 1980 and again in Nairobi in 1985 (Shalvi 2009).

22. The United States—in its effort to shore up Israel's position—objected to the paragraph because its "tendentious and unnecessary elements" have "only nominal connection with the unique concerns of women" (United Nations 1986, 62).

23. CEDAW is at once a controversial, radical manifesto and a rather conventional outline of basic needs of and goals for women worldwide. The Women's Convention originated in the creation of the UN Commission on the Status of Women in 1946. Inspired by a call that emerged during the 1975 International Women's Year World Conference, the Commission ultimately drafted an international instrument on the human rights of women. In 1977 the UN appointed a working group to finalize the Commission's draft. It was adopted by the General Assembly in December 1979 and entered into force September 1981. As of May 15, 2015, 189 states have ratified it; the US and Palau are the two signatory-only states, and six other states have taken no action (i.e., Iran, Niue, Somalia, Sudan, Tonga, and the Holy See).

24. Israel signed the International Convention on the Elimination of All Forms of Racial Discrimination on March 7, 1966, and ratified it on January 3, 1979. Israel then ratified five UN Conventions on October 3, 1991: International Convention on Civil and Political Rights (signed December 19, 1966); International Covenant on Economic, Social and Cultural Rights (signed December 19, 1966); Convention Against Torture and Other Cruel, Inhuman or Degrading Treatment (signed October 22, 1986); Convention on the Elimination of All Forms of Discrimination against Women (signed July 17, 1980); and Convention on the Rights of the Child (signed July 3, 1990).

25. Committee of CEDAW, General Recommendation 19, January 29, 1992.

26. Based on his opposition to Israel's negotiations for peace with Palestinian Chairman Yassir Arafat, a Jewish religious extremist killed Rabin (see Peri 2000).

27. Menachem Begin (Likud) ruled the government between 1977 and 1983; Yitzhak Shamir (Likud) ruled between 1983 and 1992, except for the unity government held by Labor and Likud between 1984 and 1986.

28. Kayan, Women's League for Israel, Rape Crisis Center of Tel Aviv, Woman for Woman Haifa Feminist Center, National Hotline for Battered Women, KLAF (Lesbian Feminist Community), Bat Shalom, Forum of Directors of Battered Women's Shelters, Kol Isha (Jerusalem), Women Against Violence (Nazareth).

29. For an analysis of the representation of rape in Israel media, see Korn and Efrat (2004).

30. Her case inspired a controversial 1995 legal reform that allowed a judge to not sentence a person to life imprisonment if the offender had suffered from extreme mental distress following the murder victim's abuse. Amendment 300a allowed judicial consideration that "due to a severe mental disorder . . . the defendant's ability is significantly restricted" when the defendant experienced severe and ongoing domestic violence (for analyses of its limitations, see Zarchin 2008, and Touma-Sliman 2005).

31. Nili Tal's story is a summary of her newspaper column published on February 17, 1992.

32. Bat Melech shelters for religious and haredi Jewish women in Jerusalem (1996) (and later, Beit Shemesh in 2005).

33. Today there are fourteen shelters for battered women in Israel: two designed for and by Palestinian women (not counting another one for girls and young women), two intended for religious Jewish women, and twelve that serve a diverse population, including the emergency shelter in Haifa.

34. The Haifa Women's Coalition is another enduring partnership model where several organizations leverage space, talent, legitimacy, and other resources to strengthen all its members: Isha l'Isha: Haifa Feminist Center, Haifa Rape Crisis Center, Kayan Feminist Organization, and Aswat: Palestinian Gay Women.

35. Jewish women formed a coalition to reform the personal status law system as well. Already possessing equitable access to family courts, Jewish women focused on divorce denial in rabbinical courts. The International Coalition for Aguna Rights (ICAR), formed in October 1992, led in January 1993 to an Israeli network comprising organizations across the religious and political spectrum. As a result, divorce denial was transformed from a wretched but inevitable condition to the top problem facing Jewish women in Israel. A decade into the coalition's work, the film *Sentenced to Marriage*, which followed women denied divorce in Israel and the women pleaders who advocate for them (*toenet rabbanit*), was recognized as the Best Documentary at the Jerusalem Film Festival (2004); another decade passed, still with no satisfying solution, and the feature film *Gett: The Trial of Viviane Amsalem* won the Audience Award and Best Israeli Feature at the same festival (2014) and was nominated for a Golden Globe (see Chapter 3).

36. The coalition members as of 2010 are Adalah, the Legal Center for Arab Minority Rights in Israel; Al-Tufula—Pedagogical and Multipurpose Women's Center; Al Zahraa, the Organization for the Advancement of Women; Assiwar— Arab Feminist Movement in Support of Victims of Sexual Abuse; AWC—Arab Women in the Center; Kayan—Feminist Organization; Ma'an—Forum of Arab Women's Organizations in the Negev; Mada al-Carmel Arab Center for Applied Social Research; Mossawa Center for the Rights of the Arab Citizens of Israel; Muntada—The Arab Forum for Sexuality, Education and Health; Sidreh; The Working Group for Equality in Personal Status Issues; Women Against Violence (WAV); and Yasmin Al-Nagab for the Health of Women and Family.

37. This is based on the report prepared by Itach-Maaki entitled "Report on Violence against Bedouin Women: Conspiracy of Silence: Domestic Violence against Arab Bedouin Women in the Negev."

CHAPTER 3

1. On legal pluralism, see Merry (1988).

2. Family courts are the gateway to civil management of issues such as spousal maintenance, property division, child custody, and child support. Family court judges draw on a mixture of civil and religious law. Similar to other civil courts, family court judges are selected by an appointed committee whose nine members include

two government ministers selected by the executive branch, two members of Parliament, two lawyers selected by the Israeli Bar Association, and three Supreme Court justices. In contrast to religious courts, which exclusively employ men as judges, the civil court judiciary is gender balanced. However only about 7 percent of judges are Palestinian Arabs, and about 25 percent of its judges graduated from Jewish religious-affiliated high schools (Bogoch 1999; Hofnung 2011). Judges serving in the Haifa Family Court are disproportionately women.

3. I use the term "religion" rather than "religious" to signal that not all members of these officially recognized groups are religious in terms of belief or practice. Instead, they are state-mandated identity categories.

4. State-sponsored rabbinical courts oversee the family life of Jewish Israelis, regardless of religiosity. Rabbinical courts enjoy concurrent jurisdiction with civil family courts in matters pertaining to divorce such as property division and child custody, but divorces are finalized in rabbinical courts. Twelve regional rabbinical courts and an appeals court serve a Jewish population numbering about six million (Central Bureau of Statistics 2013b, table 2.1). Within the rabbinical court a panel of three judges, known as *dayyanim*, hear cases. Dayyanim are appointed with a salary commensurate of a civil court judge by a commission composed exclusively of men, until the contested appointments of several women starting in 1996. Legislation passed in June 2013 requires that at least four women be elected or appointed to the commission of ten members, with a new eleventh member to be a *toenet rabbanit*, a female pleader; the transfer of oversight from the Ministry of Justice and back to the Ministry of Religious Services, as part of the government coalition agreement between PM Netanyahu's Likud Party and Shas, may influence appointments. Dayyanim must be citizens, men who are at least thirty years of age and ordained as an Orthodox rabbi certified by the Chief Rabbinate Council. No secular education or professional development related to family life is required of dayyanim, who are trained in gender-segregated Orthodox Jewish schools, although preferred qualifications now include military or public service and higher education. Critics argue that rather than meritorious assessment, crony and party politics determine appointment to these highly coveted positions, including but not limited to backroom agreements to vote for judicial candidates in exchange for political support.

State-sponsored sharia courts enjoyed the broadest exclusive jurisdiction among religious courts in Israel until 2001, when the Working Group for Equality in Personal Status Issues, a coalition of Palestinian Israeli women's and human rights organizations, secured reform of the Family Courts Law (Amendment 5). Since 2001, exclusive jurisdiction of sharia courts pertains only to marriage and divorce, unless both parties agreed to link the termination of the marriage to related family matters such as property division and child custody. Eight regional sharia courts and one appeals court serve a Muslim population numbering about 1.4 million (CBS 2013, table 2.1). Within sharia courts, one judge, known as a *qadi*, presides over hearings. Qadis are selected by a nine-person committee, and at least five of whom must be Muslims. In 2013, the first woman was appointed to the nominating committee. Qadis must be Muslim, married (or formerly married), over the age of thirty, and suitably trained in sharia law (notably, there is no gender requirement, although only men have served in this role thus far). Reforms to the Qadi Law in 2002 raised the minimum education qualifications, but did not require formal sharia training. No professional development related to family life is required. Similar to the appointment of dayyanim, local and national politics informs the appointment and work of qadis (Abou Ramadan 2003). Scholars debate the role of sharia courts in amplifying or muting Muslim religious autonomy in Israel (Abou Ramadan 2008; Shahar 2006).

The Druze community, made up of extended kinship factions, and numbering about 130,000, lives primarily in the north of Israel (Central Bureau of Statistics 2013b, table 2.1; Lang 2005). Between 1956 and 1963, the State of Israel conscripted Druze men; recognized the Druze first as a religion distinct from Islam, and then as a nationality apart from Arabs; approved the establishment of a Druze religious council and granted the council control over personal status (Hajjar 2000). Prior to state recognition, Druze families turned to sharia courts or community leaders to resolve family disputes. The contemporary Druze religious court of first instance and its court of appeal are in Acco; the court in the Golan Heights has not been continuously operational. Since 2001 Druze families have access to the concurrent jurisdiction of the civil family courts in matters associated with marriage and divorce. A Druze qadi is known as a *qadi madhab*, and the state funds the salaries of six Druze qadis (three for the court of first instance and three for the appeals court), although the number of qadis hearing cases at any one time varies. Similar to other courts of limited jurisdiction, and following the procedures enacted for the selection of Muslim qadis and Jewish dayyanim, a nine-person committee made up of Druze spiritual leaders, Knesset representatives, and other political appointees make nominations according to broad criteria: nominees must have suitable spiritual training, be Israeli citizens over the age of thirty and married; all are men. Druze qadis make judicial decisions drawing from an adapted version of the Law of Personal Status of the Druze Community in Lebanon, 1948.

Christian families in Israel belong to ten recognized and several unrecognized communities, each of which hosts its own ecclesiastical court serving a population totaling just over 330,000 (Central Bureau of Statistics 2013b, table 2.1). The majority of Christians in Israel are members of three recognized churches: Greek Catholic (Melkite), Greek Eastern Orthodox, and Latin (Roman) Catholic. Since 2001, Christian families are able to turn to civil family courts in all matters pertaining to divorce such as property division and child custody. However, Greek Orthodox couples must initiate the divorce process, and Greek Catholics and Latin Catholics must initiate dissolution, separation, or annulment procedures through ecclesiastical courts. Notably, Greek and Latin Catholics desiring a divorce can seek relief through at least one spouse's conversion to Greek Orthodoxy. Ecclesiastical courts are given the least amount of oversight by the state, and limited public information is available regarding their locations, laws, and procedures. Court judgments are not published and ecclesiastical court judges, typically priests, are selected internally. The Palestinian feminist NGO Kayan highlighted this lack of transparency with the first-ever publication of the locations, contact information, and canon laws associated with Greek Orthodox and Greek Catholic courts in Israel in 2010. Ecclesiastical courts uniquely possess full autonomy from the state in terms of "appointing judges, budget management, court proceedings, and procedural matters" (Batshon 2012, 3). They also collect higher fees in comparison to other religious courts and civil family courts (5).

5. The innovation of Family Court Social Services units attached to the family courts, launched in 1997, distinguished further between the two sets of courts, until a similar unit was developed for the communal courts. Social workers and other staff assess families and suggest a variety of future-oriented services including consultation on whether the couple wishes to remain together, explanation of how the court system works, child custody agreements, mediation, parent education programs, and referrals to community-based organizations (Laufer and Berman 2006). When litigants report domestic violence to an FCSS staff member, they discuss options and refer the individual or couple to violence prevention and intervention services in the community; they also seek to secure an agreement about the status of the relationship (e.g., will the couple stay together, separate, or pursue divorce) and make recommendations to the couple and the judge (Laufer 2004). The reorganized family courts enable families to resolve personal status issues related to their divorce and to access legal as well as nonlegal support that they otherwise might not have known about or understood.

6. Among their other push-backs against feminist reforms within family law, a fledgling movement powered by men's rights activists is afoot to shift legal practice from the tender years doctrine to one based on the "best interests of the child" (Hacker 2005; Halperin-Kaddari and Freeman 2016).

7. The term "mixed marriage" originally referred to Jewish spouses from different ethnic origins or more generally to heterogeneous marriages between Ashkenazi and Sephardi Jewry (Halevi 1956, 186). Marriages between individuals who are members of different religions, now the referent of "mixed" or "interfaith" marriages are anomalies. Rabbinical courts will not authorize a marriage between a Jewish and a non-Jewish person. Druze courts only will marry two members of the Druze community, and conversion is not an option. Sharia courts will marry a Muslim man to a Jewish or Christian woman. Family courts also administer the dissolution of marriages between couples of the same gender, again, because these marriages performed abroad are recognized by the state but not by any of the religious courts.

8. Jews and Muslims turn to compiled written and oral traditions, and regionally specific customs and laws to determine norms for everyday life. For Muslims, the *Quran* is the foundational text. Various schools of thought explain the Quran, *sunnah* (Muhammad's way of life) and *hadith* (narration of Muhammad's way of life) through jurisprudence (*fiqh*). Similarly, for Jews, the *Pentateuch* (the first five books of the Old Testament) is the foundational text for the Jewish *halacha*, or way

of life. The *Talmud*, and subsequent additional interpretations, debates, codes, case law, and commentaries make up the primary sources of Jewish law.

9. Druze divorce law has parallels to Muslim divorce law. One distinction, however, is that upon divorce, the formerly married couple is forbidden from remarrying and, in practice, is instructed to not have social interaction. The Druze community has a very low divorce rate.

10. The comparison of Jewish and Islamic personal status law is not an uncommon exercise; however, it has not always been a productive one: framing Jewish law as modern, and Islamic law as traditional, for example (see Chigier 1985; Edelman 1994, e.g.), or supposing that Islam improved upon the inherited Jewish tradition and thus "accords women a status unsurpassed in other cultures and religions" (Ahmed 1986, 666).

11. The need to track down missing or recalcitrant husbands is neither a new nor an exclusively Israeli phenomenon. It pertains to any Jewish couple requiring a kosher writ of divorce.

12. Domestic violence homicide is a complex phenomenon with several discernable patterns related to immigration, nationality, and militarism that are beyond the scope of this chapter (see Chapter 4).

13. Ben-Dahan served as the deputy minister of religious services as a member of Knesset in PM Netanyahu's government between 2013 and 2015, and then as deputy minister of defense as part of Netanyahu's May 2015 renegotiated coalition agreement with the Jewish Home party. Ben-Dahan also has served on the board of Bat Melech, the NGO that develops and delivers social services, including shelters, for Orthodox and ultra-Orthodox battered women.

14. The Knesset legislated the possibility of civil sanctions in 1995, expanded the type of sanctions available to judges in 2000, and set the sanctions within a specific time frame in 2012.

15. Rabbinical courts handed down 191 decisions for sanctions against forty men in 2014, 168 decisions for sanctions against sixty-eight men in 2013, sixty such decisions in 2012 (one-third for incarceration), and forty-one in 2011 (Ettinger 2013b).

16. Incarceration backfired miserably in an apocryphal-sounding but real case where Yihye Avraham refused to grant his wife Orah a divorce for nearly forty-five years, correctly predicting that she would be freed only upon his death. Under order of the attorney general, he was incarcerated for thirty-two years and died in prison in December 1994.

17. Palestinian Muslims in Israel benefit from the Ottoman Family Rights Law and the Ottoman Law of Procedure for Sharia Courts, reflecting the progressive reforms of the Tanzimat and Young Turk period (Eisenman 1978).

18. She referred to him as her betrothed.

19. See Roe, Ronen, Lereya, Fennig, and Fennig (2005) on how the state defines criminal culpability. See Herbst and Gez (2012) for how this reform, intended to mitigate criminal punishment for battered women who kill their abusers (i.e.,

Amendment 300a), was taken up by defendants such as Gilad Shemen who killed his girlfriend Einav Rogel when she wanted to end the relationship.

CHAPTER 4

1. The PSA also signaled the disproportionate number of Ethiopian women killed by their current or former intimate partners.
2. Mazali is also a cofounder of New Profile, a feminist antimilitarism NGO interested in creating a civil-oriented Israeli society.
3. Gun Free Kitchen Tables (GFKT) partner organizations: Association for Civil Rights in Israel, Coalition of Women for Peace, Hollaback Israel, Itach-Maaki Women Lawyers for Social Justice, Isha L'Isha Feminist Center, L.O.—Combatting Violence Against Women, Israel Women's Network, New Profile, Noga—The Israeli Center for Rights of Crime Victims, Physicians for Human Rights–Israel, Psychoactive, Tmura—The Antidiscrimination Legal Center, and Women and Their Bodies.
4. The military and the defense industry are central to its economy as well (see Chapter 5).
5. I borrow the term "martial citizenship," originally coined to refer to "the moral basis for the unique rights granted disabled veterans of the American Civil War . . . earned through personal sacrifice in the name of worthy social goals" (Gal and Bar 2000, 594).
6. However, new fissures may transform the IDF: the fight over religious conscription and related re-delegitimation of women soldiers, Druze men questioning the morality of soldiering for the Israeli state, and talk of shifting from a collective-based military to a professional one (Levy 2008, 2014).
7. In November 2015 the Knesset amended the burden equality law to defer its implementation until 2020 (Lis and Ettinger 2015; Somfolvi 2015).
8. The IDF has observed a rapid increase in the number of Religious Zionist women volunteering for army service over the last several years (Ettinger 2015a).
9. The official IDF YouTube Channel posted a video on "Women of the IDF" (*www.youtube.com/watch?v=04kjNIL8prM*). The IDF underwent reforms to better integrate women soldiers. The administrative segregation of women soldiers under *Chen* ("grace" in Hebrew and an acronym for *cheil nashim*, referring to the Women's Corps) was eliminated, and women are now eligible to apply for 92 percent of military positions, including some combat roles (IDF Spokesperson's Unit 2002; IDF 2014). Nonetheless, a highly gendered division of military labor has endured for decades, which reproduces inequality beyond the military (IWN 1995, 1999; Sasson Levy 2010). Women conscripts often perform staff support and training as depicted in the award-winning film *Zero Motivation* (2014), and face institutionalized sexual harassment (Izraeli 1997), recently addressed in the Sexual Harassment Law.

10. Israel's ambivalent relationship to the Holocaust is beyond the scope of the analysis, but note the feminization of pre-state European and Shoah Jewry in contrast to the masculinized new Jew who forged the Israeli state.

11. Israel's official activities and remembrances of those who have fallen in defense of the state are maintained here: *www.izkor.gov.il*. The current tally numbers 23,320, which does not include people wounded or disabled as a result of political violence.

12. The new memorial was at first "challenged on the basis of whether or not to consider the violent deaths of victims of hostile activities as a national sacrifice similar to that of the dead soldiers" (Shay 2005, 714).

13. Yagil Levy's (2012) insightful analysis of Israel's "death hierarchy" does not consider domestic violence homicide.

14. According to Hannah Safran, the resolution stemmed from a discussion in the "Feminism and Socialism" workshop (2006, 104).

15. In 1995 his organization, Zu Artzenu, led protests against the Oslo Accords; in 2005 he called for civil disobedience in the face of Prime Minister Ariel Sharon's planned unilateral withdrawal from the Gaza Strip; in 2015 Netanyahu's Likud party voted his rival Feiglin off the party list in the primary election.

16. Hamas claimed responsibility for both attacks.

17. Advocates, aided by research reports and media coverage in the mid-to-late 1990s, persuaded policy makers that domestic violence constituted a social problem specifically for the US military.

18. In the past, Israelis took cover in bomb shelters, but during the first Gulf War, fear of Iraq launching a chemical attack had Israelis fashioning what were called "sealed rooms," where windows and doors were taped off with plastic. Since about 2002, new buildings are required to have a "safe room" constructed with reinforced concrete, sealed windows, and a steel door.

19. Domestic violence homicide rates in Israel have varied over time, with politically and economically marginalized communities, such as Ethiopian and Palestinian Arab Israelis, overrepresented in the perpetrator and victim columns of relevant databases (Adelman 2003; Landau 1997, 2003; Landau and Hattis-Rolef 1998; Sela-Shayovitz 2010a and 2010b). Several NGOs, including WIZO, NO2Violence, Isha L'Isha, Na'amat, and Israel Women's Network, maintain lists of domestic violence homicides. The police publish a total number in their annual reports.

20. During the summer of 1999, I met with Palestinian women activists associated with the Women's Centre for Legal Aid and Counseling in Ramallah. They explained that awareness of and women seeking assistance for domestic violence among Palestinians had steadily increased, although limited research existed in the occupied territories, and articulated a direct relationship between national security, military occupation, and domestic violence (see Shalhoub-Kevorkian 2004).

21. Israel Police hosted its first summit on "personal security" in May 2014 to launch the new Violence Index.

22. The phrase "Herzilya conferences" refers to those convened annually by the Interdisciplinary Center (IDC) Herzliya that address global security issues.

CHAPTER 5

1. John Maynard Keynes argued that economic recession could be alleviated by public investment, primarily aimed at unemployment. Among others, his student Sir Henry William Beveridge is credited with helping to form the welfare state in postwar Britain (Backhouse and Nishizawa 2010).

2. Friedman was awarded the Nobel Prize in 1976 and elected president of the American Economics Association in 1977.

3. For additional analyses of the Israeli economy, see Aharoni (1991, 1998), Y. Ben-Porat (1986), Lewin-Epstein and Semyonov (1993), Rivlin (2011), and Sharkansky (1987).

4. Socialist Zionism was but one of competing visions for the new state. Revisionist Zionists, for example, were less concerned with economic models, although they turned toward capitalism, and became more intent on securing political control over territory. Dissent, too, was present among the Jewish people as to whether they should create a state at all.

5. Palestinian land was expropriated as well through the Absentees' Property Law (1950) (see Adalah for database of discriminatory laws).

6. For Druze women the fear is based on the expectation that, when divorced, they will lose the right to live in the family home (along with child custody) because of Druze religious law and marital housing and building patterns. Druze men build marital homes, prior to marriage, with their own land and resources. Married Druze women purchase appliances and furniture from her family's monies for the marital home. Upon divorce, the house devolves as the husband's property. In a related way, Jewish women fear that, if they leave the marital home in the process of seeking safety, be it a shelter or the home of a relative or friend, they will be declared a *moredet*, a rebellious wife, and potentially lose legal rights to the family home. Thus physically staying in the home is a legal mode of retaining property rights.

7. Today cellphones can remedy the barrier of shared telephone lines, but monitoring calls or removing the phone is made even easier with new technologies.

8. The Orr Commission investigated the causes and outcomes of solidarity demonstrations that escalated during the Second Intifada in October 2000, when Israel police killed twelve Palestinian citizens and one Palestinian from Gaza, and wounded others.

9. Shalva Weil (1997) complicates the Israeli oversimplification of Ethiopian leadership.

10. The US offered Israel $1.5 billion, over and above its annual $3 billion in aid, if it would implement liberal economic policies. The US underwent a similar transformation via the Consolidated Omnibus Budget Reconciliation Act of 1985 (Lavie 2014, 7).

11. Prior to taxes and transfers, Israel's Gini coefficient was 0.50 (OECD 2013a and 2013b); the National Insurance Institute reports that only the US, Mexico, and Turkey have higher levels of income inequality.

12. According to the Israel National Insurance Institute, Israel's poverty line—less than half of the median disposable income weighted by household size—for a one-person household was NIS 2,989 a month in 2013 (about $830 in US dollars, based on the 2013 exchange rate, which fluctuated between 3.5 and 3.7); a family of four with a monthly income under NIS 7,653 was classified as poor (about $2,125 in US dollars) (Barkali et al. 2013, 6).

13. Typically 90 to 95 percent of solo parent families are woman-headed families, hence the term "solo mothers" (Herbst 2013).

14. About 14.25 percent of solo mothers with children under the age of eighteen are tracked as "never married," although this does not mean they were not partnered (CBS 2014, 268).

15. Several researchers provide overviews of welfare reform, which I draw on for this discussion (e.g., Swirski, Kraus, Konor-Attias, and Herbst 2003). Note that polygyny among Bedouin women in the Naqab/Negev is common. The NII seeks to eliminate duplication of benefits within "one family," penalizing women in polygynous families.

16. Missing in the analysis here is the accommodated polygyny among Bedouin in the Naqab/Negev. A battered woman divorced from her husband (who then remarries) will remain physically within his compound so as not to lose contact with her children. Because of their co-location, the NII considers her ineligible for benefits. If her husband simply takes another wife and neither divorces the battered woman nor provides spousal support, again, she is determined to be ineligible for benefits based on her status as married.

17. Social benefit recipients were required to "pay back" the state the difference between when the cuts went into effect (the beginning of the year) and when the cuts kicked in (not until mid-year).

18. Lavie (2014, 10) noted that the ceasefire went into effect the same day the cuts to welfare benefits also went into effect.

19. When Israel was accepted as an OECD member, the OECD recommended that it favor "cross border workers" over foreign workers. Between 2012 and 2014, the number of Palestinians working in construction in Israel doubled, mainly due to authorization of permits, although the number of foreign workers in this sector remained at about the same level (Ministry of Economy 2015).

20. Today about 60,000 caregivers work in Israel who migrated from the Philippines (50 percent), Nepal (15 percent), India (10 percent), Sri Lanka (10 percent), Moldova (10 percent), and Eastern Europe (Kav LaOved 2015; Kolker 2015). According to Kav LaOved (Workers' Hotline), there are an additional 25,000 men who work in agriculture (primarily from Thailand) and 60,000 Palestinian men who work in construction, half from within Israel and half from over the Green Line.

21. See Kemp (2007) and Kemp and Kfir (2016) for analyses of policies (or lack of policies) that impinge on foreign or migrant workers' rights.

22. Some women may arrive already pregnant; if not, women would have to have sex (or be sexually assaulted while on a work permit in Israel [see Natan and Rabinovitz

2011]). Kav LaOved reports that Thai women employed in the agricultural sector, where they are a gender minority, get a "boyfriend" to help prevent rampant harassment and assault by fellow migrant workers. Some find themselves "abused or harassed by their 'boyfriends.'" With limited Hebrew or English language skills, no translator, and fear of deportation, the rate of reported crime is severely limited.

23. In May 2002 Israel barred Palestinians from the West Bank and Gaza from gaining permanent residency or citizenship status when married to an Israeli permanent resident or citizen (family unification). The ban was incorporated into the Nationality and Entry into Israel Law (Temporary Order) in July 2003; it has been extended, and expanded to cover spouses from Iran, Iraq, Lebanon, and Syria as well. Primarily Palestinian women citizens are affected by the bans (WGSPWCI 2005, 15).

24. See Kemp (2007) and Kemp and Kfir (2016) for policies regulating legal status for non-Jewish foreign spouses.

25. This is a summary of Isabella's story, published on November 24, 2009, in honor of the IDEVAW (Vilnai 2009).

26. This is a summary of a newspaper story entitled "Non-Israeli Battered Wives Face Deportation and Custody Battles" (Lis 2013a).

27. Unlike many international agreements, the US Trafficking Victims Protection Act of 2000 also relies on the threat of material sanctions to inspire compliance (Efrat 2012, 175–76).

28. See summary of the committee's report: *knesset.gov.il/committees/eng/docs/vaadat_chakira_shahar_eng.htm*.

29. Israel's first report on trafficking was submitted by Martina Vandenberg (1997). The Knesset rapidly responded to Amnesty International's May 2000 report on criminal sex trafficking (Weisz-Rind 2000), but it did not preclude the Tier 3 ranking.

30. The National Inspector of Treatment for Domestic Violence in the Ministry of Social Services' Individual and Family Welfare Division is responsible for supervising the shelter. In 2009, with a rise in public concern for those trafficked for forced labor, and upon threat of demotion by the United States back to Tier 3, Atlas Shelter was established for men (Hacker and Cohen 2012, 33, 36, 39).

31. This is a summary of Roslana's story, published in Hacker and Cohen (2012, 135).

32. According to new research, about 12,000 women work in prostitution, mainly in Tel Aviv; 43 percent of prostitutes work in what are called "discrete apartments," 18 percent in escort services, and another 18 percent at strip clubs and other adult businesses, with only 6 percent of prostitutes engaged in street sex work (*Times of Israel*, 2016b). Just over half were immigrants from the FSU, and over 70 percent of those surveyed reported that financial hardship and the rising cost of living pulled them into sex work (ibid.). It is a NIS 1.2 billion (about $308 million in US dollars) industry (Lee and Kashti 2016).

33. The term "infiltrators" was used by the state to refer to Palestinians externally displaced after the 1948 War who sought to return to their homes and to Palestinians entering illegally to commit political violence.

34. Limited information is shared with detainees about the unnamed "third country" to which they would be deported (Rozen 2015a, 14, 15; Rozen 2015b).
35. This policy is not upheld systematically, and men with girlfriends and wives have been summoned to Holot.
36. Several advocacy groups work with African refugees, including ACRI, African Refugee Development Center, Aid Organization for Refugees and Asylum Seekers in Israel, Amnesty International–Israel, Kav LaOved, Physicians for Human Rights Open Clinic, and Hotline for Refugees and Migrants. In addition to the EWCC, battered women are referred to the private Carmel Shelter in the north, the state's Ma'agan Shelter and the ARDC shelter.
37. Drawn from Lazareva (2013).
38. In 2012, 15.1 percent of government expenditures were allocated to defense (CBS 2013, 22).
39. Housing costs and economic opportunity tend to correspond with population density, which ranges from a high of 7657.5 persons per square kilometer in the Tel Aviv district to 80.8 in the Southern District (CBS 2013, 5).
40. Final election results did not bear this out: Likud (30), Zionist Union (24), Joint List (13), Yesh Atid (11), Kulanu (10), Habayit Hayehudi (8), Shas (7), United Torah Judaism (6), Yisrael Beitenu (6), and Meretz (5) (Pfeffer 2015).
41. These data from the emergency shelter in Haifa, officially designated as "multicultural," jibe with data from the same year (2010) presented by the Israel Women's Network (Wilmovsky and Tamir 2012, 86): Jewish (56 percent), Muslim (25 percent), Bedouin (6 percent), Christian (7 percent), Druze (2 percent), and No Religion (3 percent). Overall, women from the FSU made up 14 percent, and women from Ethiopia made up 12 percent of women in shelter that year.

CHAPTER 6

1. Recent estimates indicate about 11 percent of Jewish Israeli couples get married abroad (Ilan 2016). Those disqualified by the rabbinut include hundreds of thousands of immigrants from the former Soviet Union whose Jewishness qualified them only for citizenship but not for marriage, and tens of thousands of other Israeli Jews who breach Jewish law. Calls for religious pluralism by non-Orthodox Jewry are echoed by calls for civil marriage by some feminists and the LGBT movement.
2. Despite variations in data collection, higher levels of household firearm ownership are correlated with higher rates of female homicide victimization in general and even higher rates of firearm homicide victimization around the world (Hemenway, Shinoda-Tagawa, and Miller 2002; UNODC 2014). Dangerousness and lethality assessments point to men's previous use of a firearm to threaten or harm and/or access to a firearm as significant risk factors for battered women (Campbell 2007). A high risk of lethality for women is associated with firearms in the home (Campbell et al. 2003; Websdale 1999).
3. Seventy-two firearm dealers operate in the state whose population is about 8.1 million. In contrast, according to the US Bureau of Alcohol, Tobacco, Firearms and Explosives, in January 2013, there were over 58,725 federally licensed gun

dealers for a population numbering about 316 million. Nevertheless, "the super-vision and issuing of firearms licenses was severely lacking" until a single public crime committed in September 1992 by a former psychiatric patient stunned the country (Amit 2012, 11). Eitan Mor, a twenty-five-year-old man living in Jerusalem, returned to the mental health clinic where he had been treated and, armed with a 9mm Beretta automatic pistol and Uzi submachine gun, shot and killed four women, including his former counselor, and injured two others; it was reported that he blamed the counselor for being denied a truck driver's license and that he had been inadvertently hired and armed as a security guard because of inadequate oversight (JTA, 1992; National Organization of Parents of Murdered Children n.d.).

4. Recommendations from the Cohen Committee were put into place by 1995, the same year Prime Minister Rabin was assassinated by Jewish extremist Yigal Amir, another twenty-five-year-old man armed with a 9mm Beretta. Eligibility for a license depends on age, residency, occupation (e.g., bus driver), security history (e.g., type, length of, and rank in service), and arrest record (e.g., drug use or domestic violence) (Rosenbaum 2012, 49). An applicant must also be certified medically, demonstrate a reasonable need for a gun, complete a shooting range training and test, provide proof of a home storage safe, and if awarded eligibility, renew the license every three years. Once awarded, a gun license typically allows a person one handgun. As of September 2013, private gun licenses numbered 153,044 (in contrast to the late 1990s when there were about 300,000 such licenses garnered in response to the First Intifada), and security guard licenses num-bered 132,959 for a total of 296,003 licenses (Ministry of Public Security 2014).

References

Abraham, Margaret. 2000. *Speaking the Unspeakable: Marital Violence among South Asian Immigrants in the United States*. New Brunswick: Rutgers University Press.

Abramov, S. Zalman. 1976. *Perpetual Dilemma: Jewish Religion in the Jewish State*. Rutherford, NJ: Fairleigh Dickinson University Press.

Abdu, Janan. 2009. "Mada al-Carmel/Arab Center for Applied Research Information Papers. Resisting Subjugation: Palestinian Women's and Feminist Organizations with the 1948 Green Line." *Jadal* 4:1–15.

Abou Ramadan, Mousa. 2003. "Judicial Activism of the Shari'ah Appeals Court in Israel (1994–2001): Rise and Crisis." *Fordham International Law Journal* 27:254–98.

———. 2006. "Divorce Reform in the Sharia Court of Appeals in Israel (1992–2003)." *Islamic Law and Society* 13 (2): 242–74.

———. 2008. "Notes on the Anomaly of the Sharia Field in Israel." *Islamic Law and Society* 15 (1): 84–111.

Abou-Tabickh, Lilian. 2010. "Women's Masked Migration: Palestinian Women Explain Their Move upon Marriage." In *Displaced at Home: Ethnicity and Gender among Palestinians in Israel*, edited by Rhoda Kanaaneh and Isis Nusair, 189–205. Albany: SUNY Press.

Abramovitz, Mimi. 1996. *Regulating the Lives of Women: Social Welfare Policy from Colonial Times to the Present*. Boston: South End Press.

Abulafia, Judith. n.d. "The Social Construction of Violence against Women as a Social Problem in Israel" (unpublished manuscript).

Abu-Rabia-Queder, Sarab. 2007. "The Activism of Bedouin Women: Social and Political Resistance." *HAGAR Studies in Culture, Polity and Identities* 7 (2): 67–84.

Abu-Rabia-Queder, Sarab, and Naomi Weiner-Levy. 2013. "Between Local and Foreign Structures: Exploring the Agency of Palestinian Women in Israel." *Social Politics* 20 (1): 88–108.

Adelman, Madelaine. "Gender, Law and Nation: The Politics of Domestic Violence in Israel" PhD diss., Duke University, 1997.

———. 2000. "No Way Out: Divorce-Related Domestic Violence in Israel." *Violence Against Women* 6 (11): 1223–54.

———. 2003. "The Military, Militarism and the Militarization of Domestic Violence." *Violence Against Women* 9 (9): 1118–52.

———. 2004a. "The Battering State: Towards a Political Economy of Domestic Violence." *Journal of Poverty: Innovations on Social, Political and Economic Inequalities* 8 (3): 55–74.

———. 2004b. "Domestic Violence and Difference." *American Ethnologist* 31 (1): 131–141.

———. 2005a. "Domestic Violence." In *Companion to Gender Studies*, edited by Philomena Essed, Audrey Kobayashi, and David Theo Goldberg, 192–201. Oxford, UK: Blackwell Publishers.

————. 2005b. "Domestic Violence in Israel." In *Encyclopedia of Women and Islamic Cultures*. Vol. 2, edited by Suad Joseph, 199–121. Leiden, the Netherlands: Brill Academic Publishers.

————. 2010. "Anthropologies of Domestic Violence: Studying Crime in Situ." In *International Handbook of Criminology*, edited by Shlomo Giora Shoham, Paul Knepper, and Martin Kett, 183–209. Oxford, UK: Taylor & Francis.

————. 2014. "Sex and the City: The Politics of Gay Pride in Jerusalem." In *Jerusalem: Conflict and Cooperation in a Contested City*, edited by Madelaine Adelman and Miriam Elman, 233–60. Syracuse, NY: Syracuse University Press.

Adelman, Madelaine, Edna Erez, and Nadera Shalhoub-Kevorkian. 2003. "Policing Violence against Minority Women in Multicultural Societies: 'Community' and the Politics of Exclusion." *Police and Society: An Interdisciplinary Journal of Law Enforcement and Criminology* 7: 105–33.

Adelman, Madelaine, Hillary Haldane, and Jennifer Wies. 2012. "A Transdisciplinary Effort to Mobilize Culture as an Asset against Gender Violence." *Violence Against Women* 18 (6): 691–700.

Adelman, Madelaine, Margaret Hobart, and Karen Rosenberg. 2016. "Simulations and Social Empathy: Domestic Violence Education in the New Millennium." *Violence Against Women* 22 (12):1451–62.

Adelman, Madelaine, and Miriam Elman, eds. 2014. *Jerusalem: Conflict and Cooperation in a Contested City*. Syracuse: Syracuse University Press.

Adelman, Madelaine, and Phoebe Morgan. 2006. "Law Enforcement versus Battered Women." *Affilia: Journal of Women and Social Work* 21 (1): 28–45.

Adva Center. 2014. *Cherchez la femme in the National Budget of Israel*. Tel Aviv: Adva Center.

Adwan, Sami, Dan Bar-On, and Eyal Naveh, eds. 2012. *Side by Side: Parallel Histories of Israel-Palestine*. New York: New Press.

Agmon, Iris. 2006. *Family and Court: Legal Culture and Modernity in Late Ottoman Palestine*. Syracuse: Syracuse University Press.

Aharoni, Sarai. 2006. *The Impact of War in the North on the Israeli Women and Girls Lives: Gender Analysis*. Haifa: Isha L'Isha. [Hebrew]

————. 2014. "Internal Variation in Norm Localization: Implementing Security Council Resolution 1325 in Israel." *Social Politics* 21 (1): 1–25.

Aharoni, Sarai, and Rula Deeb. 2004. *Where Are All the Women? UN Security Council Resolution 1325: Gender Perspectives of the Israeli-Palestinian Conflict*. Haifa: Isha L'Isha—Haifa Feminist Center and Kayan-Feminist Organization.

Aharoni, Sarai, Anat Saragusti, and Nurit Haghagh, eds. 2009. *Women Confronting Peace: Voices from Israel*. Jerusalem: Israeli Branch of the International Women's Commission (IWC).

Aharoni, Yair. 1991. *The Israeli Economy: Dreams and Realities*. New York: Routledge.

————. 1998. "The Changing Political Economy of Israel." *Annals of the American Academy of Political and Social Science* 555: 127–46.

Ahmed, Leila. 1986. "Women and the Advent of Islam." *Signs* 11 (4): 665–91.

Aiken, Jane. 2001. "Provocateurs for Justice." *Clinical Law Review* 7 (2): 287–306.

Ajzenstadt, Mimi. 1998. "The Study of Crime and Social Control in Israel: Some Theoretical Observations." In *Crime and Criminal Justice in Israel: Assessing the Knowledge Base toward the Twenty-First Century*, edited by Robert Friedmann, 3–25. Binghamton, NY: SUNY Press.

————. 2002. "Crime, Social Control and the Process of Social Classification: Juvenile Delinquency/Justice Discourse in Israel, 1948–1970." *Social Problems* 49 (3): 585–604.

———. 2009. "Moral Panic and Neoliberalism: The Case of Single Mothers on Welfare in Israel." *British Journal of Criminology* 49: 68–87.

———. 2010. "Children, Families and Women in the Israeli State, 1880s–2008." In *Children, Gender and Families in Mediterranean Welfare States*, edited by Mimi Ajzenstadt and John Gal, 143–163. New York: Springer.

Ajzenstadt, Mimi, and Ariel Barak. 2008. "Terrorism and Risk Management." *Punishment and Society* 10 (4): 355–74.

Ajzenstadt, Mimi, and John Gal. 2001. "Appearances Can Be Deceptive: Gender in the Israeli Welfare State." *Social Politics* 8 (3): 292–324.

———, eds. 2010. *Children, Gender and Families in Mediterranean Welfare States*. New York: Springer.

Alahmad, Tgreed, and Maha El Taji. 2008. *Women Demand Mobility: Documenting Local Women's Experience in the Village of Maghar*. Haifa: Kayan Feminist Organization and Pardes Publishing House.

Alcalde, M. Cristina. 2007. "Going Home: A Feminist Anthropologist's Reflections on Dilemmas of Power and Positionality in the Field." *Meridians: Feminism, Race, Transnationalism* 7 (2): 143–162.

———. 2010a. "Violence across Borders: Familism, Hegemonic Masculinity, and Self-Sacrificing Femininity in the Lives of Mexican and Peruvian Migrants." *Latino Studies* 8 (1): 48–68.

———. 2010b. *The Woman in the Violence: Gender, Poverty, and Resistance in Peru*. Nashville, TN: Vanderbilt University Press.

Al-Krenawi, Alean, and John R. Graham. 1998. "Divorce among Muslim Arab Women in Israel." *Journal of Divorce & Remarriage* 29 (3/4): 103–119.

Alon, Gideon. 2005. "Knesset, IDF Tackle Taboo of Soldier Suicides." *Haaretz*, June 29. *www.haaretz.com*.

Altheide, David. 2002. *Creating Fear: News and the Construction of Crisis*. Chicago: Aldine Transaction Publishers.

Altinbas, Nihan. 2014. "Marriage and Divorce in the Late Ottoman Empire: Social Upheaval, Women's Rights and the Need for New Family Law." *Journal of Family History* 39 (2): 114–25.

Amir, Shmuel. 2002. "Overseas Foreign Workers in Israel: Policy Aims and Labor Market Outcomes." *International Migration Review* 36 (1): 41–57.

Amit, Yakov. 2012. "Gun Control in Israel: A Short History." Jerusalem: Ministry of Public Security.

Anderson, Benedict. 1983. *Imagined Communities: Reflections on the Origin and Spread of Nationalism*. New York: Verso.

Aretxaga, Begoña. 2003. "Maddening States." *Annual Review of Anthropology* 32: 393–410.

Arlosoroff, Meirav. 2015. "July 1, 1985: The Day Israeli Capitalism Was Born." *Haaretz*, July 3. *www.haaretz.com*.

Arnold, Gretchen, and Jami Ake. 2013. "Reframing the Narrative of the Battered Women's Movement." *Violence Against Women* 19 (5): 557–78.

Aronoff, Myron, and Jan Kubik. 2013. *Anthropology and Political Science: A Convergent Approach*. New York: Berghahn Books.

Avni, Noga. 1990. "Battered Wives and Policemen: Victims of the System." *Plilim, Israeli Journal of Criminal Justice* 1:171–84. [Hebrew]

———. 1991a. "Battered Wives: The Home as a Total Institution." *Violence and Victims* 6 (2): 137–49.

———. 1991b. "Battered Wives: The Phenomenon and the Causes." *Crime and Social Deviance* 18: 13–29. [Hebrew]

———. 1991c. "Economic Exchange between Battered Wives and Their Husbands in Israel." *International Review of Victimology* 2: 117–35.

———. 1991d. "Battered Wives: Characteristics of Their Courtship Days." *Journal of Interpersonal Violence* 6 (2): 232–39.

Azaryahu, Maoz. (1992). "War Memorials and the Commemoration of the Israeli War of Independence, 1948–1956." *Studies in Zionism* 13: 57–77.

Azaryahu, Sarah. (1948) 1980. *The Union of Hebrew Women for Equal Rights in Eretz Yisrael: A Selected History of the Women's Movement in Israel 1900–1947.* Translated by Marcia Freedman. Haifa: Women's Aid Fund.

Backhouse, Roger, and Tamotsu Nishizawa, eds. 2010. *No Wealth but Life: Welfare Economics and the Welfare State in Britain, 1880–1845.* Cambridge: Cambridge University Press.

Badi, Joseph. 1959. *Religion in Israel Today: The Relationship between State and Religion.* New York: Bookman Associates.

Bancroft, Lundy, and Jay Silverman. 2011. *The Batterer as Parent: Addressing the Impact of Domestic Violence on Family Dynamics.* Thousand Oaks, CA: Sage.

Bank of Israel. 2014. *Bank of Israel Annual Report, 2013.* Jerusalem: Bank of Israel.

Barak, Oren, and Gabriel Sheffer. 2006. "Israel's 'Security Network' and Its Impact: An Exploration of a New Approach." *International Journal of Middle East Studies* 38 (2): 235–61.

———. 2007. "The Study of Civil-Military Relations in Israel: A New Perspective." *Israel Studies* 12 (1): 1–27.

Barkali, Netanela, Miri Endeweld, Daniel Gottlieb, and Oren Heller. 2013. *Poverty and Social Gaps Annual Report, 2013.* Jerusalem: National Insurance Institute, Research and Planning Administration.

Barnett, Ola, Cindy Miller-Perrin, and Robin Perrin. 2011. *Family Violence across the Life Span,* 3rd ed. Thousand Oaks, CA: Sage.

Barrett, Michele, and Mary McIntosh. 1982. *The Anti-Social Family.* London: NLB.

Bartram, David. 1998. "Foreign Workers in Israel: History and Theory." *International Migration Review* 32 (2): 303–25.

Barzilai, Gad. 1996. *Wars, Internal Conflicts and Political Order: A Jewish Democracy in the Middle East.* Albany: SUNY Press.

Bassock, Moti. 2013a. "Israel Shells Out Almost a Fifth of National Budget on Defense, Figures Show." *Haaretz,* Feb. 14. *www.haaretz.com.*

———. 2013b. "Defense Spending on Staff Exceeds Entire Israeli Welfare Budget." *Haaretz,* Nov. 3. *www.haaretz.com.*

———. 2015. "After 40 Years of Decline, Israel Defense Burden Still High." *Haaretz,* Feb. 13. *www.haaretz.com.*

Bassock, Moti, and Zvi Zrahiya. 2015. "Much of Israel's Budget Windfall Likely to Go to Defense. *Haaretz,* Oct. 12. *www.haaretz.com.*

Batshon, Shirin. 2010. *Spousal Obedience in the Religious Courts.* Haifa: Kayan-Feminist Organization.

———. 2012. *Ecclesiastical Courts in Israel: A Gender-Responsive Analysis.* Haifa: Kayan-Feminist Organization.

Bayyadi-Shaloun. 2014. "Mada al-Carmel Report: Feminist Associations' Activism Regarding Femicide in Palestinian Society." *Jadal* 19: 1–4.

Beck, Connie J. A., Michele E. Walsh, Mindy Mechanic, Aurelio Figueredo, and Mei-Kuang Chen. 2011. *Intimate Partner Abuse in Divorce Mediation: Outcomes from a Long-Term Multi-Cultural Study*. Washington, DC: National Institute of Justice.

Beilin, Yossi. 1992. *Israel: A Concise History*. New York: St. Martin's Press.

Ben-Ari, Eyal. 1987. "On Acknowledgements in Ethnographies." *Journal of Anthropological Research* 43 (1): 63–84.

———. 1998. *Mastering Soldiers: Conflict, Emotions, and the Enemy in an Israeli Military Unit*. New York: Berghahn Books.

Ben-Eliezer, Uri. 1998. *The Making of Israeli Militarism*. Bloomington: Indiana University Press.

Ben Natan, Merav. 2011. "Perceived Factors Affecting Decision to Report Incidents of Domestic Violence Among Ethiopian Women in Israel." *Journal of Trauma Nursing* 18 (2): 121–26.

Ben Natan, Smadar, and Rela Mazali. 2014. *Gun Free Kitchen Tables Annual Report, 2013*. Haifa: Isha L'Isha.

Benn, Aluf. 2002. "In Israel, Too Much to Leave to the Generals." *Washington Post*. Aug. 18. *www.washingtonpost.com*.

Ben Porat, Anat, and Haya Itzhaky. 2008. "Factors That Influence Life Satisfaction among Battered Women in Shelters: Those Who Stay versus Those Who Leave." *Journal of Family Violence* 23: 597–604.

Ben-Porat, Guy. 2008. "Political Economy: Liberalization and Globalization." In *Israel Since 1980*, Guy Pen-Porat, Yagil Levy, Shlomo Mizrahi, Arye Naor, and Erez Tzfadia, 91–116. Cambridge: Cambridge University Press.

Ben-Porat, Guy, and Fany Yuval. 2012. "Minorities in Democracy and Policing Policy: From Alienation to Cooperation." *Policing and Society* 22 (2): 235–52.

Ben-Porat, Yoram. 1986. *The Israeli Economy: Maturing through Crises*. Cambridge, MA: Harvard University Press.

Benson, Miriam, and Harverd, Dorit, eds. 1988. *The Status of Women in Israel: The Implementation of the Recommendations of the Israeli Government Commission of Investigation*. Jerusalem: Israel Women's Network.

Ben-Yehuda, Dana, and Orly Shafir. 2006. "House of Hope: Group Treatment with Violent Men." *Apeture* 10: 21–34. [Hebrew]

Ben-Ze'ev, Efrat, and Eyal Ben-Ari. 1999. "War, Heroism, and Public Representations: The Case of a Museum of 'Coexistence' in Jerusalem." In *The Military and Militarism in Israeli Society*, edited by Edna Lomsky-Feder and Eyal Ben-Ari, 117–138. Albany: State University of New York Press.

Berheide, Catherine W. 1992. "Women Still 'Stuck' in Low-Level Jobs." *Women in Public Service* 3 (1): 1–4.

Berkovitch, Nitza. 1999. *From Motherhood to Citizenship: Women's Rights and International Organizations*. Baltimore: Johns Hopkins University Press.

Berkovitch, Nitza, and Neve Gordon. 2008. "The Political Economy of Transnational Regimes: The Case of Human Rights." *International Studies Quarterly* 52 (4): 881–904.

Bernstein, Deborah. 1987. *The Struggle for Equality: Urban Women Workers in Prestate Israeli Society*. New York: Praeger.

Bertone, Andrea Marie. 2000. "Sexual Trafficking in Women: International Political Economy and the Politics of Sex." *Gender Issues* 18 (1): 4–22.

Best, Joel. 2008. *Social Problems*. New York: W. W. Norton & Co.

Biale, Rachel. 1984. *Women & Jewish Law: An Exploration of Issues in Halakhic Sources.* New York: Schocken Books.

Bichler, Shomshon, and Jonathan Nitzan. 1996. "Military Spending and Differential Accumulation: A New Approach to the Political Economy of Armament: The Case of Israel." *Review of Radical Political Economics* 28 (1): 51–95.

Birenbaum-Carmeli, Daphna, and Yoram Carmeli. 2010. *Kin, Gene, Community: Reproductive Technologies among Jewish Israelis.* New York: Berghahn Books.

Black, Michelle C., Kathleen Basile, Matthew Breiding, Sharon Smith, Mikel Walters, Melissa Merrick, Jieru Chen, and Mark Stevens. 2011. *The National Intimate Partner and Sexual Violence Survey (NISVS): 2010 Summary Report.* Atlanta: National Center for Injury Prevention and Control, Centers for Disease Control and Prevention.

Blackman, Shane. 2007. "'Hidden Ethnography': Crossing Emotional Borders in Qualitative Accounts of Young People's Lives." *Sociology* 41 (4): 699–716.

Blee, Kathleen. 1998. "White-Knuckle Research: Emotional Dynamics in Fieldwork with Racist Activists." *Qualitative Sociology* 21 (4): 381–99.

Blim, Michael. 2000. "Capitalisms in Late Modernity." *Annual Review of Anthropology* 29: 25–38.

Blumberg, Arnold. 1985. *Zion before Zionism 1838–1880.* Syracuse, NY: Syracuse University Press.

Blumenfeld, Revital. 2012. "Israel's Immigration Ministry to Combat Domestic Violence among Ethiopians." *Haaretz*, Jan. 26. *www.haaretz.com.*

Bogoch, Bryna. 1999. "'Judging in a 'Different Voice': Gender and the Sentencing of Violent Offences in Israel." *International Journal of the Sociology of Law* 27: 51–78.

Bogoch, Bryna, and Rachelle Don-Yechiya. 1999. *The Gender of Justice: Bias against Women in Israeli Courts.* Jerusalem: Jerusalem Institute for Israel Research.

Bogoch, Byrna, and Ruth Halperin-Kaddari. 2006. "Divorce Israeli Style: Professional Perceptions of Gender and Power in Mediated and Lawyer-Negotiated Divorces." *Law and Policy* 28 (2): 137–63.

Bornstein, Avram. 2002. *Crossing the Green Line Between the West Bank and Israel.* Philadelphia: University of Pennsylvania Press.

Bowers, Liora. Aug. 2014. "Family Structure and Well-Being Across Israel's Diverse Population." Jerusalem: Taub Center for Social Policy Studies in Israel.

Boyarin, Daniel. 1997. *Unheroic Conduct: The Rise of Heterosexuality and the Invention of the Jewish Man.* Berkeley: University of California Press.

Brady, David. 2008. *Rich Democracies, Poor People: How Politics Explain Poverty.* New York: Oxford University.

Braudo, Yael. 2012. "Legislative Initiatives of Israeli Women's Organizations, 1948–1973." *Israel Studies Review* 27 (2): 166–89.

Breitowitz, Irving. 1993. *Between Civil and Religious Law: The Plight of the Agunah in American Society.* Westport, CN: Greenwood Press.

Bridger, Sue, Rebecca Kay, and Kathryn Pinnick. 1996. *No More Heroines? Russia, Women and the Market.* New York: Routledge.

British Broadcasting Corporation News. 2001. "Israel Moves towards Unity Deal." BBC News Online, Feb. 16. *www.news.bbc.co.uk.*

Bronofsky, Yael. 2007. "In the Ethiopian Community No One Speaks About Violence." *Ynet*, June 19. *www.ynet.com.*

Brown, Wendy. 1995. *States of Injury: Power and Freedom in Late Modernity.* Princeton, NJ: Princeton University Press.

Brownson, Elizabeth. 2008. "Gender, Muslim Family Law and Contesting Patriarchy in Mandate Palestine, 1925–1939." PhD diss., Department of History, University of California, Santa Barbara.

Broza, David, and Yonaton Geffen. 1978. "Yihye tov" [Things will be better] On *David Broza* (album). Jerusalem: NMC.

Brush, Lisa. 1990. "Violent Acts and Injurious Outcomes in Married Couples: Methodological Issues in the National Survey of Families and Households." *Gender and Society* 4 (1): 56–67.

———. 2011. *Poverty, Battered Women, and Work in U.S. Public Policy.* New York: Oxford University Press.

Buchbinder, Eli, and Zvi Eisikovits. 2008a. "Collaborative Discourse: The Case of Police and Social Work Relationships in Intimate Violence Intervention in Israel." *Journal of Social Service Research* 34 (4): 1–13.

———. 2008b. "Doing Treatment: Batterers' Experience of Intervention." *Children and Youth Services Review* 30: 616–30.

Bugensky, Yovel. November 2013. "Violence against Women: Aggregated Data, 2013." Presented to the Committee on the Advancement of Women. Jerusalem: Knesset Research and Information Center.

Bumiller, Kristen. 1987. *The Civil Rights Society: The Social Construction of Victims.* Baltimore: Johns Hopkins University Press.

———. 2008. *In an Abusive State: How Neoliberalism Appropriated the Feminist Movement against Sexual Violence.* Durham: Duke University Press.

Bunch, Charlotte, and Roxanne Carillo. 1991. *Gender Violence: A Development and Human Rights Issue.* New Brunswick, NJ: Center for Women's Global Leadership.

Burgansky, Michal. 1989. "A Comparison between Battered Women Living at Home and Residing in a Shelter." *Journal of Social Work and Policy in Israel* 2: 7–29.

Bush, Diane. 1992. "Women's Movements and State Policy Reform Aimed at Domestic Violence against Women: A Comparison of the Consequences of Movement Mobilization in the United States and India." *Gender and Society* 6 (4): 587–608.

Buzawa, Eve, Carl Buzawa, and Evan Stark. 2012. *Responding to Domestic Violence: The Integration of Policing and Human Services,* 4th ed. Thousand Oaks: Sage.

Campbell, Jacquelyn, ed. 2007. *Assessing Dangerous: Violence by Batterers and Child Abusers,* 2nd ed. New York: Springer Publishing.

Campbell, Jacquelyn C., Daniel Webster, Jane Koziol-McLain, Carolyn Block, Doris Campbell, Mary Ann Curry, Faye Gary et al. 2003. "Risk Factors for Femicide in Abusive Relationships: Results from a Multisite Case Control Study." *American Journal of Public Health* 93 (7): 1089–97.

Canaday, Margot. 2009. *The Straight State: Sexuality and Citizenship in Twentieth Century America.* Princeton, NJ: Princeton University Press.

Carey, David, Jr., and M. Gabriela Torres. 2010. "Precursors to Femicide: Guatemalan Women in a Vortex of Violence." *Latin American Research Review* 45 (3): 142–64.

Carmi, Shulamit, and Henry Rosenfeld. 2010. "Israel's Political Economy and the Widening Class Gap between Its National Groups." In *Perspectives on Israeli Anthropology,* edited by Esther Herzog, Orit Abuhav, Harvey Goldberg, and Emmanuel Marx, 377–412. Detroit, MI: Wayne State University Press.

Carmeli, Yoram, and Kalman Applebaum, eds. 2004. *Consumption and Market Society in Israel.* New York: Berg.

Carrier, James, and Daniel Miller, eds. 1998. *Virtualism: A New Political Economy.* Oxford, UK: Berg Publishers.

Cavaglion, Gabriel. 2010. "Trafficking in Women for Sex in a Glocal Context: The Case of Israel." In *Social Issues, Justice and Status: Who Pays the Price? Foreign Workers, Society, Crime and the Law*, edited by Mally Shechory, Sarah Ben David, and Dan Soen, 201–12. New York: Nova Science Publishers.

Cavender, Gray, and Nancy Jurik. 2012. *Justice Provocateur: Jane Tennison and Policing in Prime Suspect*. Urbana: University of Illinois Press.

Central Bureau of Statistics. 2013a. *Israel in Figures, 2013*. Jerusalem: CBS. *cbs.gov.il/www/publications/isr_in_n13e.pdf*.

———. 2013b. *Statistical Abstract of Israel 2013, no. 64*. Jerusalem: CBS.

———. 2014. *Statistical Abstract of Israel 2014, no. 65*. Jerusalem: CBS.

———. 2015. *Statistical Abstract of Israel 2015, no. 66*. Jerusalem: CBS.

Central Intelligence Agency (CIA). 2016. *The World Factbook: Israel*. Langley, VA: CIA. *www.cia.gov/library/publications/resources/the-world-factbook/index.html*.

Chadburn, Melissa. 2015. "Resilience Is Futile: How Well-Meaning Nonprofits Perpetuate Poverty." *Jezebel*. July 14. *jezebel.com/resilience-is-futile-how-well-meaning-nonprofits-perpe-1716461384*.

Chatterjee, Partha. 1989. "Colonialism, Nationalism, and Colonized Women: The Contest in India." *American Ethnologist* 16 (4): 622–33.

Chazan, Naomi. 1991. "Israeli Women and Peace Activism." In *Calling the Equality Bluff: Women in Israel*, edited by Marilyn Safir and Barbara Swirski, 152–61. New York: Pergamon Press.

———. 2004. "Strategies for the Inclusion of Women in Conflict Resolution." In *Where Are All the Women? U.N. Security Council Resolution 1325: Gender Perspectives of the Israeli-Palestinian Conflict*, edited by Sarai Aharoni and Rula Deeb, 54–58. Haifa: Pardes Publishing House.

———. 2014. "Israel's Gender Revolution." *Times of Israel*, Dec. 22. *www.timesofisrael.com*.

Chief Rabbinate. "Rabbinical Courts Annual Report, 2014." Jerusalem: Chief Rabbinate, 2015.

Chigier, Moshe. 1967. "The Rabbinical Courts in the State of Israel." *Israel Law Review* 2 (2): 147–81.

———. 1985. *Husband and Wife in Israeli Law*. Jerusalem: Harry Fischel Institute.

Coates, Ta-Nehisi. 2014. "This Town Needs a Better Class of Racist." *The Atlantic*, May 1. *www.theatlantic.com*.

Cohen, Gili. 2014. "In the Wake of the Escalation: Ministry of Public Security Authorizes Significant Easing of Distribution of Gun Licenses." *Haaretz*, Nov. 20. *www.haaretz.com*. [Hebrew]

———. 2015. "IDF Proposes $7.8 Billion Budget: Highest in Israel's History." *Haaretz*, July 21. *www.haaretz.com*.

Cohen, Gili, Nir Hasson, and Roy Arad. 2014. "Police Looking into Easing Gun Control in Light of Terror Attacks." *Haaretz*, Nov. 19. *www.haaretz.com*.

Cohen, Gili, and Yaniv Kubovich. 2013. "Israeli Security Guards Now Required to Leave Guns at Work, Following String of Fatal Shootings." *Haaretz*, July 25. *www.haaretz.com*.

Cohen, Gili, Yaniv Kubovich, and Jonathan Lis. 2013. "Does Israel Need Gun Control? Israeli Civilians Own 292,265 Firearms—but Does That Make the Country Safer?" *Haaretz*, April 26. *www.haaretz.com*.

Cohen, Mitchell. 1987. *Zion and State: Nation, Class and the Shaping of Modern Israel*. Oxford, UK: Basil Blackwell.

Cohen, Orna, and Rivka Savaya. 2003. "Lifestyle Differences in Traditionalism and Modernity and Reasons for Divorce among Muslim Palestinian Citizens of Israel." *Journal of Comparative Family Studies* 34 (2): 283–302.

Cohen, Orna, Rivka Savaya, and Ahmed Natour. 1997. "Muslim Women's Reasons for, Ways of Dealing with, and Adjusting to Divorce in a Mixed City in Israel." *Society and Welfare: Quarterly for Social Work* 4: 395–415. [Hebrew]

Cohen, Shalva. 1995. "Domestic Violence: Treatment in Israeli Prisons." In *The Prevention of Crime and the Treatment of Offenders in Israel, A Report*, edited by Ruth Geva. Presented at the Ninth UN Congress on the Prevention of Crime and the Treatment of Offenders, April 19–May 8, Cairo, Egypt. Jerusalem: Ministry of Foreign Affairs.

Cohen, Sherrill. 1992. *The Evolution of Women's Asylums Since 1500: From Refuges for Ex-Prostitutes to Shelters for Battered Women*. New York: Oxford University Press.

Cohen, Stuart A. 2006. "Changing Civil–Military Relations in Israel: Towards an Over-Subordinate IDF?" *Israel Affairs* 12 (4): 769–88.

Cohen, Tova, and Steven Scheer. 2015. "Netanyahu Defeat Could Mean 'Peace Dividend' for Israel's Business Sector." *Haaretz*, Mar. 17. *www.haaretz.com.*

Cohen, Tzahi. 1995. "It Is the Man Who Is Afraid." *Yediot Ahronot*, January 4.

Cohen, Zoheret. 2010. "Religious, Hurt and Hopeful." *Ynet*, Sept. 12. *www.ynetnews.com.*

Coker, Donna. 2000. "Shifting Power for Battered Women: Law, Material Resources and Poor Women of Color. *University of California, Davis Law Review* 33: 1009–55.

———. 2001. "Crime Control and Feminist Law Reform in Domestic Violence Law: A Critical Review." *Buffalo Criminal Law Review* 4: 801–60.

Cole, Simon, and Michael Lynch. 2006. "The Social and Legal Construction of Suspects." *Annual Review of Law and Social Science* 2: 39–60.

Coles, Jan, Jill Astbury, Elizabeth Dartnall, and Shazneen Limjerwala. 2014. "A Qualitative Exploration of Researcher Trauma and Researchers' Responses to Investigating Sexual Violence." *Violence Against Women* 20 (1): 95–117.

Colker, Ruth. 1998. *American Law in the Age of Hypercapitalism: The Worker, the Family, and the State*. New York: NYU Press.

Commission on the Status of Women. 1978. "The Report of the Sub-Committee on the Status of Women: Discussions and Conclusions." Jerusalem: Prime Minister's Office.

Condon, Stephanie. 2013. "Communicating Prevalence Survey Results." In *Framing Sexual and Domestic Violence through Language*, edited by Renate Klein, 41–56. London: Palgrave Macmillan.

cooke, miriam. 1996. *Woman and the War Story*. Berkeley: University of California Press.

Cooke, William Smith. (1876) 1968. *The Ottoman Empire and Its Tributary States (excepting Egypt), with a Sketch of Greece*. Amsterdam: B. R. Gruner.

Curiel, Ilana. 2013. "Mother of Murdered Girls Ignored by Police Day before Tragedy." *Ynet News*, May 24. *www.ynetnews.com.*

Curtis, Karen. 2001. "Welfare Dependency in Delaware: A Study of the State's Program Reform and Advocacy for Change." *Journal of Poverty* 5 (2): 45–66.

Dahan-Kalev, Henrietta. 2001. "Tensions in Israeli Feminism: The Mizrahi-Ashkenazi Rift." *Women's Studies International Forum* 24: 1–16.

Dahan-Kalev, Henriette, and Emilie LeFebvre, with Amal El-Sana-Alh'jooj. 2012. *Palestinian Activism in Israel: A Bedouin Woman Leader in a Changing Middle East*. New York: Palgrave Macmillan.

Dahan, Nicole, and Tzipi Levi. 2011. "Spiritual Abuse among Religious Women." *Social Welfare* 7–27. [Hebrew]

Daher-Nashef, Suhad. 2014. "A Study on the Attitudes of Palestinian Youth towards the Killing of Women." Haifa: Kayan-Feminist Organization and Baladna Association for Arab Youth. *www.kayan.org.il/en*.

Dagan-Buzaglo, Noga, Yael Hasson, and Ariane Ophir. 2014. "Gender Salary Gaps in Israel." Tel Aviv: Adva Center.

Danan, Anat. 2009. "The Significance of Spiritual Experience of Orthodox Jewish Women on an Intimate Relationship." Master's thesis, Faculty of Social Welfare and Health Studies, School of Social Work, University of Haifa. [Hebrew]

Daniele, Guilia. 2014. *Women, Reconciliation and the Israeli Palestinian Conflict: The Road Not Taken*. New York: Routledge.

Daoud, Suheir Abu Oksa. 2009. *Palestinian Women and Politics in Israel*. Gainesville: University of Florida Press.

———. 2012. "Palestinian Working Women in Israel: National Oppression and Social Constraints." *Journal of Middle East Women's Studies* 8 (2): 78–101.

Davar. 1991. "'The situation is very shocking,' says Shilanski at the End of a Tour in a Shelter for Battered Women." *Davar*, Nov. 25.

Davison, Roderic. 1963. *Reform in the Ottoman Empire 1856–1876*. Princeton, NJ: Princeton University Press.

Dayan, Aryeh. 2006. "Better to Be a Mamzer or Grow Up Without a Father?" *Haaretz*, Aug. 30. *www.haaretz.com*.

Dekel, Rachel, and Einat Peled. 2000. "Staff Burnout in Israeli Battered Women's Shelters." *Journal of Social Service Research* 26 (3): 65–76.

DeKeseredy, Walter, and Schwartz, Martin. 2009. *Dangerous Exits: Escaping Abusive Relationships in Rural America*. New Brunswick, NJ: Rutgers University Press.

Dell, Pippa, and Onkar Korotana. 2000. "Accounting for Domestic Violence: A Q Methodological Study." *Violence Against Women* 6 (3): 286–310.

Deutsch, Yvonne. 1994. "Israeli Women against the Occupation: Political Growth and the Persistence of Ideology." In *Women and the Israeli Occupation: The Politics of Change*, edited by Tamar Mayer, 88–105. New York: Routledge.

Dewalt, Kathleen, Billie Dewalt, with Coral Wayland. 1998. "Participant Observation." In *Handbook of Methods in Cultural Anthropology*, edited by H. Russell Bernard, 259–99. Walnut Creek, CA: AltaMira Press.

Dirks, Nicholas B. 1997. "The Policing of Tradition: Colonialism and Anthropology in Southern India." *Comparative Studies in Society and History* 39 (1): 182–212.

Divrei Haknesset. 1962. "Questions and Answers, no. 21: Police Treatment of Incidents of Wife Beating by Husbands." *Divrei Haknesset*, 33 (Jan. 31): 1123. [Hebrew]

———. 1976. "The Beating of Wives by Their Husbands." *Divrei Haknesset*, 77 (July 14): 3537–41. [Hebrew]

Dobash, R. Emerson, and Russell P. Dobash. 1979. *Violence against Wives: A Case against the Patriarchy*. New York: Free Press.

———. 1992. *Women, Violence, and Social Change*. New York: Routledge Publishing.

———, eds. 1999. *Rethinking Violence Against Women*. Thousand Oaks, CA: Sage Publications, Inc.

———. 2011. "'What Were They Thinking?' Men Who Murder an Intimate Partner." *Violence Against Women* 17 (1): 111–34.

Dobash, Russell P., and R. Emerson Dobash. 2012 "Who Died? The Murder of Collaterals Related to Intimate Partner Conflict." *Violence Against Women* 18 (6): 662–71.

———. 2015. *When Men Murder Women*. New York: Oxford University Press.

Dobash, R. Emerson, Russell P. Dobash, Kate Cavanaugh, and Ruth Lewis. 2000. *Changing Violent Men*. Thousand Oaks, CA: Sage.

Dobash, R. Emerson, Russell P. Dobash, and Kate Cavanaugh. 2009. "'Out of the Blue:' Men Who Murder an Intimate Partner." *Feminist Criminology* 4 (3): 194–225.

Dominguez, Virginia. 1989. *People as Subject, People as Object: Selfhood and Peoplehood in Contemporary Israel*. Madison: University of Wisconsin Press.

Dovrat-Mezrich, Adi. 2015. "Within Two Weeks: A Jump of More Than 5000% in Weapon License Applications." *The Marker*, Oct. 18. *www.themarker.com*.

Drori, Israel. 2009. *Foreign Workers in Israel: Global Perspectives*. Albany, NY: SUNY Press.

Duggan, Lisa. 2003. *The Twilight of Equality? Neoliberalism, Cultural Politics and the Attack on Democracy*. Boston: Beacon Press.

Durfee, Alesha. 2011. "'I'm Not a Victim, She's an Abuser:' Masculinity, Victimization and Protection Orders." *Gender & Society* 25 (3): 316–34.

Dutton, Donald. 1995. *The Batterer: A Psychological Profile*. New York: Basic Books.

Dutton, Donald, and Kenneth Corvo. 2006. "Transforming a Flawed Policy: A Call to Revive Psychology and Science in Domestic Violence Research and Practice." *Aggression and Violent Behavior* 11 (5): 457–83.

Edelman, Martin. 1994. *Courts, Politics, and Culture in Israel*. Charlottesville: University of Virginia Press.

Edelstein, Amon. 2013. Culture Transition, Acculturation and Intimate Partner Homicide. *Springer Plus* 2 (338): 1–12. *www.springerplus.com/content/2/1/338*.

Edin, Kathryn, and Laura Lein. 1997. *Making Ends Meet: How Single Mothers Survive Welfare and Low-Wage Work*. New York: Russell Sage Foundation.

Edleson, Jeffrey, and Zvi Eisikovits, eds. 1996. *Future Interventions with Battered Women and Their Families*. Thousand Oaks, CA: Sage Publications.

Edleson, Jeffrey, Einat Peled, and Zvi Eisikovits. 1991. "Israel's Response to Battered Women." *Violence Update* 11: 4–5.

Efraim, Omri. 2015. "Government Set to Approve Final Wave of Ethiopian Aliyah." *Ynet*, Nov. 12. *www.ynetnews.com*.

Efrat, Asif. 2012. *Governing Guns, Preventing Plunder: International Cooperation against Illicit Trade*. New York: Oxford University Press.

Eichner, Itamar. 2016. "Israel to Grant Decorations of Valor to Civilians Who Died Saving Others." *Ynet*, Mar. 2. *www.ynetnews.com*.

Eisenman, Robert. 1978. *Islamic Law in Palestine and Israel: A History of the Survival of Tanzimat and Shari'a in the British Mandate and the Jewish State*. Leiden, the Netherlands: E. J. Brill.

Eisenman, Robert. 1986. "The Young Turk Legislation, 1913–17, and Its Application in Palestine/Israel." In *Palestine in the Late Ottoman Period: Political, Social and Economic Transformation*, edited by David Kushner. Jerusalem: Yad Izhak Ben-Zvi Press.

Eisikovits, Zvi, and Avi Griffel. 1998. *Police Intervention in Intimate Violence: An Evaluation Study*. Haifa: Minerva Center for Youth Studies.

Eisikovits, Zvi, Avi Griffel, Michal Grinstein, and Faisal Azaiza. 2000. "Attitudes of Israeli Arab Social Workers Concerning Woman Battering." *Journal of Social Service Research* 26 (3): 23–47.

Eisikovits, Zvi, and Eli Buchbinder. 1996. "Pathways to Disenchantment: Battered Women's Views of Their Social Workers." *Journal of Interpersonal Violence* 11 (3): 425–40.

————. 1997. "Talking Violent: A Phenomenological Study of Metaphors Battering Men Use." *Violence Against Women* 3 (5): 482–98.

Eisikovits, Zvi, Eli Buchbinder, and Amal Bshara. 2008. "Between the Person and the Culture: Israeli Arab Couple's Perceptions of Police Intervention in Intimate Partner Violence." *Journal of Ethnic and Cultural Diversity in Social Work* 17 (2): 108–29.

Eisikovits, Zvi, Eli Buchbinder, and Michal Mor. 1998. "'What It Was Won't Be Anymore': Reaching the Turning Point in Coping with Intimate Violence." *Afflia* 13 (4): 411–34.

Eisikovits, Zvi, Hadass Goldblatt, and Zeev Winstock. 1999. "Partner Accounts of Intimate Violence: Towards a Theoretical Model." *Families in Society* 80 (6): 606–19.

Eisikovits, Zvi, Tova Band-Winterstein, and Ariela Lowenstein. 2005. *The National Survey on Elder Abuse and Neglect in Israel.* Haifa, Israel: The Center for Research and Study of Aging, University of Haifa and Eshel. [Hebrew]

Eisikovits, Zvi, Zeev Winstok, and Gideon Fishman. 2004. "The First Israeli National Survey on Domestic Violence." *Violence Against Women* 10 (7): 729–48.

Eldar-Avidan, Dorit. 1998. "Battered Women: Their Experience with Violence and Divorce." Unpublished master's thesis, Paul Baerwald School of Social Work, Hebrew University of Jerusalem. [Hebrew]

Eldar-Avidan, Dorit. 1999. *Boḥarot Ha-ḥayim Nashim Mukot Govrot 'al Ha-alimut.* Yerushalayim: Hotsa'at Shoḥen.

Elgazi, Y. 1995. "Organization of Women Against Violence: A Refuge for Battered Women in Taibe—Essential." *Haaretz*, Feb. 12, 7a.

Ellsberg Mary, and Lori Heise. 2005. *Researching Violence Against Women: A Practical Guide for Researchers and Advocates.* Washington: WHO, Program for Appropriate Technology in Health (PATH), Center for Health and Gender Equity.

Ellsberg, Mary, Lori Heise, Rodolfo Pena, Sonia Agurto, and Anna Winkvist. 2001. "Researching Domestic Violence against Women: Methodological and Ethical Considerations." *Studies in Family Planning*, 32 (1): 1–16.

Elman, Miriam, and Madelaine Adelman. 2014. "Knowing Jerusalem." In *Jerusalem: Conflict and Cooperation in a Contested City*, edited by Madelaine Adelman and Miriam Elman, 1–46. Syracuse: Syracuse University Press.

Elon, Menachem, ed. 1974. *The Principles of Jewish Law.* Jerusalem: Keter Publishing House Jerusalem Ltd.

El Or, Tamar, and Atran, Gideon. 1997. "Giving Birth to a Settlement: Maternal Thinking and Political Action of Jewish Women on the West Bank." In *Mixed Blessings: Gender and Religious Fundamentalism Cross Culturally*, edited by Judy Brink and Joan Mencher, 159–78. New York: Routledge.

Engel, David. 2001. "The Damaged Self in Three Cultures." In *Between Law and Culture: Relocating Legal Studies*, edited by Lisa Bower, David Theo Goldberg, and Michael Musheno, 3–21. Minneapolis: University of Minnesota Press.

Enloe, Cynthia. 2000. *Maneuvers: The International Politics of Militarizing Women's Lives.* Berkeley: University of California Press.

————. 2007. *Globalization and Militarism: Feminists Make the Link.* New York: Rowman & Littlefield Publishers.

Enosh, Guy. 2008. "Resistance to Evaluation in Batterers' Programs in Israel." *Children and Youth Services* 30 (6): 647–53.

Epstein, Maxine, and Reggie Marder. 1986. *Shalom bayit: A Follow-Up Study of Battered Women in Israel.* Haifa, Israel: Breirot. [Hebrew]

Erez, Edna, Madelaine Adelman, and Carol Gregory. 2009. "Intersections of Immigration and Domestic Violence: Voices of Battered Immigrant Women." *Feminist Criminology* 4 (1): 32–56.

Erez, Edna, and Nadera Shalhoub-Kevorkian. 2004. "Benign Respect or Malign Neglect? Policing Violence against Women in the Arab/Palestinian Community in Israel." *Israel Studies in Criminology* 8: 135–50.

Erez, Edna, Peter Ibarra, and Oren Gur. 2015. "At the Intersection of Private and Public Conflict Zones: Policing Domestic Violence in the Arab Community in Israel." *International Journal of Offender Therapy and Comparative Criminology* 59 (9): 930–63.

Esmaquel, Paterno, II. 2016. "32,360 Overseas Voters in First 3 Days Alone." *Rappler*, April 14. *www.rappler.com*.

Espanioly, Nabila. 1991. "Palestinian Women in Israel Respond to the Intifada." In *Calling the Equality Bluff: Women in Israel*, edited by Barbara Swirski and Marilyn Safir, 147–51. New York: Pergamon Press.

Estrin, Daniel. 2015. "Here's How Israel Gets Its Music and News—From Teenaged Soldiers." *PRI's The World*, Jan. 5. *www.pri.org*.

Ettinger, Yair. 2013a. "Israeli Divorce Refusnik Breaks Out of Jerusalem Rabbinical Court." *Haaretz*, Mar. 6. *www.haaretz.com*.

———. 2013b. "Number of Divorces in Israel Hit All-Time High." *Haaretz*, Jan. 23. *www.haaretz.com*.

Ettinger, Yair. 2014. "Divorce Rate Among Jewish Israelis Rising." *Haaretz*, Feb. 19. *www.haaretz.com*.

———. 2015a. "The Military Coup of Orthodox Israeli Women." *Haaretz*, Sept. 25. *www.haaretz.com*.

———. 2015b. "Government Opposes Appointment of Women as Sharia Judges to Avoid Precedent for Rabbinic Courts." *Haaretz*, Dec. 9. *www.haaretz.com*.

———. 2016. "Israel's High Court Delays Detention of Recalcitrant Father-in-Law." *Haaretz*, Mar. 22. *www.haaretz.com*.

Ewick, Patricia, and Susan Silbey. 1998. *The Common Place of Law: Stories from Everyday Life*. Chicago: University of Chicago Press.

Faier, Elizabeth. 2002. "Domestic Matters: Feminism and Activism among Palestinian Women in Israel." In *Ethnography in Unstable Places: Everyday Lives in Contexts of Dramatic Political Change*, edited by Elizabeth Mertz, Kay Warren, and Carol Greenhouse, 178–209. Durham: Duke University.

———. 2013. *Organizations, Gender and the Culture of Palestinian Activism in Haifa, Israel*. New York: Routledge.

Farmer, Paul. 1996. "On Suffering and Structural Violence: A View from Below." *Daedalus* 125 (1): 261–83.

———. 2004. "An Anthropology of Structural Violence." *Current Anthropology* 45 (3): 305–25.

Farrell, Stephen, and Ian Cobain. 2002. "Images of War Force Children to Confront Their Nightmares." *The Times*, May 18, 20.

Feeley, Malcolm. 1979. *The Process Is the Punishment: Handling Cases in a Lower Criminal Court*. New York: Russell Sage Foundation.

Felstiner, William, Richard L. Abel, and Austin Sarat. 1980–1981. "The Emergence and Transformation of Disputes: Naming, Blaming, Claiming . . ." *Law and Society Review* 15 (3/4): 631–54.

Fendel, Hillel. 2007. "Rabbinate Stats: 180 Women, 185 Men 'Chained' by Spouses." *Arutz Sheva, Israel National News*, Aug. 23. *www.israelnationalnews.com*.

Ferraro, Kathleen. 1996. "The Dance of Dependency: A Genealogy of Domestic Violence Discourse." *Hypatia* 11 (4): 78–91.

———. 2003. "The Words Change, but the Melody Lingers: The Persistence of the Battered Woman Syndrome in Criminal Cases Involving Battered Women." *Violence Against Women* 9 (1): 110–29.

———. 2006. *Neither Angels nor Demons: Women, Crime, and Victimization*. Boston, MA: Northeastern University Press.

Fineman, Martha. 1991. *The Illusion of Equality: The Rhetoric and Reality of Divorce Reform*. Chicago: University of Chicago Press.

———. 1995. *The Neutered Mother, the Sexual Family, and Other Twentieth Century Tragedies*. New York: Routledge.

———. 2010. "The Vulnerable Subject and the Responsive State." *Emory Law Journal* 60 (2): 251–75.

Fineman, Martha Albertson, and Roxanne Mykitiuk, eds. 1994. *The Public Nature of Private Violence*. New York: Routledge.

Fischer, Karla, and Mary Rose. 1995. "When 'Enough Is Enough': Battered Women's Decision Making Around Court Orders of Protection." *Crime and Delinquency* 41 (4): 414–29.

Fisher-Ilan, Allyn. 2015. "Persistent Israeli Ethnic Divide May Split Vote for Netanyahu." Reuters, Mar. 10. *www.reuters.com*.

Fishkoff, Sue. 1992. "The Fight Begins at Home." *Jerusalem Post Magazine*, July 10, 6–9.

Fleischmann, Ellen. 2003. *The Nation and Its "New" Women: The Palestinian Women's Movement, 1920–1948*. Berkeley: University of California Press.

Fogiel-Bijaoui, Sylvia. 1992. "Women's Organizations: Current Picture." *International Problems—Society and Problems* 31: 65–75. [Hebrew]

Fogiel-Bijaoui, Sylvia, and Reina Rutlinger-Renier. 2013. "Guest Editors' Introduction: Rethinking the Family in Israel." *Israel Studies Review* 28 (2): vii–xii.

Forte, Tania. 2003. "Sifting People, Sorting Papers: Academic Practice and the Notion of State Security in Israel." *Comparative Studies of South Asia, Africa and the Middle East* 23 (1&2): 215–23.

Founier, Pascale, Pascal McDougall, and Merissa Lichtsztral. 2012. "Secular Rights and Religious Wrongs? Family Law, Religion and Women in Israel." *William & Mary Journal of Women and the Law* 18 (2): 333–62.

Franke, Katherine M. 2012. "Dating the State: The Moral Hazards of Winning Gay Rights." *Columbia Human Rights Law Review* 44 (1): 1–46.

Frankel, Billie, and Meirav Crystal. 2011. "Real Estate Protest: We Will Fill Up Tel Aviv with Tents." *Ynet*, July 15. *www.Ynetnews.com*.

Freedman, Marcia. 1990. *Exile in the Promised Land, a Memoir*. Ithaca, NY: Firebrand Books.

Freeman, Marsha A., Christine Chinkin, and Rudolf Beate, eds. 2012. *The UN Convention on the Elimination of All Forms of Discrimination against Women: A Commentary*. New York: Oxford University Press.

Friedman, Menachem. 1995. "The Structural Foundation for Religious-Political Accommodation in Israel: Fallacy and Reality." In *Israel: The First Decade of Independence*, edited by Ilan Troen and Noah Lucas, 51–82. Albany: SUNY Press.

Gal, John, and Michael Bar. 2000. "The Needed and the Needy: The Policy Legacies of Benefits for Disabled War Veterans in Israel." *Journal of Social Policy* 29 (4): 577–98.

Galilee Society. 2014. *Violence in Families and the Community*. Shefa-Amr, Israel: Galilee Society.

García-Moreno, Claudia, Henrica Jansen, Mary Ellsberg, Lori Heise, and Charlotte Watts. 2005. *WHO Multi-Country Study on Women's Health and Domestic Violence against Women: Initial Results on Prevalence, Health Outcomes and Women's Responses*. Geneva, Switzerland: WHO.

Gavriely-Nuri, Dalia. 2013. *The Normalization of War in Israeli Discourse, 1967–2008*. Lanham, MD: Lexington Books.

Geiger, Brenda. 2013. "Ethiopian Males Account for the Double Acts of Murder and Suicide Committed by Males in Ethiopian Families Postmigration to Israel." *International Criminal Justice Review* 23 (3): 233–51.

Ghanem, Asad. 2001. *The Palestinian Arab Minority in Israel, 1948–2000*. Albany: State University of New York Press.

Gibson-Graham, J. K. 1996. *The End of Capitalism (as We Knew It): A Feminist Critique of Political Economy*. Oxford, UK: Blackwell.

Gidron, Benjamin, Michal Bar, and Hagai Katz. 2004. *The Israeli Third Sector: Between Welfare State and Civil Society*. New York: Springer Science and Business Media.

Gilbert, Martin. 2008. *Israel: A History*. Rev. ed. New York: Harper Collins.

Glazer, Ilsa, and Wahiba Abu Ras. 1994. "On Aggression, Human Rights and Hegemonic Discourse: The Case of a Murder for Family Honor in Israel." *Sex Roles* 30 (3/4): 269–88.

Gleit, Heidi. 2000. "Dayan: Current Unrest No Reason to Excuse Violence against Women." *Jerusalem Post*, Nov. 26, 2.

Goldblatt, Hadass, and Michal Granot. 2005. "Domestic Violence among Druze Women in Israel as Reflected by Health Status and Somatization Level." *Women and Health* 42 (3): 19–36.

Gondolf, Edward. 2007. "Theoretical and Research Support for the Duluth Model: A Reply to Dutton and Corvo." Indiana, PA: Mid-Atlantic Addiction Training Institute, Indian University of Pennsylvania.

———. 2012. *The Future of Batterer Programs*. Boston: Northeastern University Press.

Goode, Judith, and Jeff Maskovsky, eds. 2001. *The New Poverty Studies: The Ethnography of Power, Politics and Impoverished People in the United States*. New York: New York University Press.

Goodman, Susan Tumarkin. 1989. *In the Shadow of the Conflict: Israeli Art 1980–1989*. New York: The Jewish Museum.

———. 1998. *After Rabin: New Art from Israel*. New York: The Jewish Museum.

Goodmark, Leigh. 2010. *A Troubled Marriage: Domestic Violence and the Legal System*. New York: New York University Press.

Gordon, Linda. 1988. *Heroes of Their Own Lives: The Politics and History of Family Violence*. New York: Penguin Books.

Gozansky, Tamar. 2015. *Between Dispossession and Exploitation: Arab Laborers—Their Situation and Struggles*. Haifa, Israel: Pardes Publishing. [Hebrew]

Graetz, Naomi. 1998. *Silence Is Deadly: Judaism Confronts Wife-Beating*. Northvale, New Jersey: Jason Aronson.

Grave-Lazi, Lidar. 2014. "In Poverty Report, Arab Sector Sees Improvement While Haredi Sector Gets Poorer." *Jerusalem Post*, Dec. 16. *www.jpost.com*.

Greenberg, Susan, and Theodore Stanger. 1991. "Israel's Men on the Verge." *Newsweek*, Aug. 19, 15.

Grinberg, Lev Luis. 2010. *Politics and Violence in Israel/Palestine: Democracy versus Military Rule*. New York: Routledge.

———. 2014. *Mo(ve)ments of Resistance: Politics, Economy and Society in Israel/Palestine, 1931–2013*. Boston: Academic Studies Press.

Gross, Judah Ari. 2016. "Rather Than Save Lives, Arming Off-duty Soldiers Could Bring Greater Risk." *Times of Israel*, Feb. 23. *www.timesofisrael.com*.

Gross, Judah Ari, and Joshua Davidovich. 2016. "IDF Probing Why Soldier Killed in Supermarket Attack Was Unarmed." *Times of Israel*, Feb. 22. *www.timesofisrael.com*.

Gross, Netty C. 1997. "PR or Priority, Netanyahu's Stance on Domestic Violence." *Jerusalem Report*, July 10, 24.

Gun Free Kitchen Tables (GFKT). 2015. "In Memoriam." Haifa: GFKT. *www.isha.org.il*.

Haaretz. 2014. "Filipina Migrant Worker Wins Israeli X-Factor." Jan. 15. *www.haaretz. com*.

———. 2009. "Father Indicted for First Degree Murder of His Daughter, 3." Aug. 13. *www.haaretz.com*.

———. 2008. "Poverty Report Shows Poor Are Working, and Staying in Poverty." Feb. 19. *www.haaretz.com*.

———. 2015. "Live Blog: Obama to Netanyahu: U.S. Will Reassess Israeli Palestinian Peace Policy." Mar. 19. *www.haaretz.com*.

Hacker, Daphna. 2005. "Motherhood, Fatherhood and Law: Child Custody and Visiting in Israel." *Social and Legal Studies* 14 (3): 409–33.

Hacker, Daphna, and Orna Cohen. 2012. *Research Report: The Shelters in Israel for Survivors of Human Trafficking*. Submitted to the U.S. Department of State. Tel Aviv: Hotline for Migrant Workers and Keshet.

Haghagh, Nurit. 2009. "The Public Hearings: A Personal Viewpoint." In *Women Confronting Peace: Voices from Israel*, edited by Sarai Aharoni, Anat Saragusti, and Nurit Haghagh, 45–49. Jerusalem: Israeli Branch of the International Women's Commission.

Haider, Ali. 2010. *The Equality Index of Jewish and Arab Citizens of Israel*. Jerusalem-Haifa: Sikkuy: The Association for the Advancement of Civic Equality.

Haiduc-Dale, Noah. 2013. *Arab Christians in British Mandate Palestine*. Edinburgh, UK: Edinburgh University Press.

Haifa Women's Coalition. 1994. "Landmark Decision in Shomrat Case." *New Initiatives by Women Newsletter* (Fall).

Haifa Women's Crisis Shelter. 2011. *Crisis Shelter for Women: Annual Activity Report, 2010*. Haifa: Haifa Women's Crisis Shelter.

Hajjar, Lisa. 1996. "Israel's Interventions among the Druze." *Middle East Report* July/September: 2–6, 10.

———. 2000. "Speaking the Conflict, or How the Druze Became Bilingual: A Study of Druze Translators in the Israeli Military Courts in the West Bank and Gaza." *Ethnic and Racial Studies* 23 (2): 299–328.

———. 2004. "Religion, State Power and Domestic Violence in Muslim Societies: A Framework for Comparative Analysis." *Law and Social Inquiry* 29 (1): 1–38.

Haj-Yahia, Muhammad. 1995. "Toward Cultural Sensitive Intervention with Arab Families in Israel." *Contemporary Family Therapy* 17 (4): 429–47.

———. 1998. "Beliefs about Wife Beating among Palestinian Women. *Violence Against Women* 4 (5): 533–58.

———. 2000a. "Patterns of Violence against Engaged Arab Women from Israel and Some Psychological Implications." *Psychology of Women Quarterly* 24: 209–19.

———. 2000b. "Wife Abuse and Battering in the Sociocultural Context of Arab Society." *Family Process* 39 (2): 237–55.

———. 2003. "Beliefs about Wife Beating among Arab Men from Israel: The Influence of Their Patriarchal Ideology." *Journal of Family Violence* 18 (4): 193–206.

Haj-Yahia, Muhammad, and Dorit Eldar-Avidan. 2001. "Formerly Battered Women: A Qualitative Study of Their Experiences in Making a Decision to Divorce and Carrying It Out." *Journal of Divorce and Remarriage* 36 (1/2): 37–65.

Halevi, H. S. 1956. "Divorce in Israel." *Population Studies* 10 (2): 184–192.

Hall, Stuart. 1997. "The Work of Representation." In *Representation: Cultural Representations and Signifying Practices*, edited by Stuart Hall, 13–74. Thousand Oaks, CA: Sage.

Halperin-Kaddari, Ruth. 2000–2001. "Women, Religion and Multiculturalism in Israel." *UCLA Journal of International Law and Foreign Affairs* 5 (2): 339–66.

———. 2004 *Women in Israel: A State of Their Own*. Philadelphia: University of Pennsylvania Press.

Halperin-Kaddari, Ruth, and Marsha A. Freeman. 2012. "Economic Consequences of Marriage and Its Dissolution: Applying a Universal Equality Norm in a Fragmented Universe." *Theoretical Inquiries in Law.* 13 (1): 323–60.

———. 2016. "Backlash Goes Global: Men's Groups, Patriarchal Family Policy, and the False Promise of Gender Neutral Laws." *Canadian Journal of Women & the Law* 28 (1): 182–210.

Halperin-Kaddari, Ruth, and Yaacov Yadgar. 2010. "Between Universal Feminism and Particular Nationalism: Politics, Religion and Gender (In)Equality in Israel." *Third World Quarterly* 31 (6): 905–20.

Hamai, Michal, Eli Buchbinder, Guy Enosh, Gali Dotan, and Yael Barzilai. 2009. "The *Maftehot* ("Keys") Hostel for Released Male-Batterer Prisoners, 2005–2008." Jerusalem: National Insurance Institute. *www.btl.gov.il*. [Hebrew]

Handelman, Don. 1998. *Models and Mirrors: Towards an Anthropology of Public Events*. New York: Berghahn Books.

———. 2003. *Nationalism and the Israeli State: Bureaucratic Logic in Public Events*. New York: Berg.

Handelman, Don, and Elihu Katz. 1995. "State Ceremonies of Israel: Remembrance Day and Independence Day." *Israeli Judaism: The Sociology of Religion in Israel* 7: 75–86.

Handelman, Don, and Lea Shamgar-Handelman. 1997. "The Presence of Absence: The Memorialism of National Death in Israel." In *Grasping Land: Space and Place in Contemporary Israeli Discourse and Experience*, edited by Eyal Ben-Ari and Yoram Bilu, 85–128. Albany: State University of New York Press.

Haney, Lynne, and Lisa Pollard. (2003) 2013. "In a Family Way: Theorizing State and Familial Relations." In *Families of a New World: Gender, Politics and State Development in a Global Context*, edited by Lynne Haney and Lisa Pollard, 1–16. New York: Routledge.

Harel, Amos. 2015. "Defense Ministry, Treasury Agree on $15.6 Billion Defense Budget for 2016." *Haaretz*, Nov. 15. *www.haaretz.com*.

Harkov, Lahav. 2013. "Knesset Extends 65-Year-Long National State of Emergency." *Jerusalem Post*, Dec. 16. *www.jpost.com*.

Harris, Emily. 2013. "Last Flight of Ethiopia-to-Israel Jewish Migration Program." *National Public Radio*, Sept. 1. *www.npr.org*.

Hartaf, Hagit, and Na'ama Bar-On. 2000. *"Beit Noam:" A New Direction for Abusive Men*. Translated from the Hebrew by Karen Gold, 2002. Jerusalem: National Insurance Institute. *www.btl.gov.il*.

Hartman, Ben. 2014. "Glaring Failures in Gun Control Enforcement in Israel, State Comptroller Finds." *Jerusalem Post*, May 14. *www.jpost.com*.

Hautzinger, Sarah. 2007. *Violence in the City of Women: Police and Batterers in Bahia, Brazil*. Berkeley: University of California Press.

Heberle, Renee. 1996. "Deconstructive Strategies and the Movement against Sexual Violence." *Hypatia* 11 (4): 63–76.

Hemenway, David, Tomoko Shinoda-Tagawa, and Matthew Miller. 2002. "Firearm Availability and Female Homicide Victimization Rates among 25 Populous High-Income Countries." *Journal of the American Medical Women's Association* 57 (2): 100–104.

Hemment, Julie. 2004. "Global Civil Society and the Local Costs of Belonging: Defining Violence against Women in Russia." *Signs* 29 (3): 815–40.

Herbst, Anat. 2013. "Welfare Mom as Warrior Mom: Discourse in the 2003 Single Mothers' Protest in Israel." *Journal of Social Policy* 42: 129–45.

Herbst, Anat, and Orly Benjamin. 2012. "It Was a Zionist Act: Feminist Politics of Single Mother Policy Votes in Israel." *Women's Studies International Forum* 35 (1): 29–37.

Herbst, Anat, and Yonatan Gez. 2012. "From 'Crime of Passion' to 'Love Does Not Kill': The Murder of Einav Rogel and the Role of Na'amat Women's Organization in the Construction of Violence against Women in Israel." *Israel Studies* 17 (2): 129–55.

Herzog, Esther. 2005. "Women's Parties in Israel: Their Unrecognized Significance and Potential." *Middle East Journal* 59 (3): 437–51.

Herzog, Hanna. 1996. "Why So Few? The Political Culture of Gender in Israel." *International Review of Women and Leadership* 2: 1–18.

———. 1998. "Homefront and Battlefront: The Status of Jewish and Palestinian Women in Israel." *Israel Studies* 3 (1): 61–84.

Herzog, Sergio. 2008. "The Lenient Social and Legal Response to Trafficking in Women: An Empirical Analysis of Public Perceptions in Israel." *Journal of Contemporary Criminal Justice* 24 (3): 314–33.

Hesketh, Katie, Suhad Bishara, Rina Rosenberg, and Sawsan Zaher. Mar. 2011. "The Inequality Report: The Palestinian Minority in Israel." Haifa, Israel: Adalah: The Legal Center for Arab Minority Rights in Israel.

Hever, Shir. 2010. *The Political Economy of Israel's Occupation: Repression Beyond Exploitation*. New York: Pluto Press.

Heyd, Uriel. 1960. *Ottoman Documents on Palestine 1552–1615: A Study of the Firman According to the Muhimme Defteri*. Oxford, UK: Oxford University Press.

Hidrobo, Melissa, and Lia Fernald. 2013. "Cash Transfers and Domestic Violence." *Journal of Health Economics* 32: 304–19.

Hilgartner, Stephen, and Charles Bosk. 1988. "The Rise and Fall of Social Problems: A Public Arenas Model." *American Journal of Sociology* 94 (1): 53–79.

Hirsch, Susan. 1998. *Pronouncing and Persevering: Gender and the Discourses of Disputing in an African Islamic Court*. Chicago. University of Chicago Press.

Hofnung, Menahem. 1994. "Ethnicity, Religion, and Politics in Applying Israel's Conscription Law." Paper presented at the annual meeting of the Law and Society Association, Phoenix, Arizona, June 16–19.

———. 1996. *Democracy, Law, and National Security in Israel*. Brookfield, VT: Dartmouth Publishing Group.

———. 2011. "The Politics of Judicial Nominations in a Polarized Society." Paper presented at the Sixth General ECPR Conference, Reykjavik, Iceland, Aug. 24–27.

Hondagneu-Sotelo, Pierrette, ed. 2003. *Gender and U.S. Immigration.* Berkeley: University of California Press.

Horowitz, Dan, and Moshe Lissak. 1989. "Democracy and National Security in a Protracted Conflict." In *Trouble in Utopia: The Overburdened Polity of Israel,* edited by Dan Horowitz and Moshe Lissak, 195–230. Albany: State University of New York Press.

Hovel, Revital. 2011. "Police: Off-Duty Security Guard Kills Ex-Wife, Self in Kiryat Motzkin." Haaretz, Dec. 12. *www.haaretz.com.*

Htun, Mala, and S. Laurel Weldon. 2012a. "The Civic Origins of Progressive Policy Change: Combating Violence against Women in Global Perspective." *American Political Science Review* 106 (3): 548–69.

———. 2012b. "Appendix A: Definitions and Approach to Measuring Strong, Autonomous Feminist Movements." Supplementary material to "The Civic Origins of Progressive Policy Change: Combating Violence against Women in Global Perspective." *American Political Science Review* 106 (3). *journals.cambridge.org.*

Huggins, Martha, and Mary Louise Glebbeek. 2009. *Women Fielding Danger: Negotiating Ethnographic Identities in Field Research.* Lanham, Maryland: Rowan and Littlefield.

Humphries, Drew. 2009. "Preface." In *Women, Violence and the Media: Readings in Feminist Criminology,* edited by Drew Humphries, ix–xiii. Boston: Northeastern University Press.

IANSA (International Action Network on Small Arms). 2009. "Women at Work: Preventing Gun Violence." Bulletin 19. London: IANSA. *www.iansa-women.org/sites/default/files/newsviews/en-wn-bulletin19-web.pdf.*

Ilan, Shahar. 2016. "Marriage Freedom in Israel: By the Numbers." Presented to the Knesset's Peoplehood, Religion & State Caucus, Jerusalem, January 13. *www.hiddush.org.*

Inalcik, Halil, ed., with Donald Quataert. 1994. *An Economic and Social History of the Ottoman Empire: 1300–1914.* Cambridge: Cambridge University Press.

INCITE! Women of Color against Violence. 2006. *Color of Violence: The Incite! Anthology.* Cambridge, MA: South End Press.

Israel Foreign Affairs. 2015. "Guidelines of the Government of Israel—June 1996." Reprint, *Israel Foreign Affairs.* Nov. 2. israelforeignaffairs.com/2015/11/guidelines-of-the-government-of-israel-june-1996.

Israel Police. 2015. "Israel Police Annual Report, 2014." Jerusalem: Israel Police Department of Planning and Organization. *www.police.gov.il.* [Hebrew]

IWN (Israel Women's Network). 1995. "Women and Military Service: Reality and Desires." Jerusalem, Israel: IWN. [Hebrew]

———. 1998. "Women in Israel: Central Statistics and Information." Jerusalem: Israel Women's Network. [Hebrew]

———. 1999. "The Status of Women in Israel: A Proposed Platform for the 15th Knesset." Jerusalem: Israel Women's Network. [Hebrew]

———. 2004. "Women in Israel: Central Statistics and Information." Jerusalem: Israel Women's Network. [Hebrew]

Israeli Feminist Conference. 1980. "A Decade of Feminism in Israel: The Third Annual National Conference, 20–21 May 1980," Jerusalem [pamphlet]. Haifa, Israel: Israeli Feminist Conference.

Itach-Maaki. 2014. "Report on Violence against Bedouin Women." Be'er Sheva: Itach-Maaki. *www.iataskforce.org/resources/view/1272.*

Iyengar, Shanto. 1991. *Is Anyone Responsible? How Television Frames Political Issues.* Chicago: University of Chicago Press.

Izraeli, Dafna. 1981. "The Zionist Women's Movement in Palestine, 1911–1927: A Sociological Analysis." *Signs* 7 (1): 87–114.

———. 1997. "Gendering Military Service in the Israel Defense Forces." *Israel Social Science Research* 12: 129–66.

Jamal, Amal. 2009. "Media Culture as Counter-Hegemonic Strategy: The Communicative Action of the Arab Minority in Israel." *Media, Culture, and Society* 31 (4): 559–77.

Jenness, Val. 1995. "Hate Crimes in the U.S.: The Transformation of Injured Persons into Victims and the Extension of Victim Status." In *Images of Issues: Typifying Contemporary Social Problems*, edited by Joel Best, 213–239. Hawthorne, NY: Aldine.

Jolly, Richard. 1991. "Adjustment with a Human Face: A UNICEF Record and Perspective on the 1980s." *World Development* 19 (12): 1807–21.

Jonathan, Tal. 2010. "Police Involvement in Counter-Terrorism and Public Attitudes towards the Police in Israel—1998–2007." *British Journal of Criminology* 50: 748–71.

Jonathan, Tal, and David Weisburd. 2010. "How Do Majority Communities View the Potential Costs of Policing Terrorism? Findings from a Community Survey in Israel." *Policing* 4 (2): 169–81.

Jones, Abigail. 2015. "In Orthodox Jewish Divorce, Men Hold All of the Cards." *Newsweek*, April 8.

JTA (Jewish Telegraphic Agency). 1973. "Goren Publishes Langer Case Ruling: Cites Halachic Basis for Decision." JTA, Jan. 5. *www.jta.org*.

———. 1992. "Disturbed Man Kills 4 at Mental Clinic in Jerusalem." JTA, Sept. 9. *www.jta.org*.

———. 1997. "Domestic Violence Campaign Launched." JTA, May 27. *www.jta.org*.

———. 2014. "Israel's President Holds Bar/Bat Mitzvah Celebration for Terror Survivors." JTA, Dec. 30. *www.jta.org*.

———2016a. "75% of Israelis Want Divorce Out of Rabbinate's Hands." *Times of Israel*, Mar. 25. *www.timesofisrael.com*.

———. 2016b. "Ethiopian Aliyah to Restart in June." *Times of Israel*, April 8. *www.timesofisrael.com*.

Judicial Authority of Israel. 2013. "Semi-Annual Report, 2013." Jerusalem: Administration of Courts.

Jurik, Nancy. 2004. "Presidential Address: Imagining Justice: Challenging the Privatization of Public Life." *Social Problems* 51 (1): 1–15.

Jurik, Nancy, Joel Blumenthal, Brian Smith, and Eddie Portillos. 2000. "Organizational Cooptation or Social Change?: A Critical Perspective On Community-Criminal Justice Partnerships." *Journal of Contemporary Criminal Justice* 16 (3): 293–320.

Kacen, Lea. 2006. "Spousal Abuse among Immigrants from Ethiopia in Israel." *Journal of Marriage and Family* 68: 1276–90.

Kafadar, Cemal. 1995. *Between Two Worlds: The Construction of the Ottoman State*. Berkeley: University of California Press.

Kahn, Susan. 2000. *Reproducing Jews: A Cultural Account of Assisted Conception in Israel*. Durham: Duke University Press.

Kamin, Debra. 2013. "'South Tel Aviv Is South Sudan Now.'" *Times of Israel*, Dec. 2. *www.timesofisrael.com*.

———. 2015. "For Israel's Migrants, a Hell Frozen Over." *Times of Israel*, Jan. 19. *www.timesofisrael.com*.

Kanaaneh, Rhoda Ann. 2002. *Birthing the Nation: Strategies of Palestinian Women in Israel*. Berkeley: University of California Press.

———. 2009. *Surrounded: Palestinian Soldiers in the Israeli Military.* Stanford: Stanford University Press.

Kanaaneh, Rhoda, and Isis Nusair, eds. 2010. *Displaced at Home: Ethnicity and Gender among Palestinians in Israel.* Albany: SUNY Press.

Kang, Alice. 2015. *Bargaining for Women's Rights: Activism in an Aspiring Muslim Democracy.* Minneapolis: University of Minnesota Press.

Kaplan, Yehiel. 2012. "Enforcement of Divorce Judgments in Jewish Courts in Israel: The Interaction between Religious and Constitutional Law." *Middle East Law and Governance* 4: 1–68.

Kashti, Or. 2014. "As War Flares, Some Women Flee from Violence at Home." *Haaretz,* Aug. 1. *www.haaretz.com.*

Kassem, Fatma. 2011. *Palestinian Women: Narrative Histories and Gendered Memories.* New York: Zed Books.

Katz, Ruth. (1990) 1993. "Widowhood in a Traditional Segment of Israeli society: The Case of the Druze War Widows." In *Women in Israel,* edited by Yael Azmon and Dafna Izraeli, 51–66. New Brunswick: Transaction.

Kaufman, Debra. 1991. *Rachel's Daughters: Newly Orthodox Jewish Women.* New Brunswick, NJ: Rutgers University Press.

Kav LaOved. 2010. "Kav LaOved's (Worker's Hotline) Shadow Report on the Situation of Female Migrant Workers in Israel." Submitted to the UN Committee for the Elimination of All Forms of Discrimination against Women, 48th Session. Tel Aviv: Kav LaOved.

———. 2014. "Supporting Eritrean Women Workers." Tel Aviv: Kav LaOved. *www. kavlaoved.org.il/en/supporting-eritrean-women-workers.*

———. 2015. "Employment Sectors: Caregivers." Tel Aviv-Jaffa: Kav LaOved. *www.kavlaoved. org.il.*

Keck, Margaret, and Kathryn Sikkink. 1998. *Activists Beyond Borders: Advocacy Networks in International Politics.* Ithaca, NY: Cornell University Press.

Kelley, Judith, and Beth Simmons. 2015. "Politics by Numbers: Indicators as Social Pressure in International Relations." *American Journal of Political Science* 59 (1): 55–70.

Kelly, Liz, Sheila Burton, and Linda Regan. 1996. "Beyond Victim or Survivor: Sexual Violence, Identity and Feminist Theory and Practice." In *Sexualizing the Social: Power and the Organization of Sexuality,* edited by Lisa Adkins and Vicki Merchant, 77–101. New York: St. Martin's Press.

Kemp, Adriana. 2007. "Managing Migration, Reprioritizing National Citizenship: Undocumented Migrant Workers' Children and Policy Reforms in Israel." *Theoretical Inquiries in Law* 8 (2): 663–92.

Kemp, Adriana, and Nelly Kfir. 2016. "Mobilizing Migrant Workers' Rights in 'Non-immigration' Countries: The Politics of Resonance and Migrants' Rights Activism in Israel and Singapore." *Law & Society Review* 50 (1): 82–116.

Kempe, C. Henry, Frederic Silverman, Brandt Steele, William Droegemueller, and Henry Silver. 1962. "The Battered Child Syndrome." *Journal of the American Medical Association* 181: 17–24.

Kershner, Isabel. 2011. "Protests Grow in Israel, with 250,000 Marching." *New York Times,* Aug. 6. *www.nytimes.com.*

———. 2014. "Emergency Routine in Israel: 30 Seconds to Run for Cover." *New York Times,* July 16. *www.nytimes.com.*

Keynan, Ofra, Hannah Rosenberg, Beni Beili, Michal Nir, Shlomit Levin, Ariel Mor, Ibrahim Agabaria, and Avi Tefelin. 2003. "Beit Noam: Residential Program for Violent Men." *Journal of Aggression, Maltreatment and Trauma* 7: 207–36.

Kezwer, Gil. 2002. "I'm Not Even Sure If They're Treatable." *Jerusalem Report*, February 25, 21.

Khalidi, Rashid. (1997) 2009. *Palestinian Identity: The Construction of Modern National Consciousness*. New York: Columbia University Press.

Khattab, Nabil, and Sami Miaari, eds. 2013. *Palestinians in the Israeli Labor Market: A Multidisciplinary Approach*. New York: Palgrave Macmillan.

Khoury, Jack. 2010. "Druze Sheikh's War against the Murder of Arab Women." *Haaretz*, Feb. 7. *www.haaretz.com*.

Kilty, Keith, and Maria Vidal de Haymes. 2000. "Racism, Nativism, and Exclusion: Public Policy, Immigration and the Latino Experience in the United States." *Journal of Poverty* 4 (1/2): 1–25.

Kimmerling, Baruch. 1985. *The Interrupted System: Israeli Civilians in War and Routine Times*. New Brunswick, NJ: Transaction Books.

———. 2001. *The Invention and Decline of Israeliness: State, Society, and the Military*. Berkeley: University of California Press.

Kingsolver, Ann. 2002. "Poverty on Purpose: Life with the Free Marketers." In *Voices: The Impoverishment of Women*, edited by Sandra Morgen, 23–26. Washington, DC: Association for Feminist Anthropology.

Kiss, Ligia, Lilia Blima Schraiber, Lori Heise, Cathy Zimmerman, Nelson Gouveia, and Charlotte Watts. 2012. "Gender-based Violence and Socioeconomic Inequalities: Does Living in More Deprived Neighbourhoods Increase Women's Risk of Intimate Partner Violence?" *Social Science and Medicine* 74: 1172–79.

Kitsuse, John, and Malcolm Spector. 1973. "Toward a Sociology of Social Problems." *Social Problems* 20: 407–19.

Kitzinger, Jenny. 2004. *Framing Abuse: Media Influence and Public Understanding of Sexual Violence against Children*. London: Pluto Press.

Klein, Bethany. 2011. "Entertaining Ideas: Social Issues in Entertainment Television." *Media, Culture and Society* 33 (6): 905–21.

Klein, Renate, ed. 2013. *Framing Sexual and Domestic Violence through Language*. New York: Palgrave Macmillan.

Klein, Shira. 2008. "An Army of Housewives: Women's Wartime Columns in Two Mainstream Israeli Newspapers." *Nashim* 15: 88–107.

Kolker, Abigail. 2015. "The Feminization of Migration." Tel Aviv: Kav LaOved. *www.kavlaoved.org.il*.

Konur, Etty. 2000. "State Funding for Organizations That Serve Victims of Violence against Women." Tel Aviv: Adva Center. *adva.org/en*.

Kopf, Shula. 2011. "Take It to (Secular) Court." *Jerusalem Post*, Aug. 29, 14.

Korn, Alina. 2000. "Crime and Legal Control: The Israeli Arab Population during the Military Government Period, 1948–66. *British Journal of Criminology* 40 (4): 570–89.

———. 2003. "Rates of Incarceration and Main Trends in Israeli Prisons." *Criminal Justice* 3 (1): 29–55.

Korn, Alina, and Sivan Efrat. 2004. "The Coverage of Rape in the Israeli Press." *Violence Against Women* 10 (9): 1056–74.

Kraft, Dina. 2007. "Domestic Violence Proves Deadly for Ethiopians Disoriented by Aliyah." *Reporter Group*, Oct. 15. *www.thereportergroup.org/Article.aspx?aID=65*.

Krugman, Paul. 2015. "Israel's Gilded Age." *New York Times*, Mar. 16. *www.nytimes.com*.

Kubovich, Yaniv. 2014. "Internal Report Faults How Police Handle Domestic Violence." *Haaretz*, Sept. 9. *www.haaretz.com*.

———2015. "Israel Relaxes Gun Regulations amid Escalating Violence." *Haaretz*, Oct. 15. *www.haaretz.com*.

Kulik, Liat, and Dana Klein. 2010. "Swimming against the Tide: Characteristics of Muslim Arab Women in Israel Who Initiate Divorce." *Journal of Community Psychology* 38 (7): 918–31.

Kurz, Demie. 1998. "Women, Welfare, and Domestic Violence." *Social Justice* 25 (1): 105–22.

Lagarde y de los Ríos, Marcela. 2010. "Preface: Feminist Keys for Understanding Feminicide: Theoretical, Political and Legal Construction." In *Terrorizing Women: Feminicide in the Americas*, edited by Rosa-Linda Fregoso and Cynthia Bejarano, xi–xxvi. Durham: Duke University Press.

Lahav, Avital. 2015. "Arab Women, Haredi Unemployment Bringing Economy Down." *Ynet*, Sept. 10. *www.ynetnews.com*.

Lancaster, Roger. 1992. *Life Is Hard: Machismo, Danger and the Intimacy of Power in Nicaragua*. Berkeley: University of California Press.

Landau, Simcha. 1997. "Homicide in Israel." *Homicide Studies* 1 (4): 377–400.

———. 2003. "Societal Costs of Political Violence: The Israeli Experience." *Palestine-Israel Journal of Politics, Economic and Culture* 10 (1): 28–35.

Landau, Simha, and Susan Rolef. 1998. "Intimate Femicide in Israel: Temporal, Social and Motivational Patterns." *European Journal on Criminal Policy and Research* 6: 75–90.

Lang, Sharon. 2005. *Sharaf Politics: Honor and Peacemaking in Israeli-Palestinian Society*. New York: Routledge.

Laufer, Hanna. 2004. "Managing Domestic Violence Cases in Family Court Social Services in Israel." *International Journal of Law, Policy and the Family* 18: 38–51.

Laufer, Hanna, and Altana Berman. 2006. "Surviving the Earthquake." *Journal of Divorce and Remarriage*, 46 (1-2): 135–49.

Lavee, Yoav, and Ruth Katz. 2003. "The Family in Israel: Between Tradition and Modernity." *Marriage and Family Review* 35: 193–217.

Lavie, Smadar. 2012. "The Knafo Chronicles: Marching on Jerusalem with Israel's Silent Majority." *Affilia*: 300–315.

———. 2014. *Wrapped in the Flag of Israel: Mizrahi Single Mothers and Bureaucratic Torture*. New York: Berghahn.

Lawrence, Bruce, and Aisha Karim, eds. 2007. *On Violence: A Reader*. Durham: Duke University Press.

Layish, Aharon. 1975. *Women and Islamic Law in a Non-Muslim state*. Jerusalem: Keter.

———. 1982. *Marriage, Divorce and Succession in the Druze Family*. Leiden, the Netherlands: Brill.

Lazavera, Inna. 2013. "Standing Up to Domestic Violence in Tel Aviv." *Al-Monitor*, April 30. *www.al-monitor.com*.

Lazarus-Black, Mindie. 1994. *Legitimate Acts and Illegal Encounters: Law and Society in Antigua and Barbuda*. Washington: Smithsonian Institution Press.

———. 2007. *Everyday Harm: Domestic Violence, Court Rites, and Cultures of Reconciliation*. Urbana and Chicago: University of Illinois Press.

Lazarus-Black, Mindie, and Sally Engle Merry. 2003. "The Politics of Gender Violence: Law Reform in Local and Global Places." *Law & Social Inquiry* 28 (4): 931–39.

Lebel, Udi. 2014. "'Second Class Loss': Political Culture as a Recovery Barrier: The Families of Terrorist Casualties' Struggle for National Honors, Recognition, and Belonging." *Death Studies* 38 (1): 9–19.

Lee, Raymond, and Claire Renzetti. 1990. "The Problems of Researching Sensitive Topics." *American Behavioral Scientist* 33 (5): 510–28.

Lee, Vered. 2012. "Women Asylum Seekers Find Refuge from Men." *Haaretz*, Dec. 24. *www.haaretz.com*.

Lee, Yaron, and Or Kashti. 2016. "Prostitution in Israel Netted $308 Million in 2014, First Ever Survey Finds." *Haaretz*, Mar. 6. *www.haaretz.com*.

Lehrner, Amy, and Nicole Allen. 2009. "Still a Movement after All These Years? Current Tensions in the Domestic Violence Movement." *Violence Against Women* 15 (6): 656–77.

Lerner, Hanna. 2009. "Entrenching the Status-Quo: Religion and State in Israel's Constitutional Proposals." *Constellations* 16 (3): 445–61.

Lev-Ari, Ronit. 1979. "Battered Women in the Lower Classes in Israel." Master of Arts thesis, Faculty of Law, Institute of Criminology and Criminal Law, Tel Aviv University, Jan.

———. 1991a. *Before the Beating*. Tel Aviv: Na'amat. [Hebrew]

———. 1991b. *After the Battering: The Struggle of Battered Women with Violence in the Family*. Tel Aviv: Na'amat. [Hebrew]

Levin, Leah. 1999. "Setting the Agenda: The Impact of the 1977 Israel Women's Party." *Israel Studies* 4 (2): 40–63.

Levinson, Chaim. 2011. "Family Tragedy as Father of Seven Kills Ex-Wife, and Then Himself, in Kiryat Arba. *Haaretz*, Dec. 18.

———. 2015. "Why Probe Just the Israeli Army's Budget? Mossad, Shin Bet Are Big Spenders Too." *Haaretz*, July 23. *www.haaretz.com*.

Levenkron, Nomi, and Yossi Dahan. 2003. "Women as Commodities: Trafficking in Women in Israel, 2003." Tel Aviv and Haifa: Hotline for Migrant Workers, Isha l'Isha and Adva Center.

Levy, Yagil. 1998. "Militarizing Inequality: A Conceptual Framework." *Theory and Society* 27 (6): 873–904.

———. 2008. "Military-Society Relations: The Demise of the 'People's Army.'" In *Israel Since 1980*, edited by Guy Ben-Porat, Yagil Levy, Shlomo Mizrahi, Arye Naor, and Erez Tsfadia, 117–45. New York: Cambridge University Press.

———. 2012. *Israel's Death Hierarchy: Casualty Aversion in a Militarized Democracy*. New York: New York University Press.

———. 2014. "Who Controls the IDF? Between an 'Over-Subordinate Army' and 'a Military That Has a State.'" *Civil-Military Relations in Israel: Essays in Honor of Stuart A. Cohen*, edited by Elisheva Rosman-Stollman and Aharon Kampinsky, 47–68. Lanham, MD: Lexington Books.

Lewellen, Ted. 2003. *Political Anthropology: An Introduction*, 3rd ed. Westport, CT: Praeger.

Lewin, Ellen, and William Leap, eds. 1996. *Out in the Field: Reflections of Lesbians and Gay Anthropologists*. Champaign, IL: University of Illinois Press.

Lewin-Epstein, Noah, and Moshe Semyonov. 1987. *Hewers of Wood and Drawers of Water: Non-Citizen Arabs in the Israeli Labor Market*. Ithaca, NY: ILR Press.

———. 1993. *The Arab Minority in Israel's Economy; Patterns of Ethnic Inequality*. Boulder, CO: Westview Press.

Lidman, Melanie. 2016. "Polygamy Is Illegal in Israel. So Why Is It Allowed to Flourish among Negev Bedouin?" *Times of Israel*, Feb. 16. *www.timesofisrael.com*.

Limor, Galia. 2009. "'Let Your Voice Be Heard': Women's Public Hearings on the Israeli-Palestinian Conflict." In *Women Confronting Peace: Voices from Israel*, edited by Sarai Aharoni, Anat Saragusti, and Nurit Haghagh, 15–44. Jerusalem: Israeli Branch of the International Women's Commission.

Lis, Jonathan. 2013a. "Non-Israeli Battered Wives Face Deportation and Custody Battles." *Haaretz*, Aug. 20. *www.haaretz.com*.

———.2013b. "Knesset Okays Speedier Grants for Battered Women Leaving Shelters." *Haaretz*, Dec. 6. *www.haaretz.com*.

———. 2014. "Labor MK: Israel Gave Extra $172m to Settlements in Winter Knesset Session." *Haaretz*, Mar. 23. *www.haaretz.com*.

Lis, Jonathan, and Ruth Sinai. 2003. "Vicki from Mitzpeh' Walks into the Nation's Heart." *Haaretz*, July 10. *www.haaretz.com*.

Lis, Jonathan, and Yair Ettinger. 2015. "Knesset Approves Extension of Ultra-Orthodox Exemptions." *Haaretz*, Nov. 25. *www.haaretz.com*.

Lissak, Moshe. 2001. "Epilogue: Uniqueness and Normalization in Military-Government Relations in Israel." In *Military, State, and Society in Israel: Theoretical and Comparative Perspectives*, edited by Daniel Maman, Eyal Ben-Ari, and Zeev Rosenhek, 395–422. Albany: State University of New York Press.

Loewenberg, Frank M. 1989. "Documents from the History of Social Welfare in Eretz Yisrael: Helene H. Thon (1886–1953) on Social Work in Palestine in the 1920s." *Journal of Social Work and Policy in Israel* 2: 111–22.

———. 1991. "Voluntary Organizations in Developing Countries and Colonial Societies: The Social Services Department of the Palestine Jewish Community in the 1930s." *Nonprofit and Voluntary Sector Quarterly* 20 (4): 415–28.

Lomsky-Feder, Edna. 1998. *As if There Was No War: Life Stories of Israeli Men*. Jerusalem, Israel: Magnes Press. [Hebrew]

Lomsky-Feder, Edna, and Eyal Ben-Ari, eds. 1999. *The Military and Militarism in Israeli Society*. Albany: State University of New York Press.

London, Scott. 1997. "Conciliation and Domestic Violence in Senegal, West Africa." *Political and Legal Anthropology Review* 20: 83–91.

Loseke, Donileen. 2003. *Thinking about Social Problems*, 2nd ed. Chicago: Aldine Publishing.

Low, Setha, and Sally Merry. 2010. "Engaged Anthropology: Diversity and Dilemmas: An Introduction to Supplement 2." *Current Anthropology* 51 (S2): S203–S226.

Lubin, Gad, Nomi Werbeloff, Demian Halperin, Mordechai Shmushkevitch, Mark Weiser, and Haim Knobler. 2010. "Decrease in Suicide Rates After a Change of Policy Reducing Access to Firearms in Adolescents: A Naturalistic Epidemiological Study." *Suicide and Life-Threatening Behavior* 40 (5): 421–24.

Lugg, Catherine, and Madelaine Adelman. 2015. "Socio-Legal Contexts of LGBTQ Issues in Education." In *LGBTQ Issues in Education: Advancing a Research Agenda*, edited by George Wimberly, 43–73. Washington, DC: AERA.

Lustick, Ian. 1980. *Arabs in the Jewish State*. Austin: University of Texas Press.

Lutz, Catherine. 2002. "Making War at Home in the United States: Militarization and the Current Crisis." *American Anthropologist* 104: 723–35.

Lynfield, Ben. 1999. "Palestinians Brace for Tough Talks with New Government." *Jerusalem Post*, July 6. *www.jpost.com*.

Madriz, Esther. 1997. *Nothing Good Happens to Bad Girls*. Berkeley: University of California Press.

Magnezi, Aviel. 2011. "Cottage Cheese Protest Battles Price Hike." *Ynet*, June 15. *www.ynetnews.com.*

Maguigan, Holly. 1991. "Battered Women and Self-Defense: Myths and Misconceptions in Current Reform Proposals." *University of Pennsylvania Law Review* 140: 379–486.

Mahoney, Martha. 1991. "Legal Images of Battered Women: Redefining the Issue of Separation." *Michigan Law Review* 90: 1–95.

Maltz, Judy. 2015a. "For New Arab Chair of Knesset Panel, Some Unlikely Partnerships." *Haaretz*, Aug. 18. *www.haaretz.com.*

———. 2015b. "Not Yet 30, Israel's Youngest Lawmaker Is Already Making Waves." *Haaretz*, Feb. 2. *www.haaretz.com.*

Maman, Daniel, and Zeev Rosenhek. 2012. "The Institutional Dynamics of a Developmental State: Change and Continuity in State-Economy Relations in Israel." *Studies in Comparative International Development* 47: 342–63.

Maoz, Moshe, ed. 1975a. *Studies on Palestine during the Ottoman Period.* Jerusalem: The Magnes Press.

———. 1975b. "Changes in the Position of the Jewish Communities of Palestine and Syria in the Mid-Nineteenth Century." In *Studies on Palestine during the Ottoman period*, edited by Moshe Maoz. Jerusalem: The Magnes Press.

Marcus, Raine. 1996. "Carmela Buhbut Released from Prison. Convicted Killer Served Less Than Two Years." *Jerusalem Post*, Jan. 3.

Martin, Del. 1976. *Battered Wives.* New York. Simon and Schuster.

Masalha, Nur, ed. 2005. *Catastrophe Remembered: Palestine, Israel and the Internal Refugees.* New York: Zed Books.

Maynes, Mary Jo, Jennifer L. Pierce, and Barbara Laslett. 2008. *Telling Stories: The Use of Personal Narratives in the Social Sciences and History.* Ithaca, NY: Cornell University Press.

Mazali, Rela. 2003. "'And What About the Girls?' What a Culture of War Genders Out of View." *Nashim: A Journal of Jewish Women's Studies & Gender Issues* 6: 39–49.

———. 2009. "The Gun on the Kitchen Table: The Sexist Subtext of Private Policing in Israel." In *Sexed Pistols: The Gendered Impacts of Small Arms & Light Weapons*, edited by Vanessa Farr, Henri Myrttinen, and Albrecht Schnabel, 246–89. New York: United Nations University Press.

———. 2016a. "Sacrificing the Fight on Domestic Violence in the Name of Security." *+972 Magazine*, Mar. 16.

———. 2016b. "Speaking of Guns." *International Feminist Journal of Politics.* 18 (2): 292–304.

McAdam, Doug, and William Sewell. 2001. "It's about Time: Temporality in the Study of Social Movements and Revolutions." In *Silence and Voice in the Study of Contentious Politics*, edited by Ronald Aminzade, Jack Goldstone, Doug McAdam, Elizabeth Perry, William Sewell, Jr., Sidney Tarrow, and Charles Tilly, 89–125. Cambridge: Cambridge University Press.

McDonald, John. 2005. "Neo-Liberalism and the Pathologising of Public Issues: The Displacement of Feminist Service Models in Domestic Violence Support Services." *Australian Social Work* 58 (3): 275–84.

McLean, Athena, and Annette Leibing. 2007. *The Shadow Side of Fieldwork: Exploring the Blurred Borders between Ethnography and Life.* Oxford, UK: Blackwell Publishing.

Mehozay, Yoav. 2012. "The Fluid Jurisprudence of Israel's Emergency Powers: Legal Patchwork as a Governing Norm." *Law and Society Review* 46 (1): 137–66.

Meler, Tal. 2013. "Israeli-Palestinian Women and Their Reasons for Divorce: A Comparative Perspective." *Israel Studies Review* 28 (2): 18–40.

Meloy, Michelle, and Susan Miller. 2009. "Words That Wound: Print Media's Presentation of Gendered Violence." In *Women, Violence and the Media: Readings in Feminist Criminology*, edited by Drew Humphries, 29–56. Lebanon, NH: Northeastern.

Menjivar, Cecilia. 2011. *Enduring Violence: Ladina Women's Lives in Guatemala*. Berkeley: University of California Press.

Merav, Michaeli. 2012. "Cancel Marriage." TEDxJaffa, Israel, Nov. 10. *www.youtube.com/watch?v=tTf8jKMGsGE*.

Meron, Gidi. 1993. "On May 23, 1948, Michael Cohen Murdered His Wife." *Yediot Ahronot*, April 25, 16, "17, 20.

Merry, Sally Engle. 1988. "Legal Pluralism." *Law and Society Review* 22 (5): 869–96.

———. 1996. "Gender Violence and Legally Engendered Selves." *Identities: Global Studies in Culture and Power* 2 (1–2): 49–73.

———. 2000. *Colonizing Hawai'i: The Cultural Power of Law*. Princeton, NJ: Princeton University Press.

———. 2001. "Rights, Religion and Community: Approaches to Violence against Women in the Context of Globalization." *Law and Society Review* 35 (1): 39–88.

———. 2006. *Human Rights and Gender Violence*. Chicago: University of Chicago Press.

———. 2008. *Gender Violence: A Cultural Perspective*. Malden, MA: Wiley-Blackwell.

Messing, Jill, Madelaine Adelman, and Alesha Durfee. 2012. "Gender Violence and Transdisciplinarity." *Violence Against Women* 18 (6): 641–52.

Meyers-JDC-Brookdale. 2012. "The Ethiopian Israeli Community: Facts and Figures." Jerusalem: Myers-JDC-Brookdale Institute, Feb. *www.brookdale.jdc.org.il*.

Migdal, Joel. 2006. "Whose State Is It, Anyway? Exclusion and the Construction of Graduated Citizenship in Israel." *Israel Studies Forum* 21 (2): 3–27.

———. 2013. "Forward." In *The Everyday Life of the State: A State-In-Society Approach*, edited by Adam White, vii–xiv. Seattle: University of Washington Press.

Miller, Susan L. 2005. *Victims as Offenders: The Paradox of Women's Violence in Relationships*. New Brunswick: Rutgers University Press.

Miller, Ylana N. 1985. *Government and Society in Rural Palestine 1920–1948*. Austin: University of Texas Press.

Milner, E. 1999. "Two Tombs, Two Children, Father Is Murderer." *Yediot Ahronot*, June 14, 13.

Mink, Gwedolynn. 1995. *Wages of Motherhood: Inequality in the Welfare State 1917–1942*. Ithaca, NY: Cornell University Press.

Ministry of Aliyah and Immigrant Absorption. 2016. "Absorption Basket—*Sal Klita*." Jerusalem: Israel Ministry of Aliyah and Immigrant Absorption. *www.moia.gov.il/english/subjects/financialassistance/pages/absorptionbasket.aspx*.

Ministry of Defense. n.d. "Services for Bereaved Families." Jerusalem: Ministry of Defense. *www.mod.gov.il*.

Ministry of Economy. 2015. "Second Progress Report of the Implementation of the OECD Recommendations: Labour Market and Social Policies." Jerusalem: Ministry of Economy. *www.brookdale.jdc.org.il*.

Ministry of Finance. 2011. "The Israeli Economy: Fundamentals, Characteristics and Historic Overview": Jerusalem: International Affairs Department, Ministry of Finance. *www.financeisrael.mof.gov.il/FinanceIsrael/Docs/En/The_Israeli_Economy.pdf*.

———. 2015. "Accountant General: Government Revenues and Expenditures." Jerusalem: Israel Ministry of Finance. *www.ag.mof.gov.il*.

Ministry of Public Security. 2014. "Ministry of Public Security, an Overview." Jerusalem: Information and Knowledge Services Unit, Ministry of Public Security, Jan. *www.mops.gov.il*.

Mir-Hosseini, Ziba. 1993. *Marriage on Trial: A Study of Islamic Family Law, Iran and Morocco Compared*. New York: I.B. Tauris Publishers.

Mizrahi, Shelly. 2013. "Data on the Murder of Women by Intimate Partners and Criminal Violence in the Family," submitted to Aliza Lavie, chair of the Committee to Advance the Status of Women, May 20. Jerusalem: Knesset Research and Information Center.

Mnookin, Robert H., and Lewis Kornhauser. 1979. "Bargaining in the Shadow of the Law: The Case of Divorce." *Yale Law Journal* 88 (5): 950–97.

Moe, Angie Moe, and Myrtle Bell. 2004. "Abject Economics: The Effects of Battering and Violence on Women's Work and Employability." *Violence Against Women* 10: 29–55.

Moghadam, Valentine, ed. 1994. *Gender and National Identity: Women and Politics in Muslim Societies*. Atlantic Highlands, NJ: Zed Books.

Montoya, Celeste. 2013. *From Global to Grassroots: The European Union, Transnational Advocacy and Combating Violence against Women*. New York: Oxford University Press.

Mor, Michal. 1995. "The Turning Point in Battered Women's Lives." Master of Arts thesis, School of Social Work, University of Haifa, Aug. [Hebrew]

Morgan, Phoebe, Madelaine Adelman, and Stephen Soli. 2008. "Dueling Tragedies: A Critical Read of the Lautenberg Story." *Law, Culture and the Humanities* 4 (3): 424–51.

Morris, Madeline. 1996. "By Force of Arms: Rape, War, and Military Culture." *Duke Law Journal* 45 (4): 651–781.

Moshe, Neta. 2013. "Report on Welfare and Health Services for State-Less Women, Victims of Sexual and Physical Abuse." Presented to the Special Committee on Foreign Workers and Public, June 4. Jerusalem: Knesset Research and Information Center.

Muhlbauer, Varda. 2006. "Domestic Violence in Israel: Changing Attitudes." *Annal New York Academy of Sciences* 1087: 301–10.

Munger, Frank, ed. 2002. *Laboring Below the Line: The New Ethnography of Poverty, Low-Wage Work and Survival in the Global Economy*. New York: Russell Sage.

Myers-JDC-Brookdale Institute. 2010. "The Ethiopian-Israeli Community: Facts and Figures." Jerusalem: Myers-JDC-Brookdale Institute.

Myrtenbaum, Dana. 2005. "Women, Armed Conflict, and Occupation: An Israeli Perspective: Implementation of the Beijing Platform of Action (Section E): A Shadow Report." Haifa: Isha L'Isha—Haifa Feminist Center. Retrieved Nov. 13, 2014. *www.peacewomen.org/sites/default/files/1325_wps_womenarmedconflictoccupation_ishalisha_2005_0.pdf*.

Nakash, Ora, Benjamin Langer, Maayan Nagar, Shahar Shoham, Ido Lurie, and Nadav Davidovitch. 2014. "Exposure to Traumatic Experiences among Asylum Seekers from Eritrea and Sudan during Migration to Israel." *Journal of Immigrant Minority Health* 17 (4): 1280–86.

Natan, Gilad, and Maria Rabinovitz. 2011. "Sexual Crimes Against Foreign Workers." Presented to the Kensset Subcommittee on the Fight against Trafficking of Women, Feb. 23. Jerusalem: Knesset Center for Research and Information. *www.knesset.gov.il/mmm*. [Hebrew]

National Organization of Parents of Murdered Children, Inc. 2016. "Wendy Lea Leiker-Gordon: 31 Years Old." Cincinnati, OH: National POMC. Accessed September 9. *www.pomc.com/mw_stories_1-19/wendy_gordon.html*.

Neria, Yuval, Margarita Bravova, and Jessica M. Halper. 2010. "Trauma and PTSD among Civilians in the Middle East." *PTSD Research Quarterly* 21: 1–8.

Newman, Marissa. 2014. "In Year of War, Rise in Domestic Violence Complaints Seen." *Times of Israel*, Nov. 25. *www.timesofisrael.com.*

Nitzan, Jonathan, and Shimshon Bichler. 2002. *The Global Political Economy: From War Profits to Peace Dividends.* London: Pluto Press.

Nordstrom, Carolyn, and Antonius Robben, eds. 1995. *Fieldwork Under Fire: Contemporary Studies of Violence and Survival.* Berkeley, CA: University of California Press.

O'Leary, Karen. 2013. "Divorce Forum Shopping." *Belfast Telegraph*, May 13.

OECD. 2013a. "Government at a Glance, 2013: Country Fact Sheet: Israel." Washington, DC: Organization for Economic Co-operation and Development.

———. 2013b. "OECD Economic Surveys: Israel: Overview." Washington, DC: Organization for Economic Co-operation and Development. *www.oecd.org.*

———. 2014. "Society at a Glance Highlights: Israel OECD Social Indicators, 2014." Washington, DC: Organization for Economic Co-operation and Development.

Oksenberg, Shai. 2009. "For We Were Strangers: Hotline for Migrant Workers: A Decade of Activism for Migrants' Rights." Tel Aviv: Hotline for Migrant Workers.

Okongwu, Anne F., and Joan Mencher. 2000. "The Anthropology of Public Policy: Shifting Terrains." *Annual Review of Anthropology* 29: 107–24.

Omanit, Irit. 2003. "Violence against Women." In *Jewish Feminism in Israel: Some Contemporary Perspectives*, edited by Kalpana Misra and Melanie Rich, 132–140. Hanover, NH: UPNE and Brandeis University Press.

Opello, Walter, and Stephen Rosow. 2004. *The Nation-State and Global Order*, 2nd ed. Boulder, CO: Lynne Reiner Publications.

Orloff, Ann Shola. 2002. "Explaining U.S. Welfare Reform: Power, Gender, Race and the U.S. Policy Legacy." *Critical Social Policy* 22 (1): 96–118.

Orpaz, Inbal. 2015. "Bubbles and Exits: Who Will Enjoy the Billions from Israeli High-Tech?" *Haaretz*, Mar. 22. *www.haaretz.com.*

Orr Commission of Inquiry. 2003. "Government Commission of Inquiry to Investigate Clashes between Security Forces and Civilians in October 2000." Jerusalem: Israel Supreme Court. *elyon1.court.gov.il/heb/veadot/or/inside_index.htm.* [Hebrew]

Ortbals, Candice, and Meg Rinker. 2009. "Fieldwork, Identities, and Intersectionality: Negotiating Gender, Race, Class, Religion, Nationality, and Age in the Research Field Abroad: Editors' Introduction." *Political Science & Politics* April 1: 287–90.

Pappe, Ilan. 2006. *A History of Modern Palestine.* Cambridge: Cambridge University Press.

Paraszczuk, Joanna. 2012. "High Court Upholds State of Emergency." *Jerusalem Post*, May 8. *www.jpost.com.*

Parson, Nia. 2013. *Traumatic States: Gendered Violence, Suffering, and Care in Chile.* Nashville, TN: Vanderbilt University Press.

Pascoe, Peggy. 2009. *What Comes Naturally: Miscegenation Law and the Making of Race in America.* New York: Oxford University Press.

Pasquetti, Silvia. 2013. "Legal Emotions: An Ethnography of Distrust and Fear in the Arab Districts of an Israeli City." *Law & Society Review* 47: 461–92.

Payes, Shany. 2005. *Palestinian NGOs in Israel: The Politics of Civil Society.* New York: I.B. Icaurus.

Peled, Alise. 2001. *Debating Islam in the Jewish State: The Development of Policy toward Islamic Institutions in Israel.* Albany: State University of New York Press.

Pence, Ellen. 2012. "Forward." In "Special Issue: Contemporary Perspectives on Battered Women's Use of Non-Fatal Force in Intimate Heterosexual Relationships–A Contextual Approach." *Violence Against Women* 18 (9): 1000–03.

Peri, Yoram, ed. 2000. *The Assassination of Yitzhak Rabin*. Palo Alto, CA: Stanford University Press.

Peteet, Julie. 1991. *Gender in Crisis: Women and the Palestinian Movement*. New York: Columbia University Press.

Peterson, V. Spike, and Anne Runyan. 2010. *Global Gender Issues in the New Millennium*, 3rd ed. Boulder, CO: Westview Press.

Pew Research Center. 2016. "Israel's Religiously Divided Society." Washington, DC: Pew Research Center.

Pfeffer, Anshel. 2015. "The Big Winners and Losers of the Israeli Election's Final Episode." *Haaretz*, May 15. *www.haaretz.com*.

Pickering, Sharon. 2001. "Undermining the Sanitized Account: Violence and Emotionality in the Field in Northern Ireland." *British Journal of Criminology* 41: 485–501.

Pierson, Chris. 1998. *Beyond the Welfare State: The New Political Economy of Welfare*, 2nd ed. University Park: Penn State University Press.

Pileggi, Tamar. 2015. "High Court Hears Petition to Strike Down Refugee Law, Again." *Times of Israel*, Feb. 4. *www.timesofisrael.com*.

Ping, Jonathan. 2005. *Middle Power Statecraft: Indonesia, Malaysia and the Asia-Pacific*. Aldershot: Ashgate Publishing Limited.

Pleck, Elizabeth. 1987. *Domestic Tyranny: The Making of American Social Policy against Family Violence from Colonial Times to the Present*. New York: Oxford University Press.

Plessner, Yakir. 1994. *The Political Economy of Israel: From Ideology to Stagnation*. Albany: State University of New York Press.

Polletta, Francesca. 2006. *It Was Like a Fever: Storytelling in Protest and Politics*. Chicago: University of Chicago Press.

———. 2009. "How to Tell a New Story about Battering." *Violence Against Women* 15 (12): 1490–1508.

Potter, Hillary. 2008. *Battle Cries: Black Women and Intimate Partner Abuse*. New York: New York University Press.

Press, Eyal. 2011. "Rising Up in Israel." *New York Review of Books* 58 (Nov. 24). *eyalpress.com/articles/rising-up-in-israel*.

Presser, Lois. 2005. "Negotiating Power and Narrative in Research: Implications for Feminist Methodology." *Signs* 30 (4): 2067–90.

Prime Minister's Office. 2011. *No One Has the Right to Hurt You! Information Booklet, 2011*. Jerusalem: Authority for the Advancement of the Status of Women, Prime Minister's Office and Ministry of Absorption, State of Israel.

Prosor, Ron. 2013. "Violence against Women and Girls." Statement presented at the 2013 Commission on the Status of Women, New York, March 11. *embassies.gov.il/un/statements/committee_statements/Pages/2013-Commission-on-the-Status-of-Women.aspx*.

Ptacek, James. 1999. *Battered Women in the Courtroom: The Power of Judicial Responses*. Boston: Northeastern University Press.

Public Knowledge Workshop ("Hasadna"). 2016. "Budget Key." Tel Aviv: Hasadna. Accessed April 23, 2016. *www.obudget.org/#budget/15/2016/main*.

Quadagno, Jill. 1994. *The Color of Welfare: How Racism Undermined the War on Poverty*. New York: Oxford University Press.

Rabho, Laila Abed. 2013. "From Victimhood to Empowerment: Muslim Women's Narratives in Shari'a Courts in Jerusalem and Taibe." *Contemporary Islam* 7: 267–81.

———. 2015. "'My Mother-in-Law Ruined My Life:' The Jealous Mother-in-Law and the Empowerment of Palestinian Women." *Contemporary Islam* 9 (3): 455–70.

Rabinowitz, Dan. 2001. "The Palestinian Citizens of Israel, the Concept of Trapped Minority and the Discourse of Transnationalism in Anthropology." *Ethnic and Racial Studies* 24 (1): 64–85.

Rabrenovic, Gordana, and Laura Roskos. 2001. "Introduction: Civil Society, Feminism, and the Gendered Politics of War and Peace." *National Women's Studies Association Journal* 13: 40–54.

Raday, Frances. 2009. "Law in Israel." *Jewish Women: A Comprehensive Historical Encyclopedia*. Jewish Women's Archive. *jwa.org/encyclopedia/article/law-in-israel*.

———. 2012. "Gender and Democratic Citizenship: The Impact of CEDAW." *International Journal of Constitutional Law* 10 (2): 512–30.

Raijman, Rebeca, and Moshe Semyonov. 2004. "Perceived Threat and Exclusionary Attitudes towards Foreign Workers in Israel." *Ethnic and Racial Studies* 27 (5): 780–99.

Raijman, Rebeca, Silvina Schammah-Gesser, and Adriana Kemp. 2003. "International Migration, Domestic Work and Care Work: Undocumented Latina Migrants in Israel." *Gender and Society* 17 (5): 727–49.

Rattner, Arye, and Gideon Fishman. 1998. *Justice for All? Jews and Arabs in the Israeli Criminal Justice System*. Westport, CT: Greenwood Publishing Group.

Raved, Ahiya. 2013. "Police Fail to Respond to Tip on Suspect in Girls' Murder." *Ynet News*, June 11. *www.ynetnews.com*.

Raz-Yurovich, Liat. 2012. "Economic Determinants of Divorce among Dual-Earner Couples: Jews in Israel." *European Journal of Population* 28: 177–203.

Regev, Besora, and Shai Amram. 2014. "The National Violence Index: Toward Evidence-Based Policy." Jerusalem: Ministry of Public Security. *mops.gov.il/documents/publications/informationcenter/innovation%20exchange/innovation%20exchange%2017/the%20national%20violence%20index.pdf*.

Regev, Besora, and Nitzan Shiri. 2012. "Violence against Women." Excerpt from publication in *Public Security* 2. Jerusalem: Ministry of Public Security, Dec. 10. *mops.gov.il/english/crimeandsocietyeng/pages/targetingwomen.aspx*.

Reiter, Rayna, ed. 1975. *Toward an Anthropology of Women*. New York: Monthly Review Press.

Reiter, Yitzhak. 2009. "Judge Reform: Facilitating Divorce by Shari'a Courts in Israel." *Journal of Islamic Law and Culture* 11 (1): 13–38.

Renzetti, Claire. 1997. "Confessions of a Reformed Positivist: Feminist Participatory Research as Good Social Science." In *Researching Sexual Violence against Women*, edited by Martin Schwartz, 131–143. Thousand Oaks, Sage.

Renzetti, Claire, and Raquel Kennedy Bergen. 2005a. "Introduction: The Emergence of Violence against Women as a Social Problem." In *Violence Against Women*, edited by Claire Renzetti and Raquel Kennedy Bergen, 1–12. New York: Rowman and Littlefield Publishers.

———, eds. 2005b. *Violence Against Women*. New York: Rowman and Littlefield Publishers.

Reuters. 2015. "Israel Needs $3.6 Billion Tax Hike to Cover Defense Costs, Central Bank Says." *Haaretz*, Feb. 5. *www.haaretz.com*.

Richie, Beth. 1995. *Compelled to Crime: The Gender Entrapment of Battered Black Women*. New York: Routledge.

————. 2012. *Arrested Justice: Black Women, Violence and America's Prison Nation*. New York: New York University Press.

————. 2015. "Reimagining the Movement to End Gender Violence: Anti-Racism, Prison Abolition, Women of Color Feminisms, and Other Radical Visions of Justice" (Transcript). Keynote presented at the Converge Conference, Miami, Florida. *University of Miami Race & Social Justice Law Review* 5: 257–73. *repository.law.miami.edu/umrsjlr/v015/iss2/6.*

Rifkin, Jeremy. 2000. *The Age of Access: The New Culture of Hypercapitalism Where All of Life Is a Paid-For Experience*. New York: Penguin Putnam.

Rivlin, Paul. 2011. *The Israeli Economy from the Foundation of the State through the 21st Century*. Cambridge: Cambridge University Press.

Robbins, Joyce, and Uri Ben-Eliezer. 2000. "New Roles or 'New Times?' Gender Inequality and Militarism in Israel's Nation-in-Arms." *Social Politics: International Studies in Gender, State & Society* 7 (3): 309–42.

Rockberger, Ingrid. 2008–2009. "A Safe Haven—25th Anniversary." *WIZO Review* 320: 10–13.

Rodriguez, Noelie. 1988. "Transcending Bureaucracy: Feminist Politics at a Shelter for Battered Women." *Gender & Society* 2 (2): 214–27.

Roe, David, Ya'ir Ronen, Jossef Lereya, Shmuel Fennig, and Silvana Fennig. 2005. "Reduced Punishment in Israel in the Case of Murder: Bridging the Medico-Legal Gap." *International Journal of Law and Psychiatry* 28 (3): 222–30.

Rosaldo, Michele, and Louise Lamphere, eds. 1974. *Women, Culture and Society*. Stanford: Stanford University Press.

Rose, Alison. 2003. "Imagining the 'New Jewish Family': Gender and Nation in Early Zionism." In *Families of a New World: Gender, Politics and State Development in a Global Context*, edited by Lynne Haney and Lisa Pollard, 64–84. New York: Routledge.

Rose, Nikolas. 1990. *Governing the Soul: The Shaping of Private Self*. New York: Routledge.

Rose, V. M. 1977. "Rape as a Social Problem: A By-Product of the Feminist Social Movement." *Social Problems* 25.

Roseberry, William. 1988. "Political Economy." *Annual Review of Anthropology* 17:161–85.

————. 1990. *Anthropologies and Histories*. New Brunswick, NJ: Rutgers University Press.

Rosen, Ruth. 1994. "MacKinnon Does Not Speak for Me: The Legal Scholar Is Wrong to Make Pornography, Not Poverty, the Most Urgent Feminist Issue." *Los Angeles Times*, Feb. 9. *www.articles.latimes.com.*

Rosenbaum, Janet. 2012. "Gun Utopias? Firearm Access and Ownership in Israel and Switzerland." *Journal of Public Health Policy* 33 (1): 46–58.

Rosenberg, David. 2015. "Nice Iran Speech, Bibi, but What about the Price of Cottage Cheese?" *Haaretz*, Mar. 11. *www.haaretz.com.*

Rosenhek, Zeev. 2000. "Migration Regimes, Intra-State Conflicts, and the Politics of Exclusion and Inclusion: Migrant Workers in the Israeli Welfare State." *Social Problems* 47 (1): 49–67.

————. 2011. "Dynamics of Inclusion and Exclusion in the Israeli Welfare State." In *The Contradictions of Israeli Citizenship: Land, Religion and State*, edited by Guy Ben-Porat and Bryan S. Turner, 63–86. New York: Routledge.

Rosenhek, Zeev, and Michael Shalev. 2014. "The Political Economy of Israel's 'Social Justice' Protests: A Class and Generational Analysis." *Contemporary Social Science* 9 (1): 31–48.

Rosen-Zvi, Ariel. 1989. "Forum Shopping between Religious and Secular Courts (and Its Impact on the Legal System)." *Tel Aviv University Studies in Law* 9: 347, 348, 355–7.

Ross, Ellen, and Rayna Rapp. 1981. "Sex and Society: A Research Note from Social History and Anthropology." *Comparative Studies in Society and History* 23 (1): 51–72.

Roth, Natasha. 2016. "Why Are So Many Israeli Women Subjected to Sexual Harassment?" *+972 Magazine*, Mar. 3. *www.972mag.com*.

Rozen, Orit. 2011. *The Rise of the Individual in 1950s Israel*. Translated by Haim Watzman. Waltham: Brandeis University Press.

Rozen, Sigal. 2015a. "Rwanda or Saharonim: Monitoring Report: Asylum Seekers at the Holot Facility." Tel Aviv: Hotline for Refugees and Migrants.

———. 2015b. "Deported to the Unknown: Monitoring Report: Summarizing Findings of Affidavits Signed by Asylum Seekers in Uganda during August 2015 and Testimonies Gathered Since by the Hotline for Refugees and Migrants." Tel Aviv: Hotline for Refugees and Migrants, Dec. 2015.

Rozen, Sigal, and Sam Kuttner. 2016. "Trafficking in Persons in Israel: Yearly Monitoring, 2015." Tel Aviv: Hotline for Refugees and Migrants. *hotline.org.il/wp-content/uploads/2016/04/TIP-report-2015-April-2016-Final-Eng-1.pdf*.

Rozovsky, Lisa. 2016. "Fleeing Abuse in Israel, Non-Jewish Women Fear Violence and Deportation." *Haaretz*, Mar. 5. *www.haaretz.com*.

Rudge, D. Barak. 1999. "Violence Is a Central Threat." *Jerusalem Post*, July 28.

Russo, Ann. 2006. "The Feminist Majority's Campaign to Stop Gender Apartheid: The Intersections of Feminism and Imperialism in the United States." *International Feminist Journal of Politics* 8 (4): 557–80.

Sa'di, Ahmed, and Lila Abu-Lughod, eds. 2007. *Nakba: 1948, and Claims of Memory*. New York: Columbia University Press.

Sa'ar Amalia. 1998. "Carefully on the Margins: Christian Palestinians in Haifa between Nation and State." *American Ethnologist* 25 (2): 215–39.

———. 2004. "Many Ways of Becoming a Woman: The Case of Unmarried Israeli-Palestinian 'Girls.'" *Ethnology* 43 (1): 1–18.

———. 2007. "Contradictory Location: Assessing the Position of Palestinian Women Citizens of Israel." *Journal of Middle East Women's Studies* 3 (3): 45–74.

———. 2009. "Low Income 'Single Moms' in Israel: Redefining the Gender Contract." *Sociological Quarterly* 50: 450–73.

Sa'ar, Amalia. 2016. *Economic Citizenship: Neoliberal Paradoxes of Empowerment*. New York: Berghahn Books.

Sa'ar, Amalia, Dalia Sachs, and Sarai Aharoni. 2011. "Between a Gender and a Feminist Analysis: The Case of Security Studies in Israel." *International Sociology* 26 (1): 50–73.

Sa'ar, Amalia, and Taghreed Yahia-Younis. 2008. "Masculinity in Crisis: The Case of Palestinians in Israel." *British Journal of Middle Eastern Studies* 35 (3): 305–23.

Sacher, Howard M. 2007. *A History of Israel: From the Rise of Zionism to Our Time*, 3rd ed. New York: Alfred A. Knopf.

Sachs, Dalia, Amalia Sa'ar, and Sarai Aharoni. 2005a. "Silent Witnesses: Women in the Israeli-Palestinian Conflict." Haifa: Isha L'Isha. [Hebrew]

———. 2005b. "The Influence of the Armed Israeli-Palestinian Conflict on Women in Israel." Haifa: Isha L'Isha—Haifa Feminist Center.

———. 2007. "'How Can I Feel for Others When I Myself am Beaten?' The Impact of the Armed Conflict on Women in Israel." *Sex Roles* 53: 593–606.

Safir, Marilyn, and Barbara Swirski, eds. 1991. *Calling the Equality Bluff: Women in Israel*. New York: Pergamon Press.

Safran, Hannah. 1994. "Alliance and Denial: Feminist Lesbian Protest Within Women in Black. Master's Thesis in Liberal Studies, Simmons College.

————. 2004. "An Observant Woman in Black." *Bridges* 10 (1): 61–63.

————. 2006. *Don't Wanna Be Nice Girls: The Struggle for Suffrage and the New Feminism in Israel*. Haifa: Pardes Publications. [Hebrew]

Safran, Nadav. 1981. *Israel: The Embattled Ally*. Cambridge, MA: Belknap Press of Harvard University Press.

Salcido, Olivia, and Madelaine Adelman. 2004. "'He Has Me Tied with the Blessed and Damned Papers': Undocumented-Immigrant Battered Women in Phoenix, Arizona." *Human Organization* 63 (2): 162–73.

Sanders, Cynthia. 2015. "Economic Abuse in the Lives of Women Abused by an Intimate Partner: A Qualitative Study." *Violence Against Women* 21 (1): 3–29.

Saraceno, Chiara. 1994. "The Ambivalent Familism of the Italian Welfare State." *Social Politics: International Studies in Gender, State and Society* 1 (1): 60–82.

Saragusti, Anat. 2009. "The Secret Revolution." In *Women Confronting Peace: Voices from Israel*, edited by Sarai Aharoni, Anat Saragusti, and Nurit Haghagh, 7–13. Jerusalem: Israeli Branch of the International Women's Commission (IWC).

Sassen, Saskia. 1998. *Globalization and Its Discontents: Essays on the Mobility of People and Money*. New York: The New Press.

Sasson-Levy, Orna. 2010. "From the 'Citizen Army' to the 'Market Army': Israel as a Case Study." In *The New Citizen Armies: Israel's Armed Forces in Comparative Perspective*, edited by Stuart Cohen, 173–195. New York: Routledge.

Savaya, Riki, and Orna Cohen. 2004. "Divorce Among 'Unmarried' Muslim Arabs in Israel." *Journal of Divorce & Remarriage* 40 (1–2): 93–109.

Scarry, Elaine. 1985. *The Body in Pain: The Making and Unmaking of the World*. New York: Oxford University Press.

Schechter, Susan. 1982. *Women and Male Violence*. New York: Pluto Press.

Schneider, Anne, and Helen Ingram. 2005. *Deserving and Entitled: Social Constructions and Public Policy*. Albany: SUNY Press.

Schneider, Elizabeth. 2000. *Battered Women and Feminist Lawmaking*. New Haven, CT: Yale University Press.

Schon, Daniel, and Martin Rein. 1994. *Frame Reflection*. New York: Basic Books.

Segal, Einat Maayan. 2013. "Protecting Our Rear." *Israel Social TV*, April 15. *www.youtube.com/watch?v=0Cz9R1QpCSE*.

Segal, Elizabeth A. 2011. "Social Empathy: A Model Built on Empathy, Contextual Understanding, and Social Responsibility That Promotes Social Justice." *Journal of Social Service Research* 37 (3): 266–77.

————. 2013. *"Social Empathy: Using Interpersonal Skills to Effect Change."* Presented by author, as keynote speaker at twenty-fifth national symposium on doctoral research in social work, Ohio State University College of Social Work, Columbus, OH.

————. 2016. *Social Welfare Policy and Social Programs: A Values Perspective*, 4th ed. Boston: Cengage Learning.

Segal, Elizabeth A., Karen Gerdes, Cindy Lietz, M. Alex Wagaman, and Jennifer Geiger. Forthcoming. *Assessing Empathy: What Is It and How Do We Measure It?* New York: Columbia University Press.

Sela-Shayovitz, Revital. 2009. "Social Control in the Face of Security and Minority Threats." *British Journal of Criminology* 49: 772–87.

———. 2010a. "External and Internal Terror: The Effects of Terrorist Acts and Economic Changes on Intimate Femicide Rates in Israel." *Feminist Criminology* 5 (2): 135–55.

———. 2010b. "The Role of Ethnicity and Context: Intimate Femicide Rates among Social Groups in Israeli Society." *Violence Against Women* 16 (2): 1424–36.

———. 2014. "Police Legitimacy under the Spotlight: Media Coverage of Police Performance in the Face of a High Terrorism Threat." *Journal of Experimental Criminology* 11 (1): 117–39.

Sella, Zohar Kadmon. 2014. "News Media and the Authority of Grief: The Journalistic Treatment of Terrorism Victims as Political Activists." Unpublished doctoral dissertation, Columbia University.

Senor, Dan, and Saul Singer. 2009. *Start-Up Nation: The Story of Israel's Economic Miracle.* New York: Twelve Press.

Sered, Susan. 2000. *What Makes Women Sick? Maternity, Modesty, and Militarism in Israeli Society.* London: Brandeis University Press, an imprint of University Press of New England.

Sezgin, Yuksel. 2010. "The Israeli Millet System: Examining Legal Pluralism through Nation-Building and Human Rights." *Israel Law Review* 43: 631–54.

———. 2013. *Human Rights and State-Enforced Religious Family Laws in Israel, Egypt and India.* Cambridge: Cambridge University Press.

Shachar, Ayelet. 2001. *Multicultural Jurisdictions: Cultural Differences and Women's Rights.* Cambridge: Cambridge University Press.

———. 2009. *The Birthright Lottery: Citizenship and Global Inequality.* Cambridge: Harvard University Press.

Shadmi, Erella. 1998. "Police and Police Reform in Israel: The Formative Role of the State." In *Crime and Criminal Justice in Israel,* edited by Robert Friedmann, 207–44. Binghamton: SUNY Press.

Shafir, Gershon, and Yoav Peled. 2002. *Being Israeli: The Dynamics of Multiple Citizenship.* Cambridge: Cambridge University Press.

Shaffir, Stav. 2015. "Stav Shaffir True Zionism Speech." Jerusalem: Knesset (Jan. 21). *www.youtube.com/watch?v=mfyFlK5bkPU.*

Shahar, Ido. 2006. "Legal Reform, Interpretive Communities, and the Quest for Legitimacy: A Contextual Analysis of a Legal Circular." In *Law, Custom and Status: Essays in Honor of Aharon Layish,* edited by Ron Shaham, 199–227. Boston: Brill.

Shalhoub-Kevorkian, Nadera. 1999. "Law, Politics, and Violence against Women: A Case Study of Palestinians in Israel." *Law and Policy* 2: 189–211.

———. 2000. "The Efficacy of Israeli Law in Preventing Violence within Palestinian Families Living in Israel." *International Review of Victimology* 7: 47–66.

———. 2003. "Reexamining Femicide: Breaking the Silence and Crossing 'Scientific' Borders." *Signs* 28 (2): 581–608.

———. 2004. "Racism, Militarization and Policing: Police Reactions to Violence against Palestinian Women in Israel." *Social Identities* 10 (2): 171–93.

———. 2009. *Militarization and Violence against Women in Conflict Zones in the Middle East: A Palestinian Case Study.* New York: Cambridge University Press.

———. 2010. "The United Nations Security Council Resolution 1325 Implementation in Palestine and Israel 2000–2009," a report submitted to the Norwegian Christian Aid.

Shalhoub-Kevorkian, Nadera, and Edna Erez. 2002. "Integrating a Victim Voice in Community Policing: A Feminist Critique." *International Review of Victimology* 9 (2): 113–35.

Shalhoub-Kevorkian, Nadera, and Sana Khsheiboun. 2015. "Going to Ecclesiastical Courts for Protection and Access to Justice: An Indigenous Reading." Haifa: Mada al-Carmel Gender Studies Program.

Shalhoub-Kevorkian, Nadera, and Suhad Daher-Nasif. 2013. "Femicide and Colonization: between the Politics of Exclusion and the Culture of Control." *Violence Against Women* 19 (3): 295–315.

Shalvi, Alice. 2002. "Fear and Fury: Personal Perspectives on the Middle East." On *The Connection* (radio program), host Dick Gordon. WBUR/National Public Radio. June 24.

Shalvi, Alice, and Tamar Eshel. 2009. "Tamar Eshel." In *Jewish Women: A Comprehensive Historical Encyclopedia*. Jewish Women's Archive. *jwa.org/encyclopedia/article/eshel-tamar*.

Shamgar-Handelman, Lea. 1981. "Administering to War Widows in Israel: The Birth of a Social Category." *Social Analysis* 9: 24–47.

———. 1983. "The Social Status of War Widows." *International Journal of Mass Emergencies and Disasters* 1 (1): 153–69.

———. 1986. *Israeli War Widows: Beyond the Glory of Heroism*. Hadley, MA: Bergin and Garvey Publishers.

Shamgar-Handelman, Lea, and Don Handelman. 1991. "Celebrations of Bureaucracy: Birthday Parties in Israeli Kindergartens." *Ethnology* 3 (4): 293–312.

Shapira, Anita. 1992. *Land and Power: The Zionist Resort to Force, 1881–1948*. Translated by William Templer. New York: Oxford University Press.

———. 2012. *Israel: A History*. Waltham, MA: Brandeis University Press.

Shapiro, Haim. 1994. "Ministry Admits It Keeps Marriage Blacklist." *Jerusalem Post*, Dec. 22.

Shapiro, R. 1998. "The Gruesome Details on Women Killed by Their Husbands." *Haaretz*, June 16.

Sharkansky, Ira. 1987. *The Political Economy of Israel*. New Brunswick, NJ: Transaction Books.

Sharma, Aradhana, and Akhil Gupta. 2006. "Introduction: Rethinking Theories of the State in an Age of Globalization." In *The Anthropology of the State: A Reader*, edited by Aradhana Sharma and Akhil Gupta, 1–41. Malden, MA: Blackwell Publishing.

Shay, Talia. 2005. "Can Our Loved Ones Rest in Peace? The Memorialization of the Victims of Hostile Activities." *Anthropological Quarterly* 78 (3): 709–23.

Shechory-Bitton, Mally. 2014. "A Glimpse into the World of Battered Ultra-Orthodox Jewish Women in Israel: A Follow-Up Study on Women Who Resided in a Shelter." *Health Care for Women International* 35 (4): 400–22.

Sheffer, Gabriel, and Oren Barak, eds. 2010. *Militarism and Israeli Society*. Bloomington, IN: Indiana University Press.

Shehada, Nahda. 2009. "House of Obedience: Social Norms, Individual Agency and Historical Contingency." *Journal of Middle East Women's Studies* 5 (1): 24–49.

Shehori, Dalia. 2001. "Ministerial Committee Formed to Promote Women's Rights." *Haaretz*, Nov. 26. *www.haaretz.com*.

Shelef, Leah, Lucian Tats-Laur, Estela Derazne, J. John Mann, and Eyal Fruchter. 2016. "An Effective Suicide Prevention Program in the Israel Defense Forces: A Cohort Study." *European Psychiatry* 31: 37–43.

Sherman, Lawrence, and Ellen Cohn. 1990. "The Effects of Research on Legal Policy in the Minneapolis Domestic Violence Experiment." In *Family Violence: Research and Public Policy Issues*, edited by Douglas Besharov, 205–27. Washington, DC: AEI Press.

Shevi, M. 1998. "Calls to Family Violence Hotline on the Rise." *Haaretz*, Feb. 19. *www. haaretzdaily.com.*

Shkolnik, Ido. 2015. "The Caregivers Choice." Kav LaOved. July 20. *www.kavlaoved.org.il/ en/the-caregivers-choice.*

Shoham, Efrat. 2000. "The Battered Wife's Perception of the Characteristics of Her Encounter with Police." *International Journal of Offender Therapy and Comparative Criminology* 44 (2): 242–57.

———. 2005. "Gender, Traditionalism, and Attitudes toward Domestic Violence within a Closed Community." *International Journal of Offender Therapy and Comparative Criminology* 49 (4): 427–49.

———. 2013a. "The Coverage of 'Spousal Homicide' in the Ethiopian Community in the Israeli Daily Press." *Law and Politics* 6 (2): 185–92.

———. 2013b. "The Role of Police Risk Assessments in Judicial Decisions Regarding Domestic Violence Offenses in Israel." *Canadian Social Science* 9 (5): 1–9.

Shostak, Marjorie. 1981. *Nisa, the Life and Words of a !Kung Woman.* Cambridge, MA: Harvard University Press.

Shteltzer-Pier, A. 2003. "Beit Hatikva: The Anti-Family-Violence Department." In *A Window to Prison: New Reviews and Studies in the Field of Imprisonment and Prisoners in Israel,* edited by A. Shteltzer-Pier, 90–97. Jerusalem: Israeli Prison Service. [Hebrew]

Shuman, Amy. 1986. *Storytelling Rights: The Uses of Oral and Written Texts by Urban Adolescents.* Cambridge: Cambridge University Press.

———. 2005. *Other People's Stories: Entitlement Claims and the Critique of Empathy.* Urbana: University of Illinois Press.

Sikkuy. 2004. "The Sikkuy Report, 2003–2004: Monitoring Civic Equality Between Arab and Jewish Citizens of Israel: The Or Commission Recommendations: One Year Later." Jerusalem and Haifa: Sikkuy: The Association for the Advancement of Civic Equality. *www.sikkuy.org.il/wp-content/uploads/2013/12/sikkuy_report-2003-4.pdf.*

Sikular, Naama. 2012. "Cottage Cheese Boycott Sours Tnuva's Bottom Line." *Ynet*, Feb. 28. *www.ynetnew.com.*

Simon, Jonathan. 2007. *Governing through Crime: How the War on Crime Transformed American Democracy and Created a Culture of Fear.* New York: Oxford University Press.

Sinai, Ruth. 2002. "Police Opened 22,000 Cases of Domestic Violence." *Haaretz*, Mar. 21. *www.haaretzdaily.com.*

Singh, Rashmee. 2012. "Grassroots Governance: Domestic Violence and Criminal Justice Partnerships in an Immigrant City. Unpublished dissertation, Centre of Criminology and Sociolegal Studies, University of Toronto.

Skocpol, Theda. 1985. "Bringing the State Back In: Strategies in the Analysis of Current Research." In *Bringing the State Back In*, edited by Peter B. Evans, Dietrich Rueschemeyer, and Theda Skocpol, 3–43. New York: Cambridge University Press.

Snell, John, Richard Rosenwald, and Ames Robey. 1964. "The Wifebeater's Wife." *Archives of General Psychiatry* 11 (6): 109–14.

Snow, David, E. Burke Rochford, Steven K. Worden, and Robert D. Benford. 1986. "Frame Alignment Processes, Micromobilization, and Movement Participation." *American Sociological Review* 51 (4): 464–81.

Soffer, Oren. 2012. "The Anomaly of Galei Tzahal: Israel's Army Radio as a Cultural Vanguard and Force for Pluralism." *Historical Journal of Film, Radio and Television* 32 (2): 225–43.

Sokoloff, Natalie, and Ida Dupont. 2005. "Domestic Violence at the Intersections of Race, Class, and Gender." *Violence Against Women* 11: 38–64.

Solomon, Zahava. 1995. *Coping with War-Induced Stress: The Gulf War and the Israeli Response*. New York: Plenum.

Somfolvi, Attila. 2015. "Government Approves Changes to Burden Equality Law." *Haaretz*, Nov. 24. *www.haaretz.com*.

Sommer, Hillel. 2003. "Providing Compensation for Harm Caused by Terrorism: Lessons Learned in the Israeli Experience." *Indiana Law Review* 36: 335–65.

Spector, Malcolm, and John I. Kitsuse (1977) 1987. *Constructing Social Problems*. Hawthorne, NY: Aldine de Gruyter.

Stanko, Elizabeth. 1985. *Intimate Intrusions: Women's Experiences of Male Violence*. London and New York: Routledge Kegan Paul.

———. 1996. "Warnings to Women: Police Advice and Women's Safety in Britain." *Violence Against Women* 2 (1): 5–24.

———. 1997. "'I Second That Emotion': Reflections on Feminism, Emotionality, and Research on Sexual Violence." In *Researching Sexual Violence against Women: Methodological and Personal Perspectives*, edited by Martin D. Schwartz, 74–85. Thousand Oaks: Sage.

———, ed. 2003. *The Meanings of Violence*. New York: Routledge.

———. 2006. "Theorizing about Violence: Observations from the Economic and Social Research Council's Violence Research Program." *Violence Against Women* 12 (6): 543–55.

Stark, Evan. 1979. "Medicine and Patriarchal Violence: The Social Construction of a 'Private' Event." *Journal of Health Services* 9: 477–89.

Starr, June. 1994. "When Empires Meet: European Trade and Ottoman Law." In *Contested States: Law, Hegemony and Resistance*, edited by Mindie Lazarus-Black and Susan Hirsch, 231–51. New York: Routledge.

State of Israel. 1997. *Combined Initial and Second Report of the State of Israel Concerning the Implementation of the United Nations Convention on the Elimination of All Forms of Discrimination against Women (CEDAW)*. Jerusalem: Ministry of Foreign Affairs and Ministry of Justice.

Statistics Canada. 2013. "Violence against Women, 2011." *The Daily*, Feb. 25. *www.statcan.gc.ca/daily-quotidien/130225/dq130225a-eng.htm*.

Steiner, Yoseffa. 1990. *The Needs and Self-Concept of Battered Women*. Tel Aviv: Breirot. [Hebrew]

Steinmetz, Suzanne, and Murray Straus, eds. 1974. *Violence in the Family*. New York: Dodd, Mead & Company.

Stern, Itay. 2015. "What Happened to the Filipina Caregiver Who Won Israel's Inaugural *X-Factor*?" *Haaretz*, June 3. *www.haaretz.com*.

Stevens, Jacqueline. 1999. *Reproducing the State*. Princeton, NJ: Princeton University Press.

Stier, Haya. 2011. *Welfare and Employment among Single Mothers: Israel from a Comparative Perspective*. Policy Paper No. 2011.07. Jerusalem: Taub Center for Social Policy Studies in Israel. *taubcenter.org.il/wp-content/files_mf/welfareandemploymentamongsinglemothers.pdf*.

Stier, Haya, and Efrat Herzberg. 2013. *Women in the Labor Force: The Impact of Education on Employment Patterns and Wages*. Jerusalem: Taub Center for Social Policy Studies in Israel. *taubcenter.org.il/wp-content/files_mf/womeninthelaborforce.pdf*.

Straus, Murray, Richard Gelles, and Suzanne Steinmetz. 1980. *Behind Closed Doors: Violence in the American Family*. Garden City, NY: Doubleday.

Suk, Jeannie. 2009. *At Home in the Law: How The Domestic Violence Revolution Is Transforming Privacy*. New Haven, CT: Yale University Press.

Swedenburg, Ted. 1995. *Memories of Revolt: The 1936–1939 Rebellion and the Palestinian National Past*. Minneapolis: University of Minnesota Press.

Swirski, Barbara. 1981. "Wife Beating in Israel." *Journal of Critical Analysis of Israeli Society* 7: 37–62. [Hebrew]

———. 1984. *Daughters of Eve, Daughters of Lilith*. Jerusalem: Women for Women and Ministry of Labour and Welfare. [Hebrew]

———. (1980) 1987. *Legal Guide for Women in Domestic Matters*, 2nd ed. Haifa: Breirot. [Hebrew]

———. 1991a. "Jews Don't Batter Their Wives: Another Myth Bites the Dust." In *Calling the Equality Bluff: Women in Israel*, edited by Barbara Swirski and Marilyn P. Safir, 319–27. New York: Pergamon Press.

———. 1991b. "Israeli Feminism New and Old." In *Calling the Equality Bluff: Women in Israel*, edited by Barbara Swirski and Marilyn Safir, 285–302. New York: Pergamon Press.

Swirski, Shlomo. 2008. *The Burden of Occupation: The Cost of the Occupation to Israeli Society, Polity and Economy, 2008 Update*. Tel Aviv: Adva Center.

———. 2010. *The Cost of Occupation: The Burden of the Israeli-Palestinian Conflict, 2010 Report*. Tel Aviv: Adva Center.

———. 2015. "Not Exactly a Start-Up Nation." Adva Center, Sept. 21. adva.org/en/not-exactly-a-start-up-nation.

Swirski, Shlomo, and Yaron Hoffmann-Dishon. 2015. *The Burden of the Israeli-Palestinian Conflict, 2015*. Tel Aviv: Adva Center.

Swirski, Shlomo, Etty Konur-Attias, and Alon Etkin. 2002. *Government Funding of the Israeli Settlements in the West Bank, Gaza Strip, and Golan Heights in the 1990s of Local Governments, Home Construction, and Road Building: Executive Summary*. Tel Aviv: Adva Center. adva.org/settele/settel.htm.

Swirski, Shlomo, Etty Konor-Attias, and Ariane Ophir. 2014. *Israel: A Social Report, 2013*. Tel Aviv: Adva Center.

Swirski, Shlomo, Etty Konor-Attias, and Rotem Zelingher. 2015. *Israel: A Social Report, 2015*. Tel Aviv: Adva Center.

Swirski, Shlomo, Vered Kraus, Etty Konor-Attias, and Anat Herbst. 2003. "Solo Mothers in Israel." *The Israel Equality Monitor*, no. 12, 1–35.

Sztokman, Elana Maryles. 2014. "It Was a Man's War." *Lilith*, Oct. 7. lilith.org/blog/tag/elana-maryles-sztokman.

———. 2015. *The War on Women in Israel: A Story of Religious Radicalism and Women Fighting for Freedom*. Naperville, IL: Sourcebooks.

Tal, Nili. 1992. "200 Battered Women Came to My House." *Yediot Ahronot*, Feb. 17.

———. 1998. "Till Death Do Us Part." Documentary. Directed by Nili Tal. Israel: Channels 1 and 8.

Tarrow, Sidney. 2011. *Power in Movement: Social Movements and Contentious Politics*, 3rd ed. Cambridge: Cambridge University Press.

Tartakovsky, Eugene, and Mezhibovsky, Sabina. 2012. "Female Immigrant Victims of Domestic Violence: A Comparison between Immigrants from the Former Soviet Union in Israel and Israeli-Born Women." *Journal of Family Violence* 27: 561–72.

Taub Center for Social Policy Studies Israel. 2015. *A Picture of the Nation: Israel's Society and Economy in Figures.* Jerusalem: Taub Center. *taubcenter.org.il/wp-content/files_mf/pictureofthenation2015english.pdf.*

Taylor, Rae. 2009. "Slain and Slandered: A Content Analysis of the Portrayal of Femicide in Crime News." *Homicide Studies* 13 (1): 21–49.

Taylor, Rae, and Jana L. Jasinski. 2011. "Femicide and the Feminist Perspective." *Homicide Studies* 15 (4): 341–62.

Taylor, Verta. 1989. "Social Movement Continuity: The Women's Movement in Abeyance." *American Sociological Review* 54 (5): 761–75.

Tedeschi, Guido (Gad). 1966. *Studies in Israel Private Law.* Jerusalem: Kiryat Sepher.

Teschner, Naama. Dec. 2013. "The Impact of Legislation on Gender Equality: Implementation and Comparative Analysis." Jerusalem: Knesset Research and Information Center.

Thomas, Dorothy Q., and Michele E. Beasley. 1993. "Domestic Violence as a Human Rights Issue." *Human Rights Quarterly* 15: 36–62.

Tierney, Kathleen. 1982. "The Battered Woman Movement and the Creation of the Wife Beating Problem." *Social Problems* 3: 207–20.

Times of Israel. 2012. "Israel Dismisses NRA's Claim about Gun Laws." *Times of Israel,* Dec. 12. *www.timesofisrael.com.*

———. 2013. "Police Nab Father Suspected of Slaying 2 Daughters." *Times of Israel,* July 7. *www.timesofisrael.com.*

———. 2014. "Israel's Filipina 'X-Factor' Champ Allowed to Work as Singer." *Times of Israel,* Jan. 20. *www.timesofisrael.com.*

———. 2015a. "Herzog Slams PM for Spending over the Green Line." *Times of Israel,* Feb. 26. *www.timesofisrael.com.*

———. 2015b. "Poverty Report Downplays Number of Poor in Israel, Says Charity." *Times of Israel,* Dec. 12. *www.timesofisrael.com.*

———. 2015c. "Gun Permit Restrictions Eased Amid Terror Wave." *Times of Israel,* Oct. 14. *www.timesofIsrael.com.*

———. 2016a. "Israel Police Appoints First Muslim Commissioner." *Times of Israel,* April 13. *www.timesofIsrael.com.*

———. 2016b. "12,000 Women Work in Prostitution in Israel, Gov't Says." *Times of Israel,* Mar. 4. *www.timesofIsrael.com.*

Torstrick, Rebecca. 2000. *The Limits of Coexistence: Identity Politics in Israel.* Ann Arbor: University of Michigan Press.

———. 2004. *Culture and Customs of Israel.* Westport, CT: Greenwood Press.

Touma-Sliman, Aida. 2005. "Culture, National Minority and the State: Working against the 'Crime of Family Honor' within the Palestinian Community in Israel." In *Honor: Crimes, Paradigms, and Violence against Women,* edited by Lynn Welchman and Sara Hossain, 181–98. New York: Zed Books.

Trajtenberg, Manuel. 2012. "Trajtenberg Report: Creating a More Just Israeli Society." Jerusalem: Prime Minister's Office.

Triger, Zvi. 2012. "Introducing the Political Family: A New Road Map for Critical Family Law." *Theoretical Inquiries in Law* 13 (1): 361–84.

Tripp, Aili Mari. 2013. "Toward a Gender Perspective on Human Security." In *Gender, Violence, and Human Security: Critical Feminist Perspectives,* edited by Aili Mari Tripp, Myra Marx Feree, and Christine Ewig, 3–32. New York: New York University Press.

Tripp, Aili Mari, Myra Marx Feree, and Christine Ewig, eds. 2013. *Gender, Violence, and Human Security: Critical Feminist Perspectives*. New York: New York University Press.

True, Jacqui. 2012. *The Political Economy of Violence against Women*. New York: Oxford University Press.

Tucker, Judith. 1998. *In the House of the Law: Gender and Islamic Law in Ottoman Syria and Palestine*. Berkeley: University of California Press.

UN (United Nations). 1976. *Report of the [First] World Conference of the International Women's Year*, Mexico City, June 19–July 2, 1975. UN Doc E/Conf.66/34. *undocs.org/E/Conf.66/34*.

———. 1979. *Convention on the Elimination of All Forms of Discrimination against Women*. GA Resolution 34/180. 34th Sess., 107th Plenary Meeting, December 18. UN Doc A/Res/34/180. *www.un-documents.net/a34r180.htm*.

———. 1980. *Report of the [Second] World Conference of the United Nations Decade for Women: Equality, Development and Peace*. Copenhagen, July 14–30. UN Doc A/Conf.94/35. *undocs.org/A/Conf.94/35*.

———. 1986. *Report of the [Third] World Conference to Review and Appraise the Achievements of the United Nations Decade for Women: Equality, Development and Peace*. Nairobi, July 15–26. UN Doc A/Conf.116/28/Rev.1. *undocs.org/A/CONF.116/28/Rev.1*.

———. 1993. *Declaration on the Elimination of Violence against Women*. GA Resolution 48/104. 48th Sess., 85th Plenary Meeting, December 20. UN Doc A/RES/48/104. *undocs.org/A/RES/48/104*.

UNHDP (United Nations Human Development Programme). 2013. "Income GINI Coefficient by Country." New York: UNHDP. *hdr.undp.org/en/content/income-gini-coefficient*.

UNICEF Office of Research. 2016. *Fairness for Children: A League Table of Inequality in Child Well-Being in Rich Countries: Innocenti Report Card 13*. Innocenti, Florence, Italy: UNICEF Office of Research. *www.unicef-irc.org*.

UNODC (United Nations Office on Drugs and Crime). 2014. *Global Study on Homicide, 2013: Trends, Contexts, Data*. Sales No. 14.IV.1. *www.unodc.org/documents/gsh/pdfs/2014_GLOBAL_HOMICIDE_BOOK_web.pdf*.

UNSRVAW (United Nations Special Rapporteur on Violence against Women). 2009. *Fifteen Years of the United Nations Special Rapporteur on Violence against Women, Its Causes and Consequences*. Geneva: OHCHR. *www2.0hchr.org/english/issues/women/rapporteur/docs/15YearReviewofVAWMandate.pdf*.

United Nations Statistics Division (UNSD). 2015. *The World's Women 2015—At a Glance*. New York: UNSD. *unstats.un.org/unsd/gender/docs/WW2015%20at%20a%20Glance.pdf*.

United Nations Women (UNW). 2015. *United Nations Trust Fund to End Violence against Women: Annual Report, 2014*. New York: UNTF to End Violence against Women. *www.unwomen.org/-/media/headquarters/attachments/sections/library/publications/2015/untf-annualreport-2014-en.pdf*.

USAID Office of Women in Development. 1999. "Women as Chattel: The Emerging Global Market in Trafficking." *Gender Matters Quarterly* 1: 1–8.

Vandenberg, Martina. 1997. "Trafficking of Women to Israel and Forced Prostitution: A Report." Jerusalem: Israel Women's Network.

Vertsberger, Rachel. 2001a. "Background Paper: Hotlines for Battered Women." Presented to the Committee for the Advancement of Women. Jerusalem: Knesset Center for Research and Information. [Hebrew]

————. 2001b. "Background Paper: Treatment of Men Who Batter." Presented to the Committee for the Advancement of Women. Jerusalem: Knesset Center for Research and Information. [Hebrew]

Vignansky, Efrat, and Uri Timor. 2015. "Domestic Violence against Partners According to Wife Beaters: Construction of Lifestyles and Meaning." *International Journal of Offender Therapy and Comparative Criminology* 1–26. doi:10.1177/0306624X15617223.

Vilnai, Orly. 2009. "Isabella's Prison." *Haaretz*, Nov. 24. *www.haaretz.com.*

Vincent, Joan. 1990. *Anthropology and Politics: Visions, Traditions, and Trends.* Tucson: University of Arizona Press.

Walker, Lenore. 1979. *The Battered Woman.* New York: Harper and Row.

Wallach, Helene, Ziv Weingram, and Orit Avitan. 2010. "Attitudes towards Domestic Violence: A Cultural Perspective." *Journal of Interpersonal Violence* 25 (7): 1284–97.

Websdale, Neil. 1999. *Understanding Domestic Homicide.* Boston: Northeastern University Press.

————. 2001. *Policing the Poor: From Slave Plantation to Public Housing.* Boston: Northeastern University Press.

Weil, Shalva. 1997. "Changing of the Guards: Leadership among Ethiopian Jews in Israel." *Journal of Social Studies* 1 (4): 301–07.

————. 2004. "Ethiopian Jewish Women: Trends and Transformations in the Context of Transnational Change." *Journal of Jewish Women's Studies and Gender Issues* 8: 73–109.

Weiler-Polak, Dana. 2010. "Despite Netanyahu's Promises, Battered Israeli Women Find No Relief." *Haaretz*, Nov. 25. *www.haaretz.com.*

————. 2011. "International Day for the Elimination of Violence against Women 2011: Figures Show Sharp Rise in Number of Women Killed by Partners." *Haaretz*, Nov. 22. *www.haaretz.com.*

Weiler-Polak, Dana, and Gilli Cohen. 2011. "State to Shutter Half of Battered Women Shelters as NGOs Fail to Meet Basic Requirements." *Haaretz*, June 24. *www.haaretz.com.*

Weimann, Gabriel. 1983. "The Theater of Terror: Effects of Press Coverage." *Journal of Communication* 33 (1): 38–45.

Weiss, Efrat. 2002. "Research: 141,710 Battered Women in Israel." *Ynet*, Nov. 3. *www.ynet.co.il.*

Weis, Lois, Michelle Fine, Amira Proweller, Corrine Bertram, and Julia Marusza. 1998. "'I've Slept in Clothes Long Enough': Excavating the Sounds of Domestic Violence among Women in the White Working Class." *The Urban Review* 30 (1): 1–27.

Weiss, Meira. 2002. *The Chosen Body: The Politics of the Body in Israeli Society.* Stanford: Stanford University Press.

Weiss, Susan. 2013. "From Religious 'Right' to Civil 'Wrong': Using Israeli Tort Law to Unravel the Knots of Gender, Equality and Jewish Divorce." In *Gender, Religion and Family Law: Theorizing Conflicts between Women's Rights and Cultural Traditions*, edited by Lisa Fishbayne-Joffee and Sylvia Neil, 125–138. Lebanon, NH: UPNE and Brandeis University Press.

————. 2015. "Women, Divorce and Mamzer Status in the State of Israel." In *Love, Marriage and Jewish Families: Paradoxes of a Social Revolution*, edited by Sylvia Barack Fishman, 256–86. Brandeis, MA: Brandeis University Press.

Weiss, Susan, and Netty C. Gross-Horowitz. 2012. *Marriage and Divorce in the Jewish State: Israel's Civil War.* Lebanon, NH: UPNE and Brandeis University Press.

Weisburd, David, Badi Hasisi, Tal Jonathan, and Gali Aviv. 2010. "Terrorist Threats and Police Performance: A Study of Israeli Communities." *British Journal of Criminology* 50 (4): 725–47.

Weisman, Gloria, and Rifka Makayes. 1992. "Family Violence: The Law to Prevent Family Violence—1991." Jerusalem: Israel Women's Network.

Weissman, Deborah. 2007. "The Personal Is Political—and Economic: Rethinking Domestic Violence." *BYU Law Review* 2: 387–450.

———. 2013. "Law, Social Movements and the Political Economy of Domestic Violence." *Duke Journal of Gender Law and Policy* 20: 221–54.

Weisz-Rind, Yael, ed. 2000. "Women as a Commodity: Violation of the Human Rights of Women Trafficked from the Former Soviet Union to the Sex Industry in Israel." London: Amnesty International.

Weldon, Laurel. 2002. *Protest, Policy and the Problem of Violence against Women: A Cross-National Comparison.* Pittsburgh: University of Pittsburgh Press.

Whittier, Nancy. 1997. "Political Generations, Micro-Cohorts, and the Transformation of Social Movements." *American Sociological Review* 62 (5): 760–78.

Wies, Jennifer, and Hilary Haldane, eds. 2015. *Applying Anthropology to Gender-Based Violence.* Lanham, MD: Lexington Books.

———, eds. 2011. *Anthropology at the Frontlines of Gender-Based Violence.* Nashville, TN: Vanderbilt University Press.

Williamson, John. 2004. "A Short History of the Washington Consensus." In *The Washington Consensus Reconsidered: Towards a New Global Governance*, edited by Narcis Serra and Joseph Stiglitz, 14–30. New York: Oxford University Press.

Wilmovsky, Inbal, and Tamir, Tal, eds. 2012. "Women in Israel—Between Theory and Reality: Data and Information, Changes and Trends." Jerusalem: Israel Women's Network.

Wilson, Margo, and Martin Daly. 1993. "Spousal Homicide Risk and Estrangement." *Violence and Victims* 8: 3–16.

Winer, Stuart. 2014. "Ministers Okay Work Permits for 5,000 Palestinians." *Times of Israel*, Sept. 14. *www.timesofisrael.com.*

Wolfsfeld, Gadi, Paul Frosh, and Maurice T. Awabdy. 2008. "Covering Death in Conflicts: Coverage of the Second Intifada on Israeli and Palestinian Television." *Journal of Peace Research* 45 (3): 401–17.

Women's Security Index. 2013. "Redefining Security, Informing Public Policy: Selected Findings from the Pilot Survey." Haifa: Isha L'Isha Feminist Center, Coalition of Women for Peace, Kayan Feminist Organization, Aswat Palestinian Gay Women, Women Against Violence and New Profile.

Woods, Patricia. 2008. *Judicial Power and National Politics: Courts and Gender in the Religious-Secular Conflict in Israel.* Albany: SUNY Press.

WGSPWCI (Working Group on the Status of Palestinian Women Citizens of Israel). 1997. "The Status of Palestinian Women Citizens of Israel." Submitted to the United Nations Committee on the Elimination of All Forms of Discrimination against Women. Nazareth: WGSPW, June. *www.adalah.org/uploads/oldfiles/eng/intladvocacy/pal_women1.pdf.*

———. 2005. *NGO Pre-Sessional Report on Israel's Implementation of the United Nations Convention on the Elimination of All Forms of Discrimination against Women (CEDAW).*

Submitted in January 2005 to the Pre-Sessional Working Group. Nazareth: WGSPW, Jan. 21. *www.adalah.org/uploads/oldfiles/newsletter/eng/feb05/CEDAW.pdf.*

———. 2010. *The Status of Palestinian Women Citizens of Israel.* Submitted to the Committee on the Elimination of All Forms of Discrimination against Women, December. Nazareth: WGSPW. *www2.0hchr.org/english/bodies/cedaw/docs/ngos/WomenCitizens_of_Israel_for_the_session_Israel_CEDAW48.pdf.*

World Bank. 2014a. "GINI Index by Country." Washington, DC: World Bank. *data.worldbank.org/indicator/SI.POV.GINI/countries/XS?display=default.*

———. 2014b. "Military Expenditure as Percent of GDP by Country." Washington, DC: World Bank. *data.worldbank.org/indicator/MS.MIL.XPND.GD.ZS.*

———. 2014c. "Military Expenditure as Percent of Central Government Expenditure by Country." Washington, DC: World Bank. *data.worldbank.org/indicator/MS.MIL.XPND.ZS.*

World Health Organization (WHO). 1999. *Putting Women's Safety First: Ethical and Safety Recommendations for Research on Domestic Violence against Women.* Geneva: World Health Organization.

World Health Organization (WHO), and Pan American Health Organization (PAHO). 2012. "Understanding and Addressing Violence against Women." Geneva: World Health Organization and Pan American Health Organization.

Yanay, Uri. 2005. "Women's Shelters in Israel: From Voluntary Innovation to State Dependency." *Social Security* 70: 77–109. [Hebrew]

Yaron, Lee. 2016. "With Rise in Domestic Violence, Israeli Victims Search for Solutions." *Haaretz*, Feb. 16. *www.haaretz.com.*

Yaron, Lee, and Or Kashti. 2016. "Prostitution in Israel Netted $308 Million in 2014, First Ever Survey Finds." *Haaretz*, Mar. 6. *www.haaretz.com.*

Yiftachel, Oren. 2000. "Social Control, Urban Planning and Ethno-Class Relations: Mizrahi Jews in Israel's 'Development Towns.'" *International Journal of Urban and Regional Research* 24 (2): 418–38.

Yishai, Yael. 1991. *Land of Paradoxes: Interest Politics in Israel.* Albany: SUNY Press.

———. 1996. *Between the Flag and the Banner: Women in Israeli politics.* Albany: SUNY Press.

Ynet. 2013. "Lapid on Benefit Cuts: Parents Responsible for Children, Not State." Aug. 19. *www.ynetnews.com.*

Yuval-Davis, Nira. 1987. "Woman/Nation/State: The Demographic Race and National Reproduction in Israel." *Radical America* 21 (6): 37–59.

Zacharia, Janine. 1995. "Behind Closed Doors." *Jerusalem Report*, Nov. 16, 16.

Zaher, Sawsan. 2005. "Palestinian Women Citizens of Israel in the Israeli Economy." Haifa: Ittihaj–Union of Arab Community-Based Associations, and Kayan-Feminist Organization.

Zarchin, Tomer, and Haaretz Correspondent. 2008. "Supreme Court Ruling Raises Questions on Definition of Battered Wife." *Haaretz*, April 17. *www.haaretz.com.*

Zilber, Neri. 2012. "Emergency Routine." *Foreign Policy*, Nov. 16. *www.foreignpolicy.com.*

Zohar, Gabi. 1995. "About 500 Men Suspected of Violence Against Their Wives Are Referred to a Treatment Unit in Haifa." *Haaretz*, Feb. 16. *www.haaretz.com.*

Zucker, Norman I., with the assistance of Naomi Flink Zucker. 1973. *The Coming Crisis in Israel: Private Faith and Public Policy.* Cambridge, MA: MIT Press.

Index

Abou Ramadan, Fouzieh, 114
Abramovich, Yitzhak, 140–41
Absentees' Property Law, 223n5
Abu Shareb, Insaf, 84
Acco/Acre, 29, 45, 217n4
Achdut, Leah, 178
Acre Arab Women's Association, 45
activism, 4–7, 12, 35, 81–82, 111, 160–61,
    222n20; AIDS, 11; anti-gender violence,
    21, 24–25, 33–34, 38–87, 190, 196, 203–5,
    207–8; antimilitarist, 147–48, 221n2; anti-
    occupation, 40; feminist, 40, 54, 77, 81, 145,
    147–48, 151, 193; grassroots, 55, 79; LGBT,
    14, 40, 70, 226n1; men's rights/antifeminist,
    57, 214n15, 219n5; Palestinian, 14, 40, 70,
    145, 155–56, 222n20; peace, 40, 70, 142–43,
    147–48, 151, 193; See also burnout; social
    movements
ACT UP, 11
Adalah, the Legal Center for Arab Minority
    Rights in Israel, 216n36
Adva Center, 57, 191
advocacy, 36–87, 95, 107, 138, 151, 167,
    205, 226n36; courtroom, 122, 216n35,;
    first-generation experts, 43, 65–66; policy,
    100–101, 109–11, 125–26, 139–41, 156–57,
    206, 208, 222n17; political economy and,
    36–37; relationship to the state, 21–22, 62,
    148–49, 162–63; research and, 1, 4–5, 8,
    12; scholar-advocates, 6, 16, 18, 57, 202;
    second-generation experts, 43, 65–66, 76–77,
    83; strategies, 10, 143–44, 198; See also
    claimsmakers
Africa, 26, 28, 185. See also individual countries
"Africa Is a Country" (blog), 12–13
African Refugee Development Center (ARDC),
    13, 226n36
African refugees, 188–90, 226n36
Agudat Yisrael Party, 30–31
agunah, 6, 100, 111, 216n35
Aid Organization for Refugees and Asylum
    Seekers in Israel, 226n36
Ajzenstadt, Mimi, 213n9
al-Badil, 77

al-Fanar, 77
al-Fora'a, 98
Ali, Mutasim, 12–13
Alignment Party, 51–53
Al-Ittihad, 85
Aliyah Bet, 213n12
Almagor (Terror Victims Association), 135
Al-Nakba Day (Palestine), 25, 132
Alrov, Itzik, 160
Al-Tufula—Pedagogical and Multipurpose
    Women's Center, 216n36
Al Zahraa, the Organization for the Advancement
    of Women, 216n36
Amendment 300a, 215n30, 220n19
American Economics Association, 223n2
Amharic (language), 88, 171
Amir, Yigal, 137, 227n4
Ammunition Hill, 136
Amnesty International, 225n29; Israel office,
    226n36
Amtirat, Ali, 97–98
Anglo-Saxons (Israeli term), 26
anthropology, 33, 36, 77, 178, 201, 211nn6–7;
    engaged, 3; feminist anthropologists, 19, 54;
    methods, 9; research on domestic violence,
    21–23; research on family, 18–19
anti–gender violence movement, 38–87, 142,
    152, 190, 196, 203–8, 222n20; global nature
    of, 21; relation to the state, 18, 24–25, 33–34
antimilitarist activism, 147–48, 221n2
Arabic (language), 1, 3, 94, 211n5; language
    barriers, 68, 83, 123, 155, 198; press, 71, 75,
    128
Arabs, 1, 113–14, 128, 197; advocacy for, 63,
    142, 147, 216n2; anti–domestic violence
    activism, 42, 71, 77, 83, 105, 167, 216n36;
    employment, 103, 165; neighborhoods, 54,
    105, 112, 167–69; poverty, 174, 222n19;
    schools for, 59; stereotypes about, 13–14,
    42, 46, 51, 75, 152–53, 155, 170; treatment
    by British Empire, 30, 44–45; treatment by
    Israeli state, 26–27, 31, 48, 131–32, 153–56,
    166–70, 195, 217n4; See also Joint Arab List
    Party; Palestinians (Israeli citizens)

www.ingramcontent.com/pod-product-compliance
Lightning Source LLC
Chambersburg PA
CBHW030643270326
41929CB00007B/180